FIRE PUNCH

7

STORY AND ART BY
TATSUKI FUJIMOTO

CHARACTERS

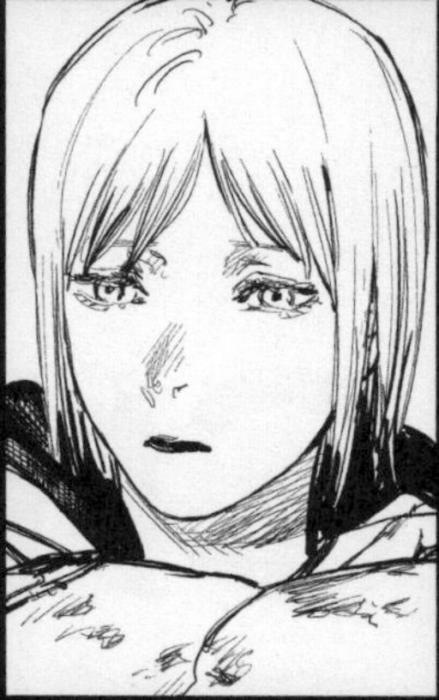

JUDAH

A Blessed with the power of regeneration, she has lost her memory and is suffering from infantile regression.

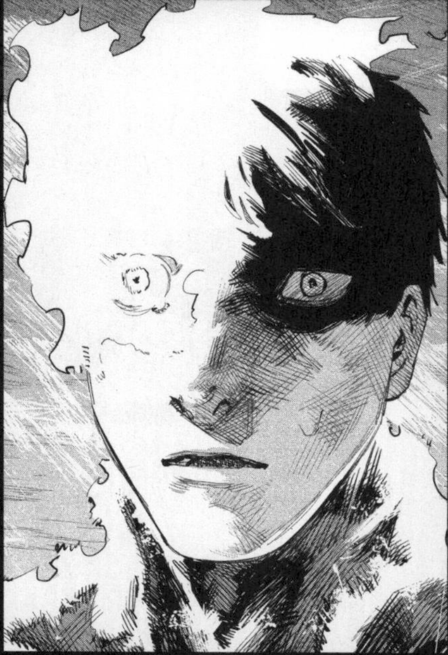

AGNI

A Blessed with the power of regeneration, his little sister is killed by Doma, who engulfs Agni in flames that will never extinguish.

SUN

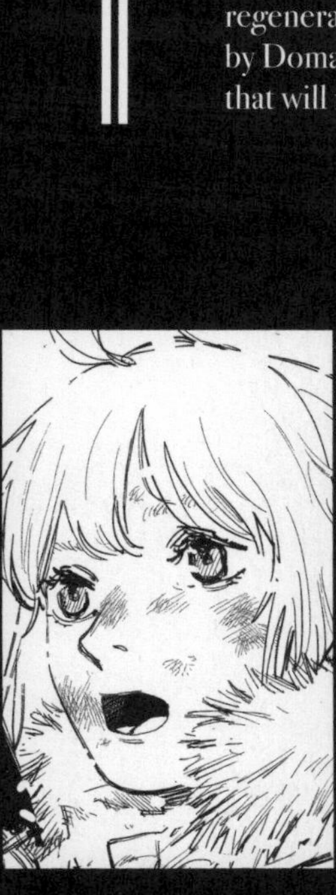

A Blessed with the power of electricity. Agni saves his life.

NENETO

A girl taken to Behemdorg with Sun.

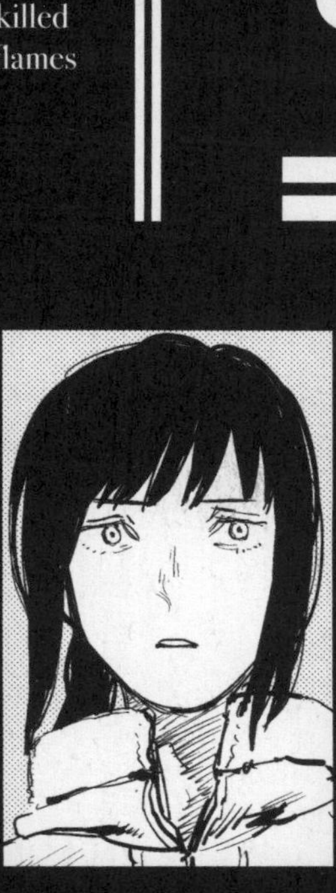

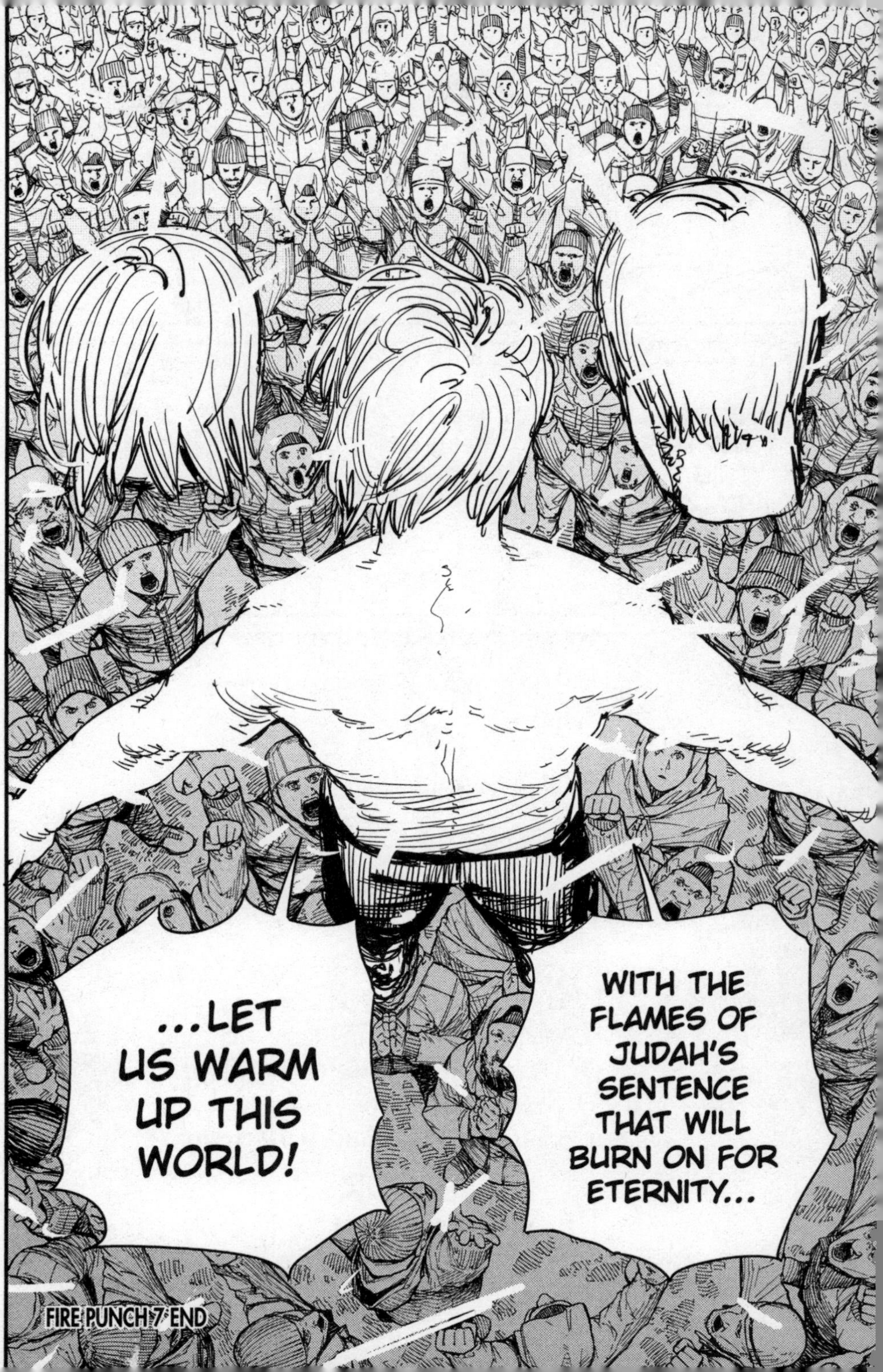
WITH THE FLAMES OF JUDAH'S SENTENCE THAT WILL BURN ON FOR ETERNITY...
...LET US WARM UP THIS WORLD!
FIRE PUNCH 7 END

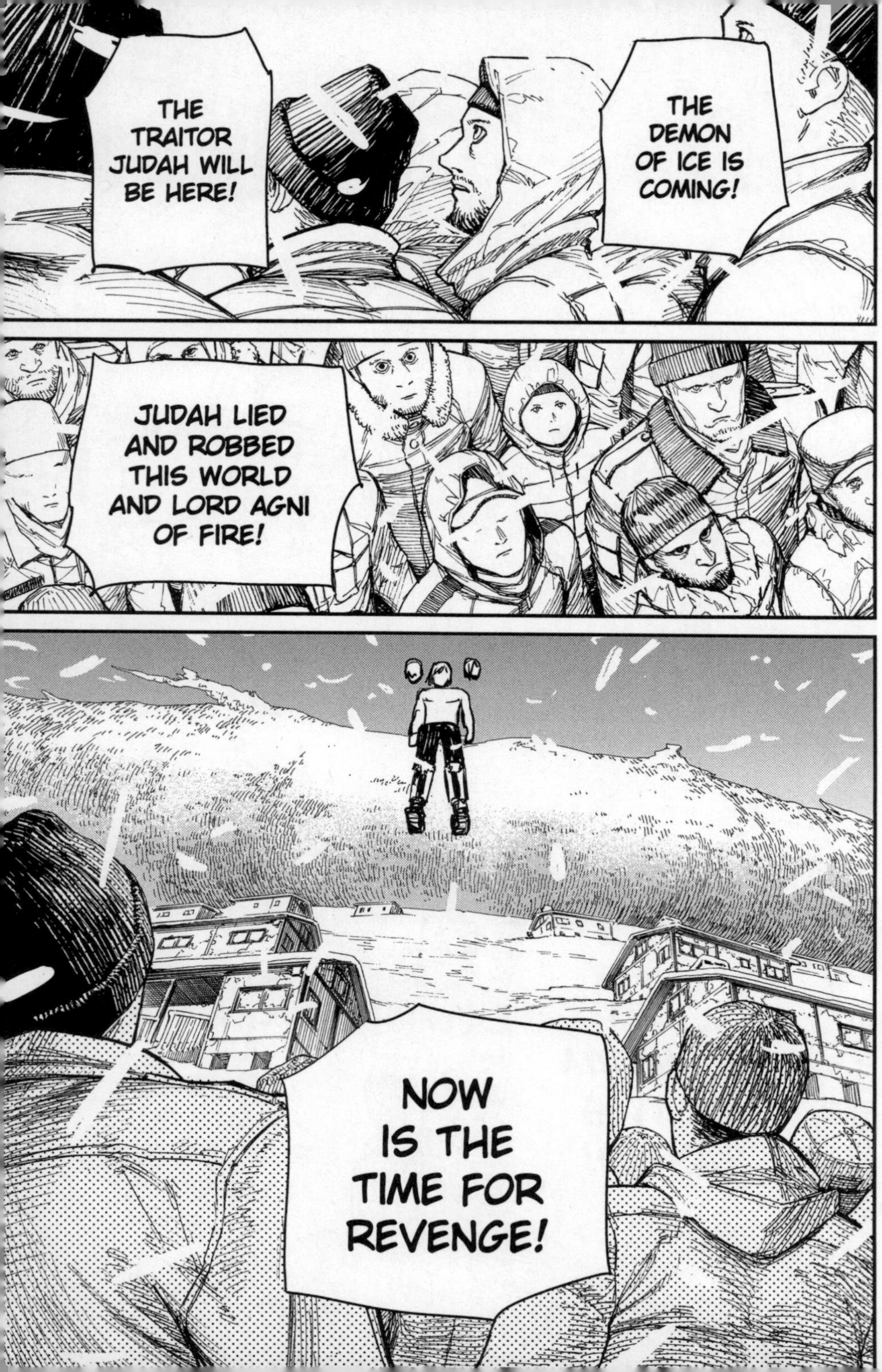
THE DEMON OF ICE IS COMING!
THE TRAITOR JUDAH WILL BE HERE!
JUDAH LIED AND ROBBED THIS WORLD AND LORD AGNI OF FIRE!
NOW IS THE TIME FOR REVENGE!

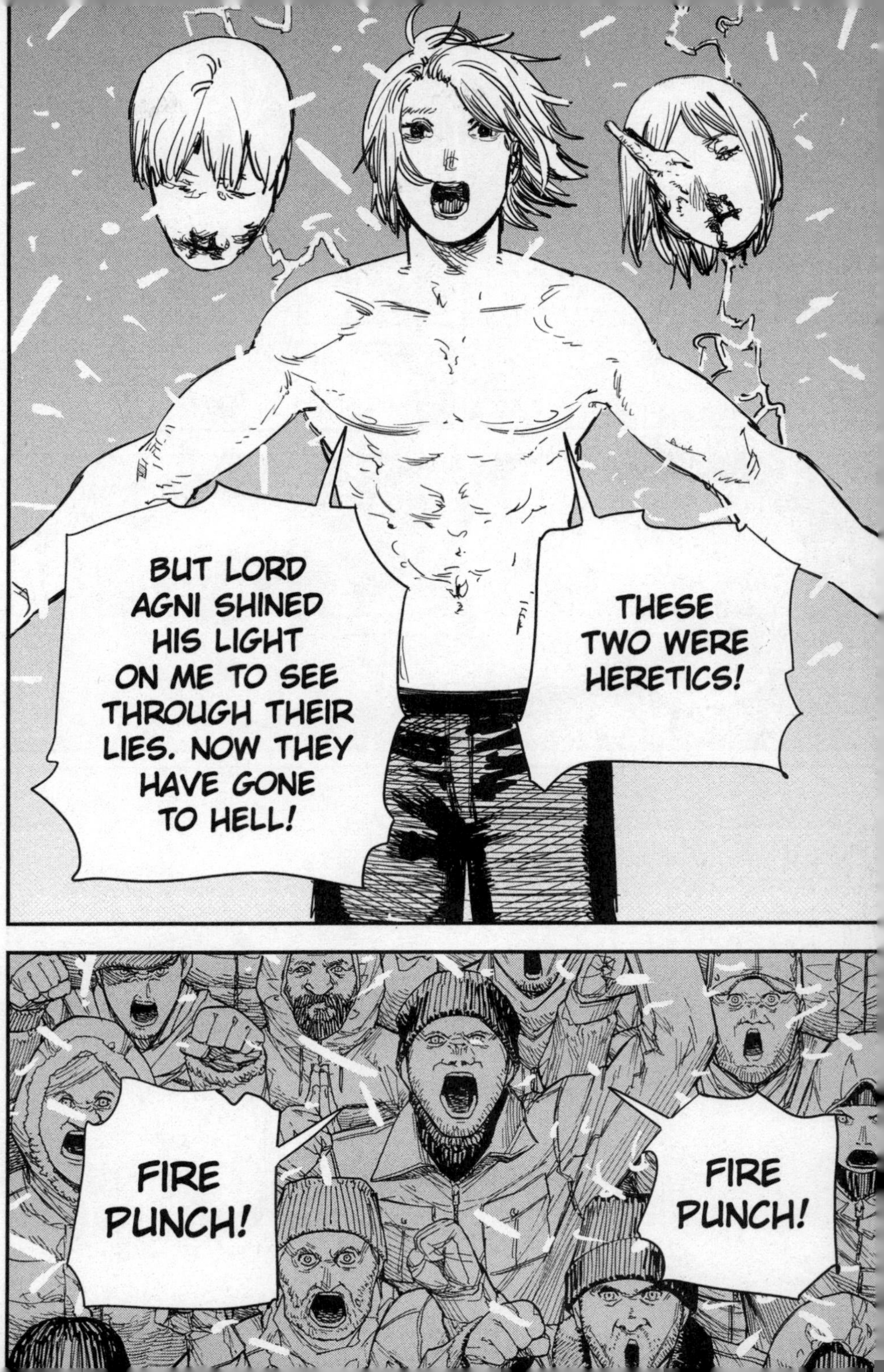
THESE TWO WERE HERETICS!
BUT LORD AGNI SHINED HIS LIGHT ON ME TO SEE THROUGH THEIR LIES. NOW THEY HAVE GONE TO HELL!
FIRE PUNCH!
FIRE PUNCH!

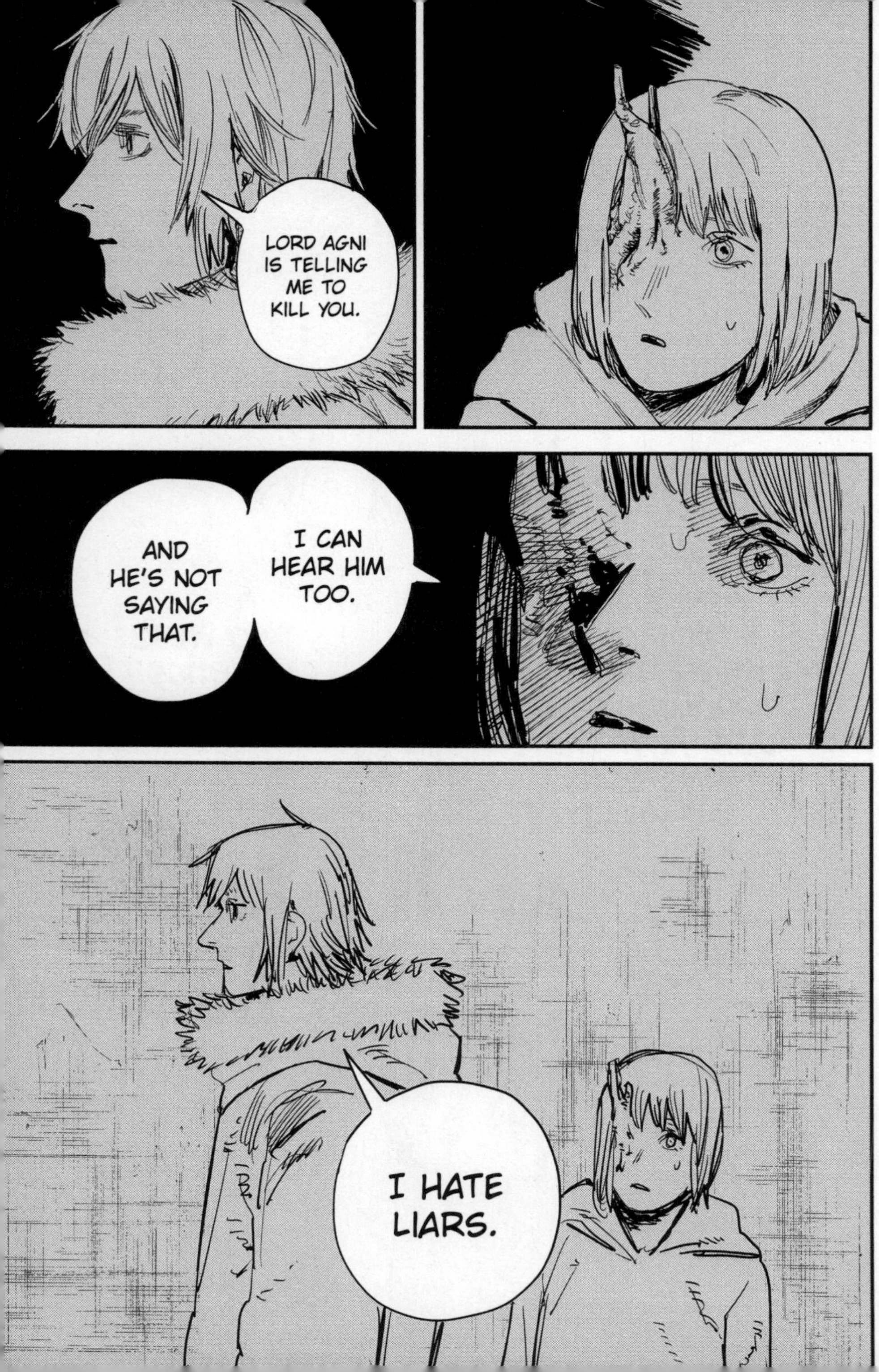
LORD AGNI IS TELLING ME TO KILL YOU.
I CAN HEAR HIM TOO.
AND HE'S NOT SAYING THAT.
I HATE LIARS.

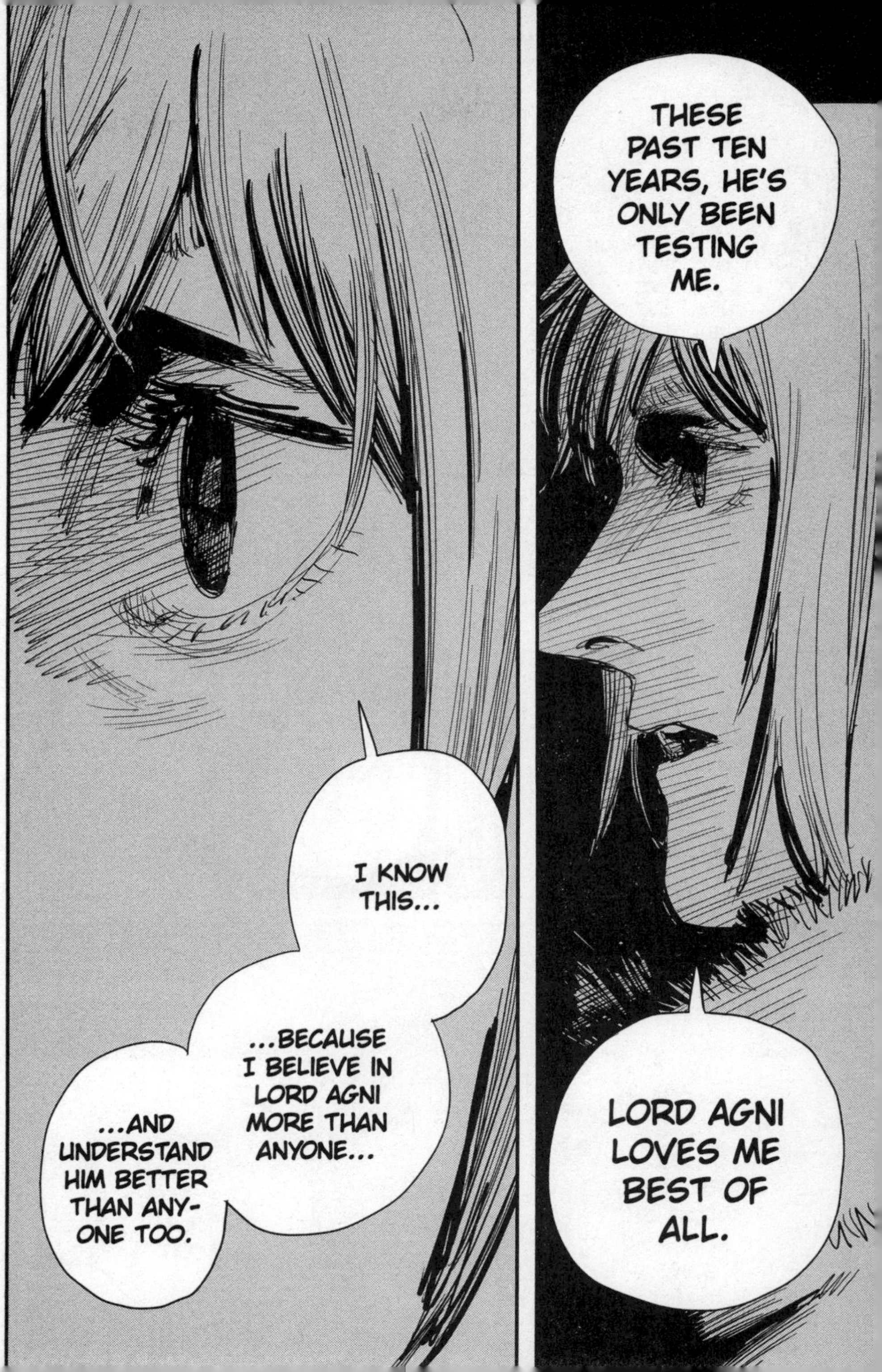
THESE PAST TEN YEARS, HE'S ONLY BEEN TESTING ME.
LORD AGNI LOVES ME BEST OF ALL.
I KNOW THIS...
...BECAUSE I BELIEVE IN LORD AGNI MORE THAN ANYONE...
...AND UNDERSTAND HIM BETTER THAN ANY-ONE TOO.

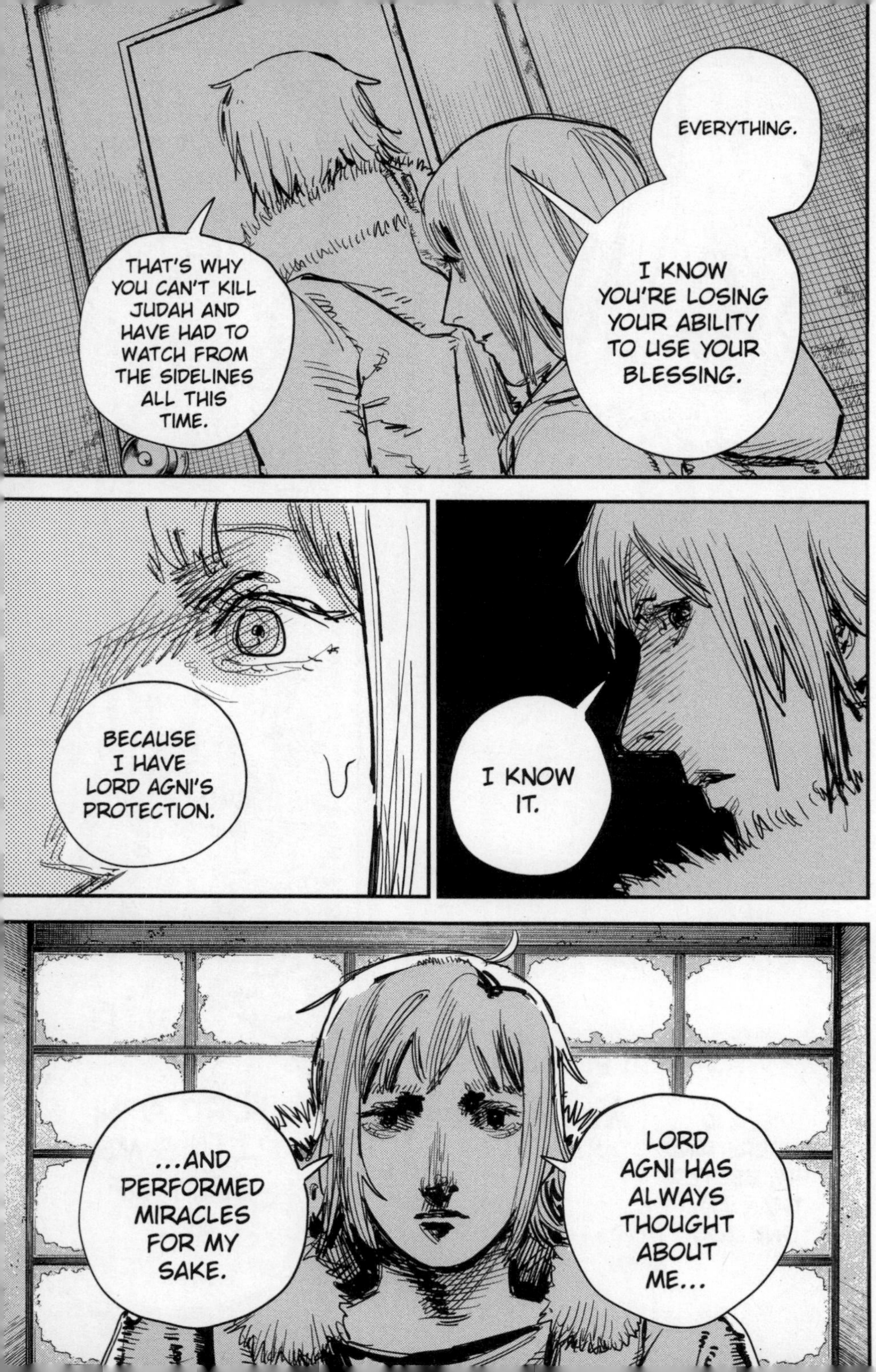
EVERYTHING.
I KNOW YOU'RE LOSING YOUR ABILITY TO USE YOUR BLESSING.
THAT'S WHY YOU CAN'T KILL JUDAH AND HAVE HAD TO WATCH FROM THE SIDELINES ALL THIS TIME.
I KNOW IT.
BECAUSE I HAVE LORD AGNI'S PROTECTION.
LORD AGNI HAS ALWAYS THOUGHT ABOUT ME...
...AND PERFORMED MIRACLES FOR MY SAKE.

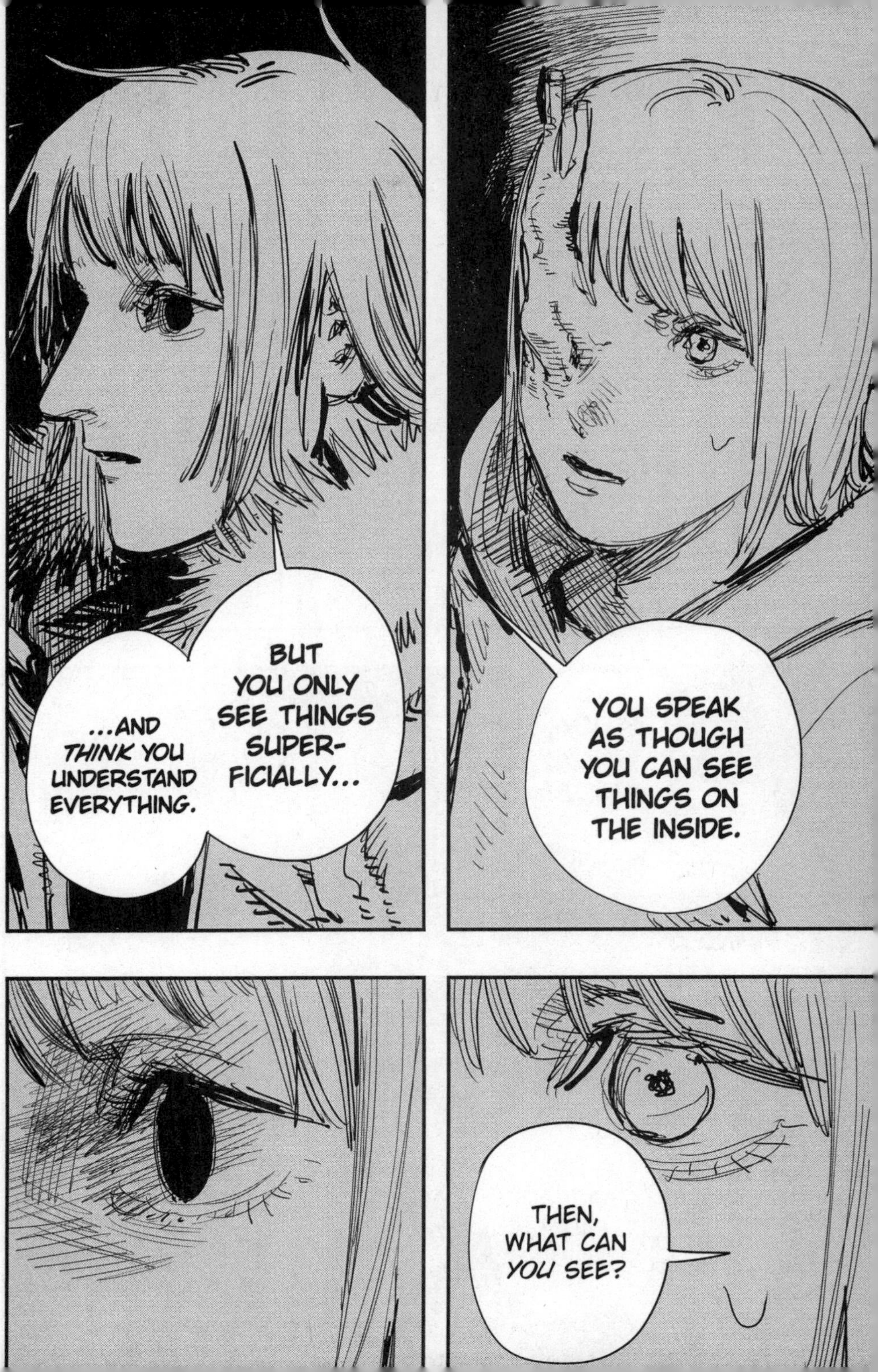
YOU SPEAK AS THOUGH YOU CAN SEE THINGS ON THE INSIDE.
BUT YOU ONLY SEE THINGS SUPER-FICIALLY...
...AND *THINK* YOU UNDERSTAND EVERYTHING.
THEN, WHAT CAN *YOU* SEE?

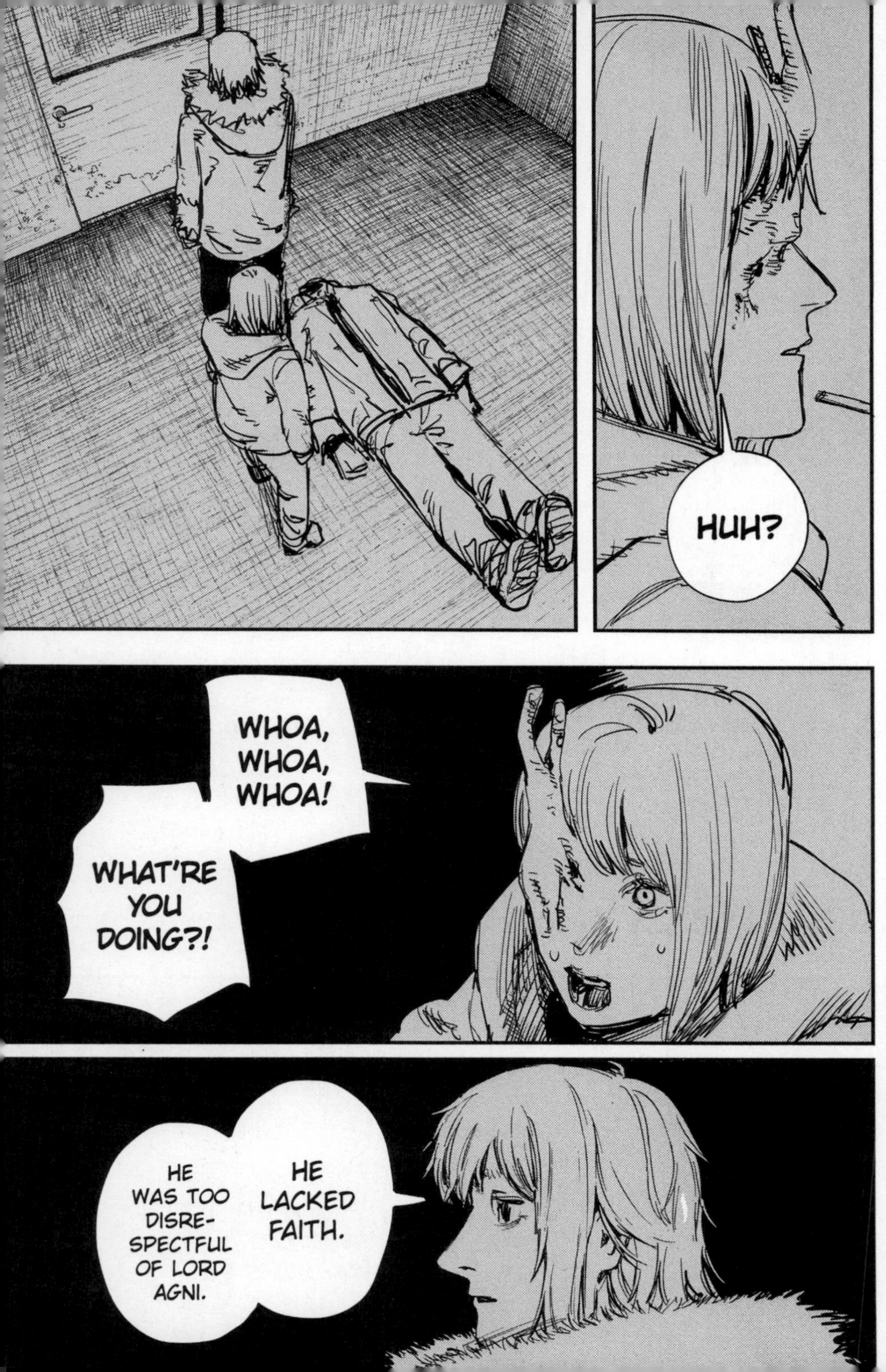
HUH?
WHOA, WHOA, WHOA!
WHAT'RE YOU DOING?!
HE LACKED FAITH.
HE WAS TOO DISRESPECTFUL OF LORD AGNI.

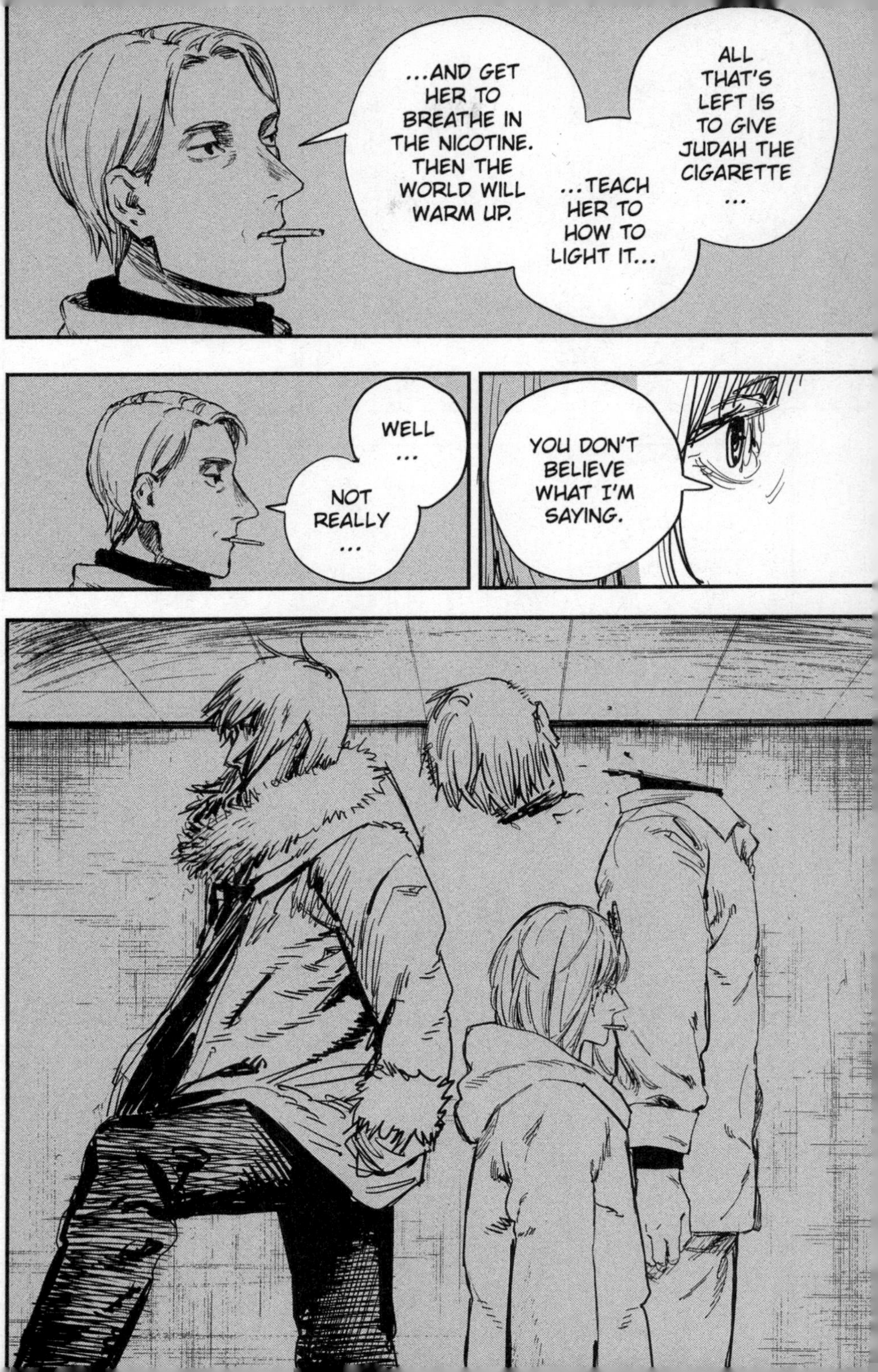
ALL THAT'S LEFT IS TO GIVE JUDAH THE CIGARETTE ...
...TEACH HER TO HOW TO LIGHT IT...
...AND GET HER TO BREATHE IN THE NICOTINE. THEN THE WORLD WILL WARM UP.
YOU DON'T BELIEVE WHAT I'M SAYING.
WELL ...
NOT REALLY ...

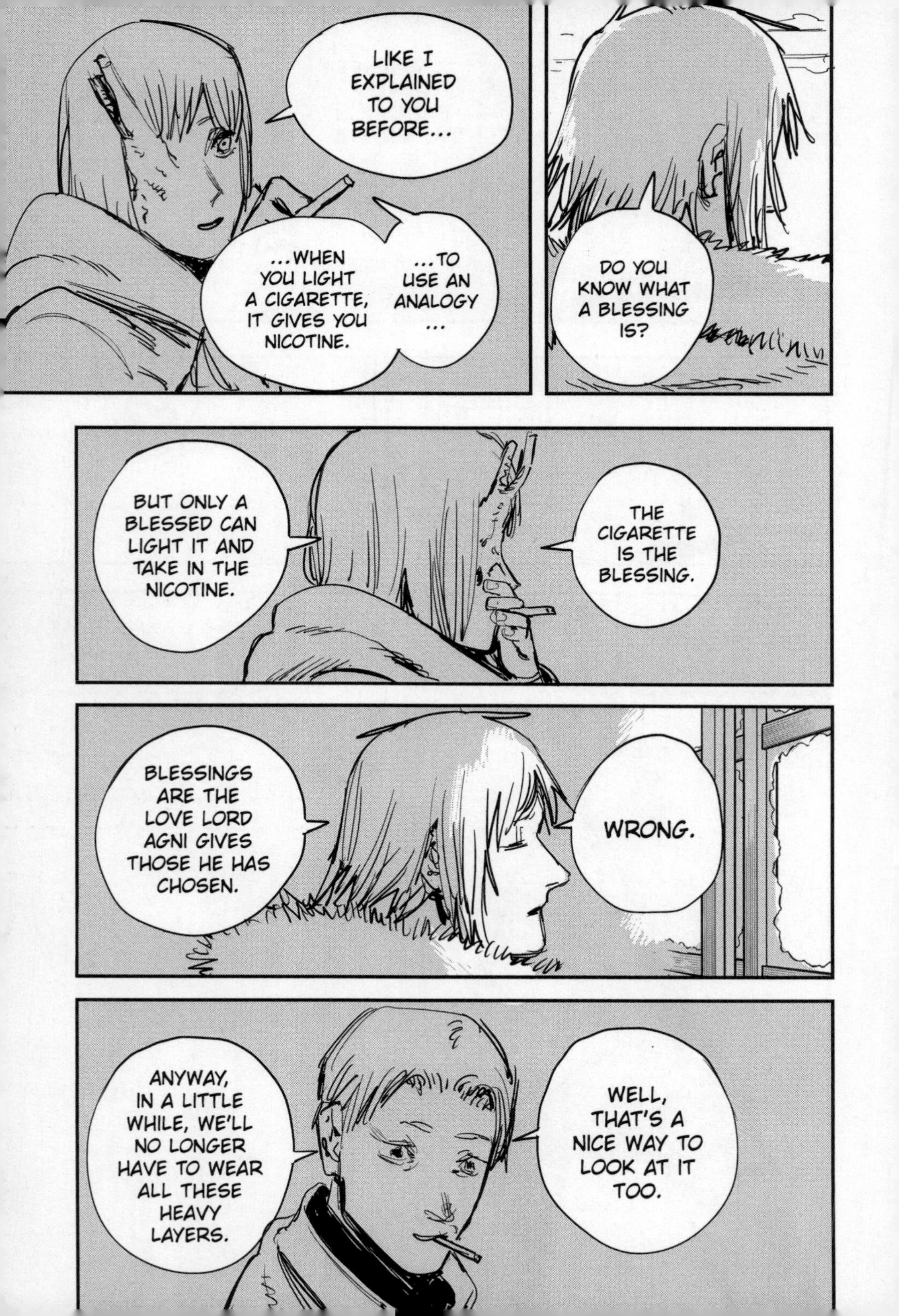
DO YOU KNOW WHAT A BLESSING IS?
LIKE I EXPLAINED TO YOU BEFORE...
...TO USE AN ANALOGY ...
...WHEN YOU LIGHT A CIGARETTE, IT GIVES YOU NICOTINE.
THE CIGARETTE IS THE BLESSING.
BUT ONLY A BLESSED CAN LIGHT IT AND TAKE IN THE NICOTINE.
WRONG.
BLESSINGS ARE THE LOVE LORD AGNI GIVES THOSE HE HAS CHOSEN.
WELL, THAT'S A NICE WAY TO LOOK AT IT TOO.
ANYWAY, IN A LITTLE WHILE, WE'LL NO LONGER HAVE TO WEAR ALL THESE HEAVY LAYERS.

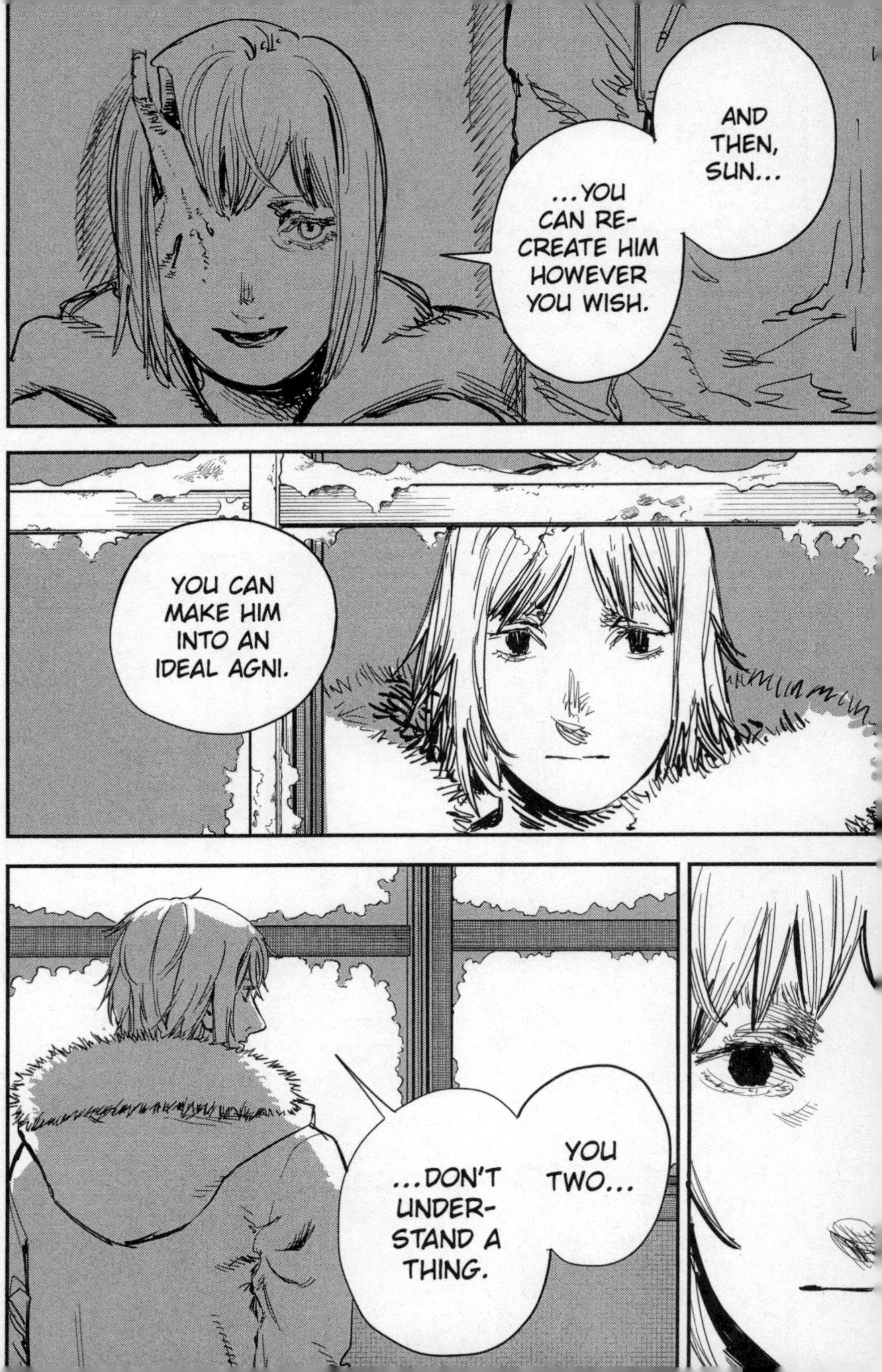
AND THEN, SUN...
...YOU CAN RE-CREATE HIM HOWEVER YOU WISH.
YOU CAN MAKE HIM INTO AN IDEAL AGNI.
YOU TWO...
...DON'T UNDERSTAND A THING.

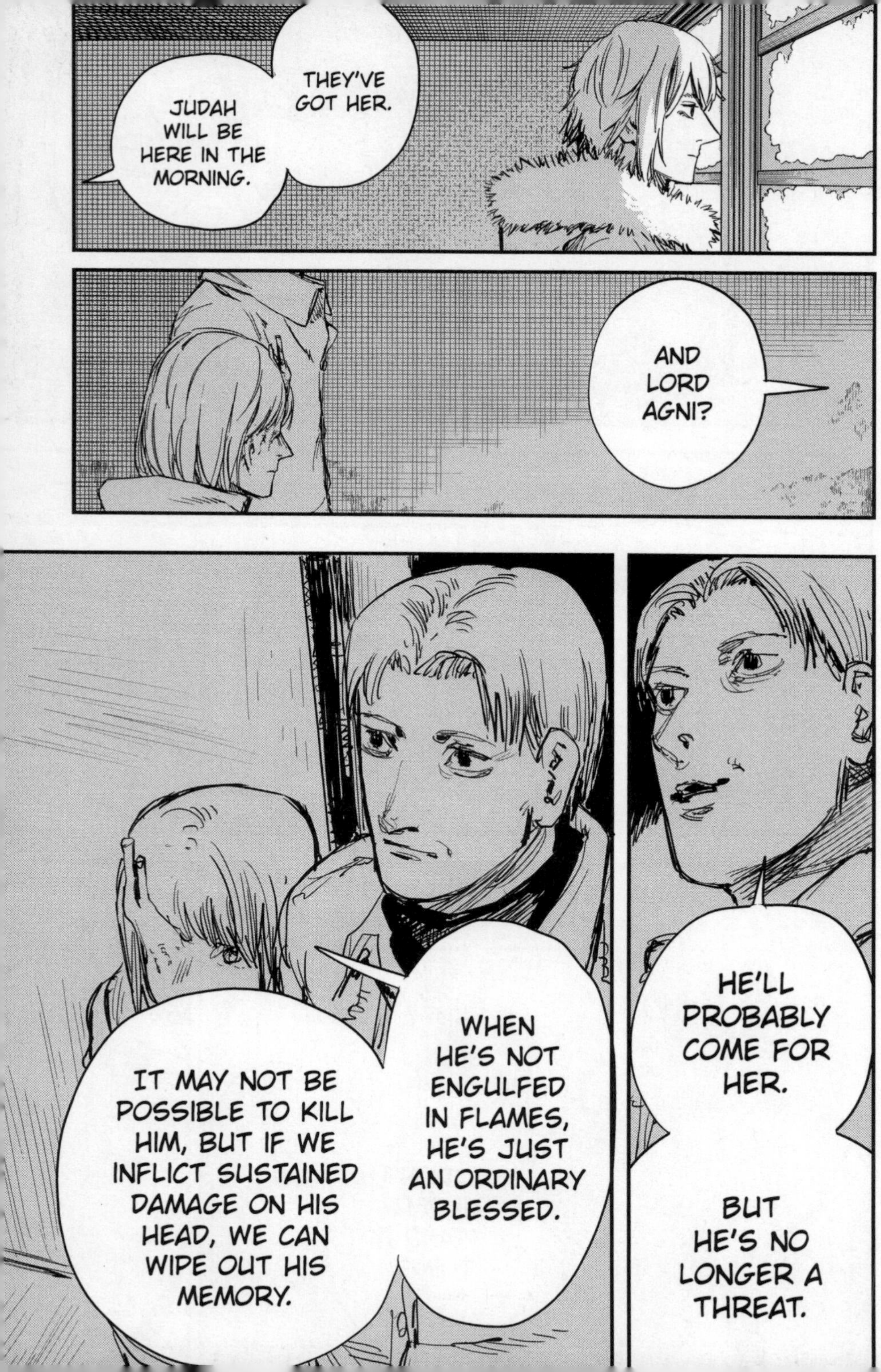
THEY'VE GOT HER.
JUDAH WILL BE HERE IN THE MORNING.
AND LORD AGNI?
HE'LL PROBABLY COME FOR HER.
BUT HE'S NO LONGER A THREAT.
WHEN HE'S NOT ENGULFED IN FLAMES, HE'S JUST AN ORDINARY BLESSED.
IT MAY NOT BE POSSIBLE TO KILL HIM, BUT IF WE INFLICT SUSTAINED DAMAGE ON HIS HEAD, WE CAN WIPE OUT HIS MEMORY.

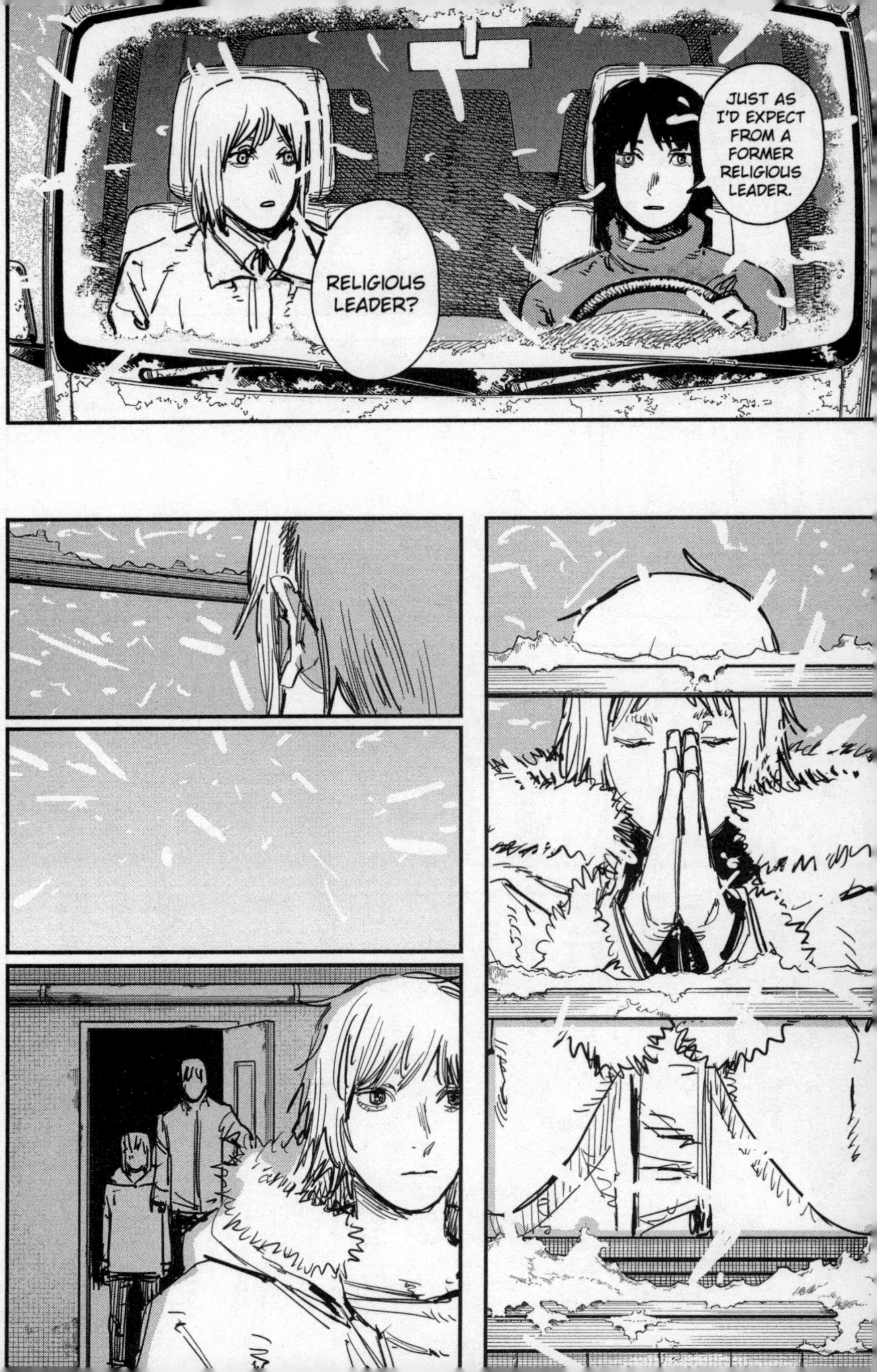
JUST AS I'D EXPECT FROM A FORMER RELIGIOUS LEADER.
RELIGIOUS LEADER?

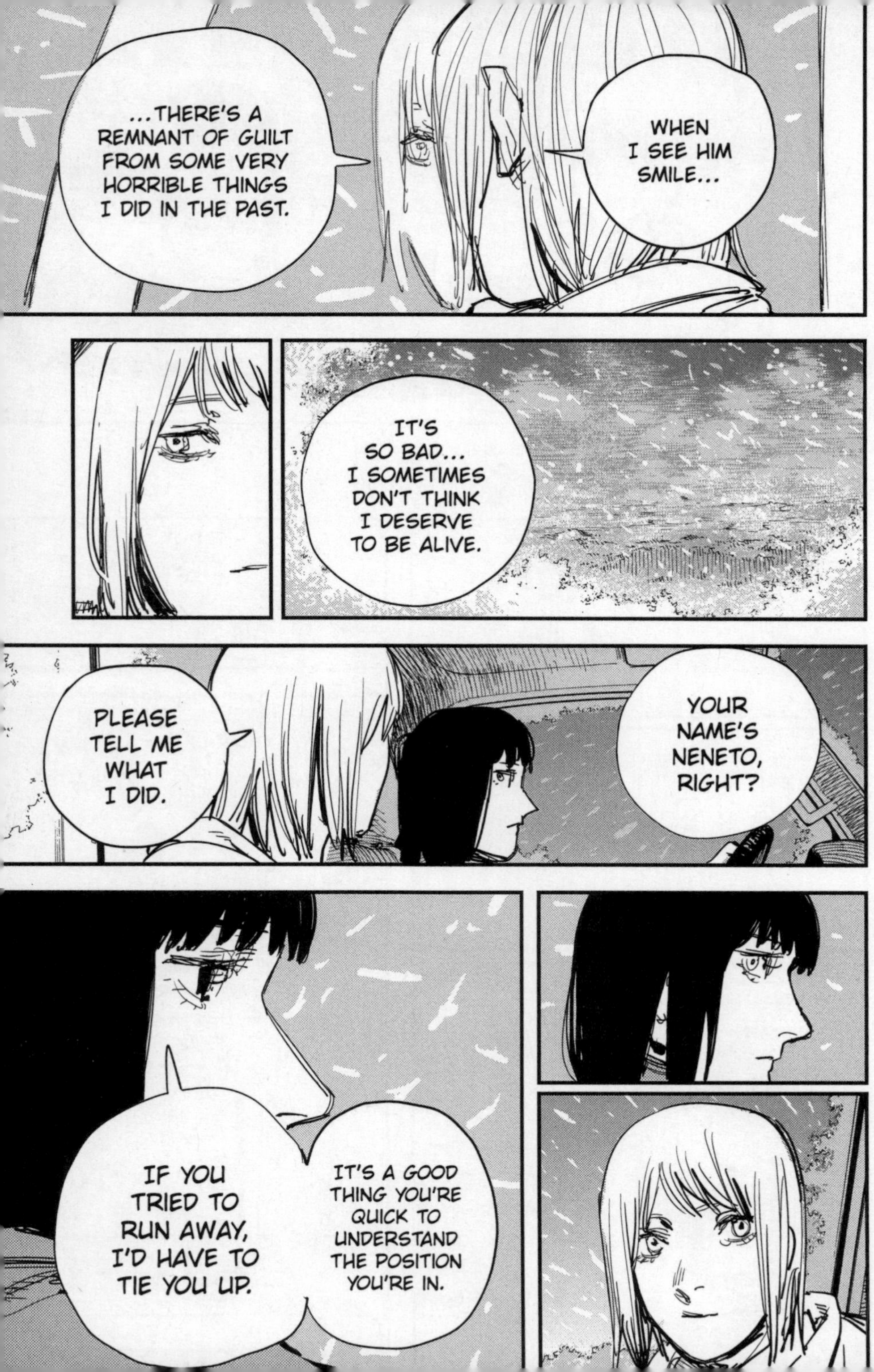
WHEN I SEE HIM SMILE...
...THERE'S A REMNANT OF GUILT FROM SOME VERY HORRIBLE THINGS I DID IN THE PAST.
IT'S SO BAD... I SOMETIMES DON'T THINK I DESERVE TO BE ALIVE.
YOUR NAME'S NENETO, RIGHT?
PLEASE TELL ME WHAT I DID.
IT'S A GOOD THING YOU'RE QUICK TO UNDERSTAND THE POSITION YOU'RE IN.
IF YOU TRIED TO RUN AWAY, I'D HAVE TO TIE YOU UP.

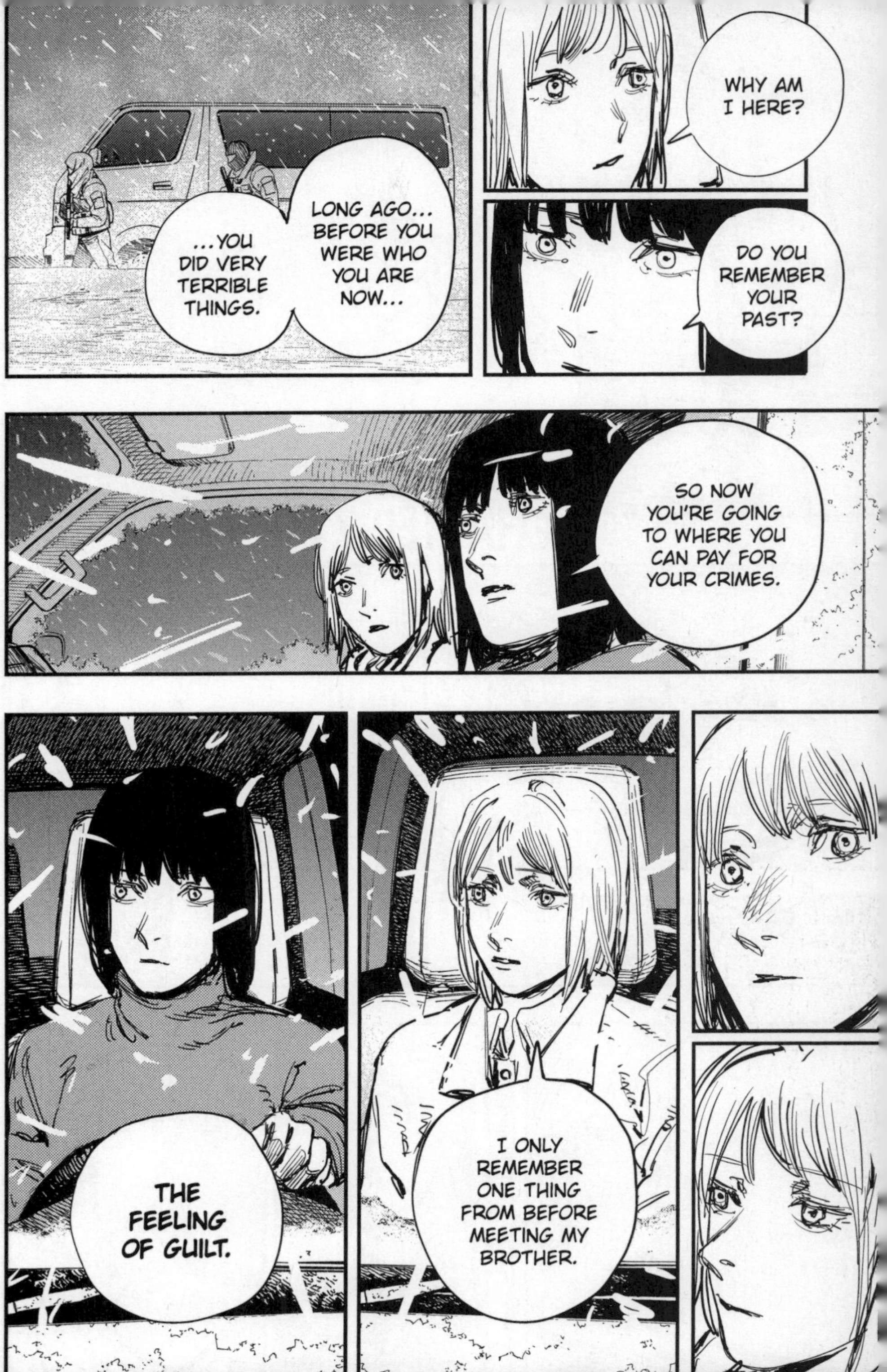
WHY AM I HERE?
DO YOU REMEMBER YOUR PAST?
LONG AGO... BEFORE YOU WERE WHO YOU ARE NOW...
...YOU DID VERY TERRIBLE THINGS.
SO NOW YOU'RE GOING TO WHERE YOU CAN PAY FOR YOUR CRIMES.
I ONLY REMEMBER ONE THING FROM BEFORE MEETING MY BROTHER.
THE FEELING OF GUILT.

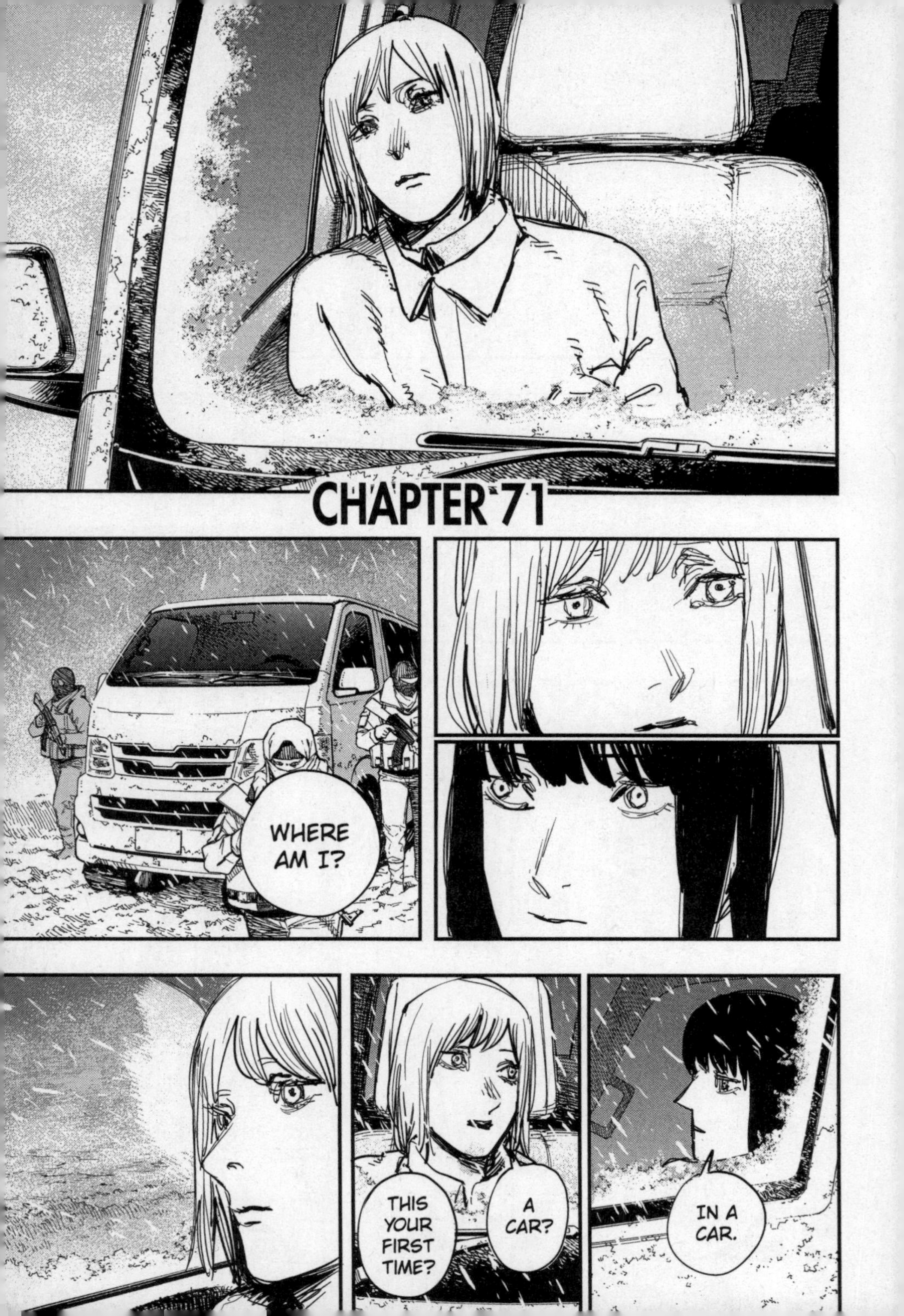
CHAPTER 71
WHERE AM I?
IN A CAR.
A CAR?
THIS YOUR FIRST TIME?

FIRE PUNCH

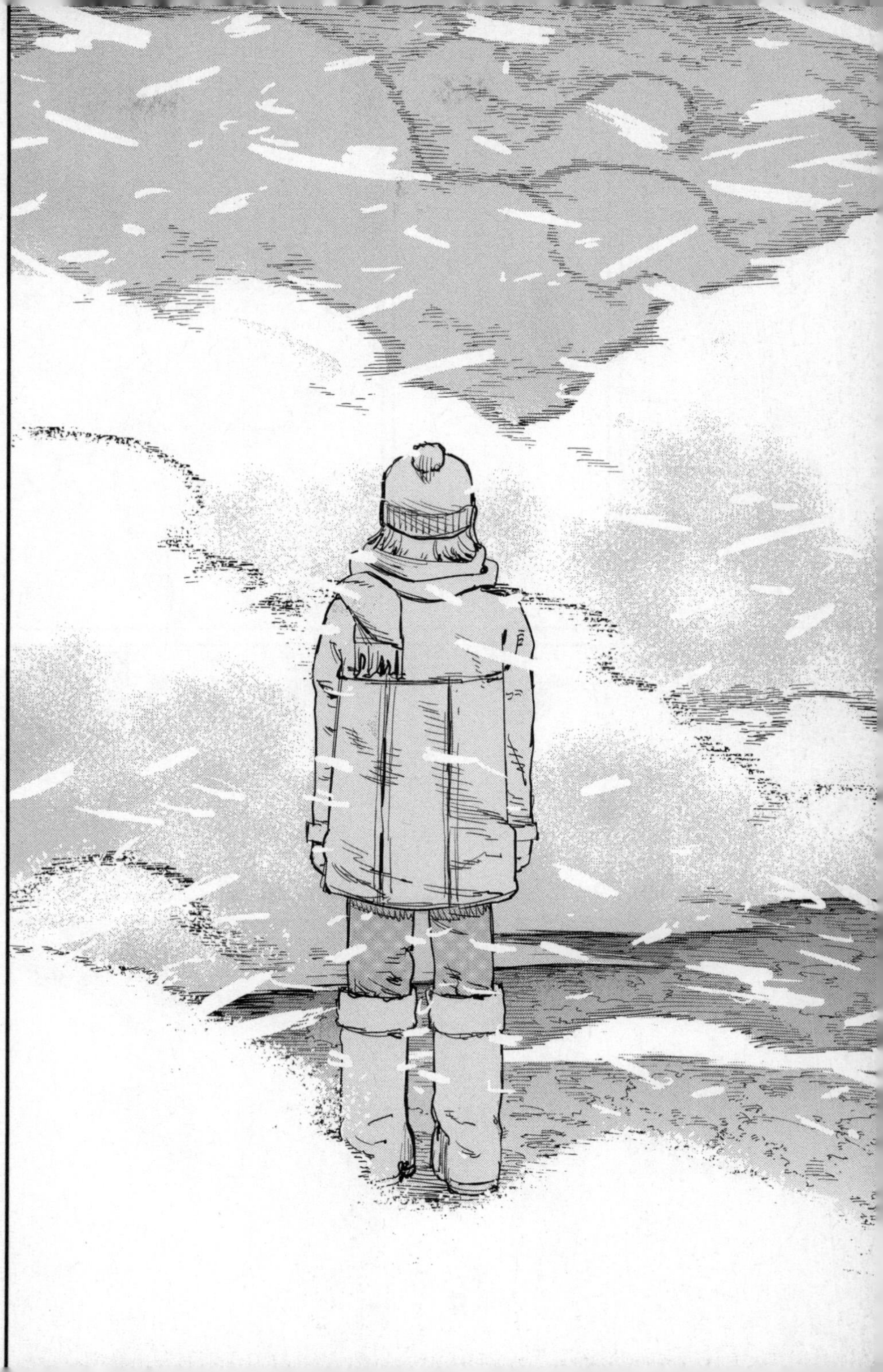

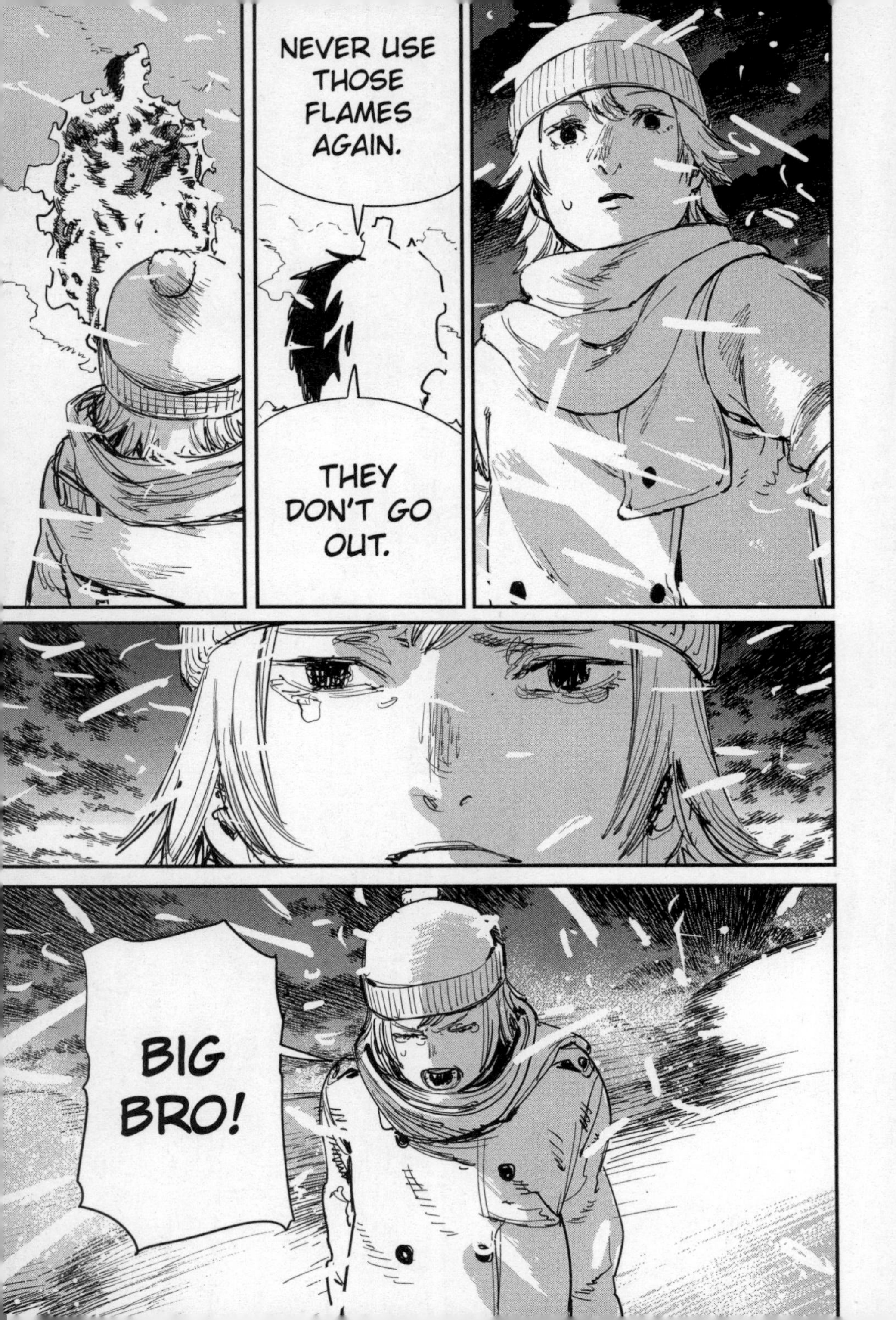
NEVER USE THOSE FLAMES AGAIN.
THEY DON'T GO OUT.
BIG BRO!

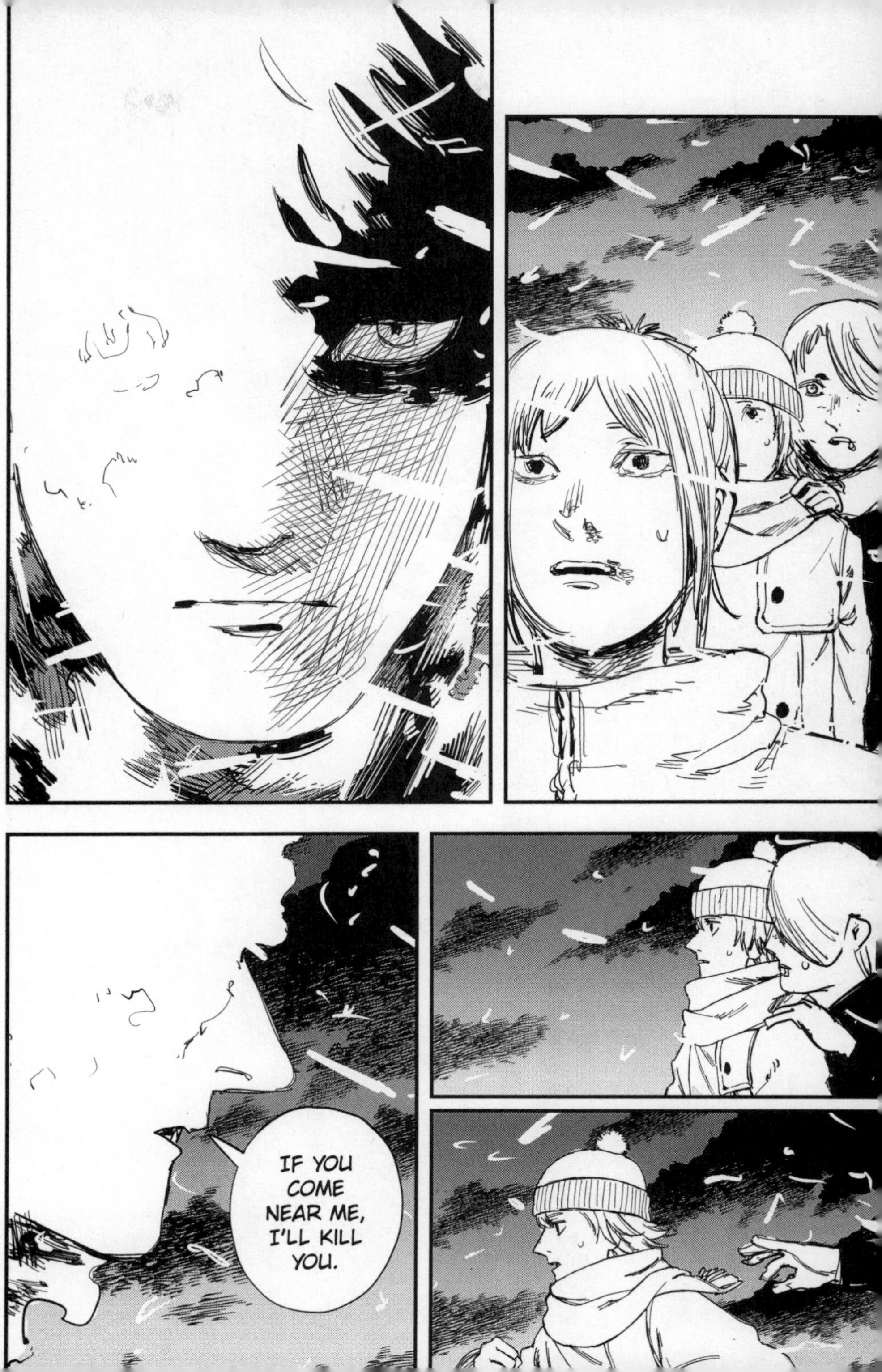
IF YOU COME NEAR ME, I'LL KILL YOU.

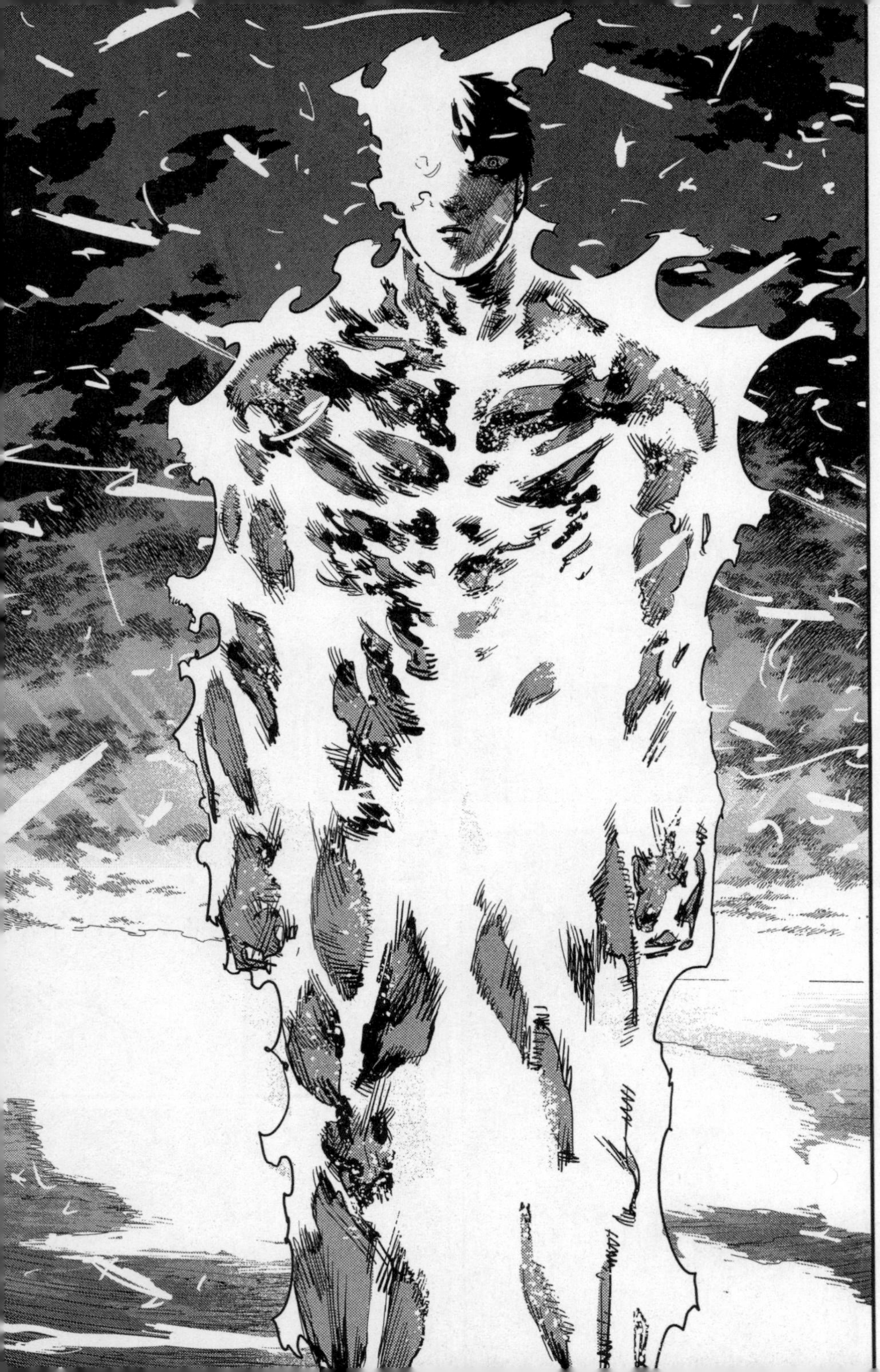

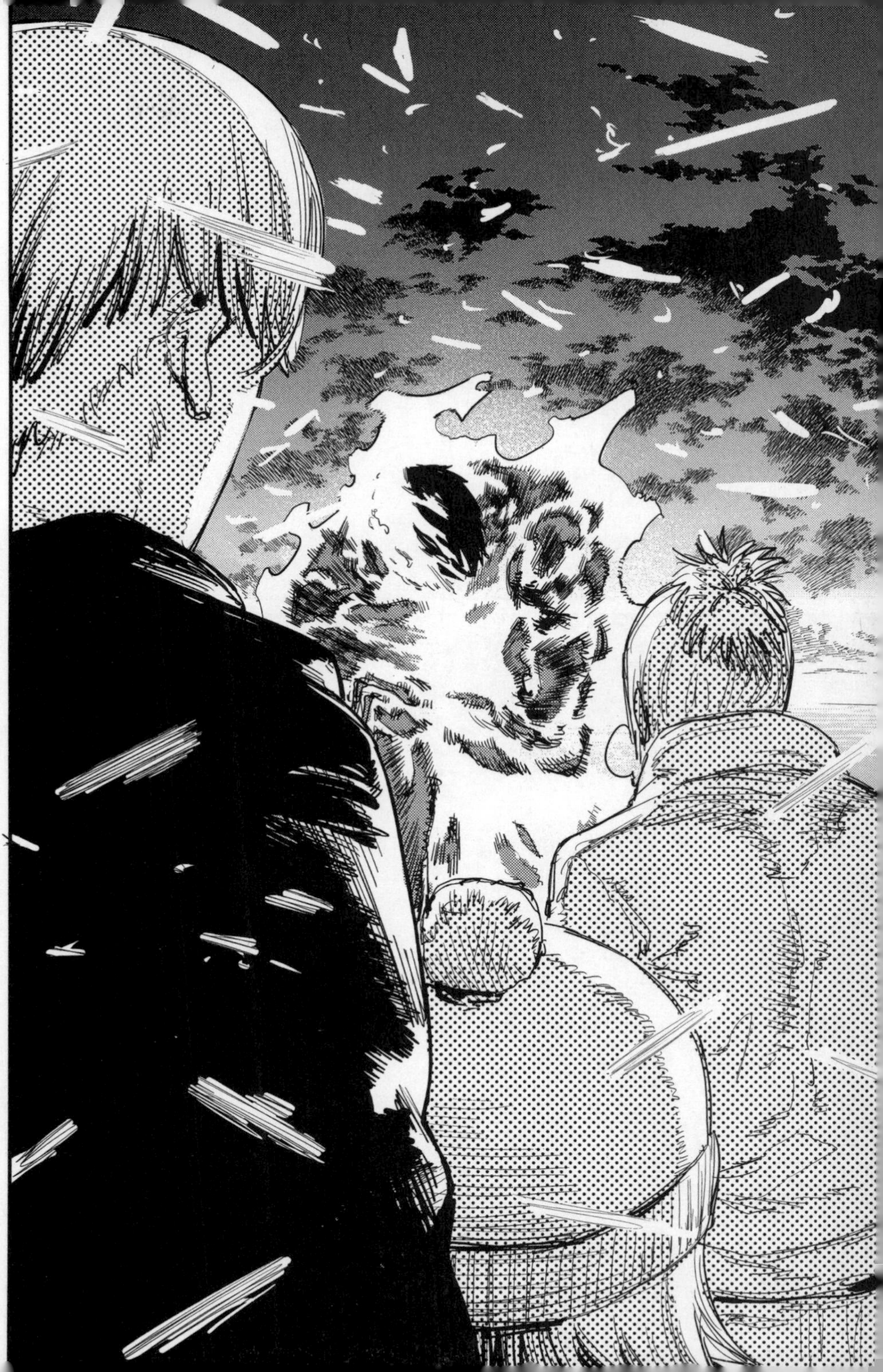

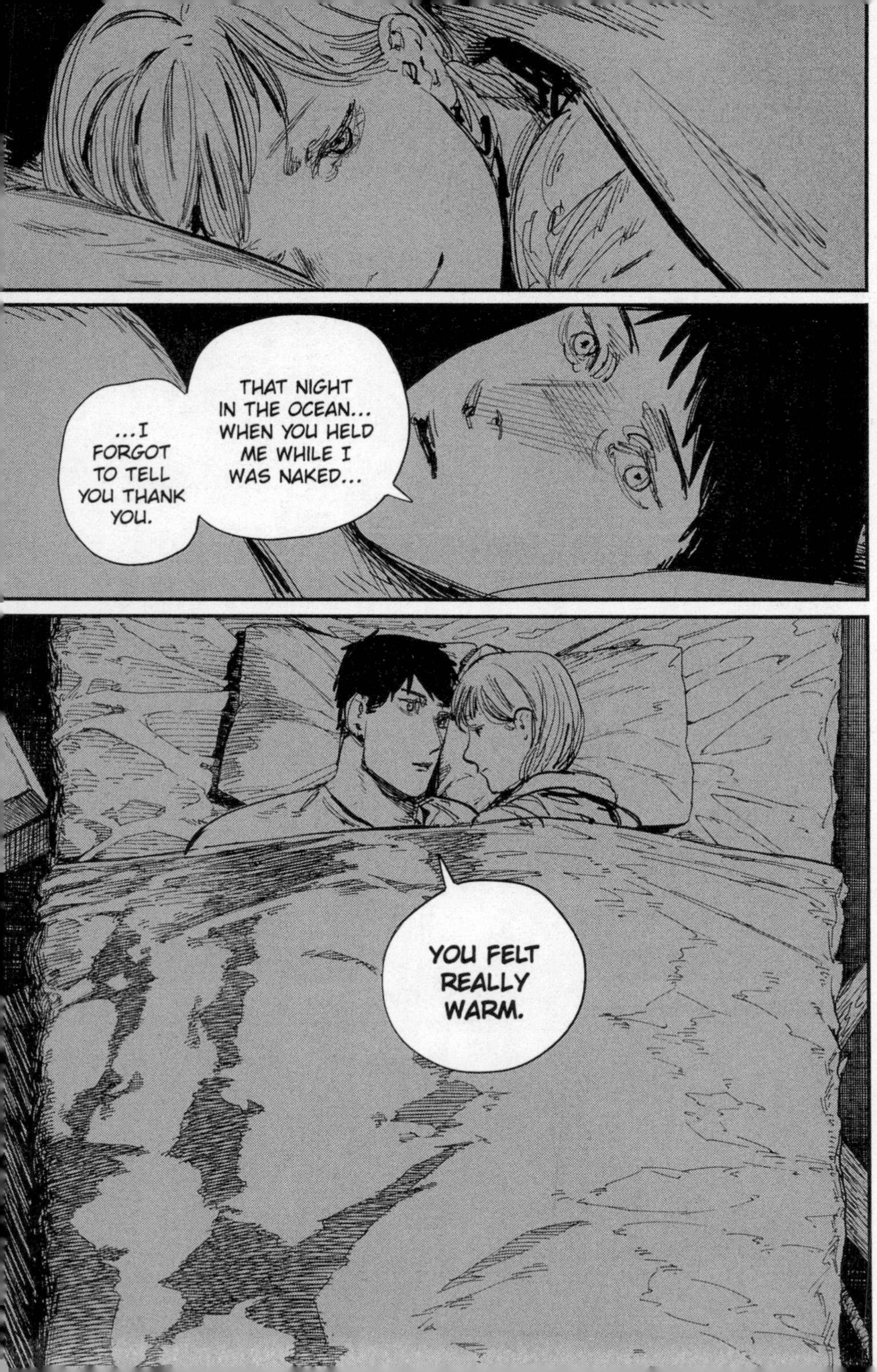
THAT NIGHT IN THE OCEAN... WHEN YOU HELD ME WHILE I WAS NAKED...
...I FORGOT TO TELL YOU THANK YOU.
YOU FELT REALLY WARM.

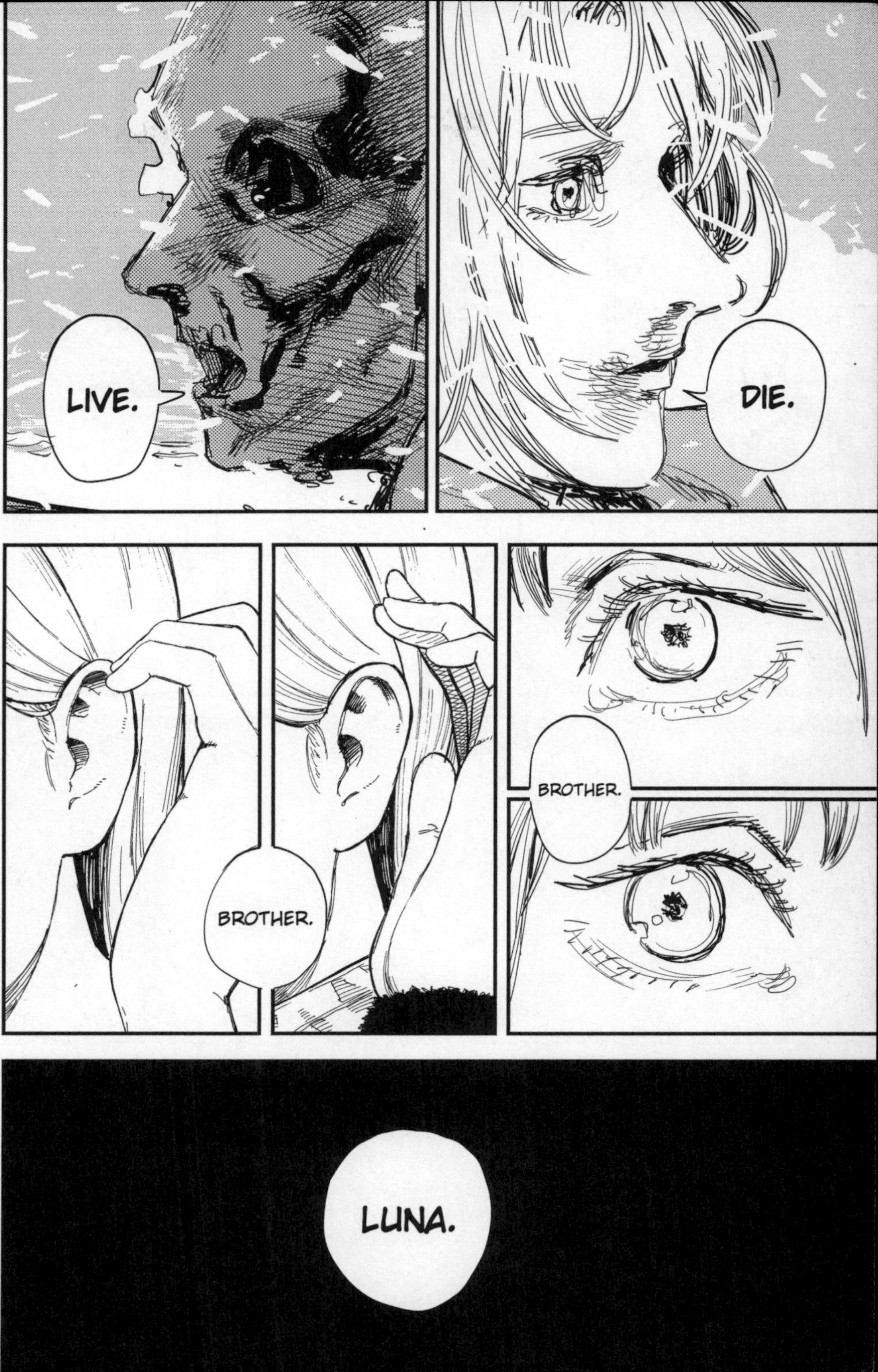
DIE.
LIVE.
BROTHER.
BROTHER.
LUNA.

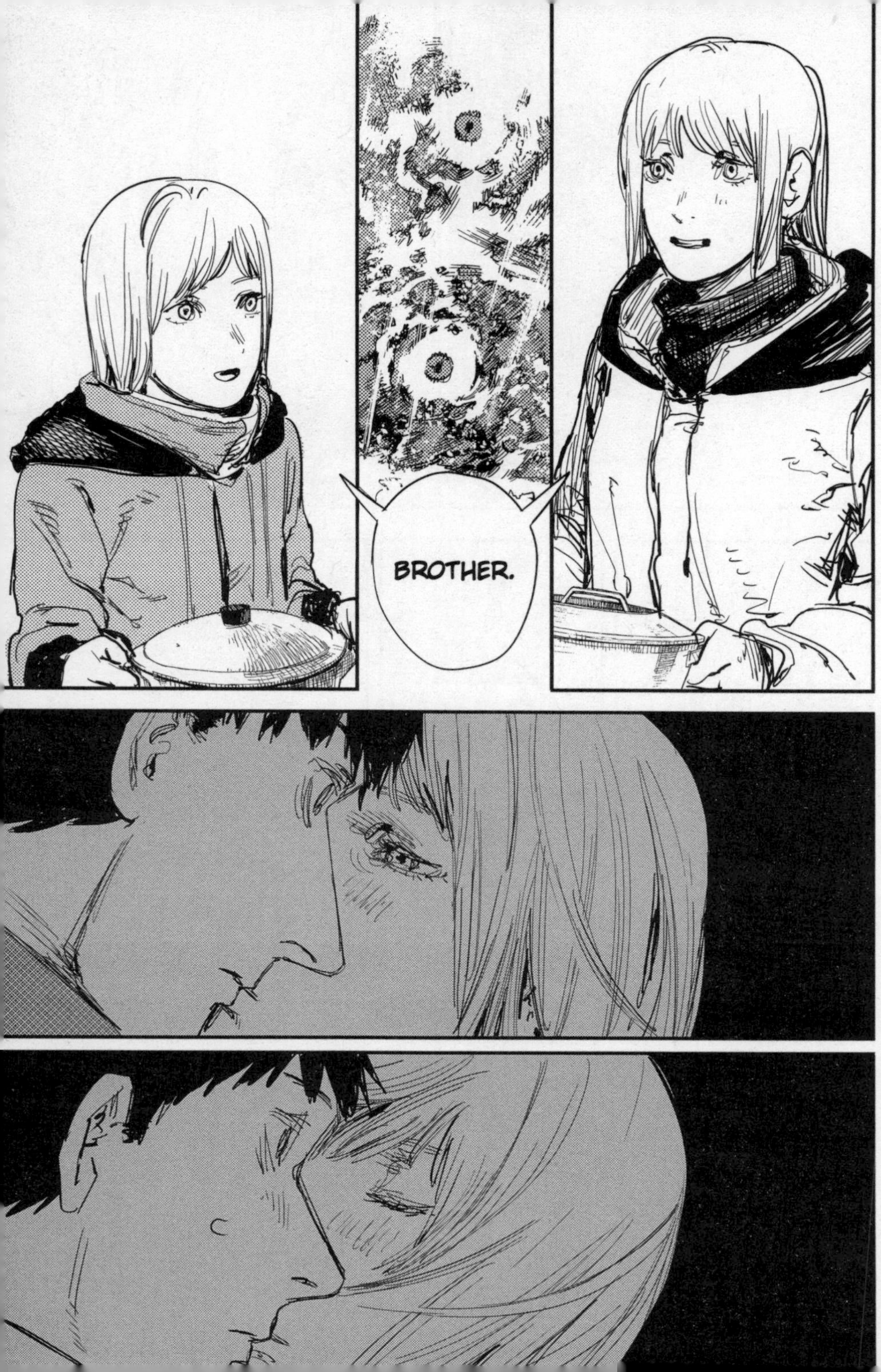
BROTHER.

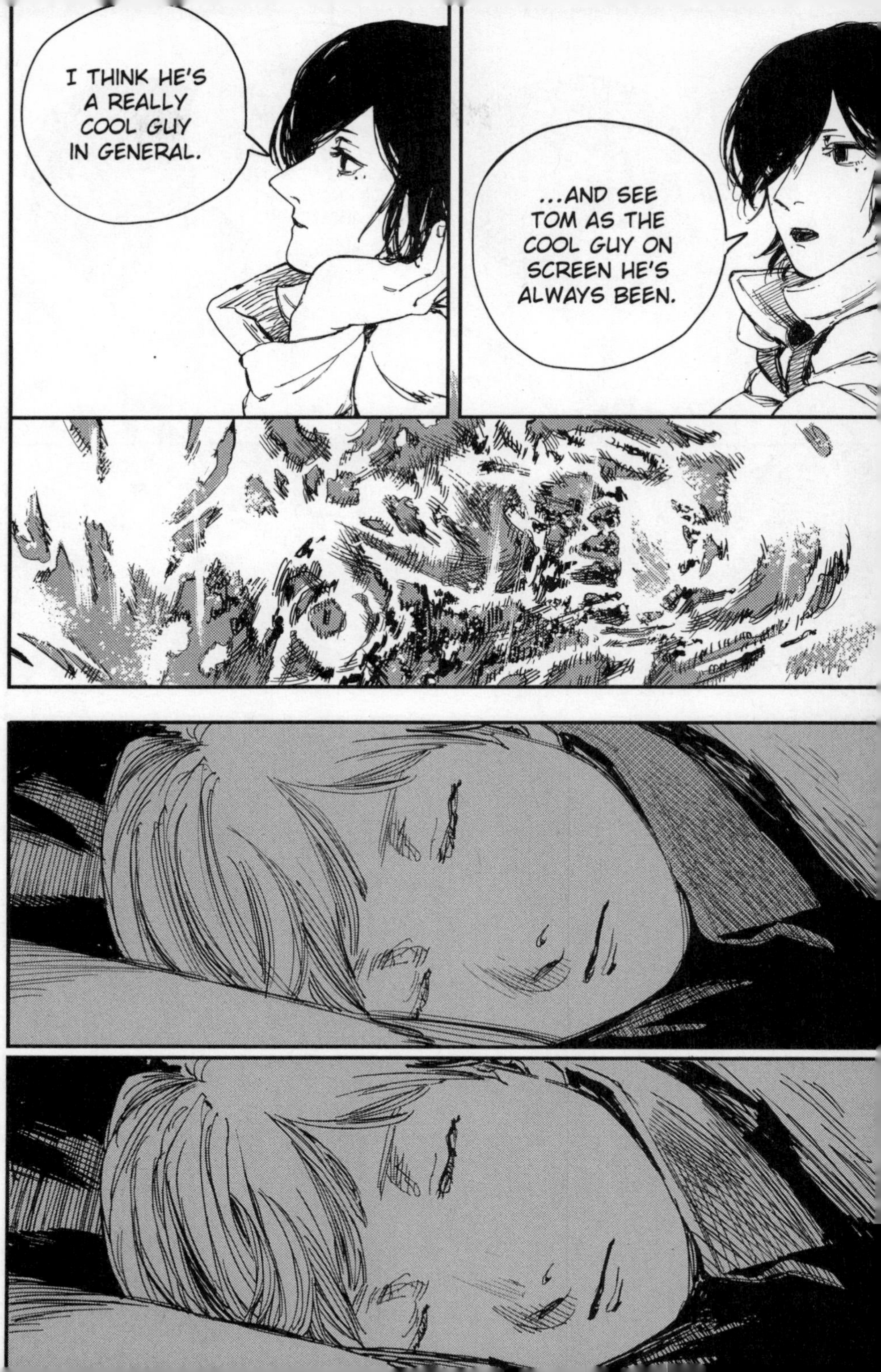
...AND SEE TOM AS THE COOL GUY ON SCREEN HE'S ALWAYS BEEN.
I THINK HE'S A REALLY COOL GUY IN GENERAL.

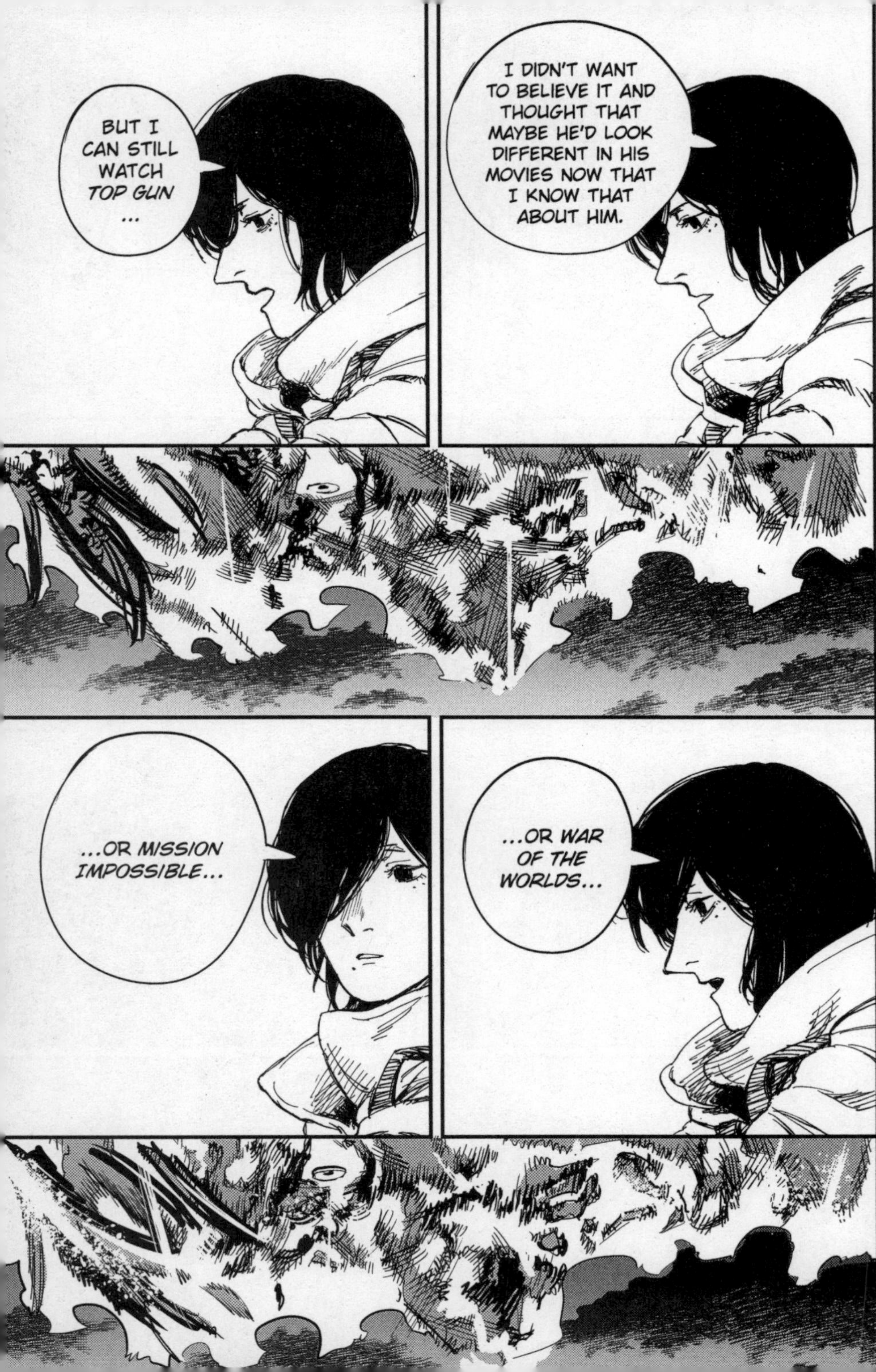
I DIDN'T WANT TO BELIEVE IT AND THOUGHT THAT MAYBE HE'D LOOK DIFFERENT IN HIS MOVIES NOW THAT I KNOW THAT ABOUT HIM.
BUT I CAN STILL WATCH *TOP GUN* ...
...OR *WAR OF THE WORLDS*...
...OR *MISSION IMPOSSIBLE*...

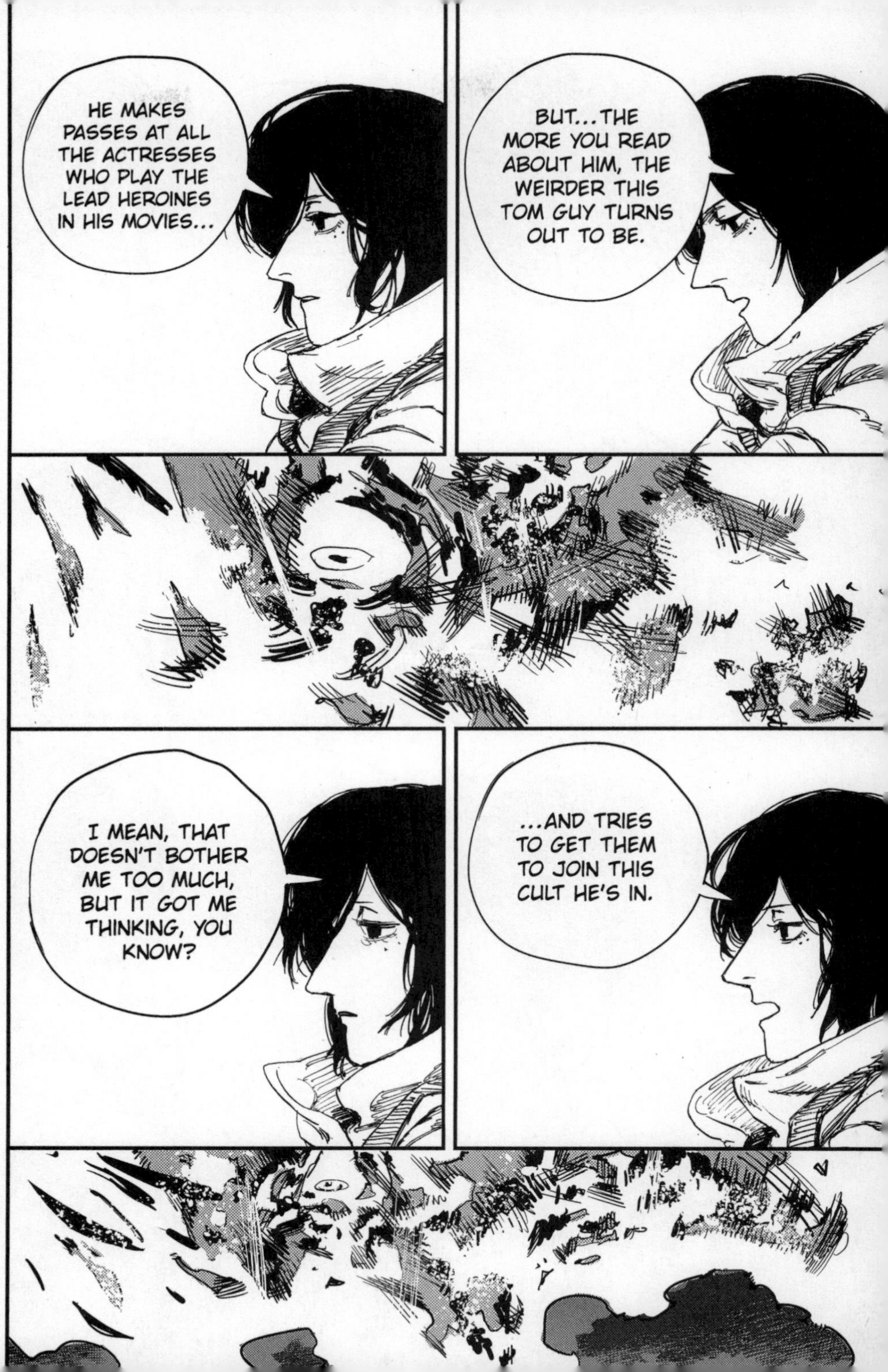
BUT...THE MORE YOU READ ABOUT HIM, THE WEIRDER THIS TOM GUY TURNS OUT TO BE.
HE MAKES PASSES AT ALL THE ACTRESSES WHO PLAY THE LEAD HEROINES IN HIS MOVIES...
...AND TRIES TO GET THEM TO JOIN THIS CULT HE'S IN.
I MEAN, THAT DOESN'T BOTHER ME TOO MUCH, BUT IT GOT ME THINKING, YOU KNOW?

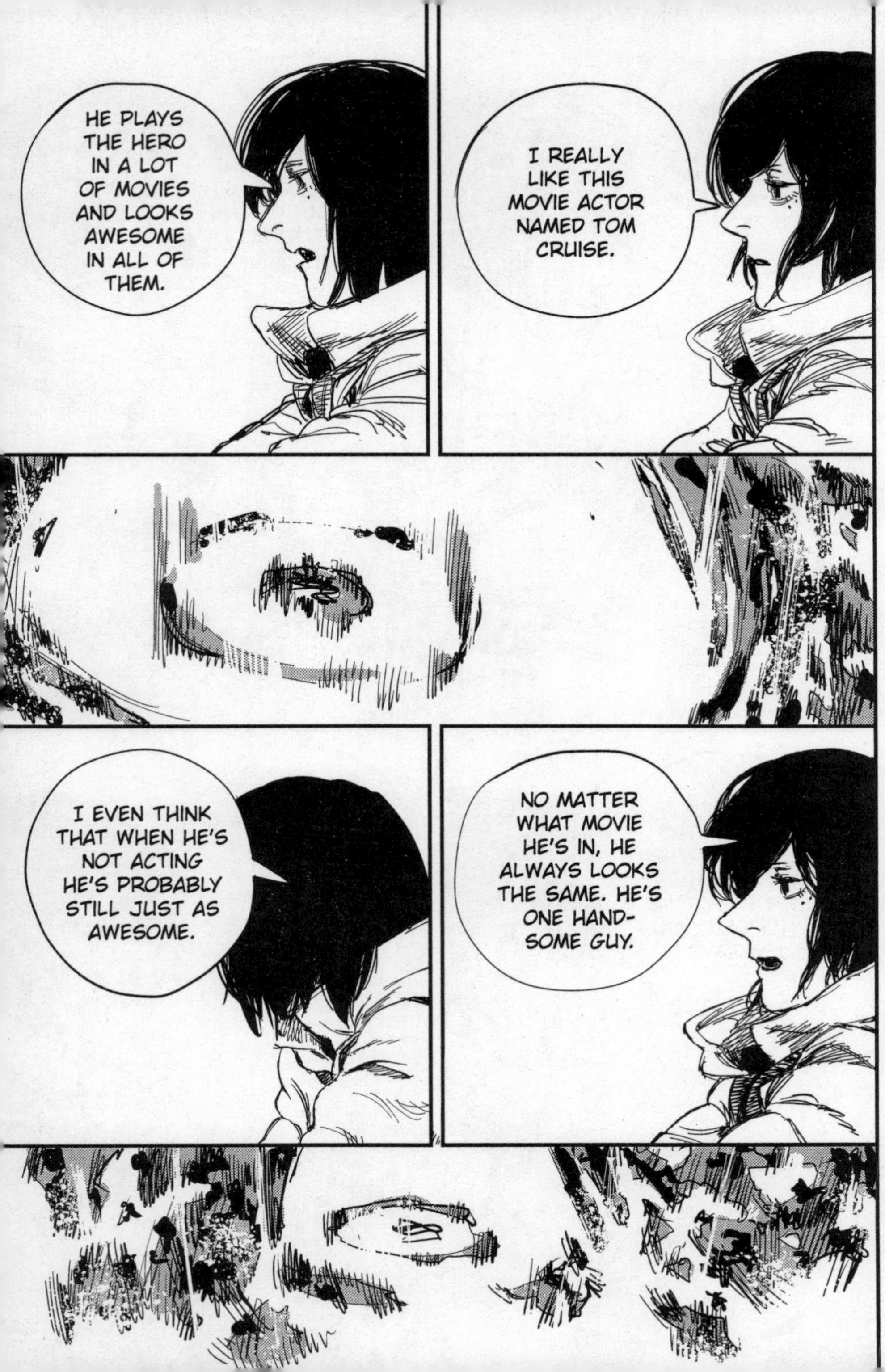
I REALLY LIKE THIS MOVIE ACTOR NAMED TOM CRUISE.
HE PLAYS THE HERO IN A LOT OF MOVIES AND LOOKS AWESOME IN ALL OF THEM.
NO MATTER WHAT MOVIE HE'S IN, HE ALWAYS LOOKS THE SAME. HE'S ONE HAND-SOME GUY.
I EVEN THINK THAT WHEN HE'S NOT ACTING HE'S PROBABLY STILL JUST AS AWESOME.

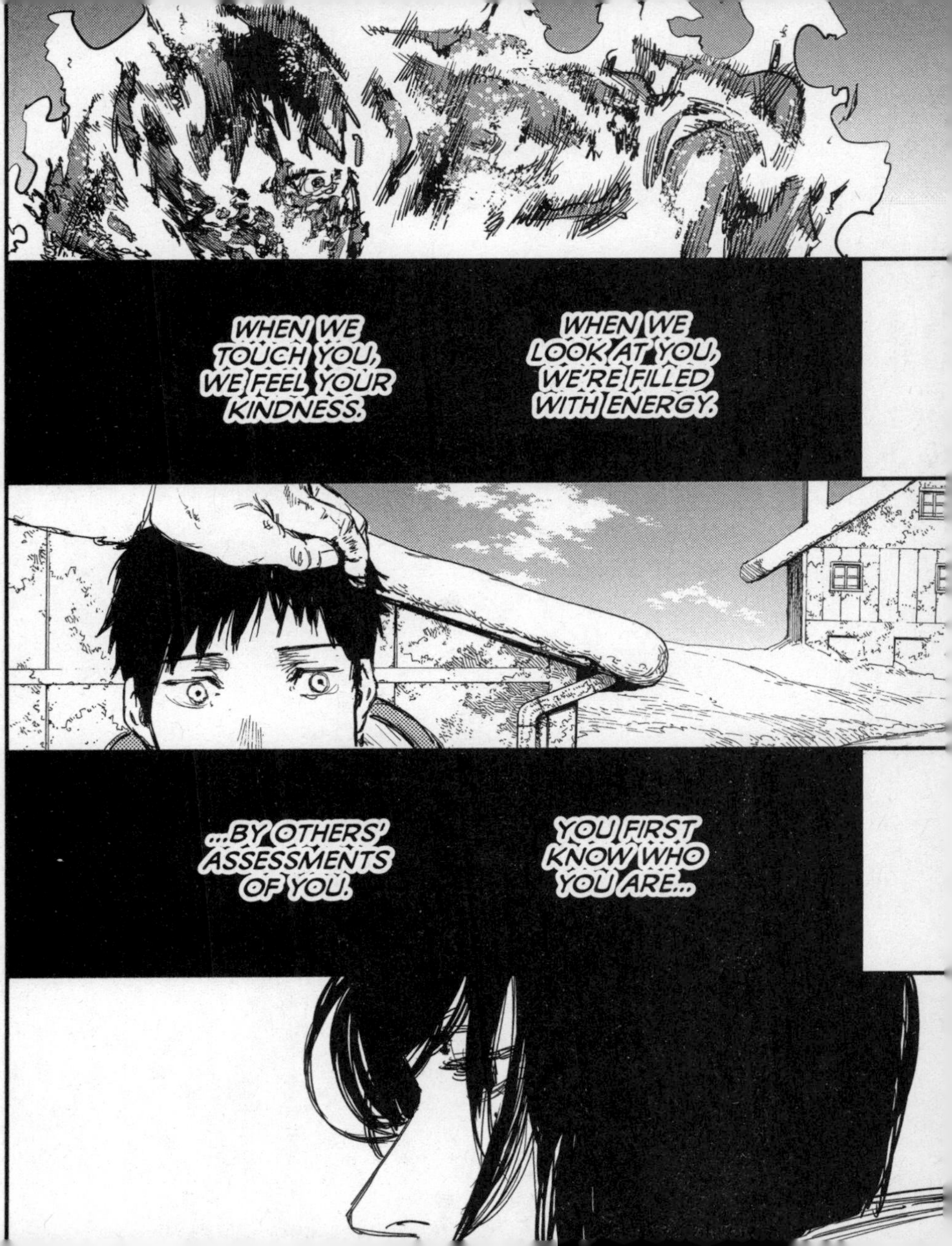
WHEN WE LOOK AT YOU, WE'RE FILLED WITH ENERGY.
WHEN WE TOUCH YOU, WE FEEL YOUR KINDNESS.
YOU FIRST KNOW WHO YOU ARE...
...BY OTHERS' ASSESSMENTS OF YOU.

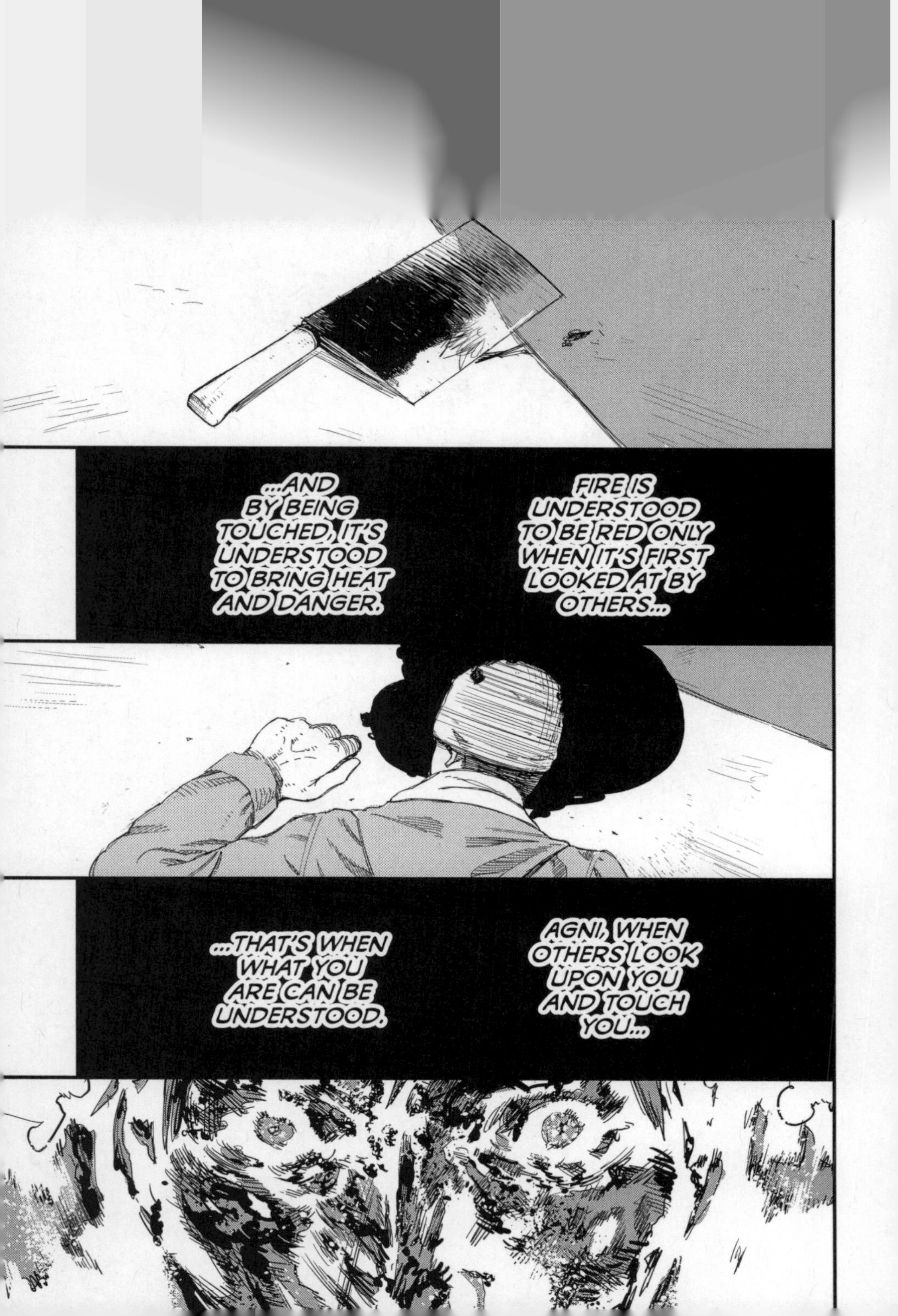
FIRE IS UNDERSTOOD TO BE RED ONLY WHEN IT'S FIRST LOOKED AT BY OTHERS...
...AND BY BEING TOUCHED, IT'S UNDERSTOOD TO BRING HEAT AND DANGER.
AGNI, WHEN OTHERS LOOK UPON YOU AND TOUCH YOU...
...THAT'S WHEN WHAT YOU ARE CAN BE UNDERSTOOD.

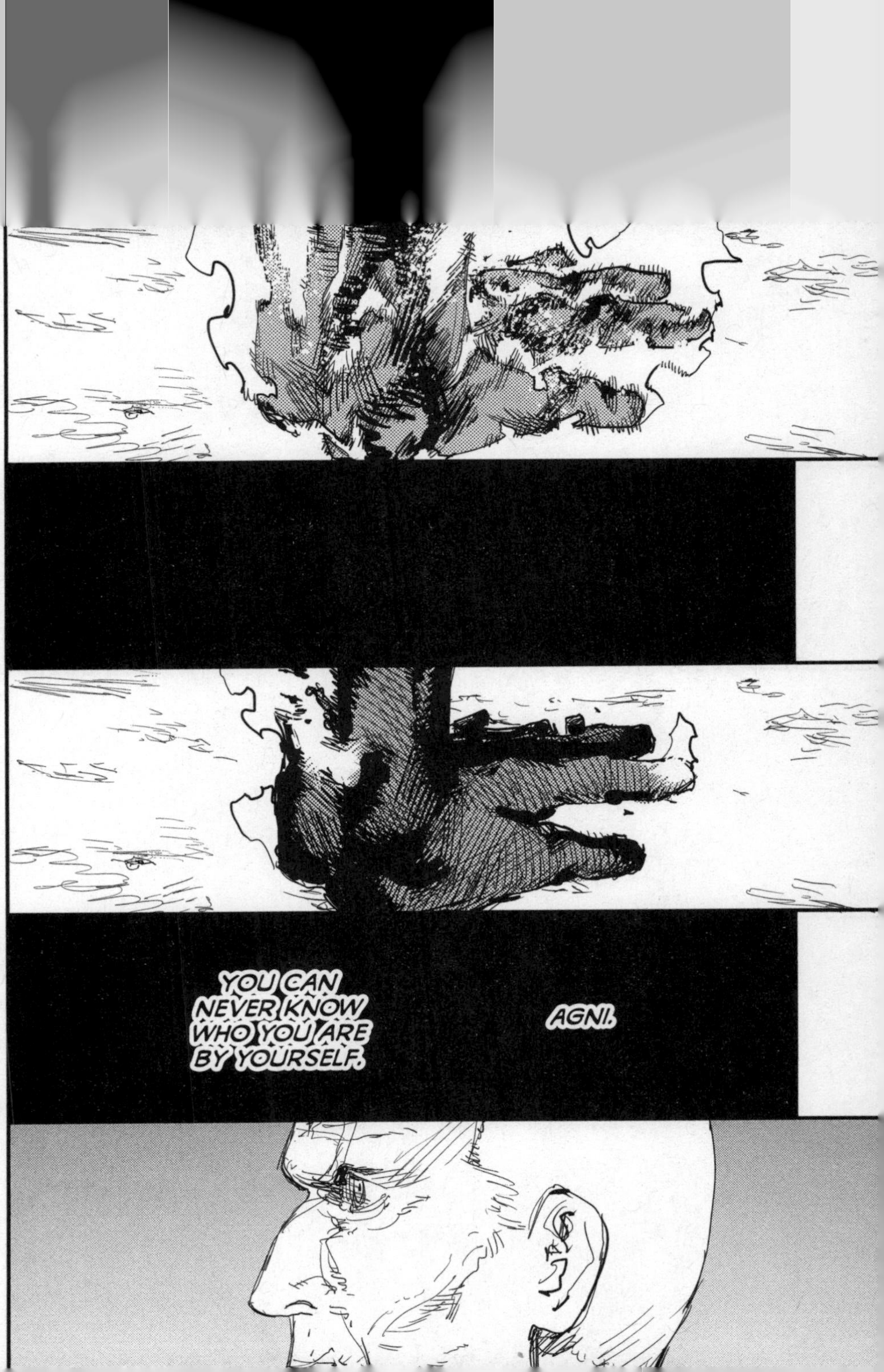
AGNI.
YOU CAN NEVER KNOW WHO YOU ARE BY YOURSELF.

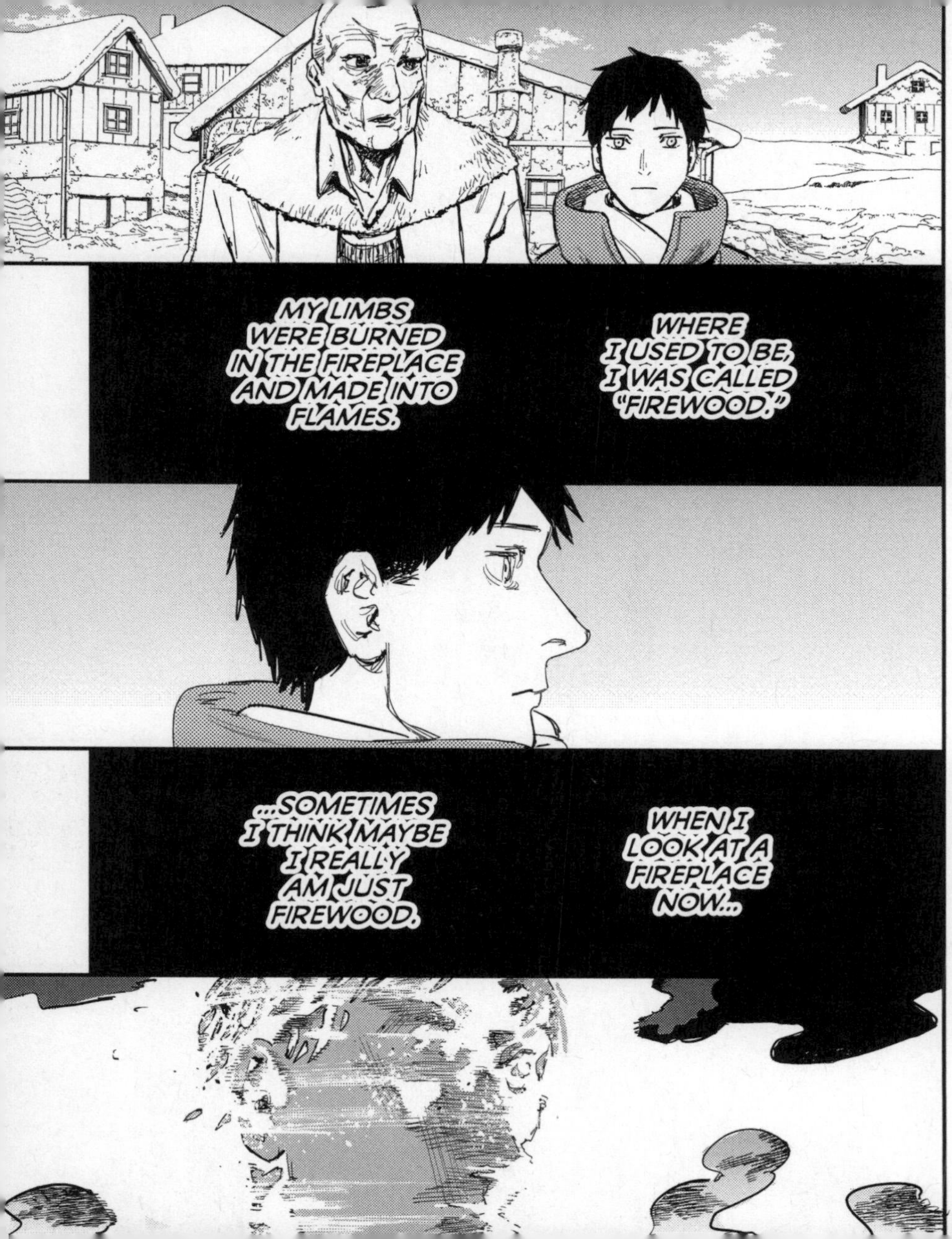
WHERE I USED TO BE, I WAS CALLED "FIREWOOD."
MY LIMBS WERE BURNED IN THE FIREPLACE AND MADE INTO FLAMES.
WHEN I LOOK AT A FIREPLACE NOW...
...SOMETIMES I THINK MAYBE I REALLY AM JUST FIREWOOD.

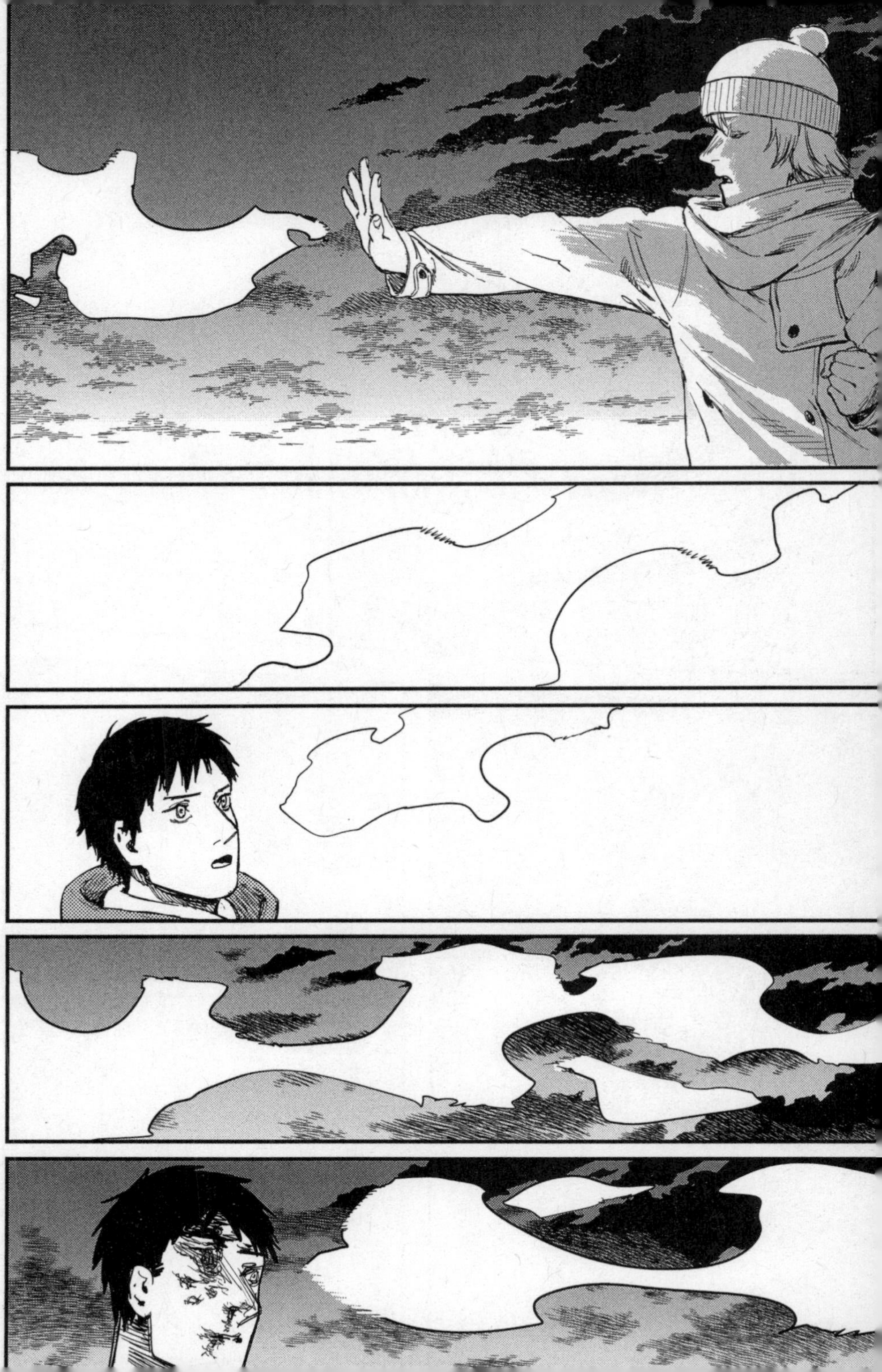

DON'T BULLY MY MOMMY!

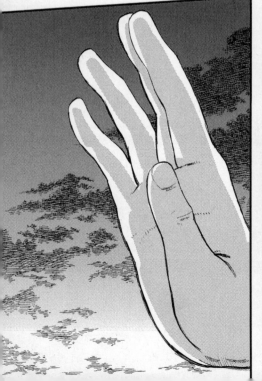

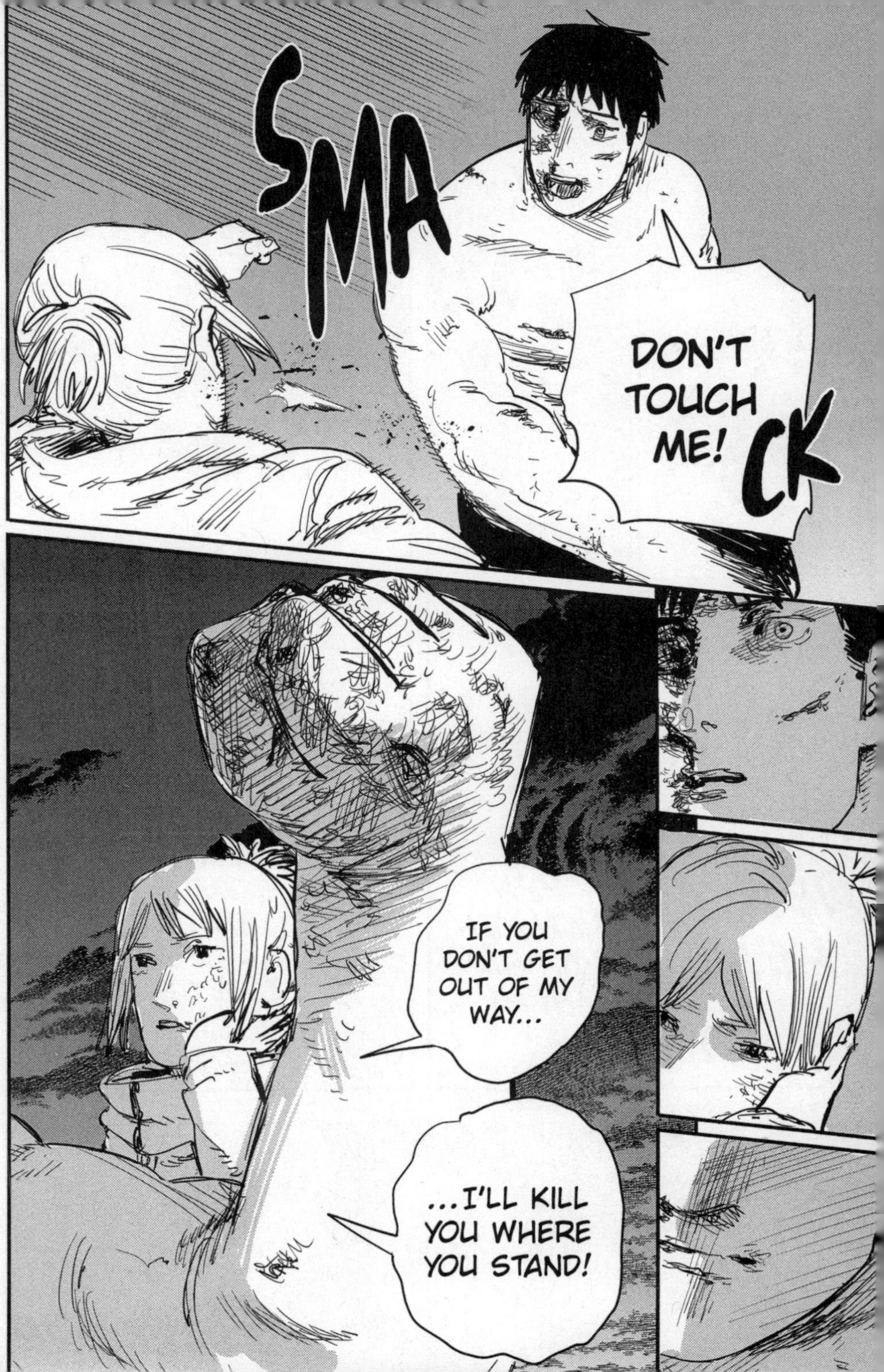
DON'T TOUCH ME!
SMA
CK
IF YOU DON'T GET OUT OF MY WAY...
...I'LL KILL YOU WHERE YOU STAND!

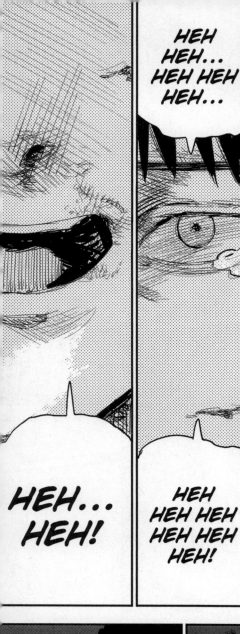

HEH
HEH...
HEH HEH
HEH...

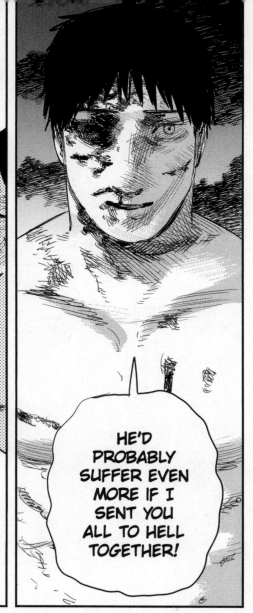

HE'D
PROBABLY
SUFFER EVEN
MORE IF I
SENT YOU
ALL TO HELL
TOGETHER!

HEH...
HEH!

HEH
HEH HEH
HEH HEH
HEH!

AGNI!

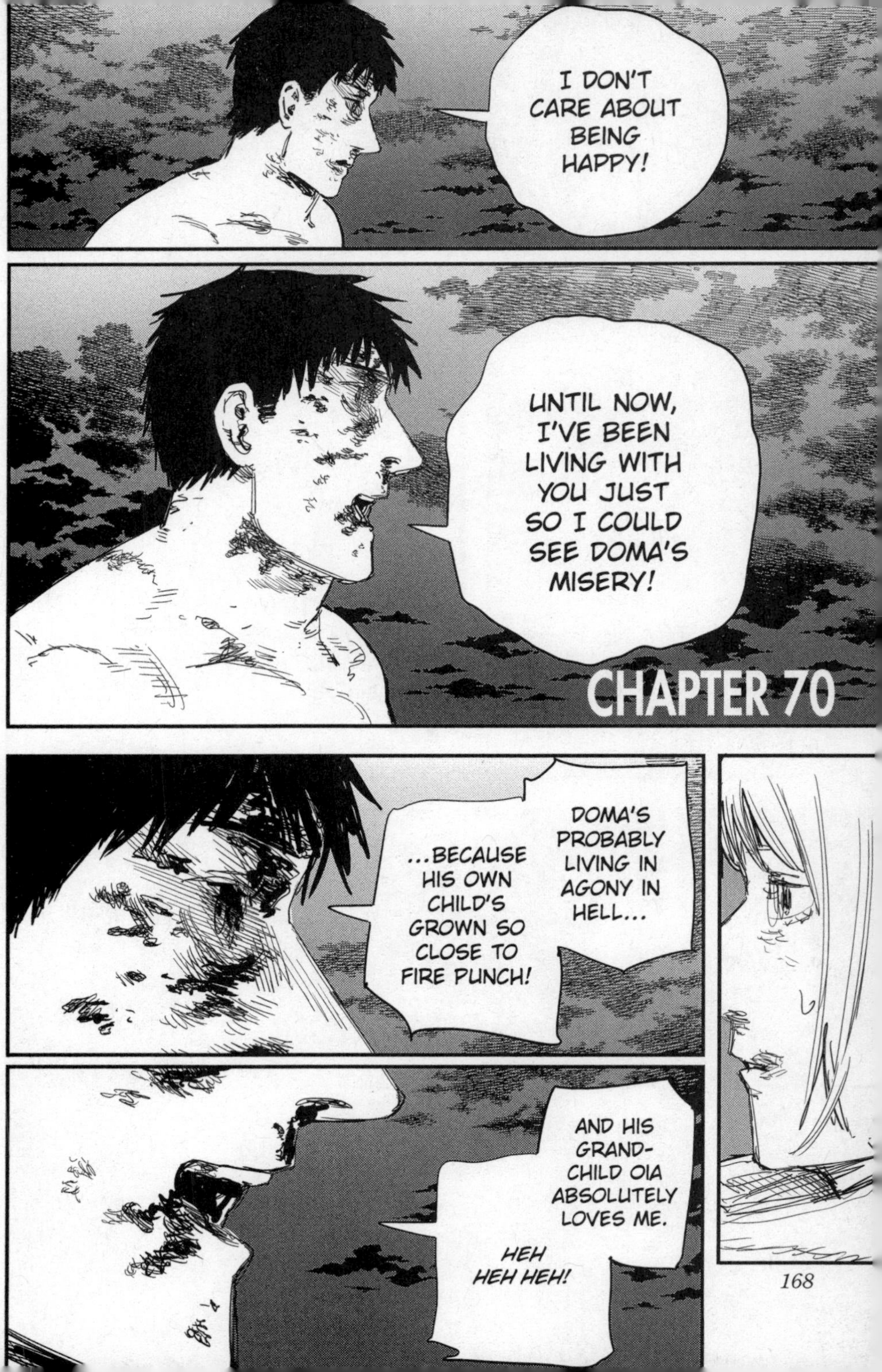
I DON'T CARE ABOUT BEING HAPPY!
UNTIL NOW, I'VE BEEN LIVING WITH YOU JUST SO I COULD SEE DOMA'S MISERY!
CHAPTER 70
DOMA'S PROBABLY LIVING IN AGONY IN HELL...
...BECAUSE HIS OWN CHILD'S GROWN SO CLOSE TO FIRE PUNCH!
AND HIS GRAND-CHILD OIA ABSOLUTELY LOVES ME.
HEH HEH HEH!

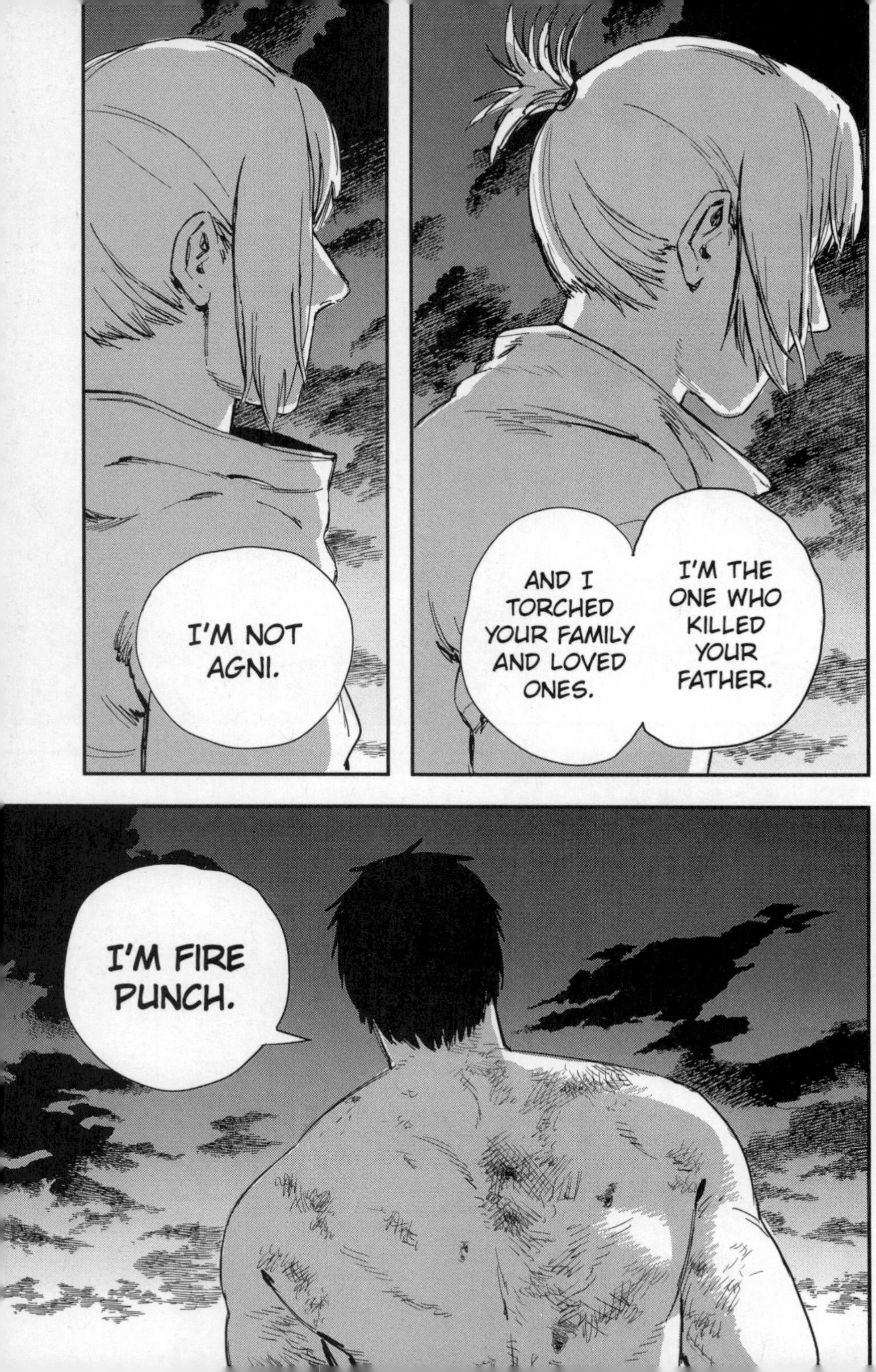

I'M THE ONE WHO KILLED YOUR FATHER.
AND I TORCHED YOUR FAMILY AND LOVED ONES.
I'M NOT AGNI.
I'M FIRE PUNCH.

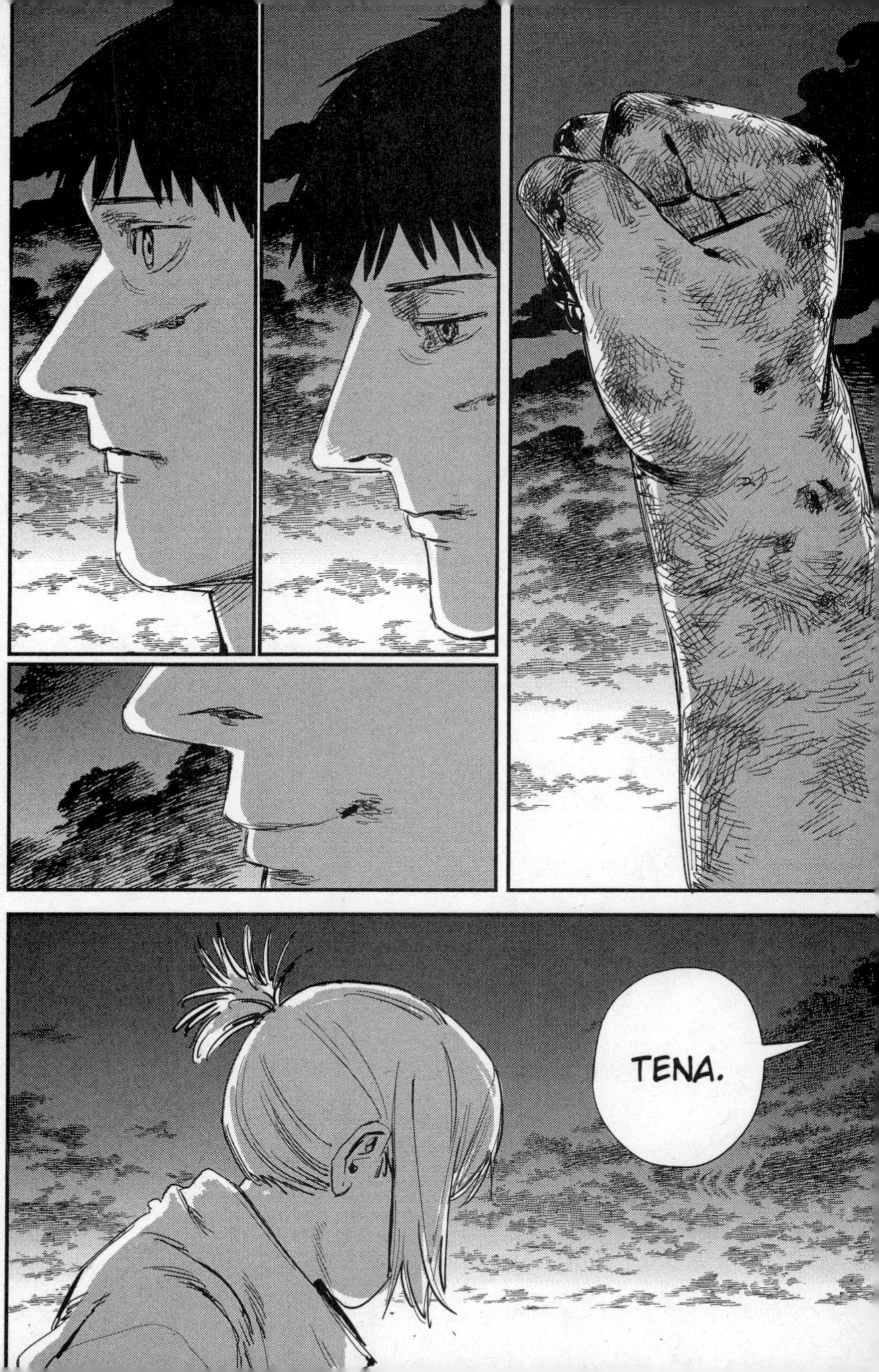
TENA.

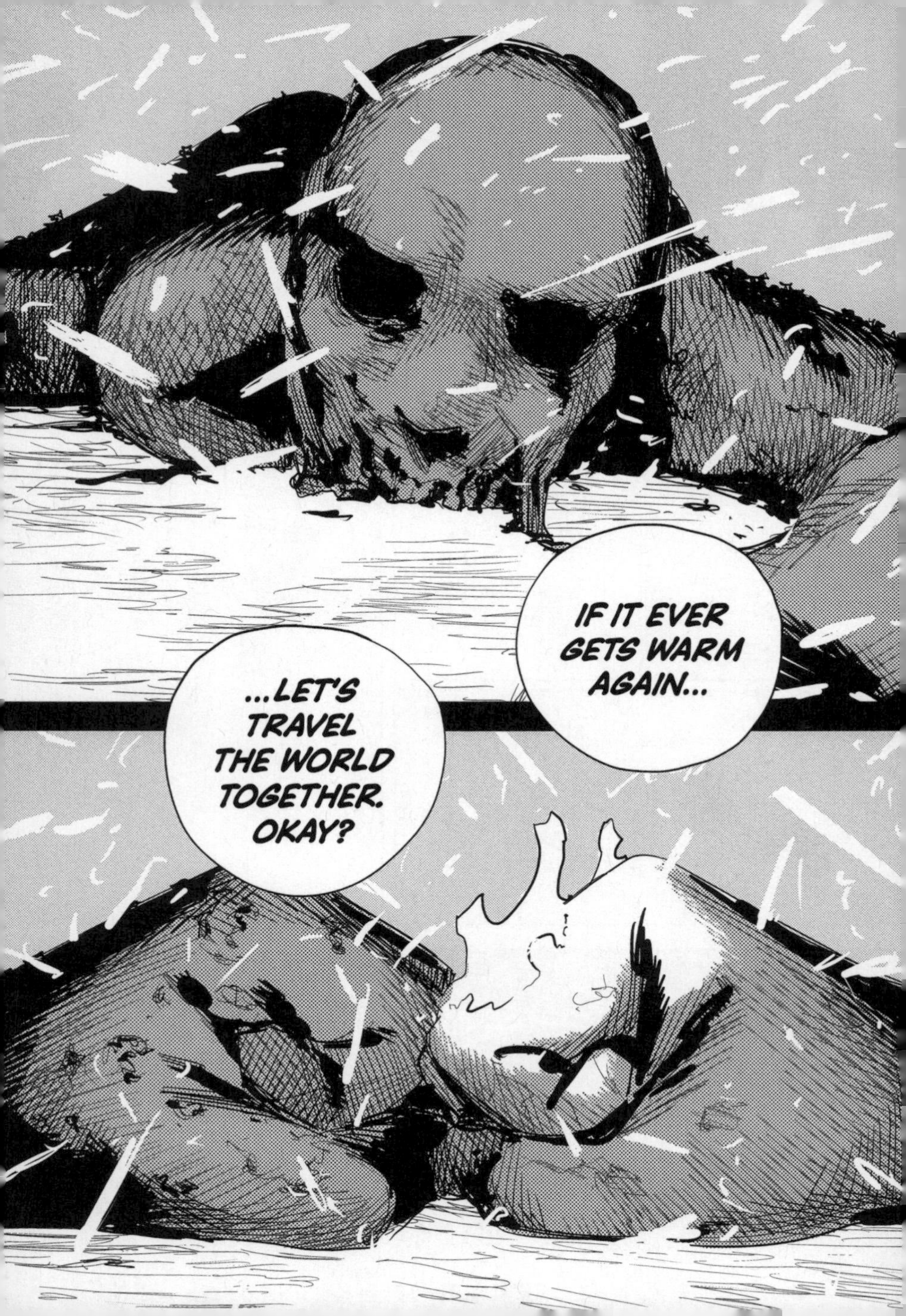
IF IT EVER GETS WARM AGAIN...
...LET'S TRAVEL THE WORLD TOGETHER. OKAY?

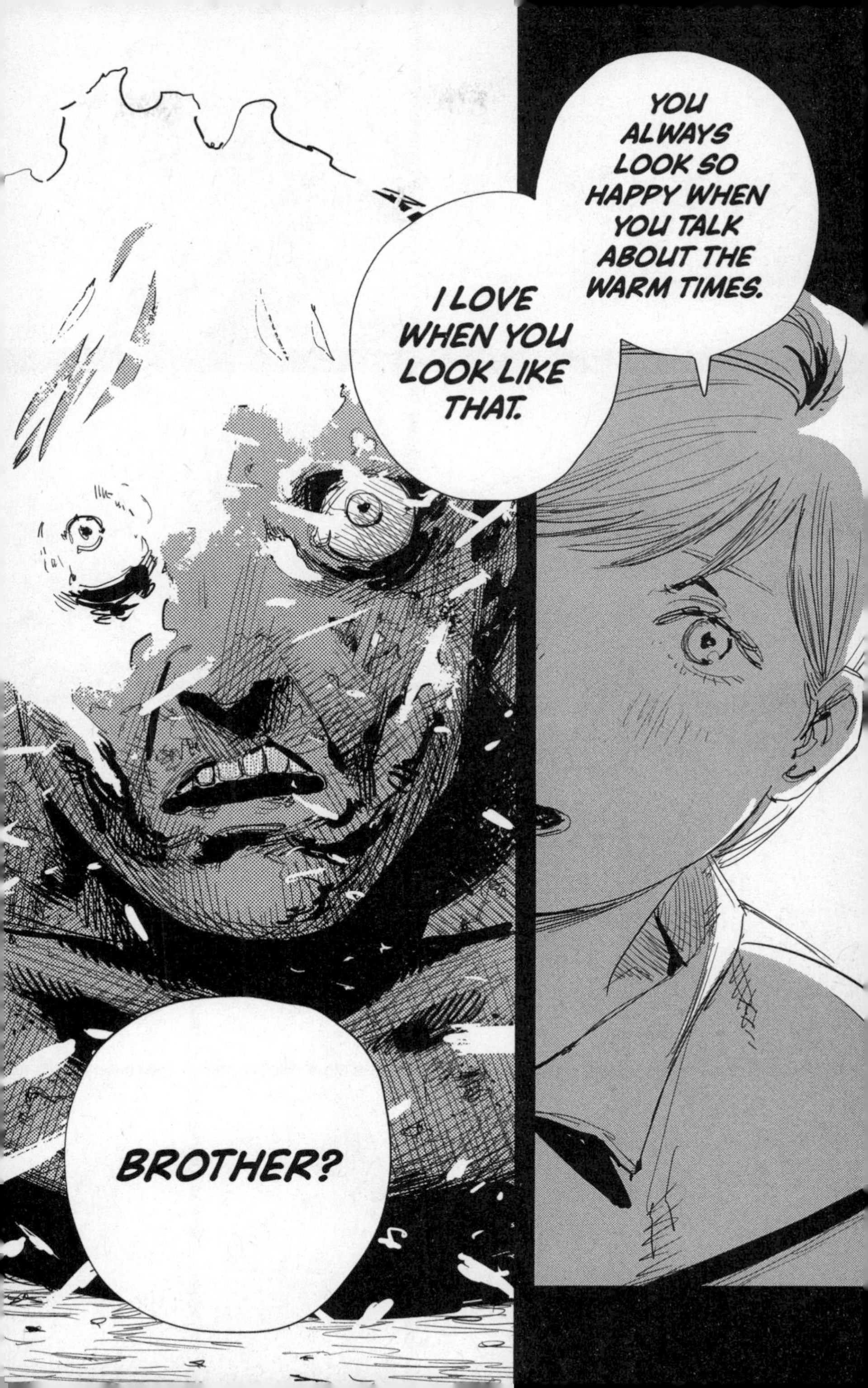
YOU ALWAYS LOOK SO HAPPY WHEN YOU TALK ABOUT THE WARM TIMES.
I LOVE WHEN YOU LOOK LIKE THAT.
BROTHER?

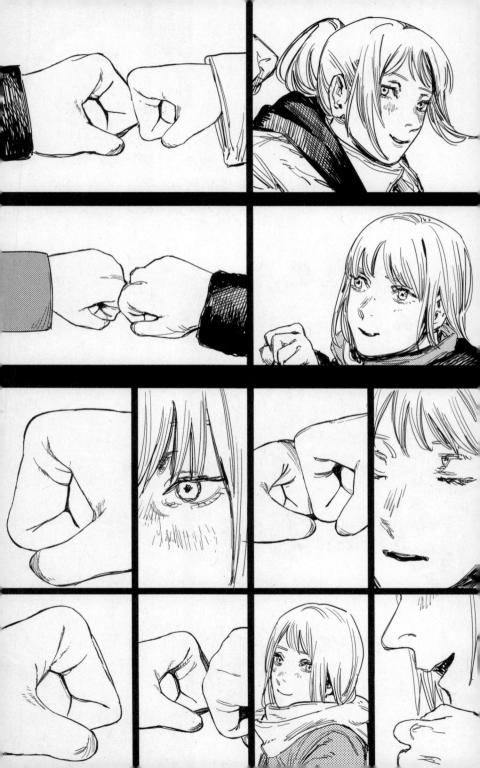

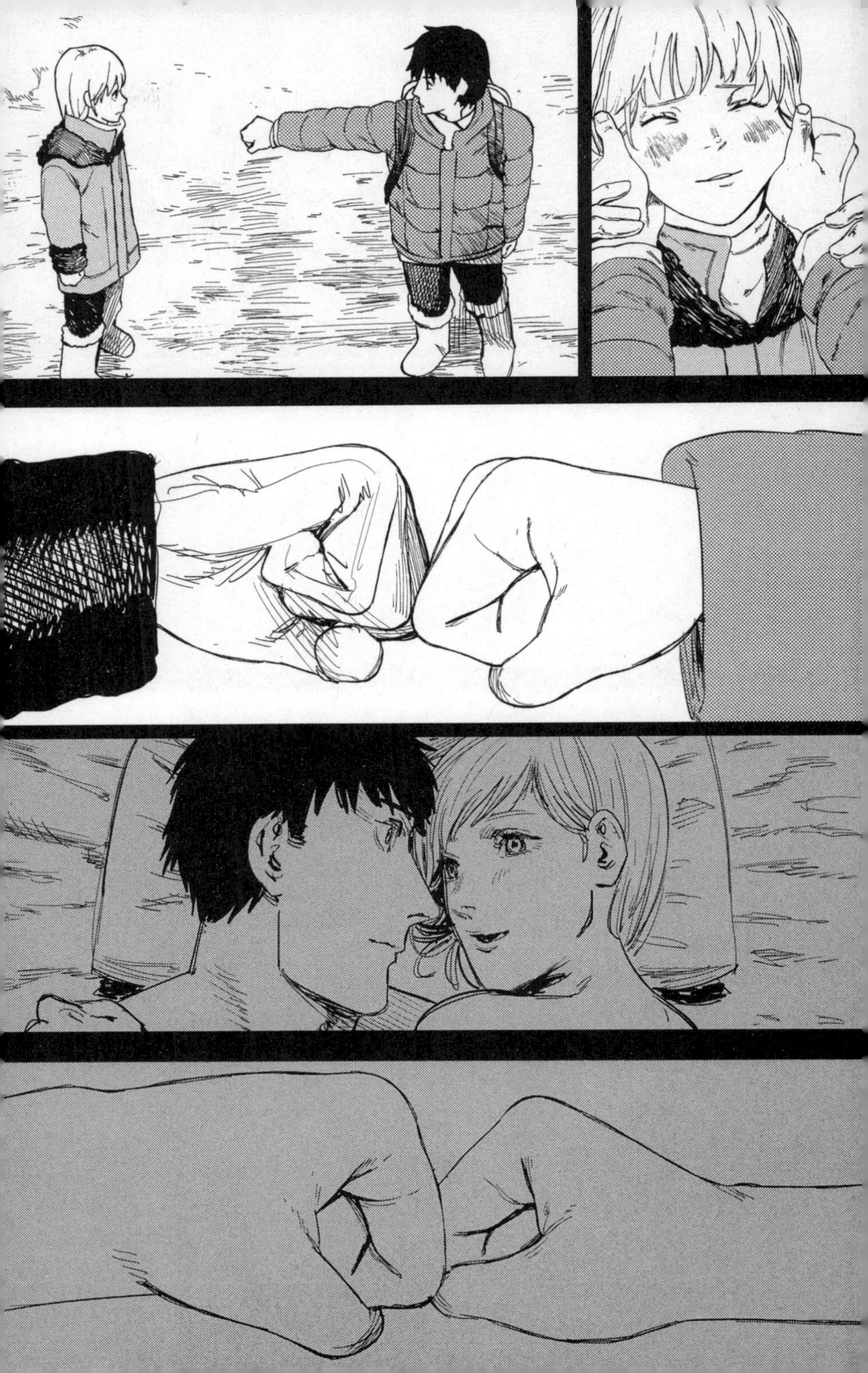

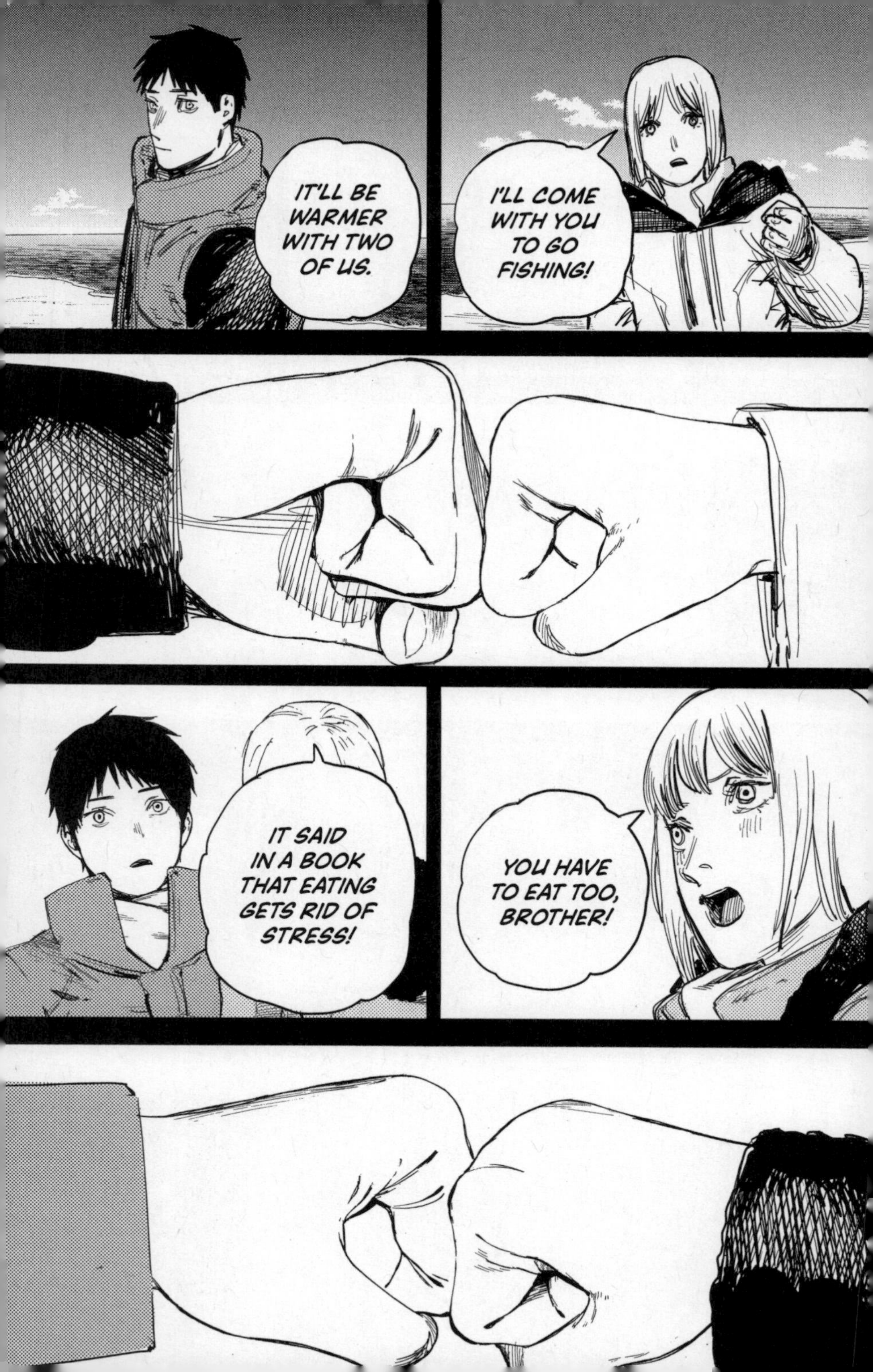
I'LL COME WITH YOU TO GO FISHING!
IT'LL BE WARMER WITH TWO OF US.
YOU HAVE TO EAT TOO, BROTHER!
IT SAID IN A BOOK THAT EATING GETS RID OF STRESS!

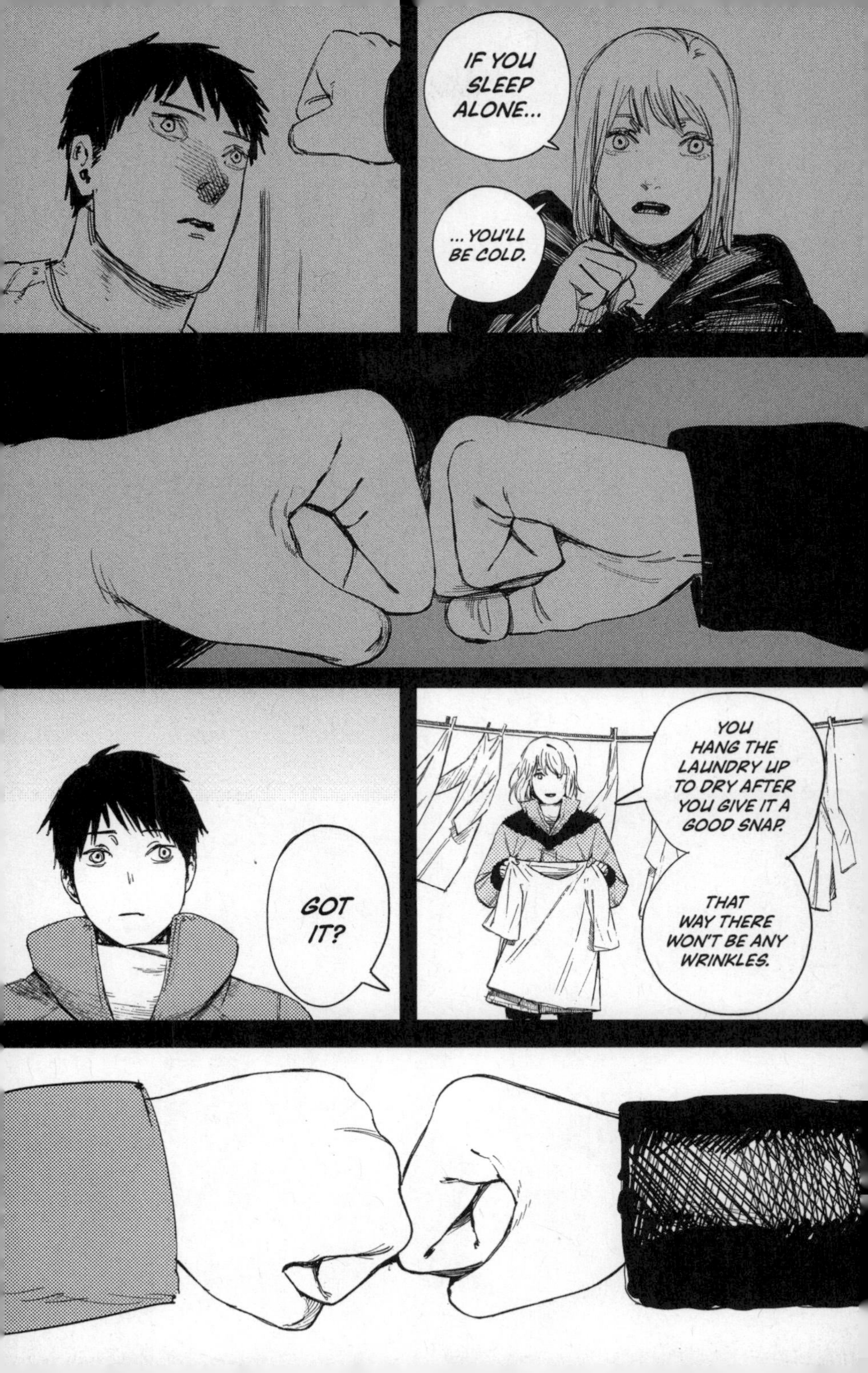
IF YOU SLEEP ALONE...
...YOU'LL BE COLD.
YOU HANG THE LAUNDRY UP TO DRY AFTER YOU GIVE IT A GOOD SNAP.
THAT WAY THERE WON'T BE ANY WRINKLES.
GOT IT?

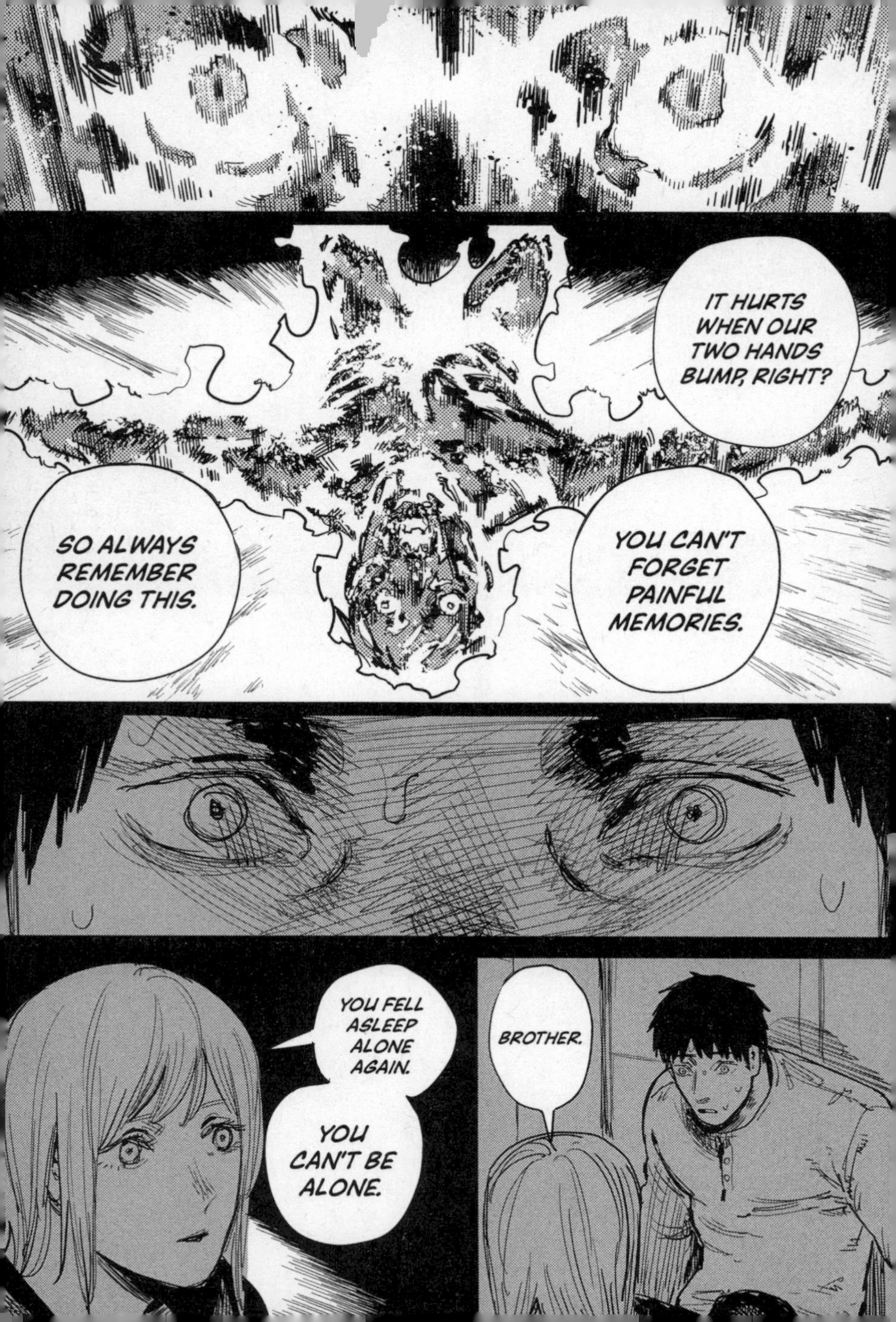
IT HURTS WHEN OUR TWO HANDS BUMP, RIGHT?
YOU CAN'T FORGET PAINFUL MEMORIES.
SO ALWAYS REMEMBER DOING THIS.
BROTHER.
YOU FELL ASLEEP ALONE AGAIN.
YOU CAN'T BE ALONE.

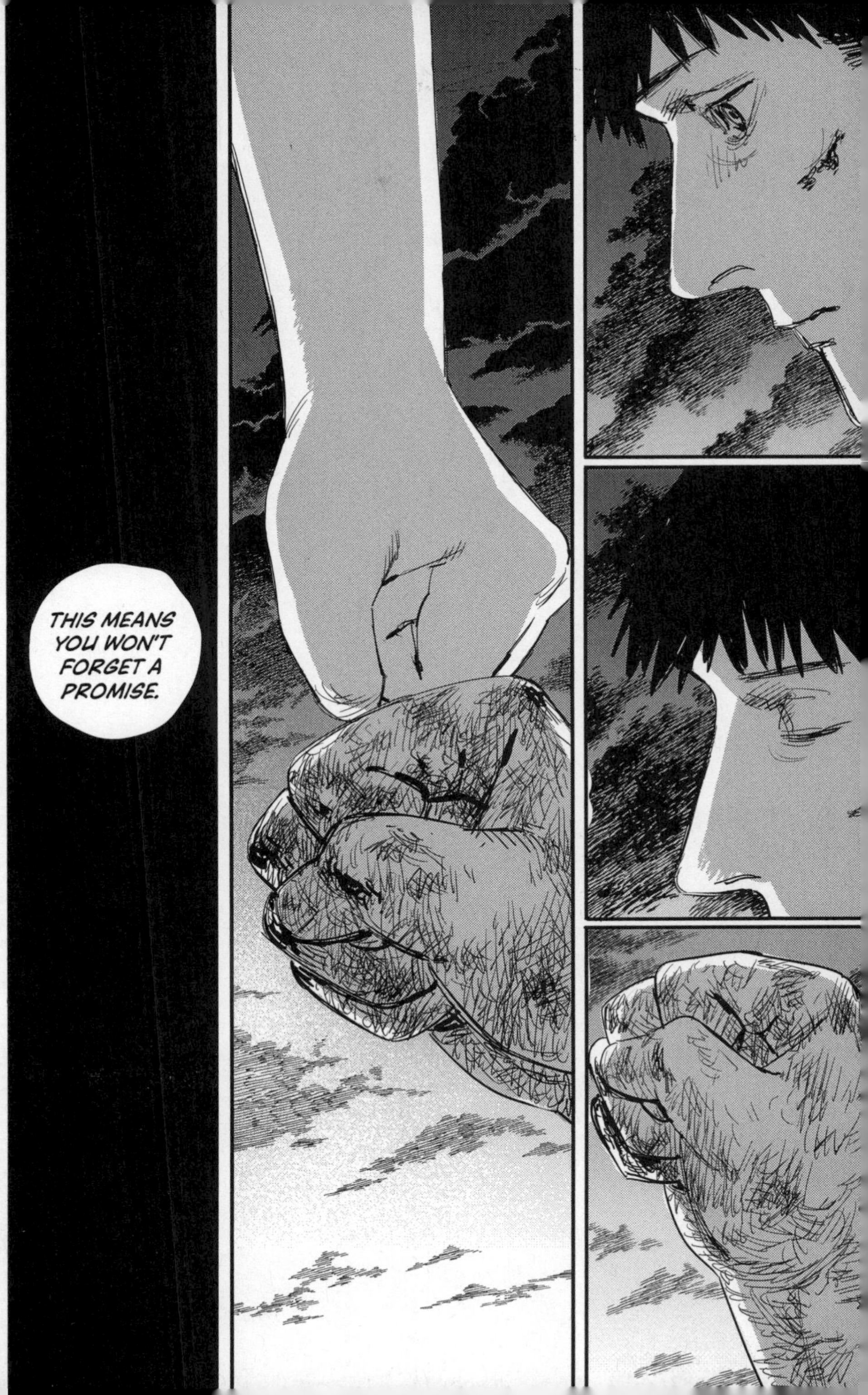
THIS MEANS YOU WON'T FORGET A PROMISE.

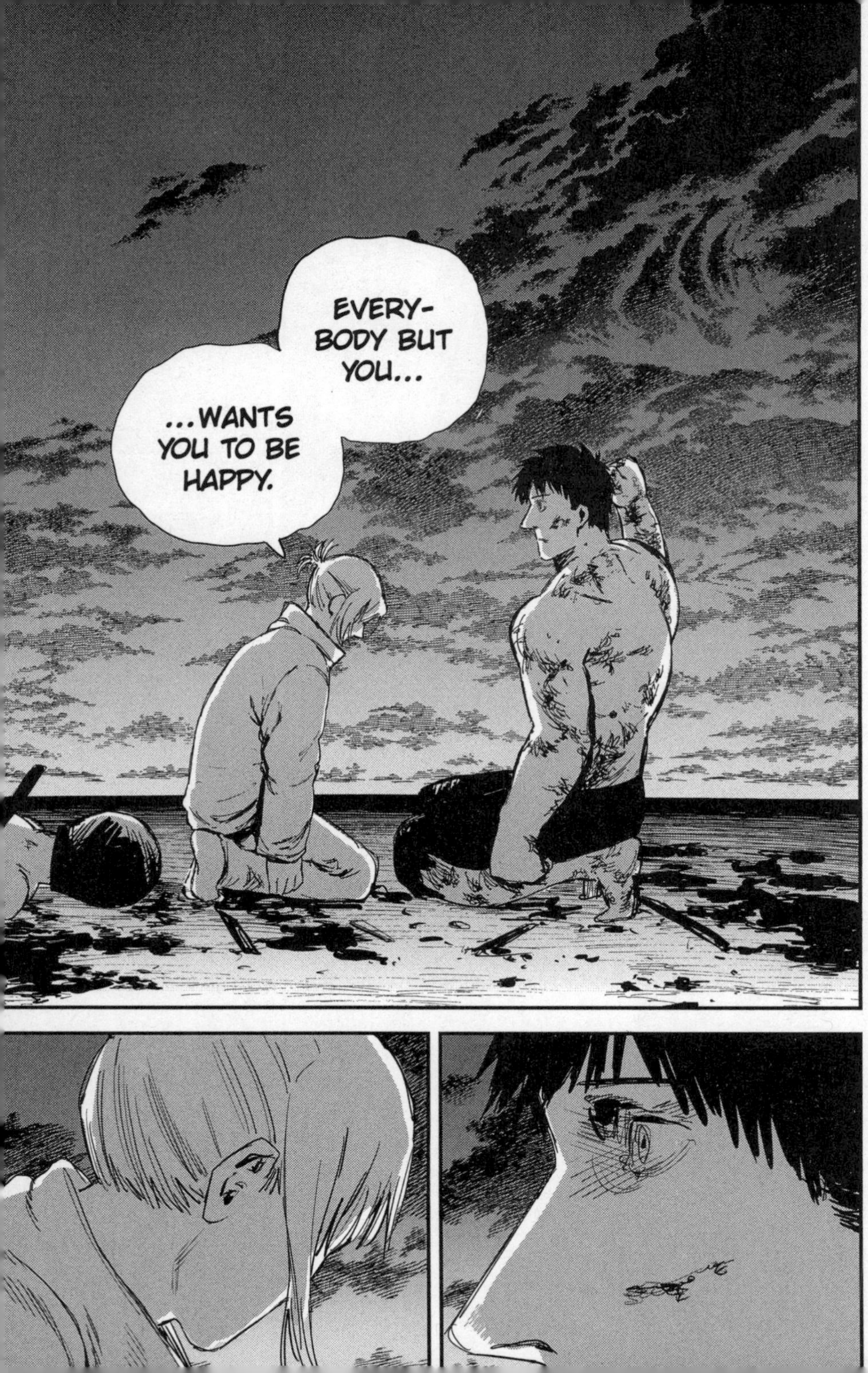
EVERY-BODY BUT YOU...
...WANTS YOU TO BE HAPPY.

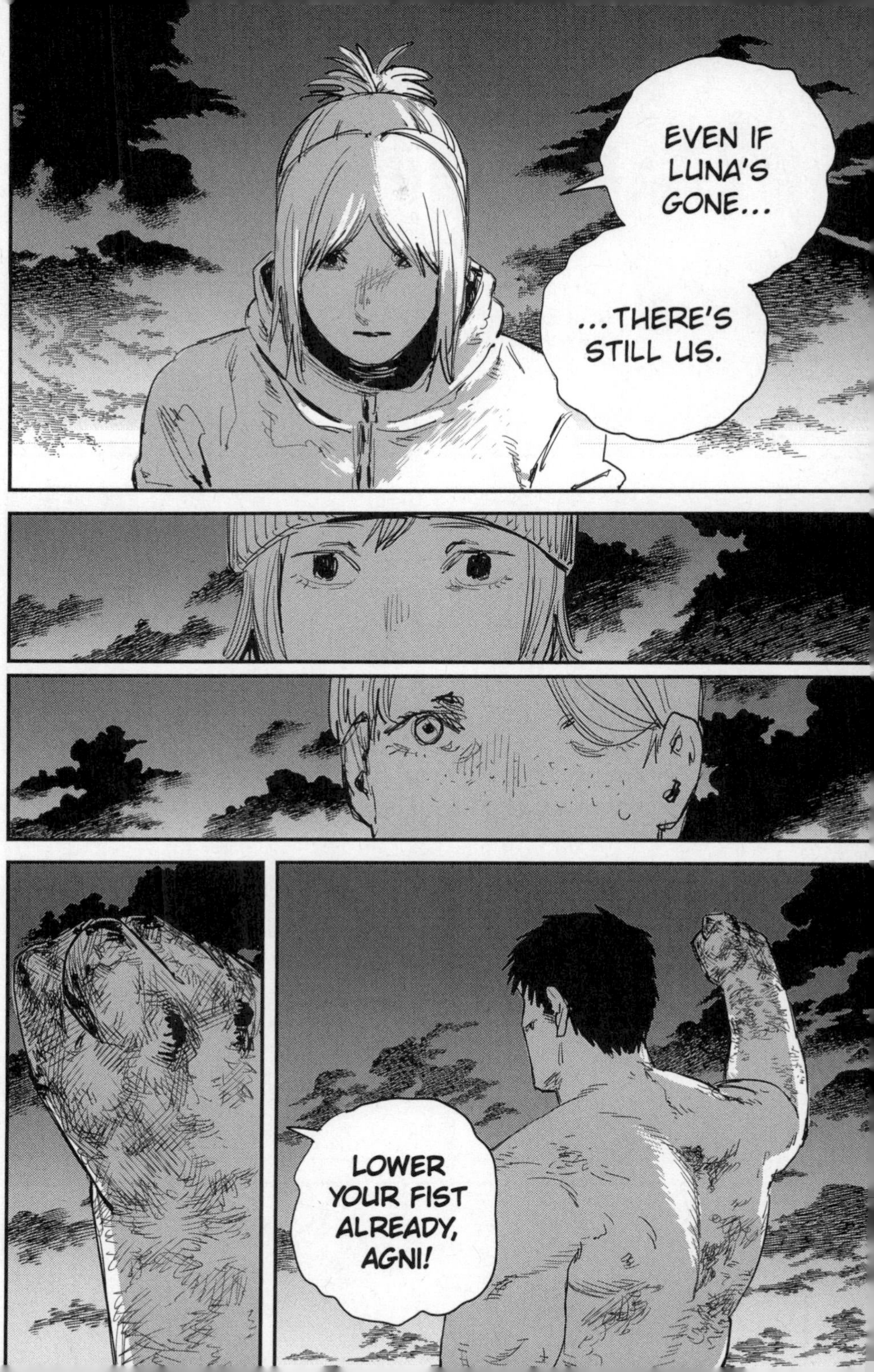
EVEN IF LUNA'S GONE...
...THERE'S STILL US.
LOWER YOUR FIST ALREADY, AGNI!

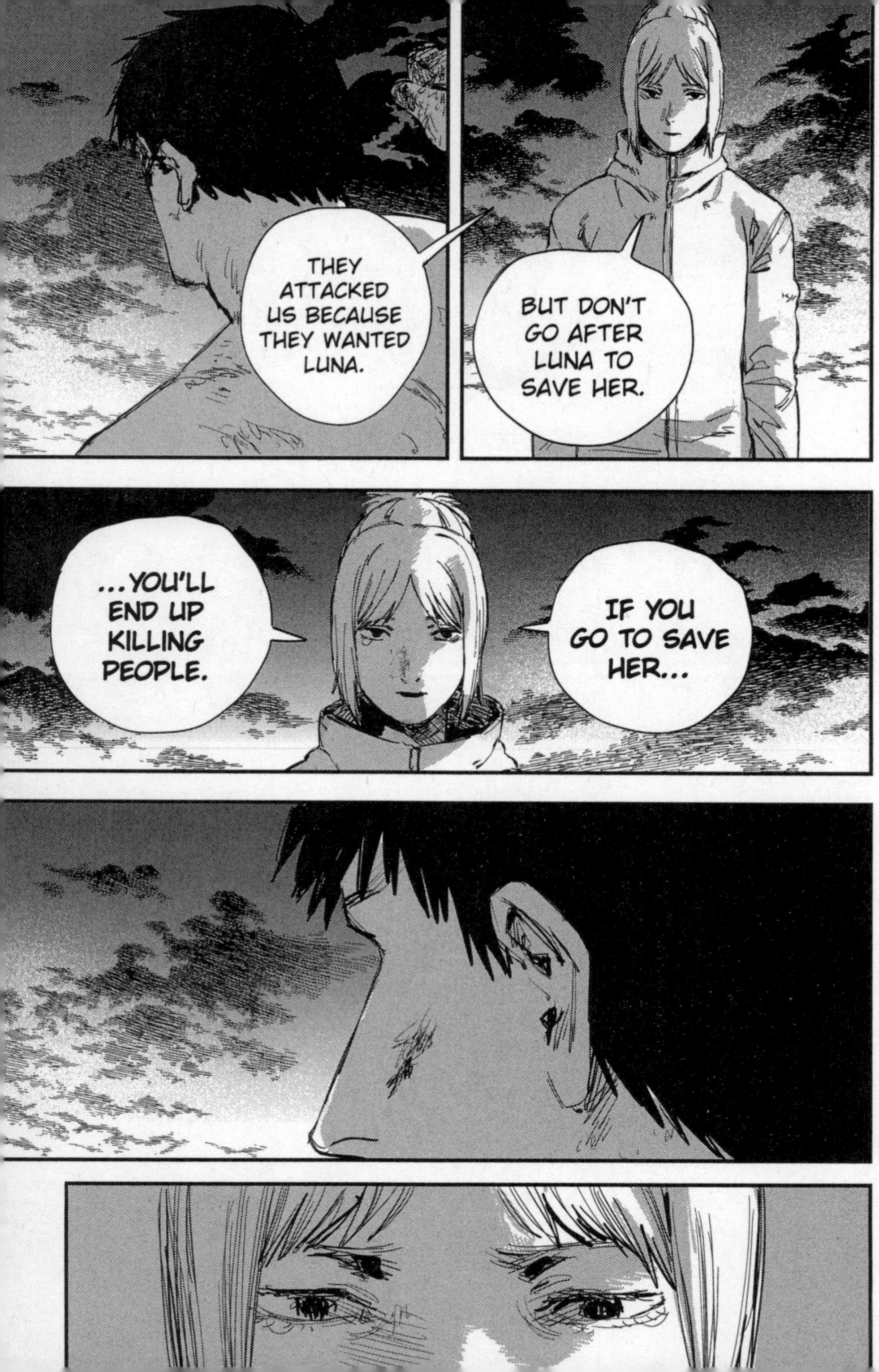
BUT DON'T GO AFTER LUNA TO SAVE HER.
THEY ATTACKED US BECAUSE THEY WANTED LUNA.
IF YOU GO TO SAVE HER...
...YOU'LL END UP KILLING PEOPLE.

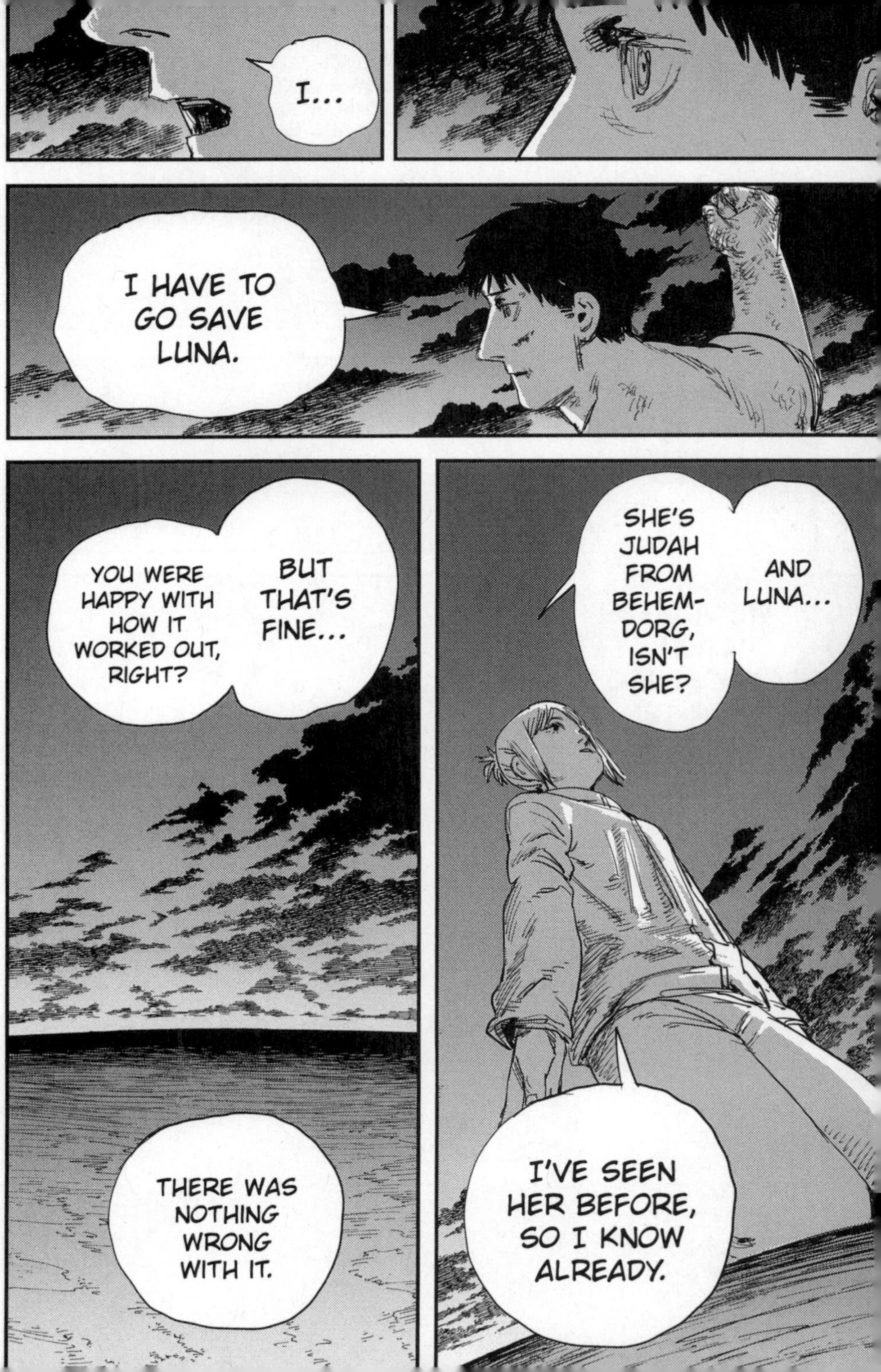
I...
I HAVE TO GO SAVE LUNA.
AND LUNA...
SHE'S JUDAH FROM BEHEMDORG, ISN'T SHE?
I'VE SEEN HER BEFORE, SO I KNOW ALREADY.
BUT THAT'S FINE...
YOU WERE HAPPY WITH HOW IT WORKED OUT, RIGHT?
THERE WAS NOTHING WRONG WITH IT.

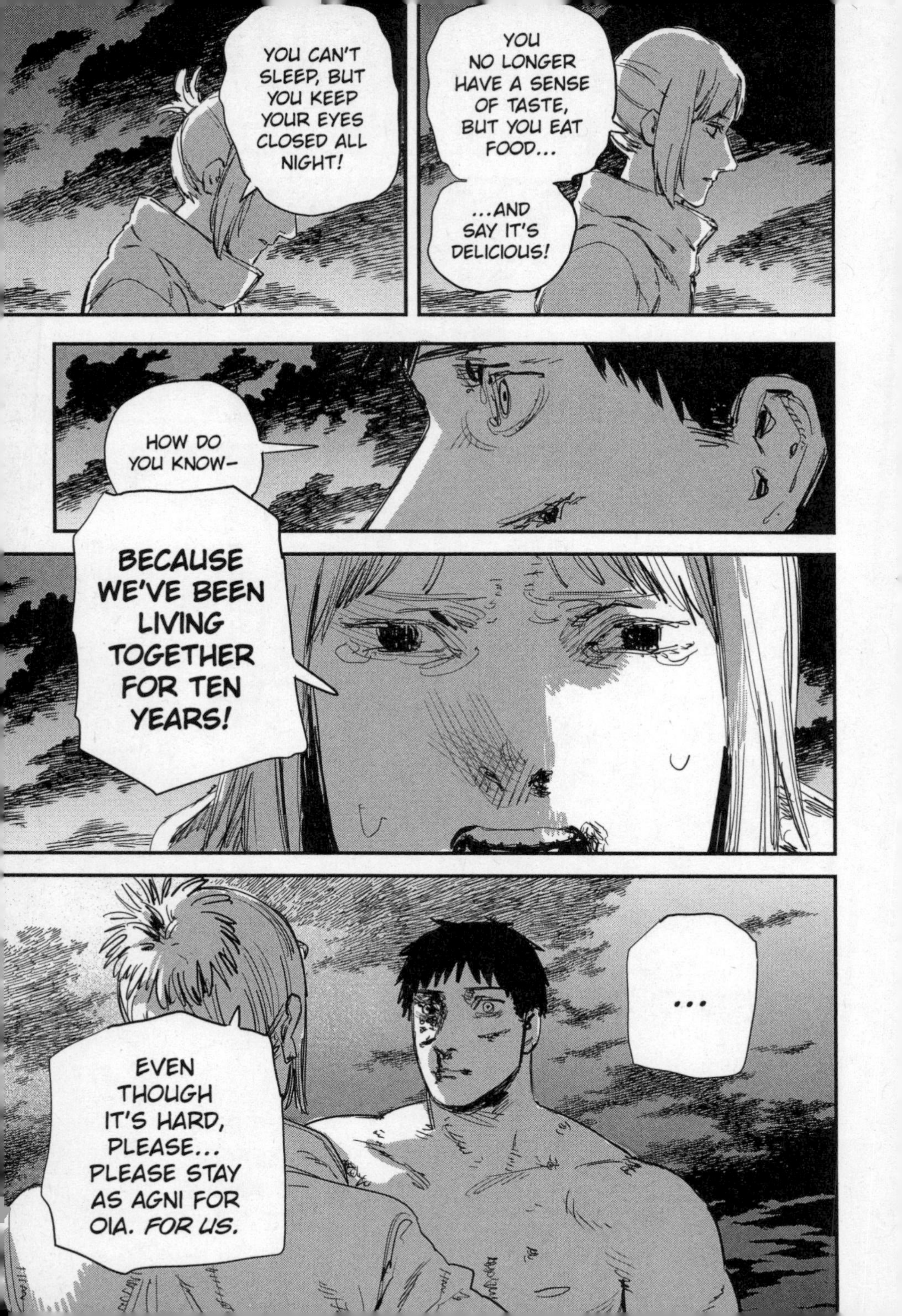
YOU NO LONGER HAVE A SENSE OF TASTE, BUT YOU EAT FOOD...
...AND SAY IT'S DELICIOUS!
YOU CAN'T SLEEP, BUT YOU KEEP YOUR EYES CLOSED ALL NIGHT!
HOW DO YOU KNOW—
BECAUSE WE'VE BEEN LIVING TOGETHER FOR TEN YEARS!
...
EVEN THOUGH IT'S HARD, PLEASE... PLEASE STAY AS AGNI FOR OIA. *FOR US.*

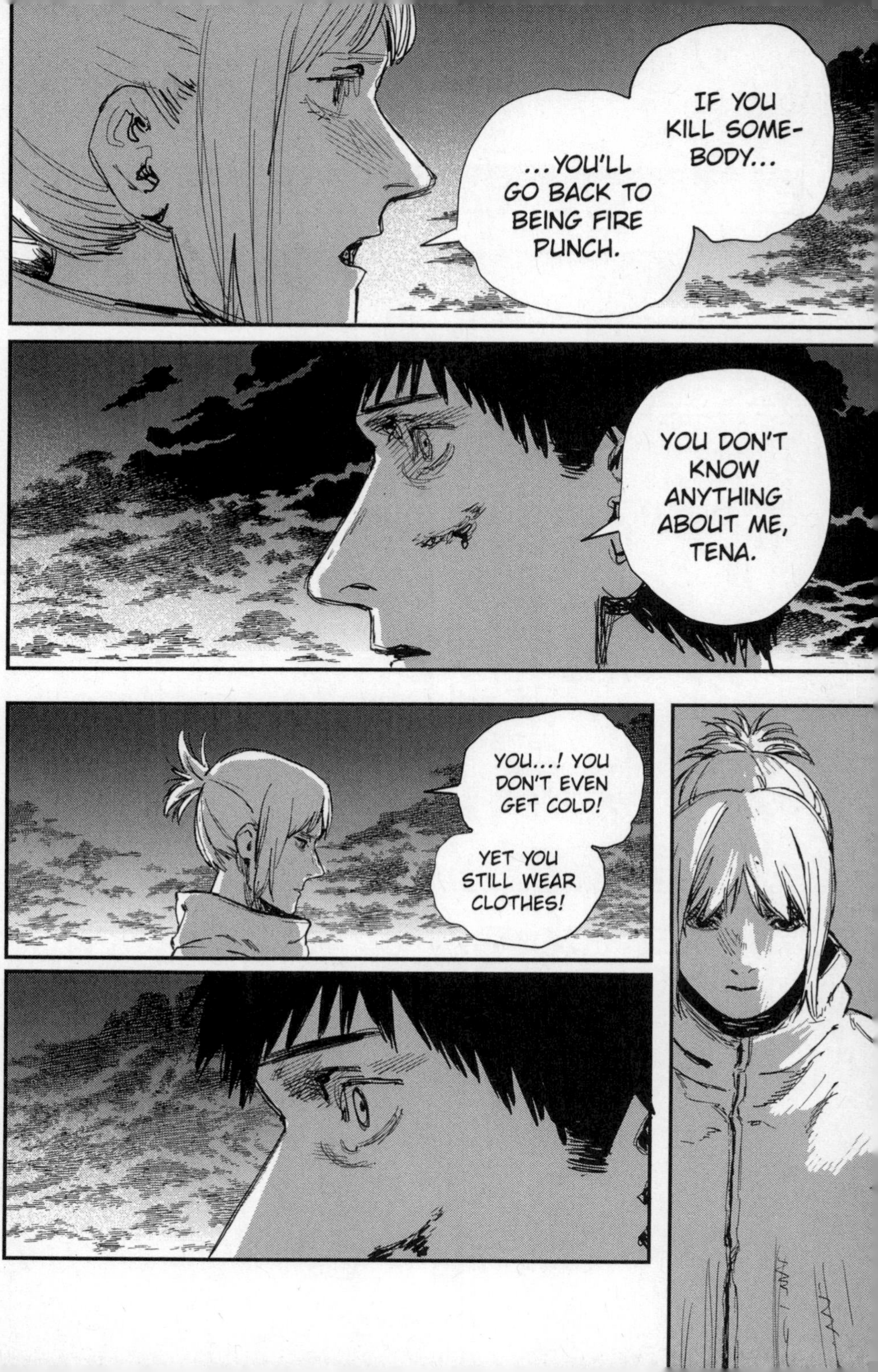
IF YOU KILL SOME-BODY...
...YOU'LL GO BACK TO BEING FIRE PUNCH.
YOU DON'T KNOW ANYTHING ABOUT ME, TENA.
YOU...! YOU DON'T EVEN GET COLD!
YET YOU STILL WEAR CLOTHES!

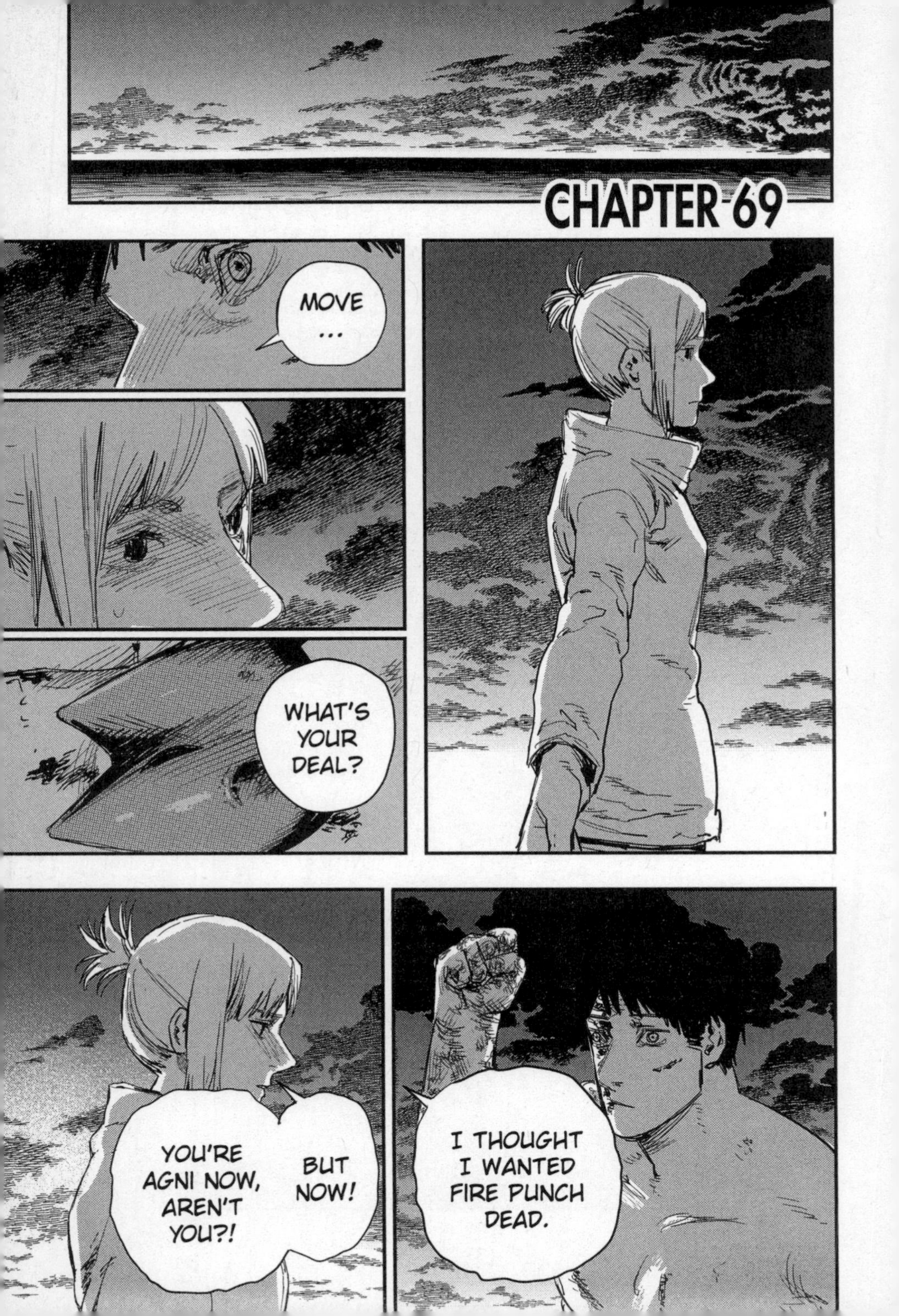
CHAPTER 69
MOVE ...
WHAT'S YOUR DEAL?
I THOUGHT I WANTED FIRE PUNCH DEAD.
BUT NOW!
YOU'RE AGNI NOW, AREN'T YOU?!

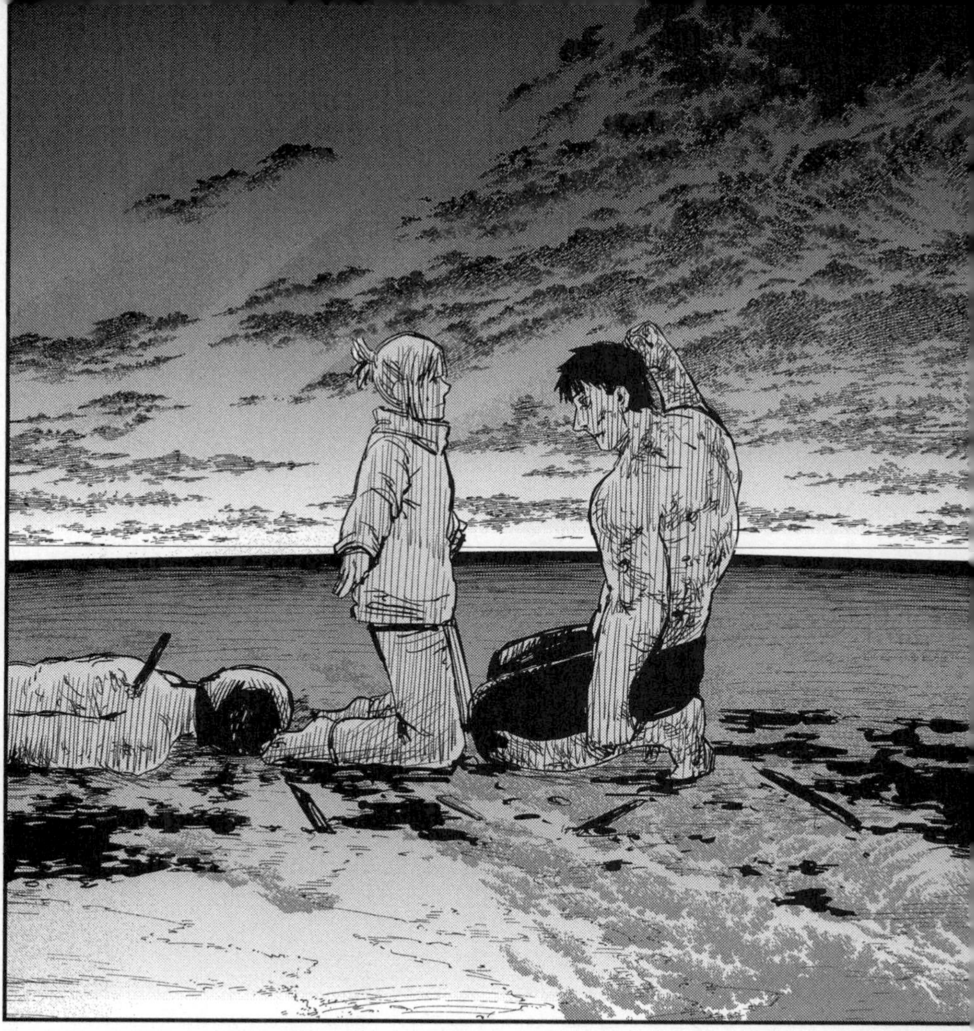
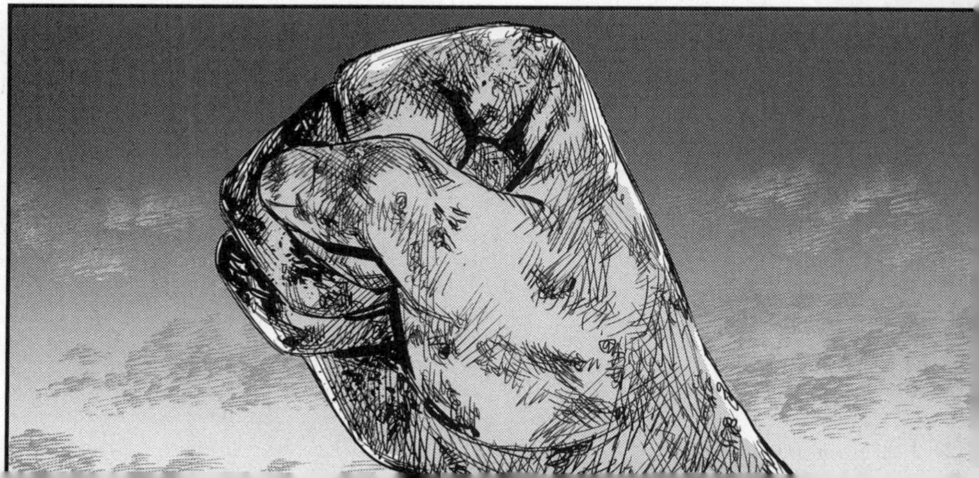

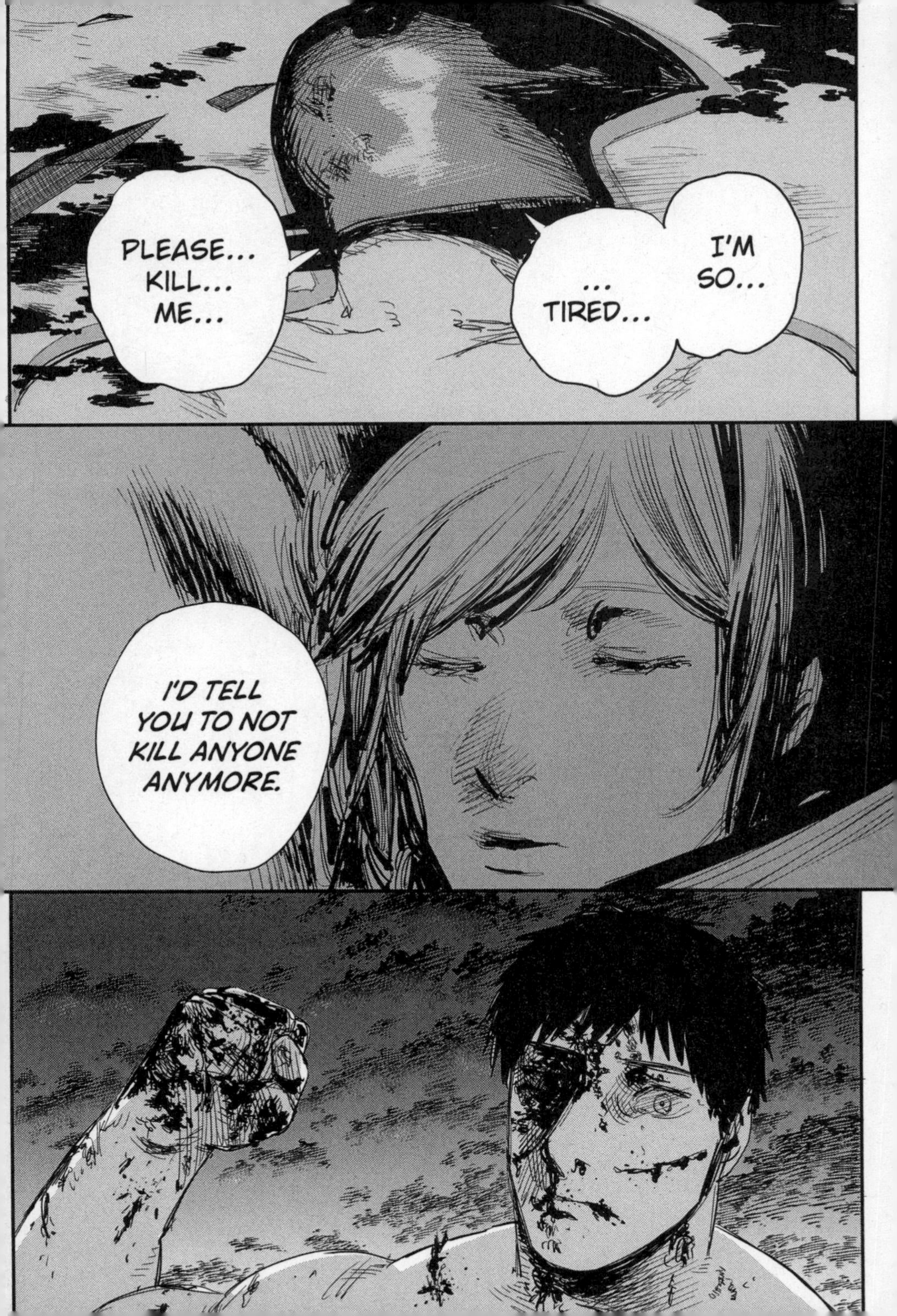
I'M SO... ... TIRED...
PLEASE... KILL... ME...
I'D TELL YOU TO NOT KILL ANYONE ANYMORE.

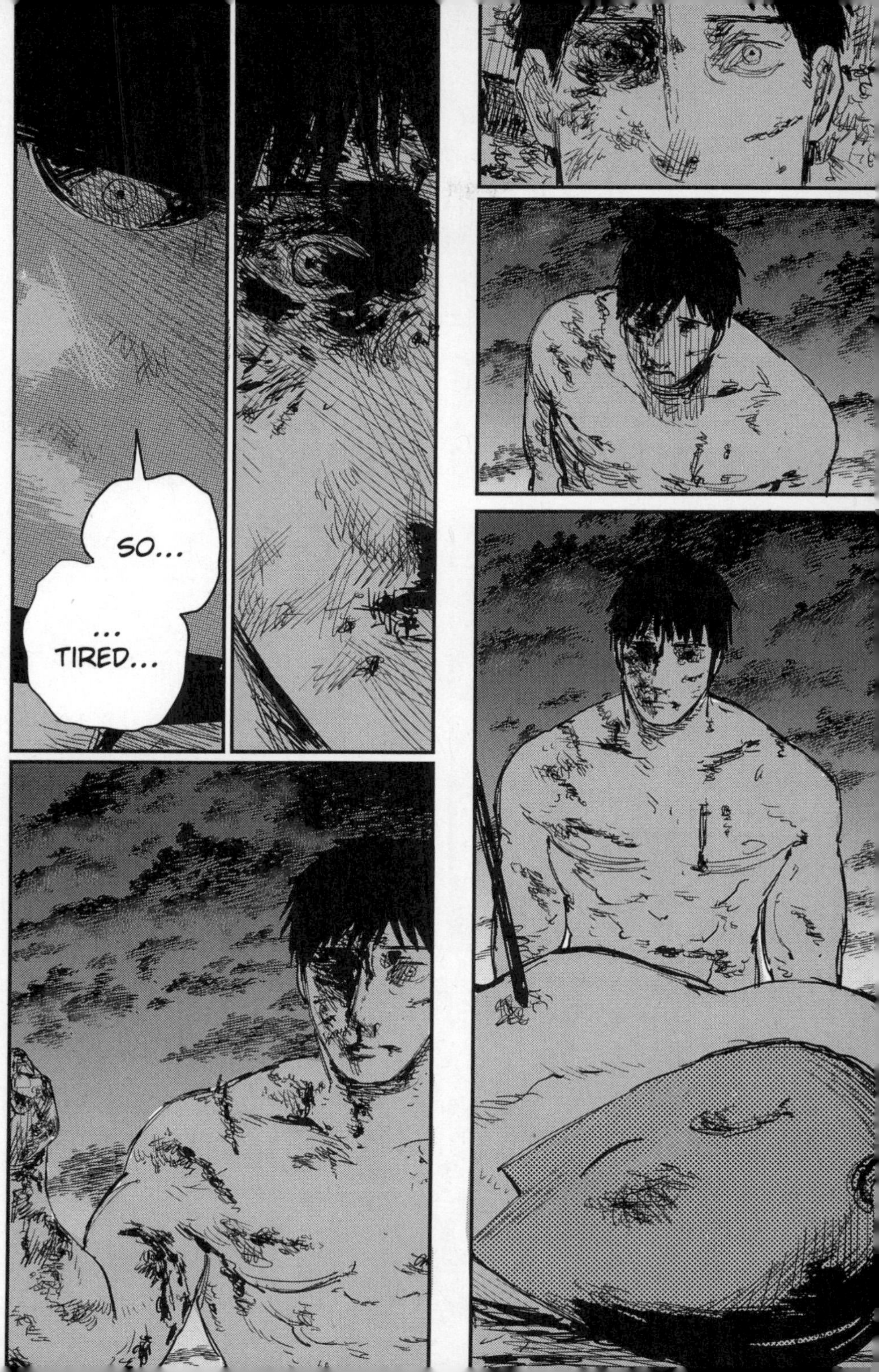
SO...
... TIRED...

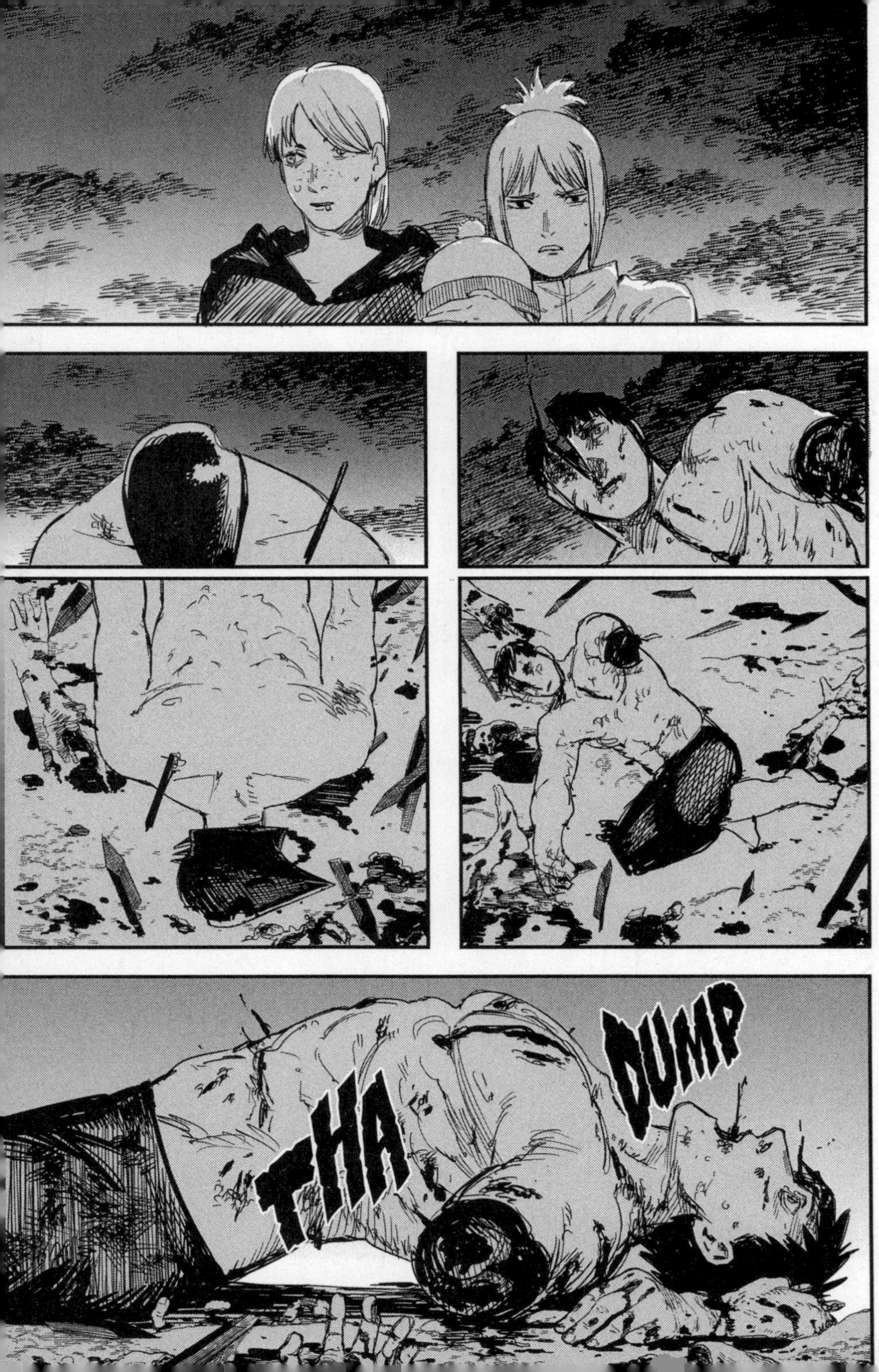
DUMP
THA

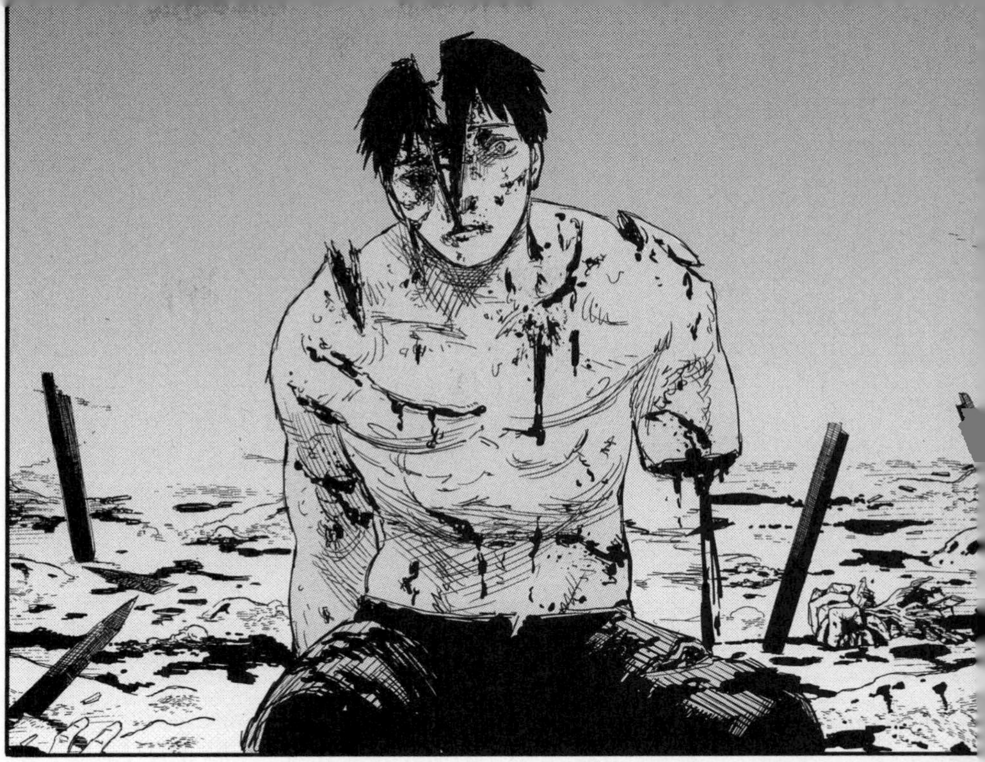
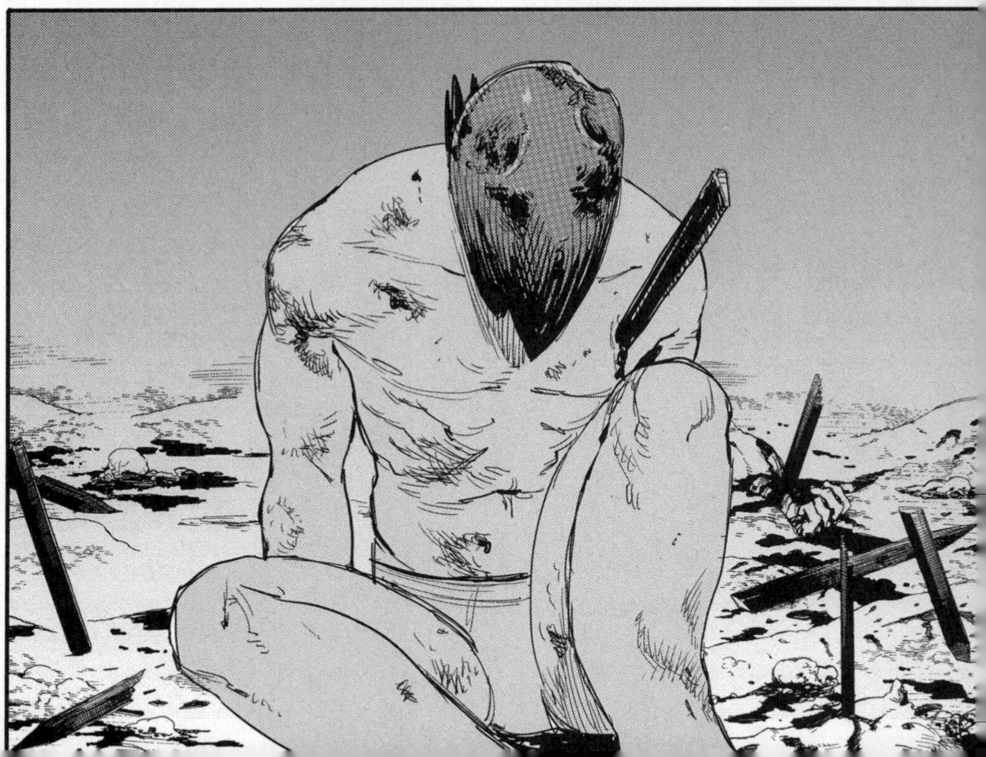

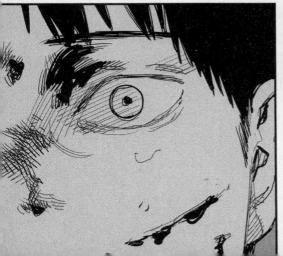

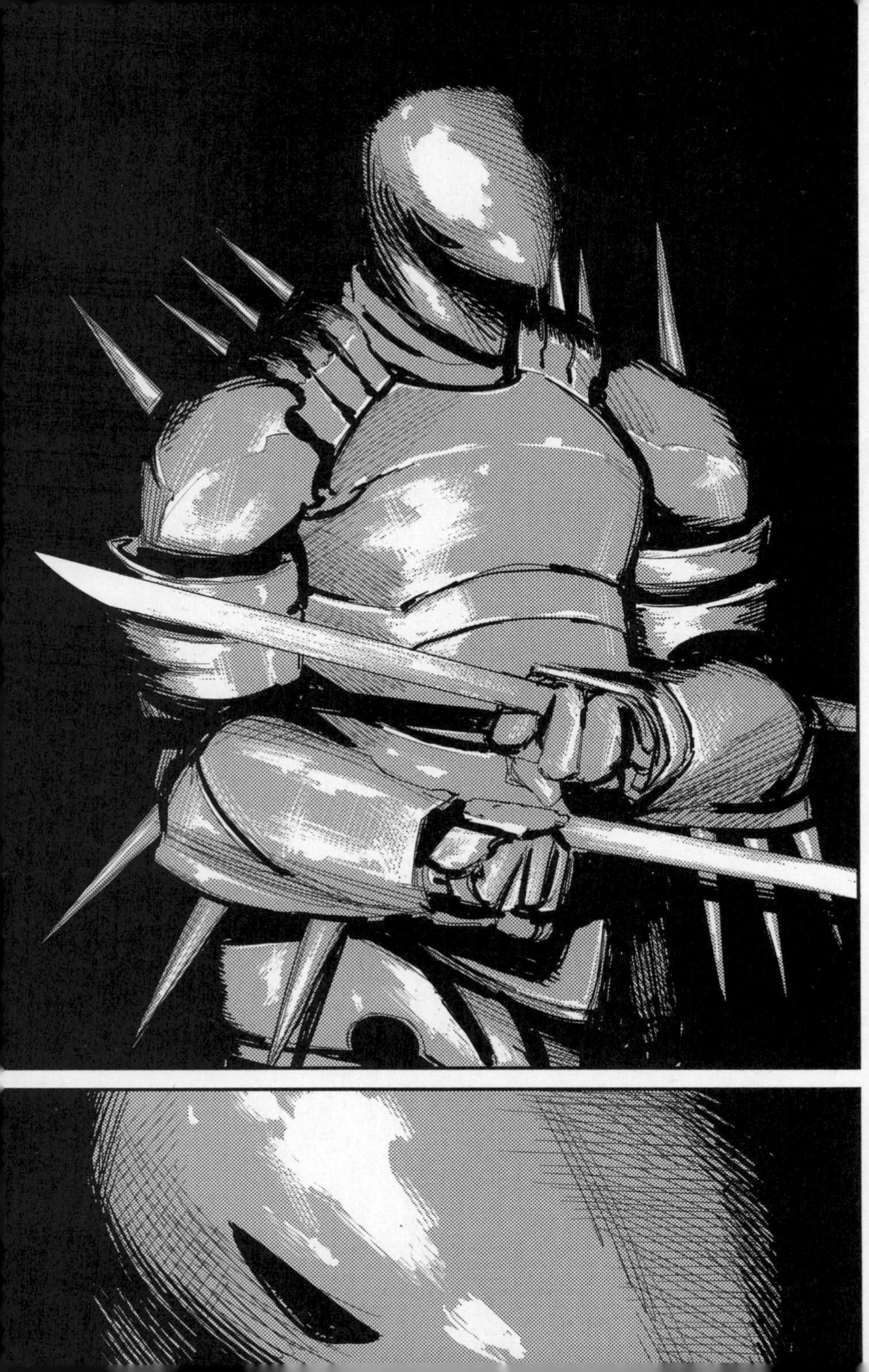

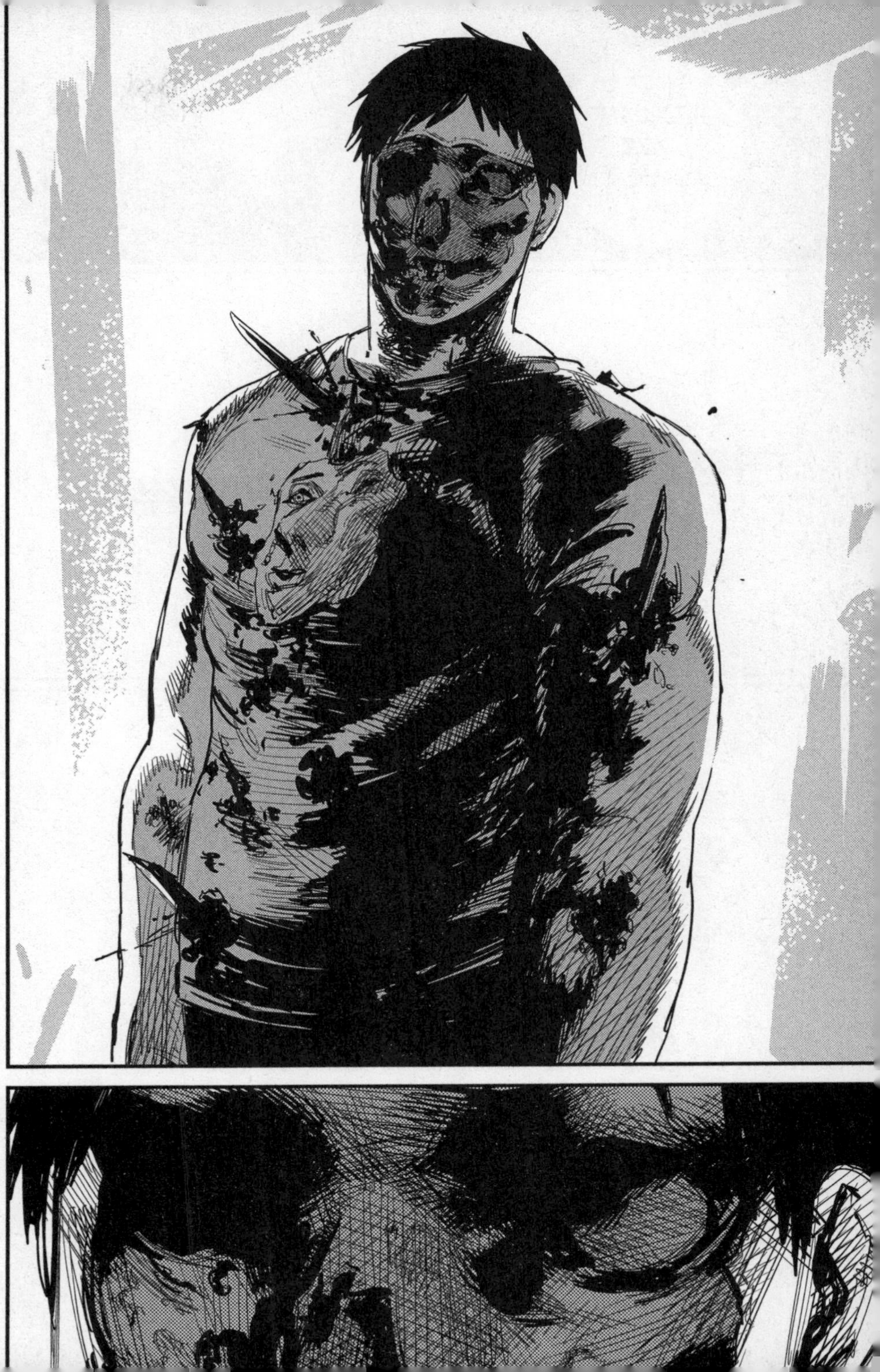

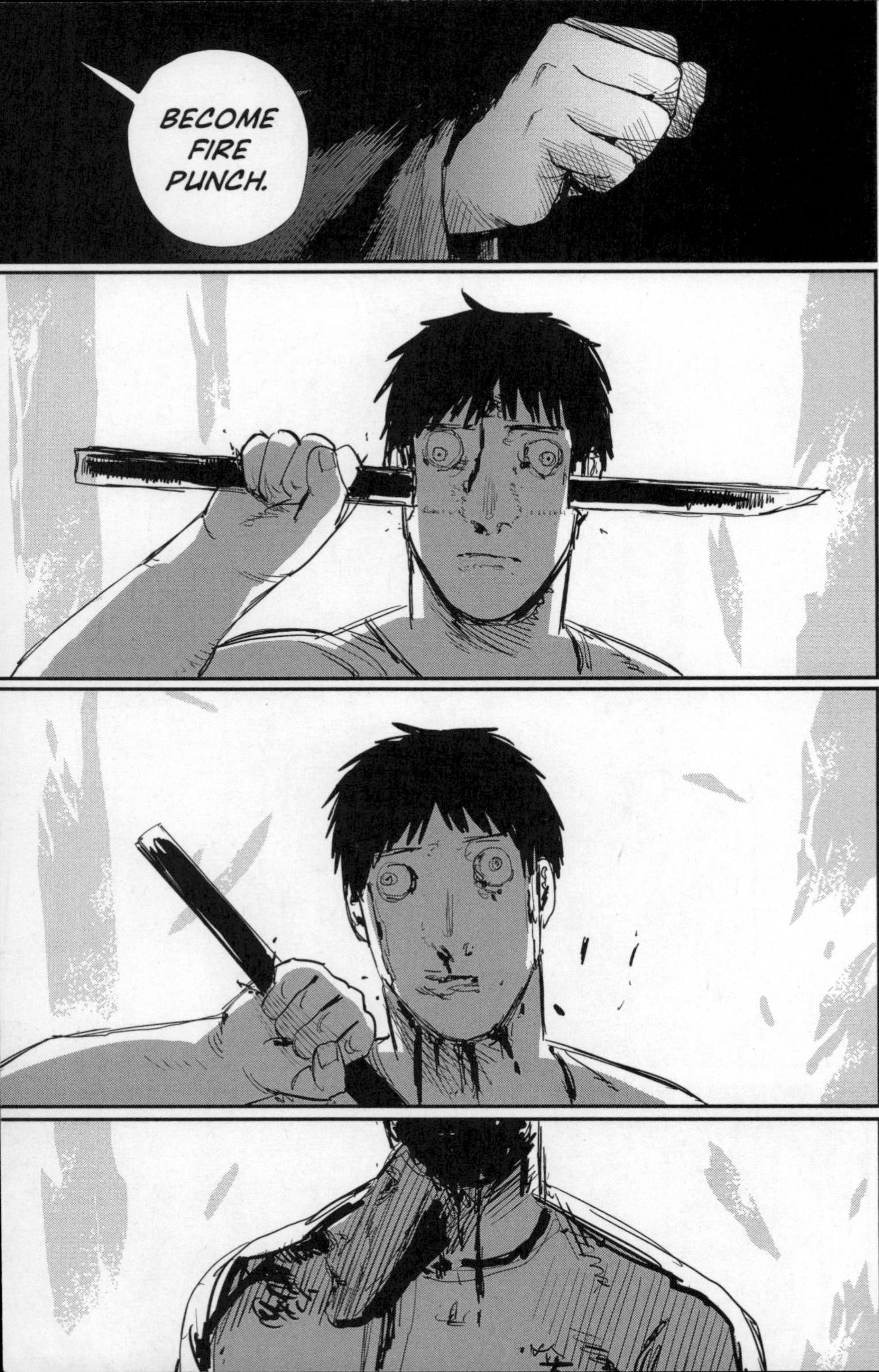
BECOME FIRE PUNCH.

ＺＳＨ

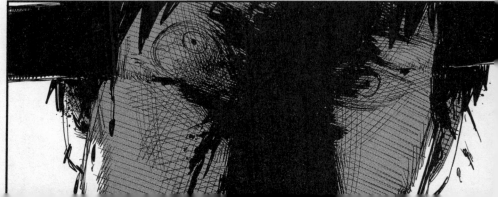

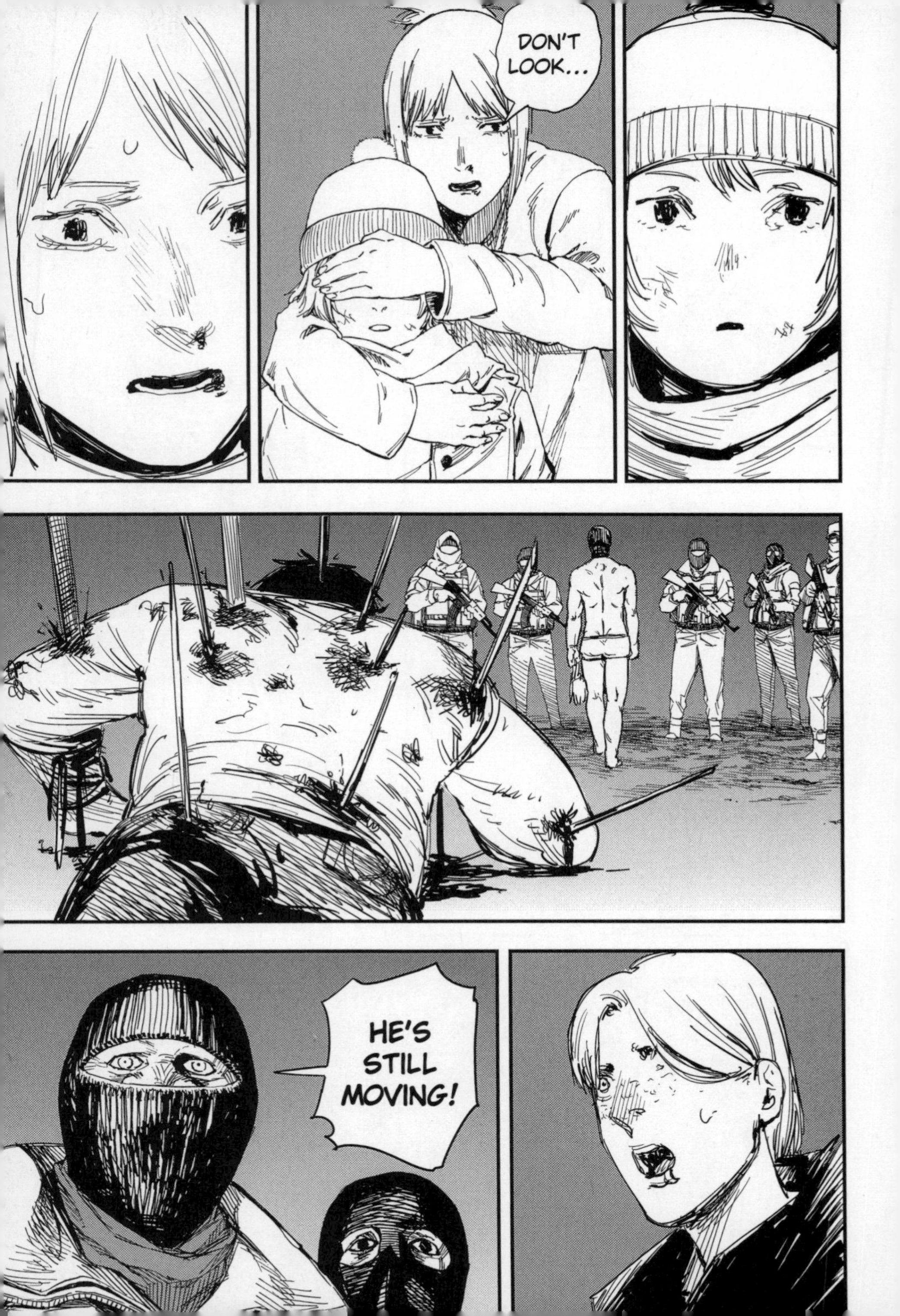
DON'T LOOK...
HE'S STILL MOVING!

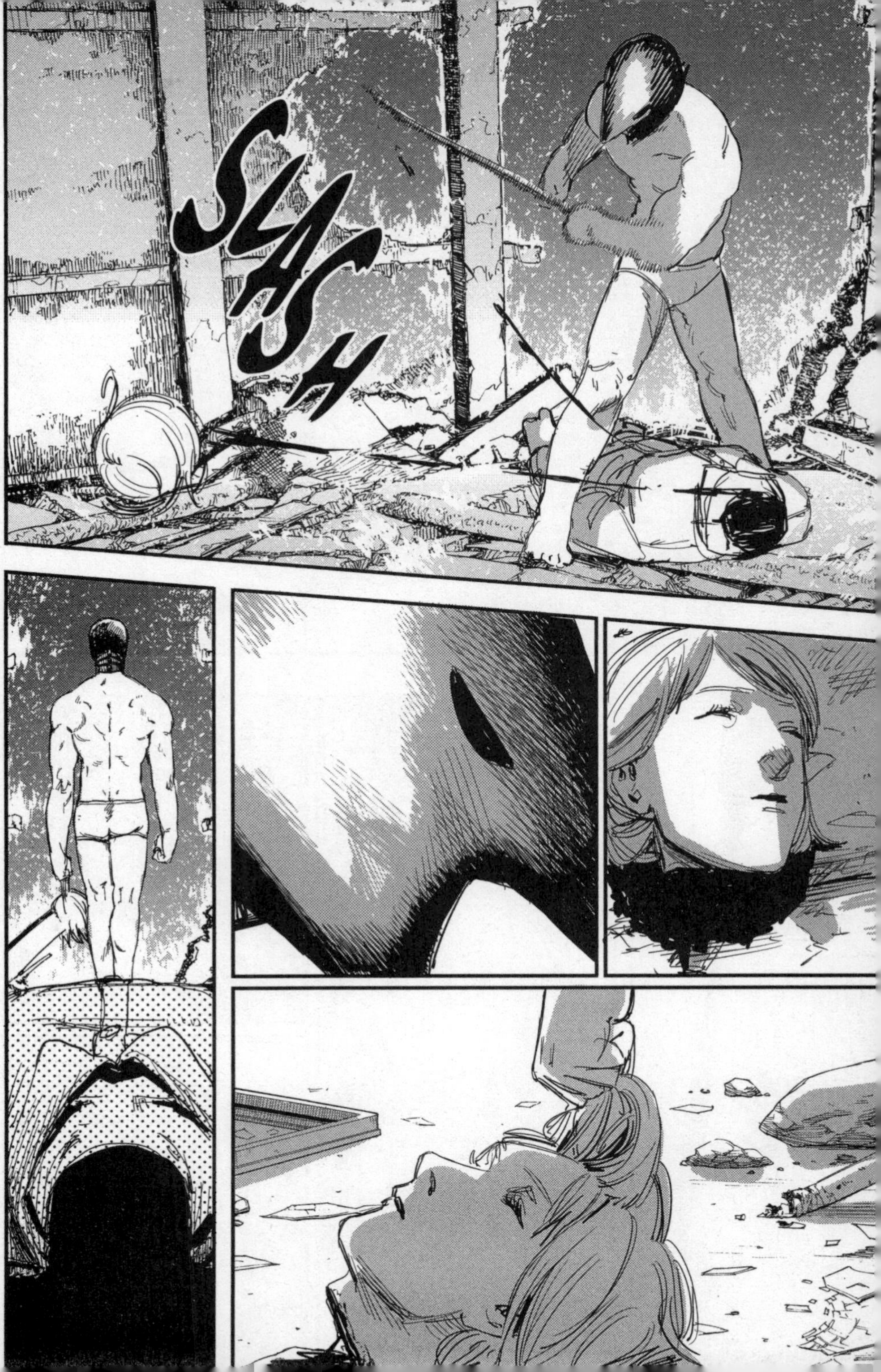
SLASH

SHNKT

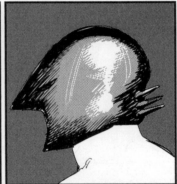

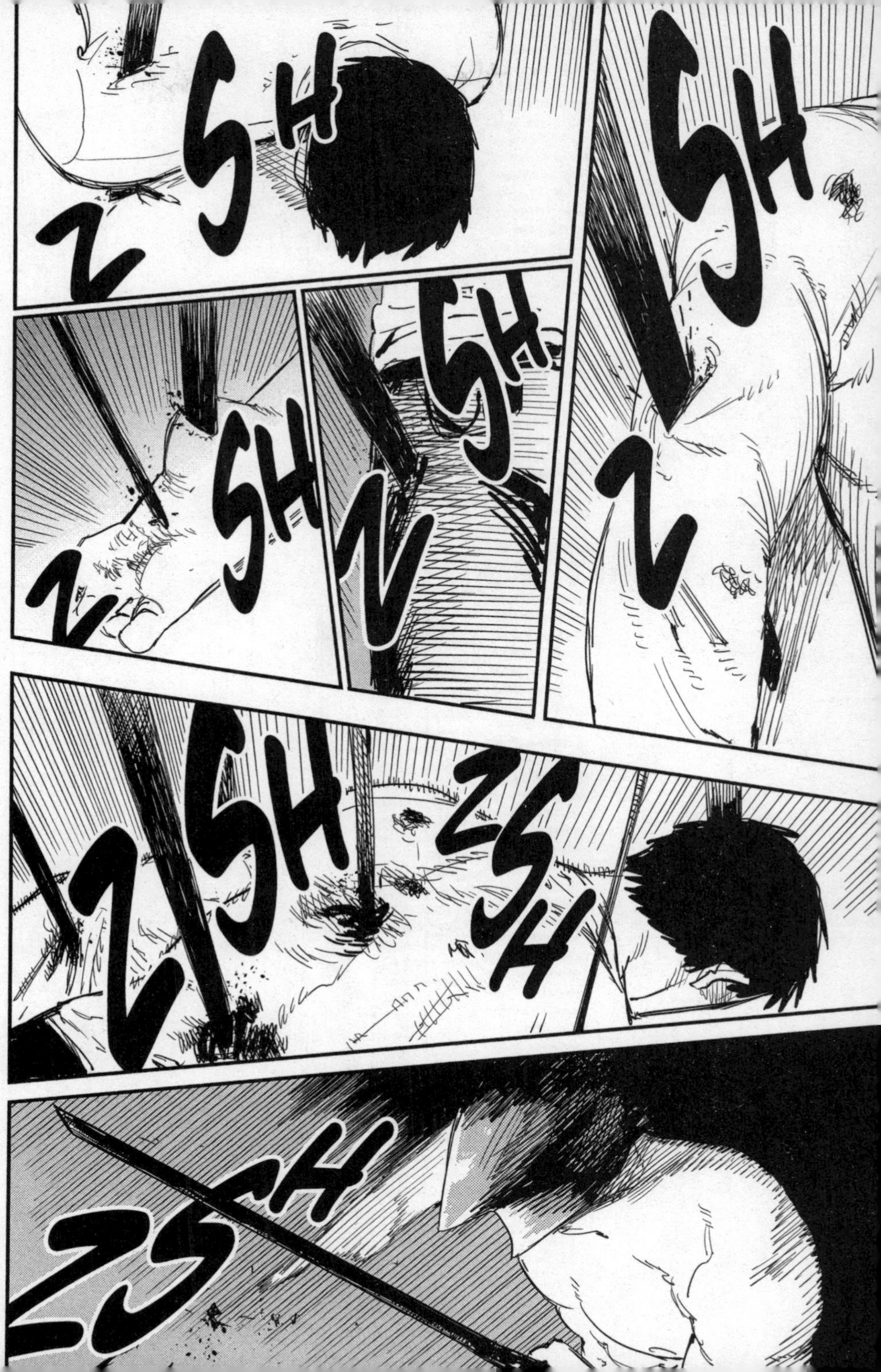
ZSH
ZSH
ZSH
ZSH
ZSH
ZSH
ZSH

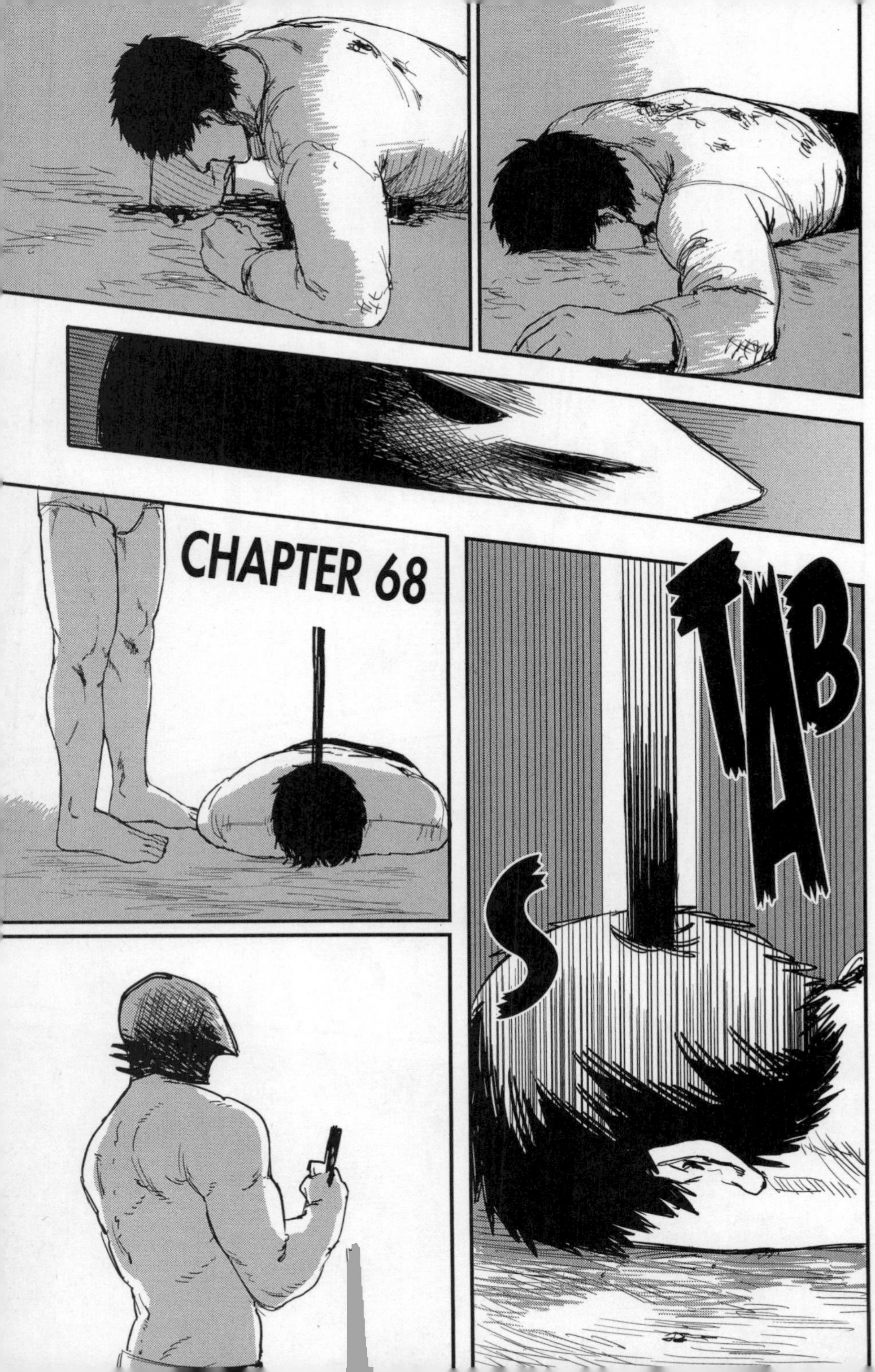
STAB
CHAPTER 68

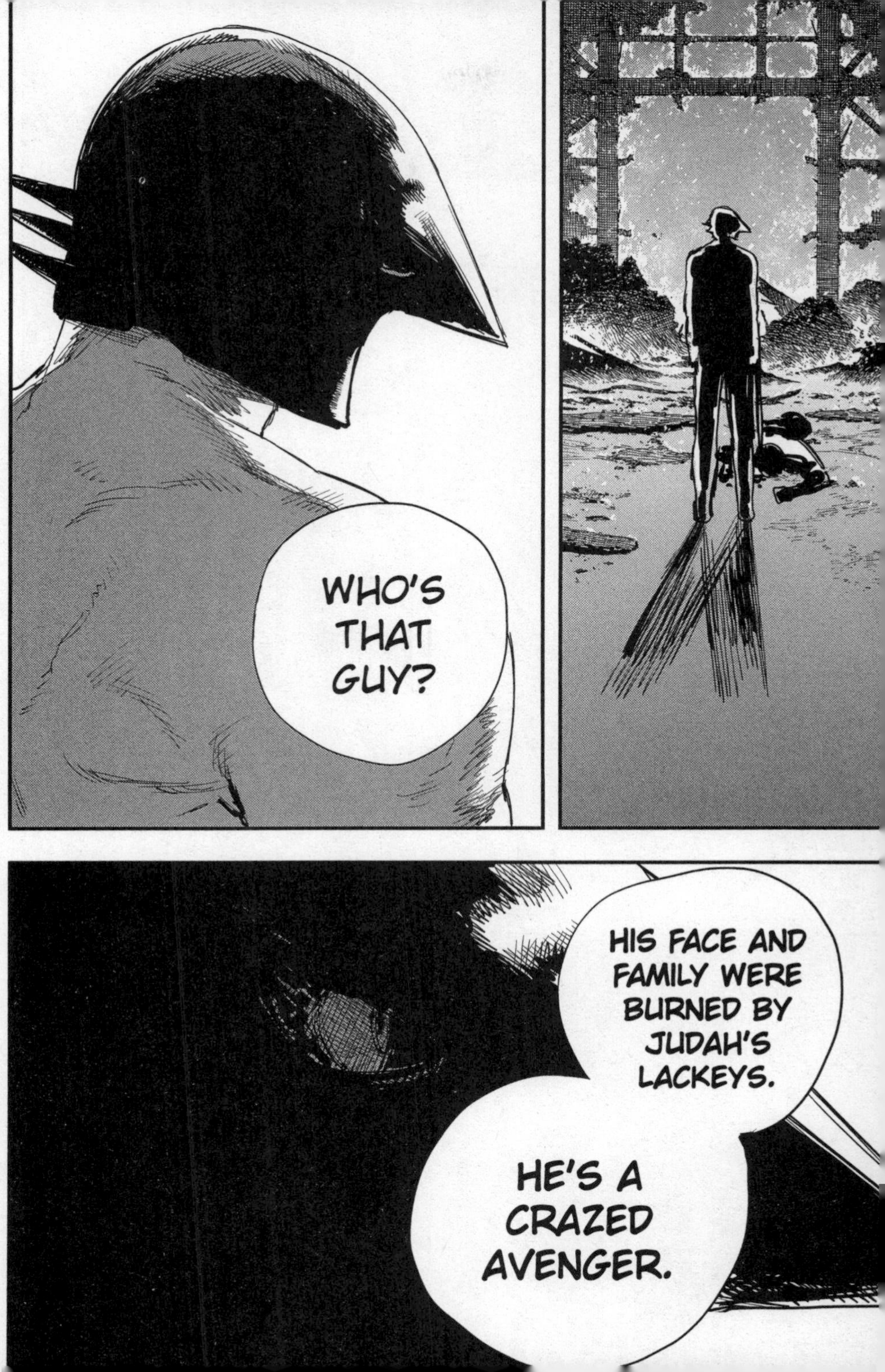
WHO'S THAT GUY?
HIS FACE AND FAMILY WERE BURNED BY JUDAH'S LACKEYS.
HE'S A CRAZED AVENGER.

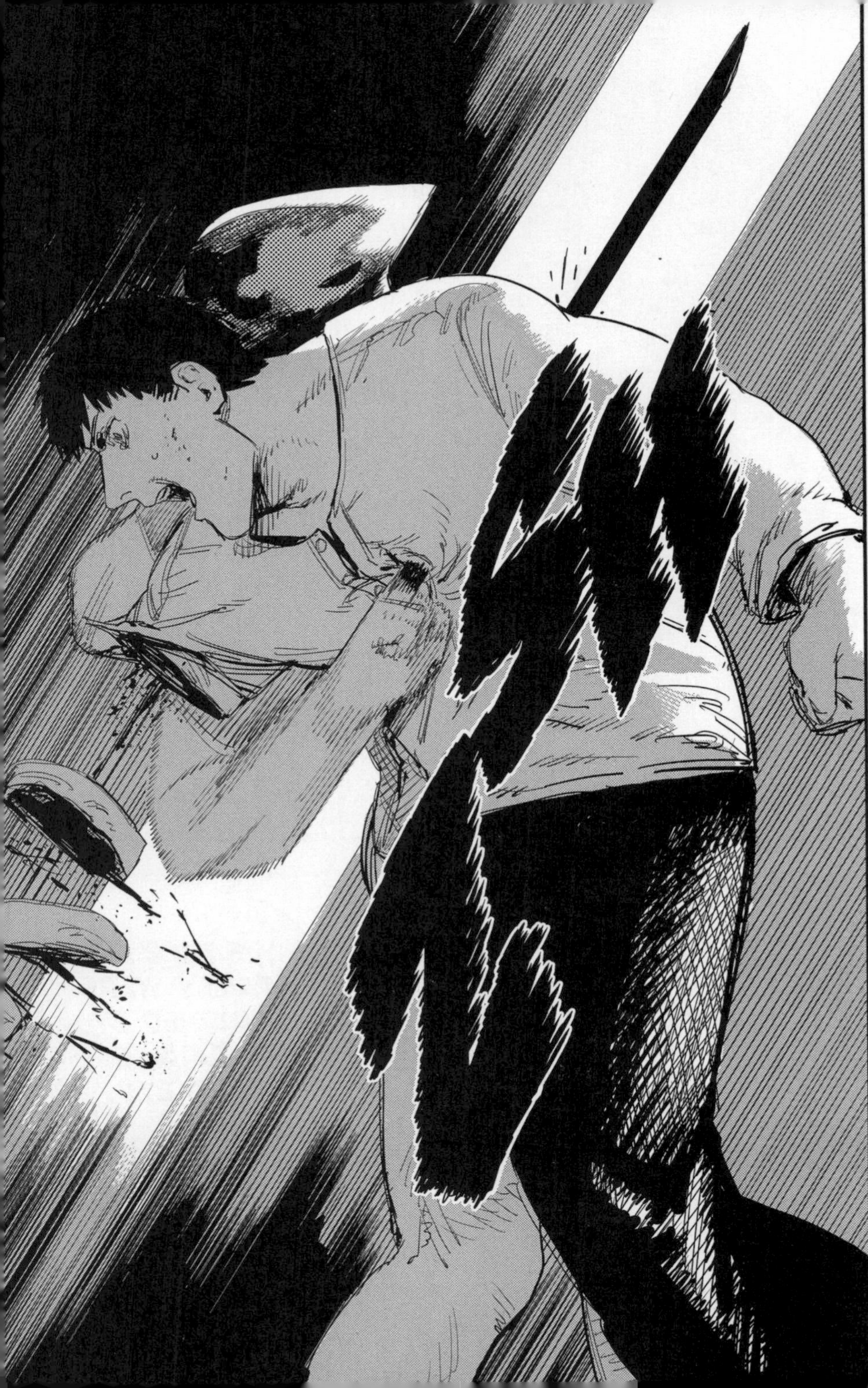

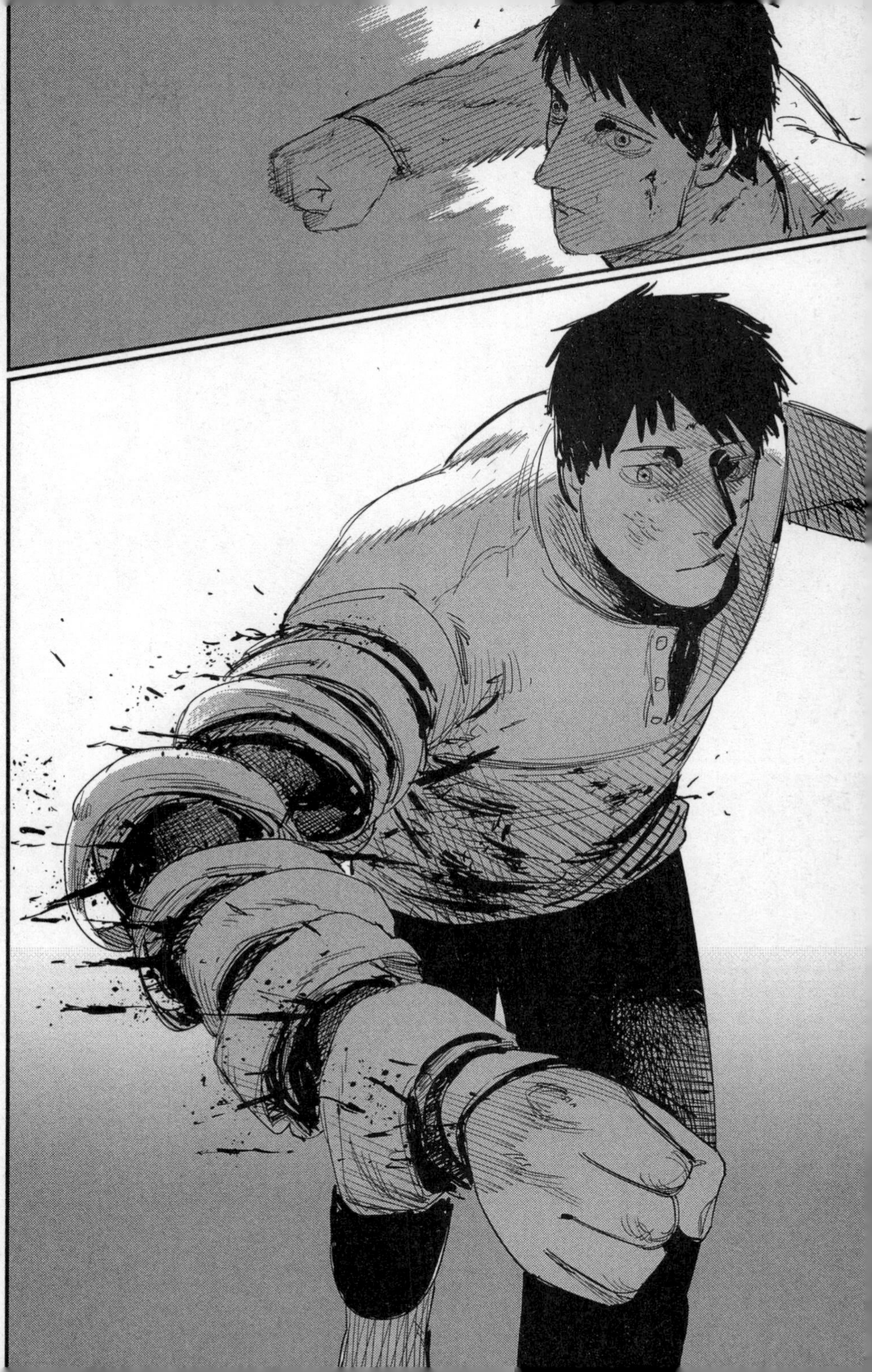

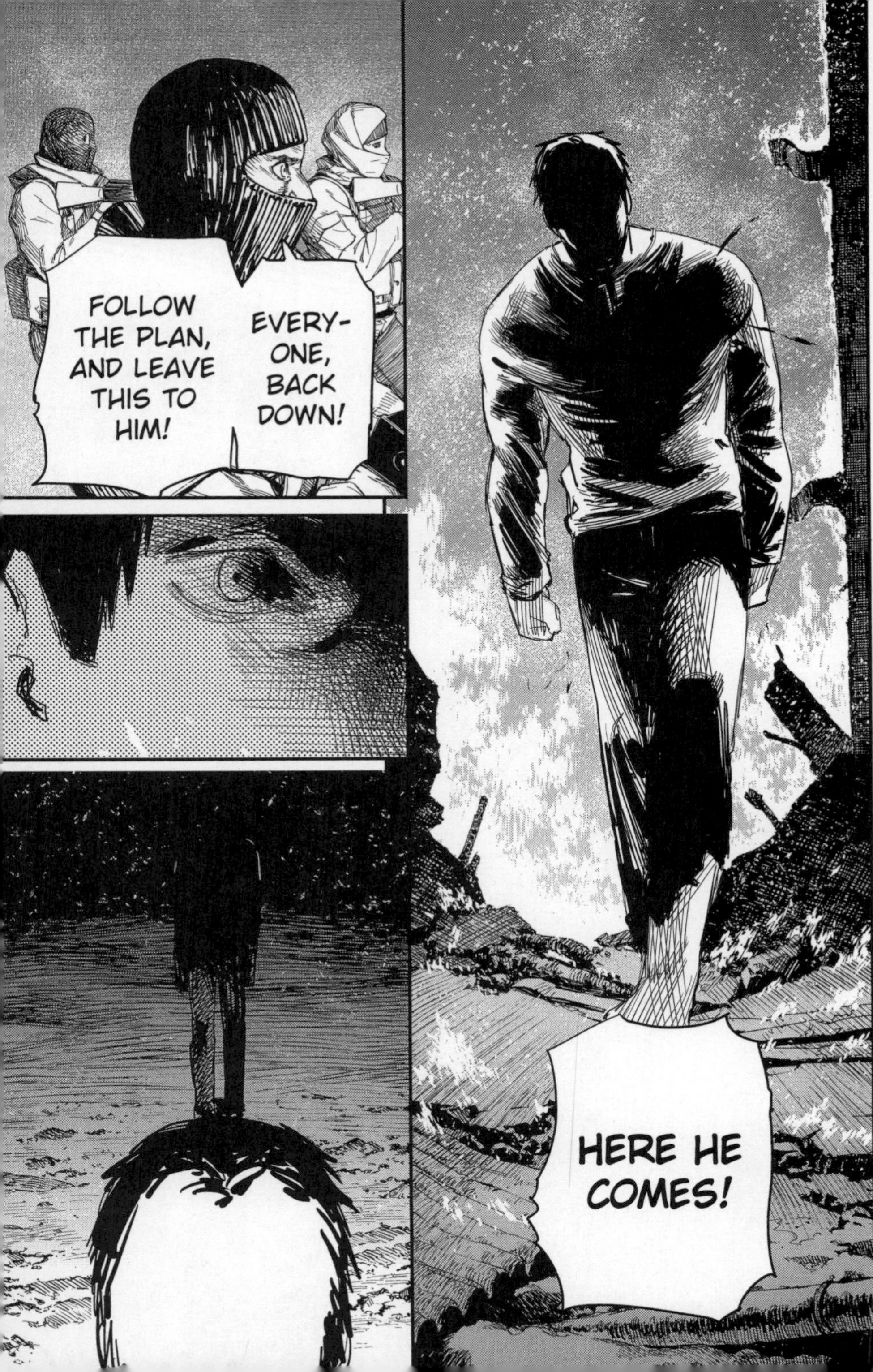
HERE HE COMES!
EVERY-ONE, BACK DOWN!
FOLLOW THE PLAN, AND LEAVE THIS TO HIM!

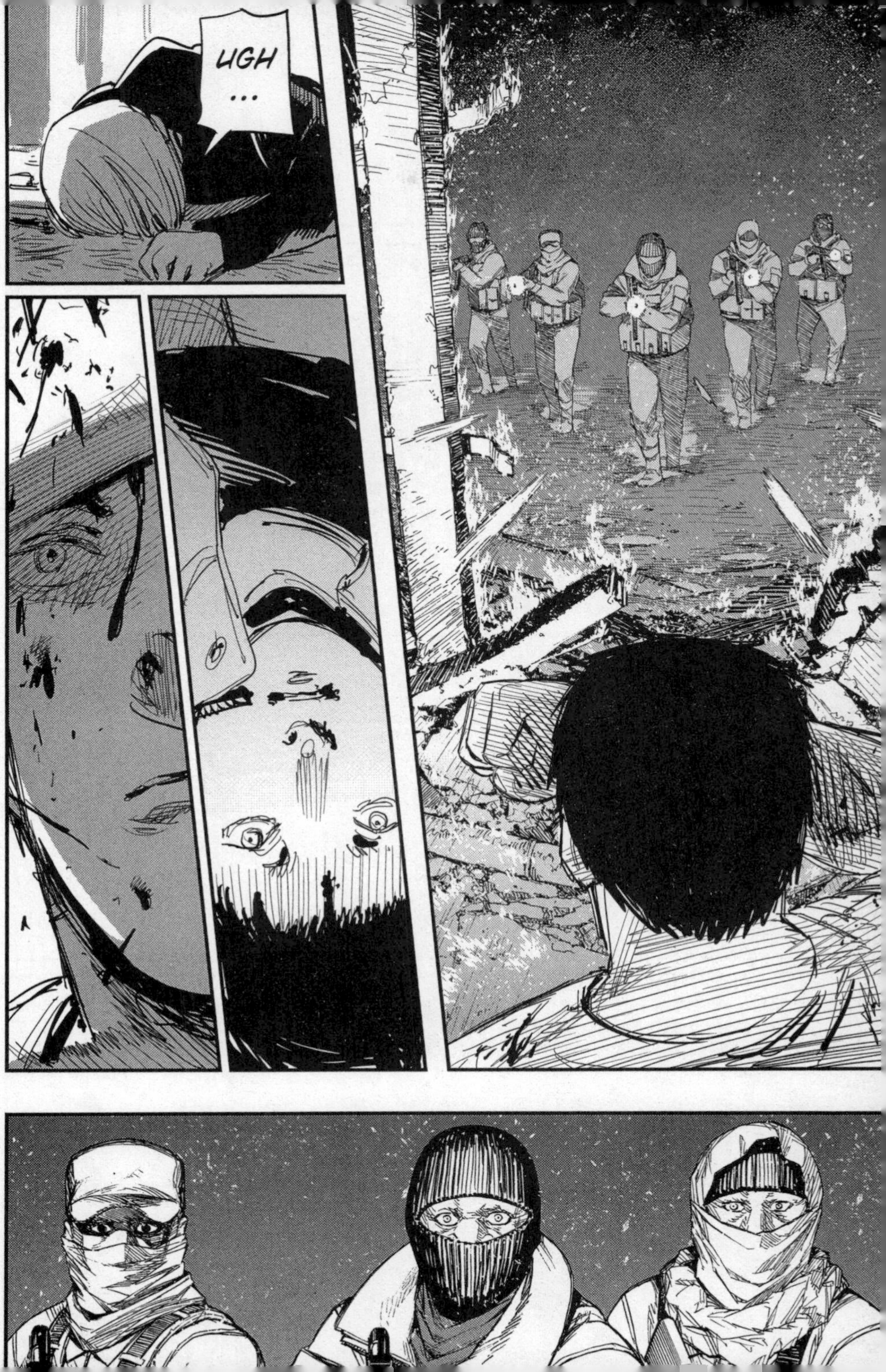
UGH ...

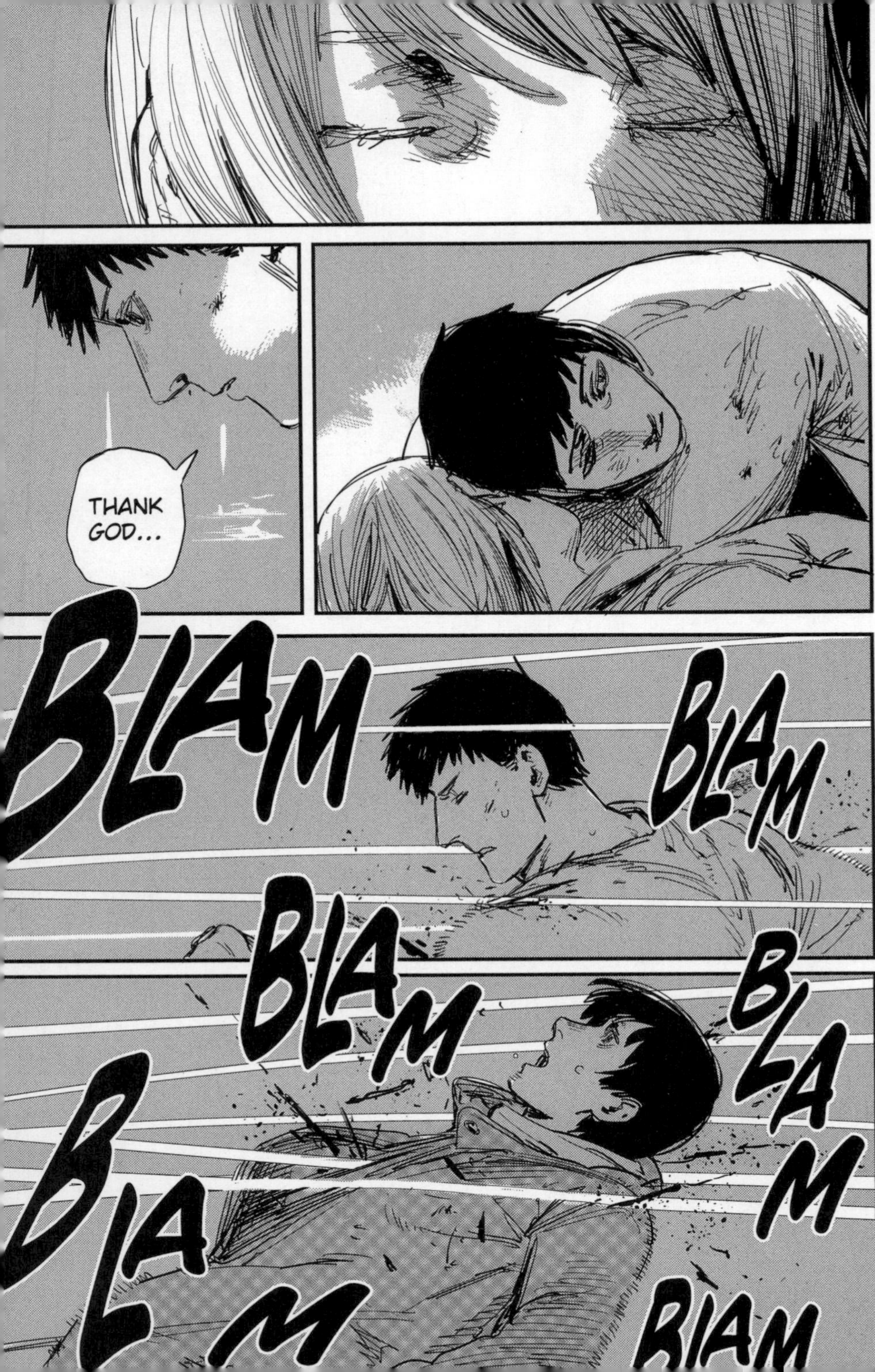

THANK GOD...
BLAM
BLAM
BLAM
BLAM
BLAM
BLAM

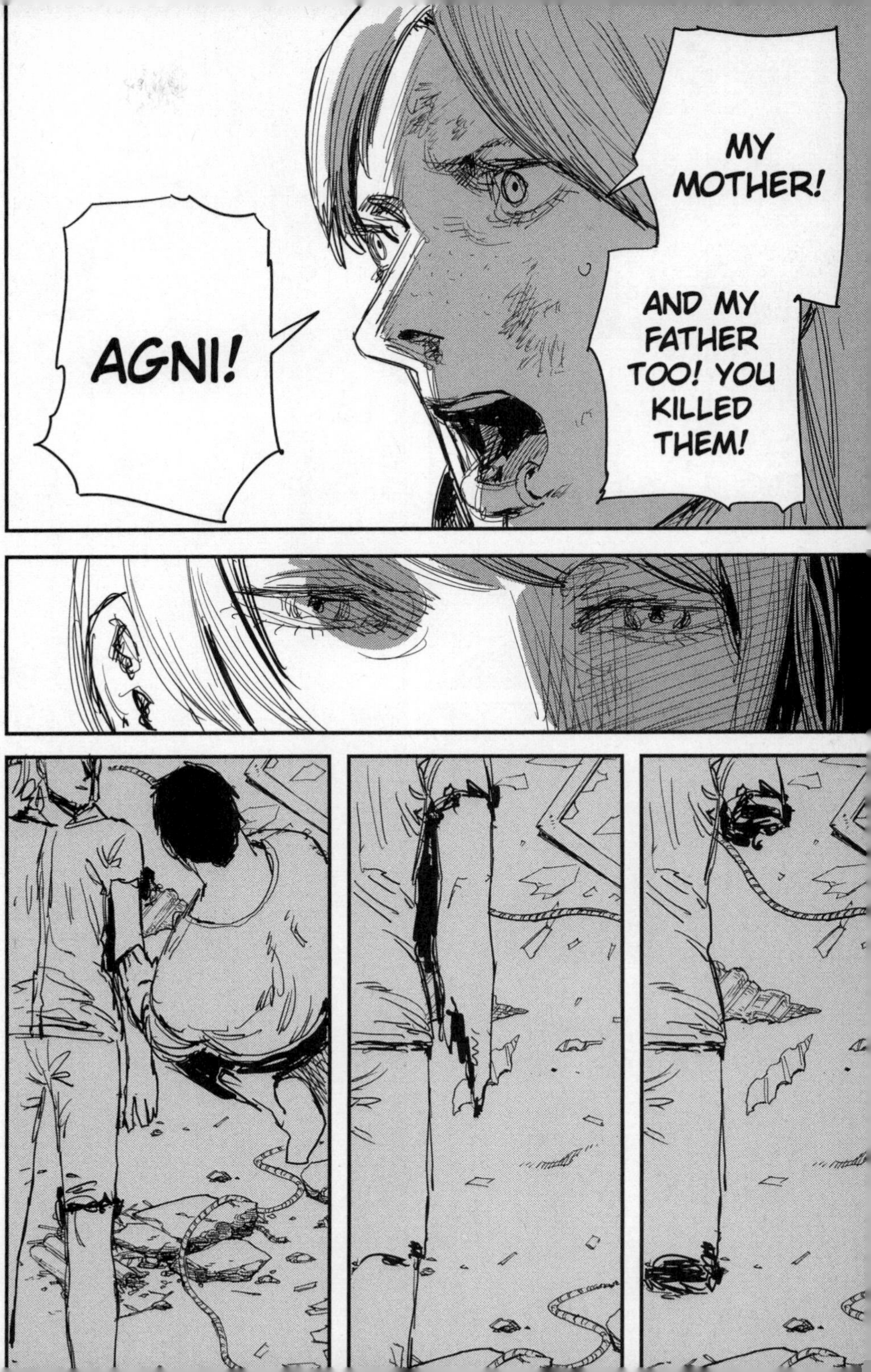
MY MOTHER!
AND MY FATHER TOO! YOU KILLED THEM!
AGNI!

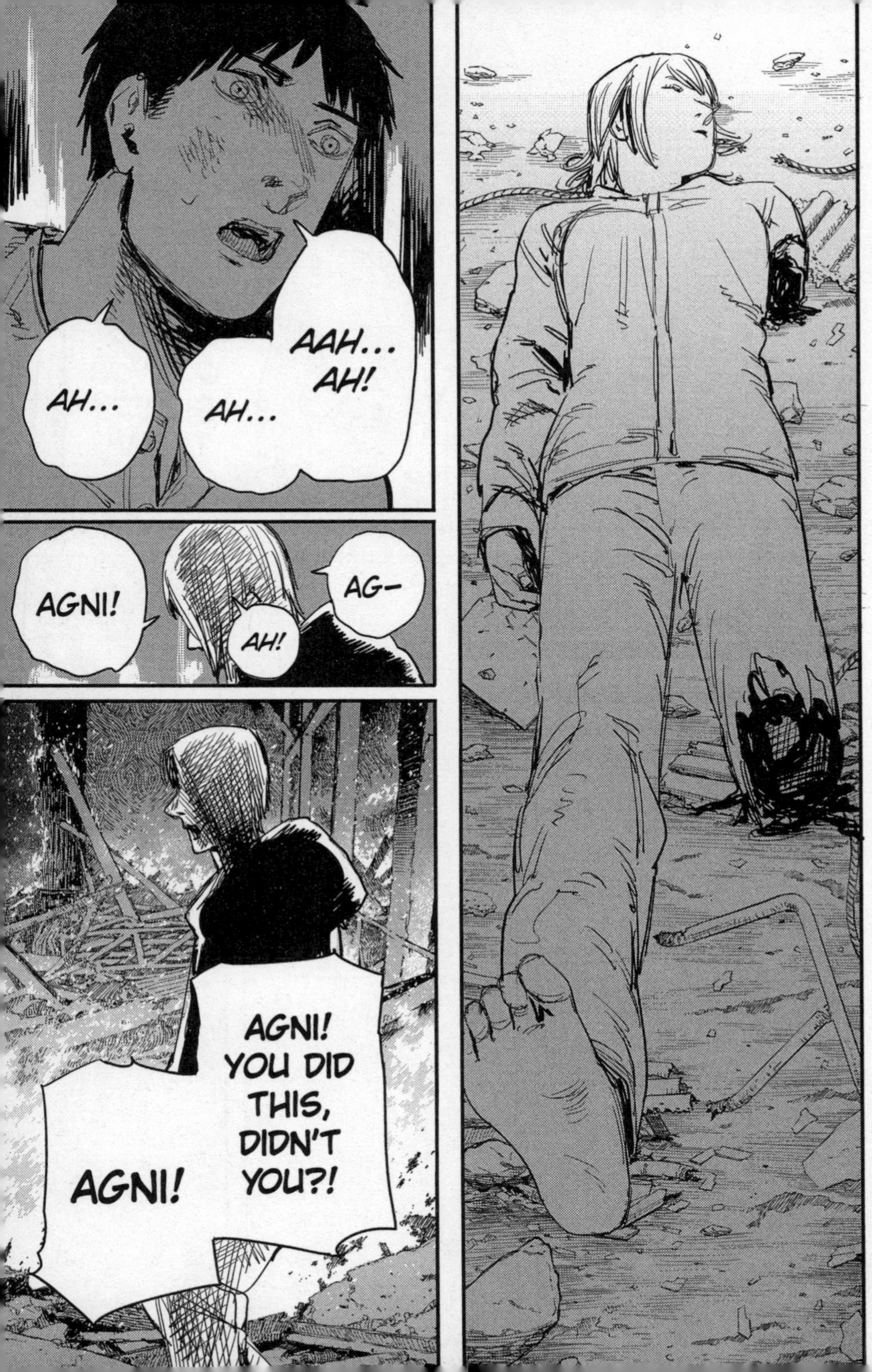
AAH... AH!
AH...
AH...
AG-
AH!
AGNI!
AGNI! YOU DID THIS, DIDN'T YOU?!
AGNI!

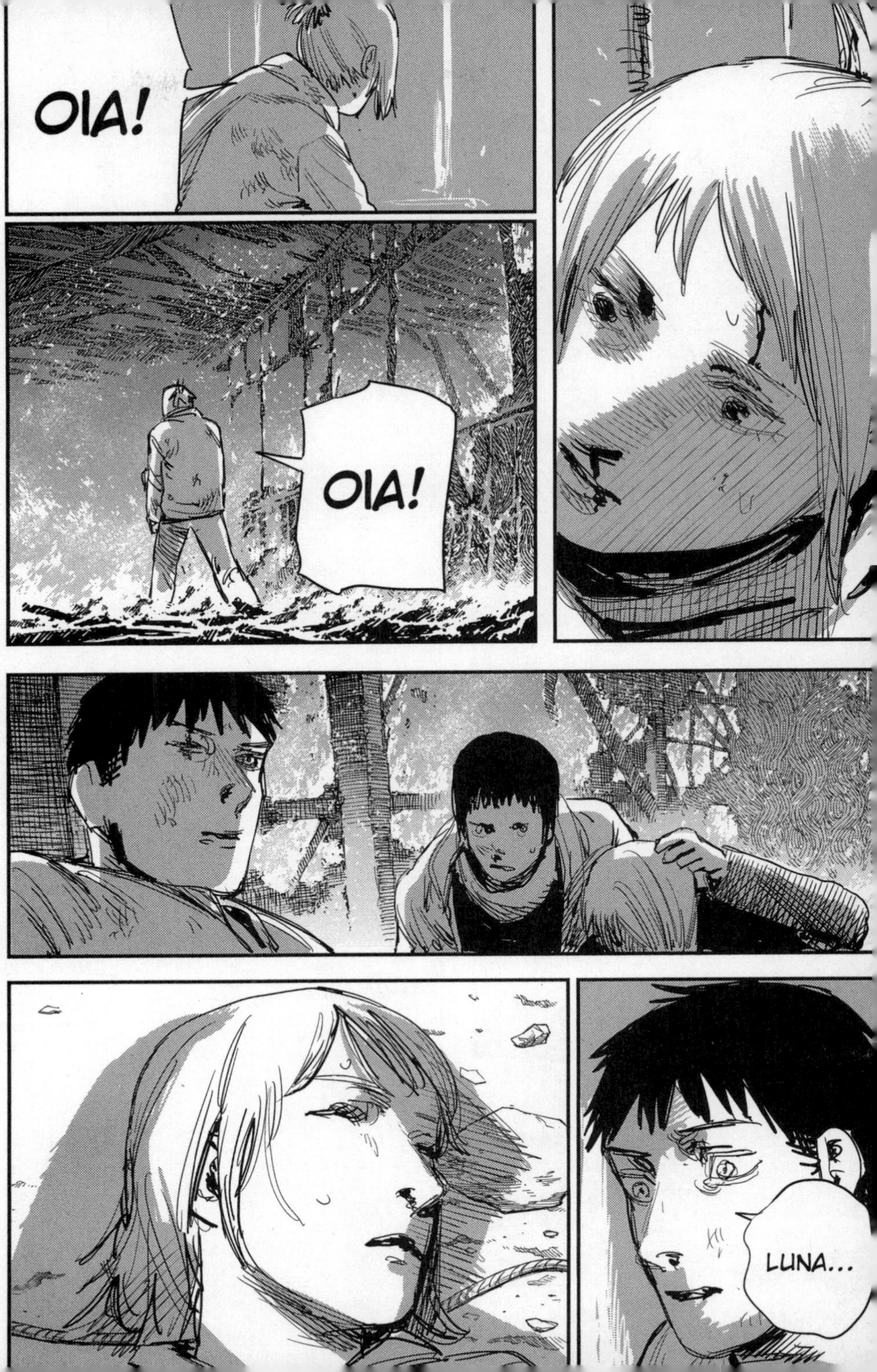
OIA!
OIA!
LUNA...

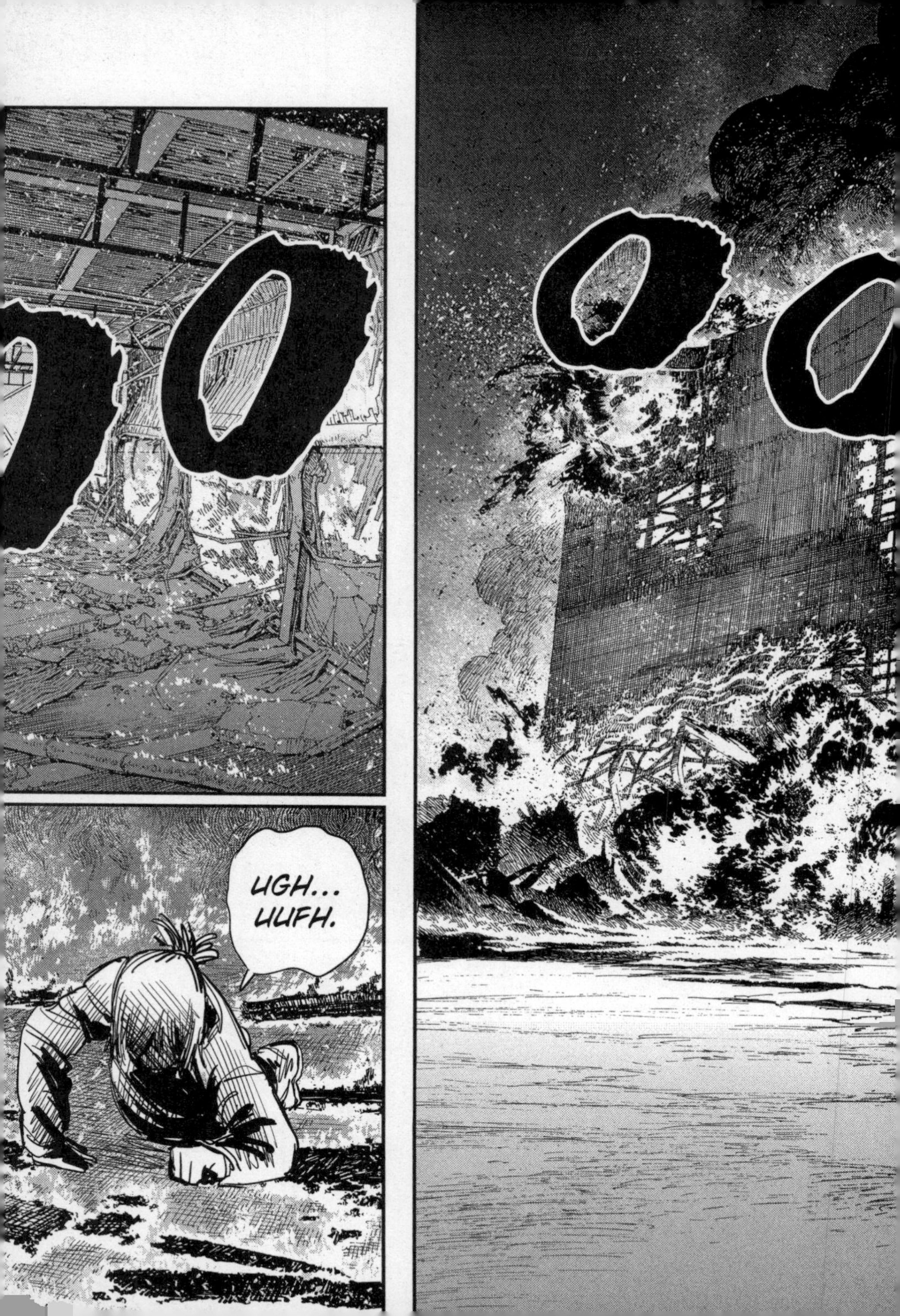
UGH... UUFH.

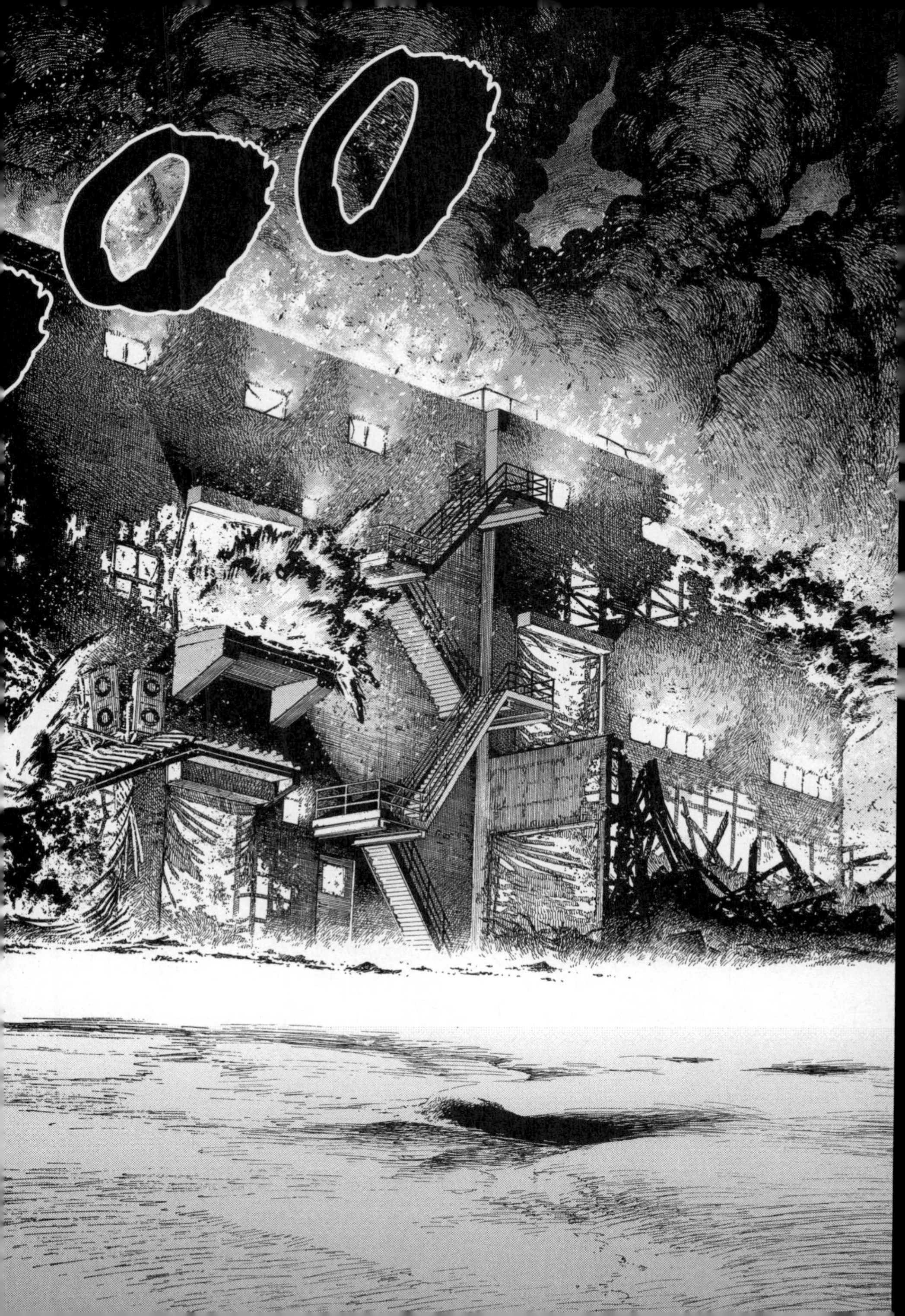
OO

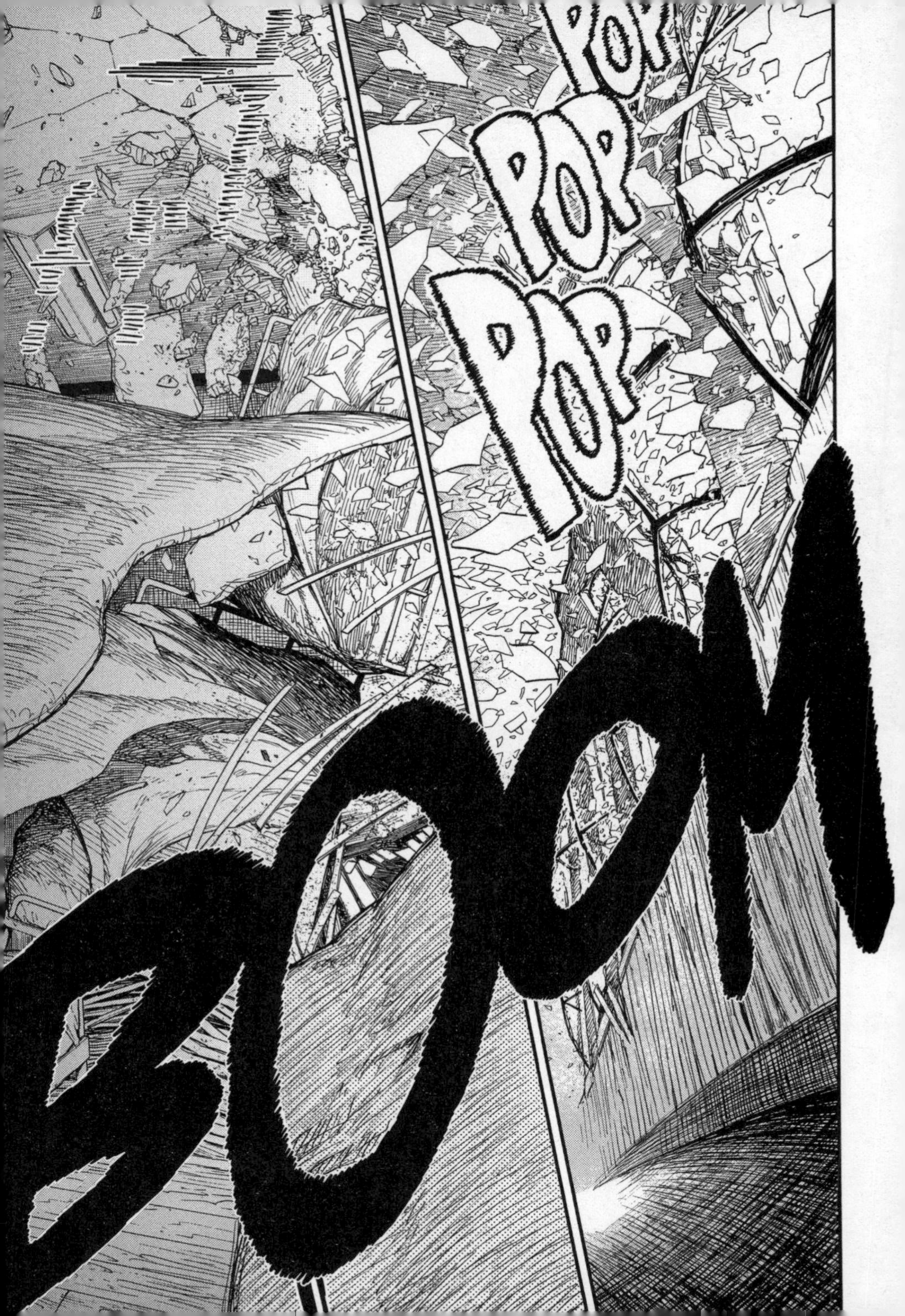
POP POP POP POP-
BOOOM

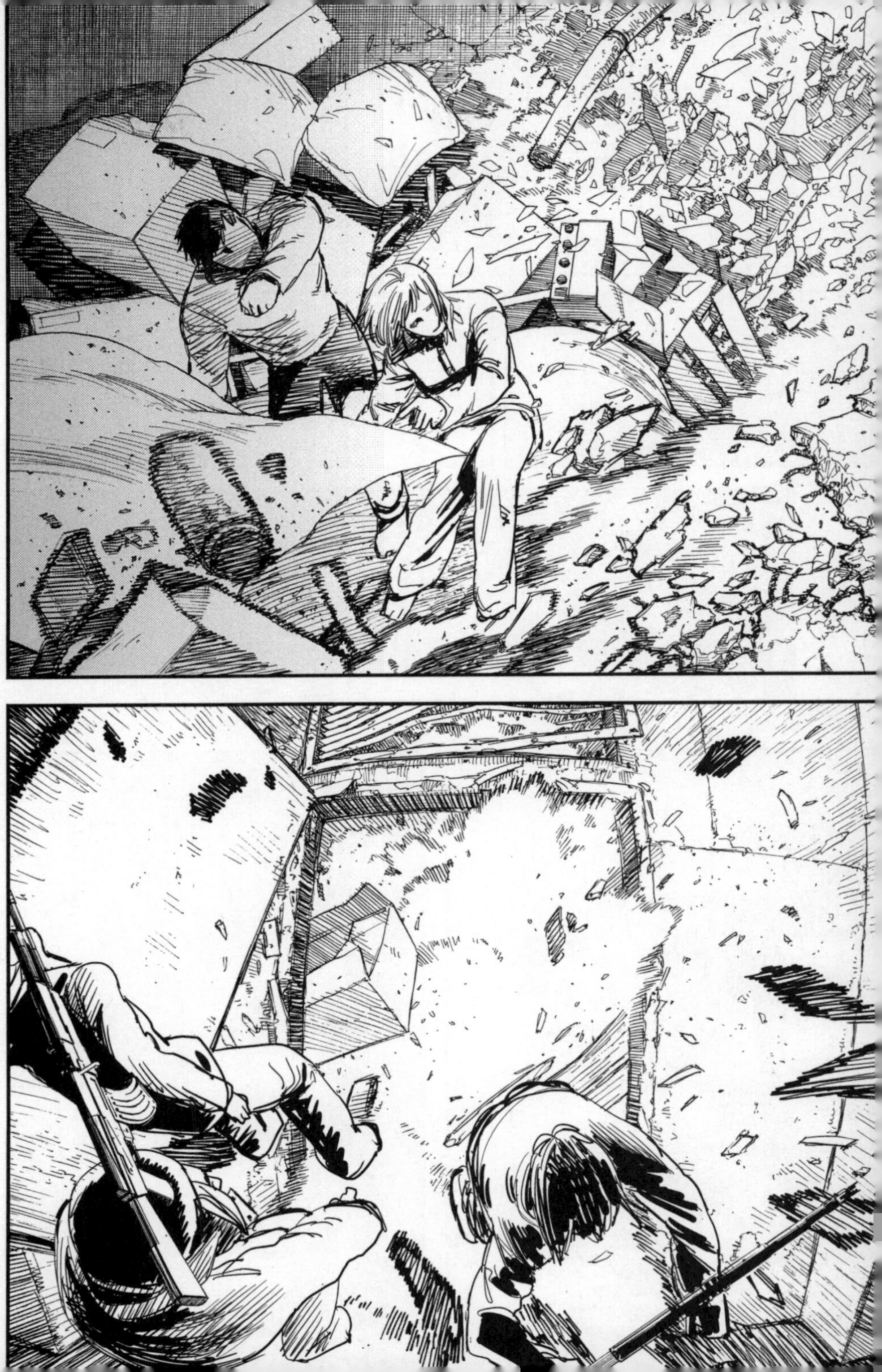

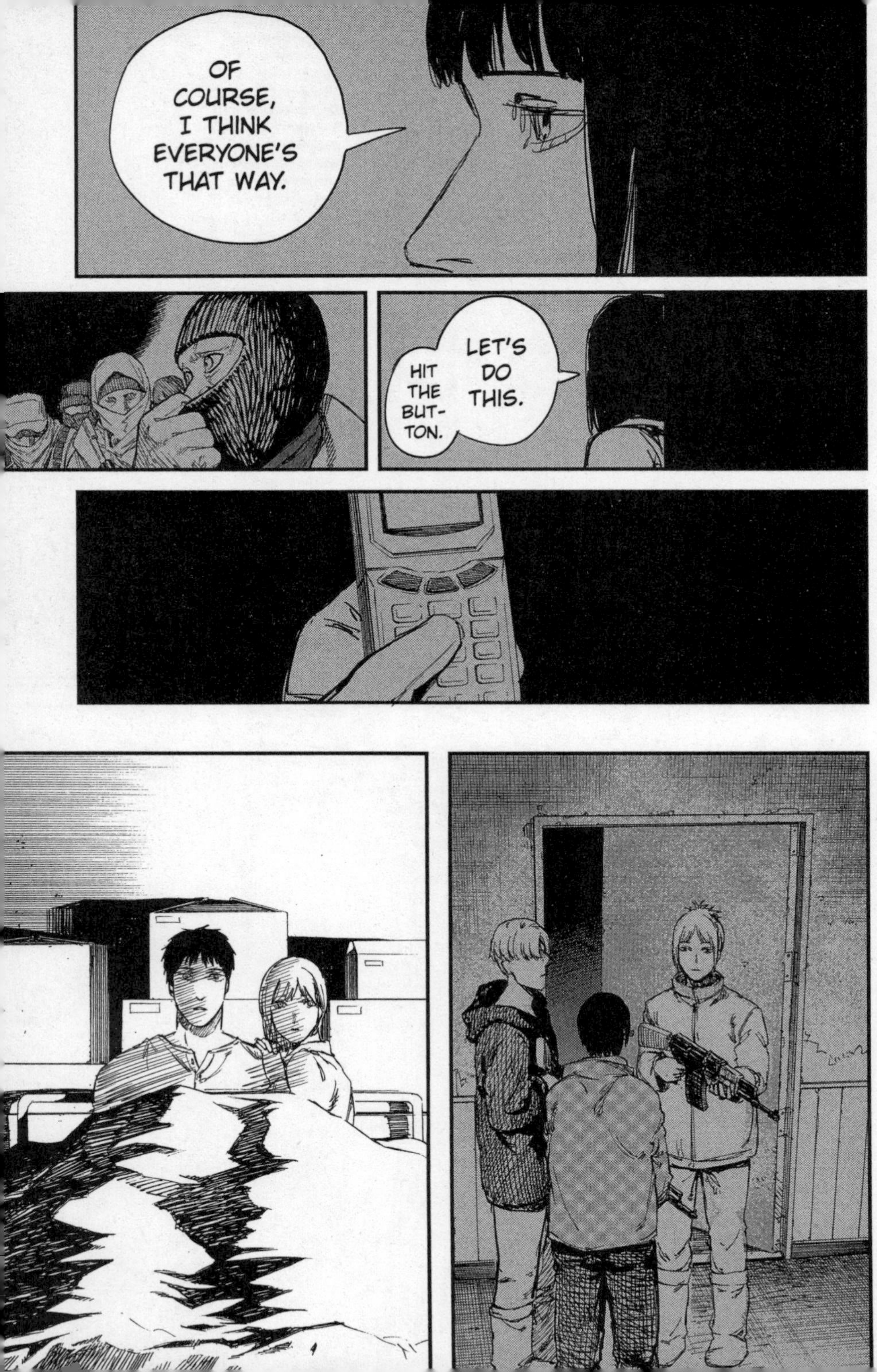
OF COURSE, I THINK EVERYONE'S THAT WAY.
LET'S DO THIS.
HIT THE BUT-TON.

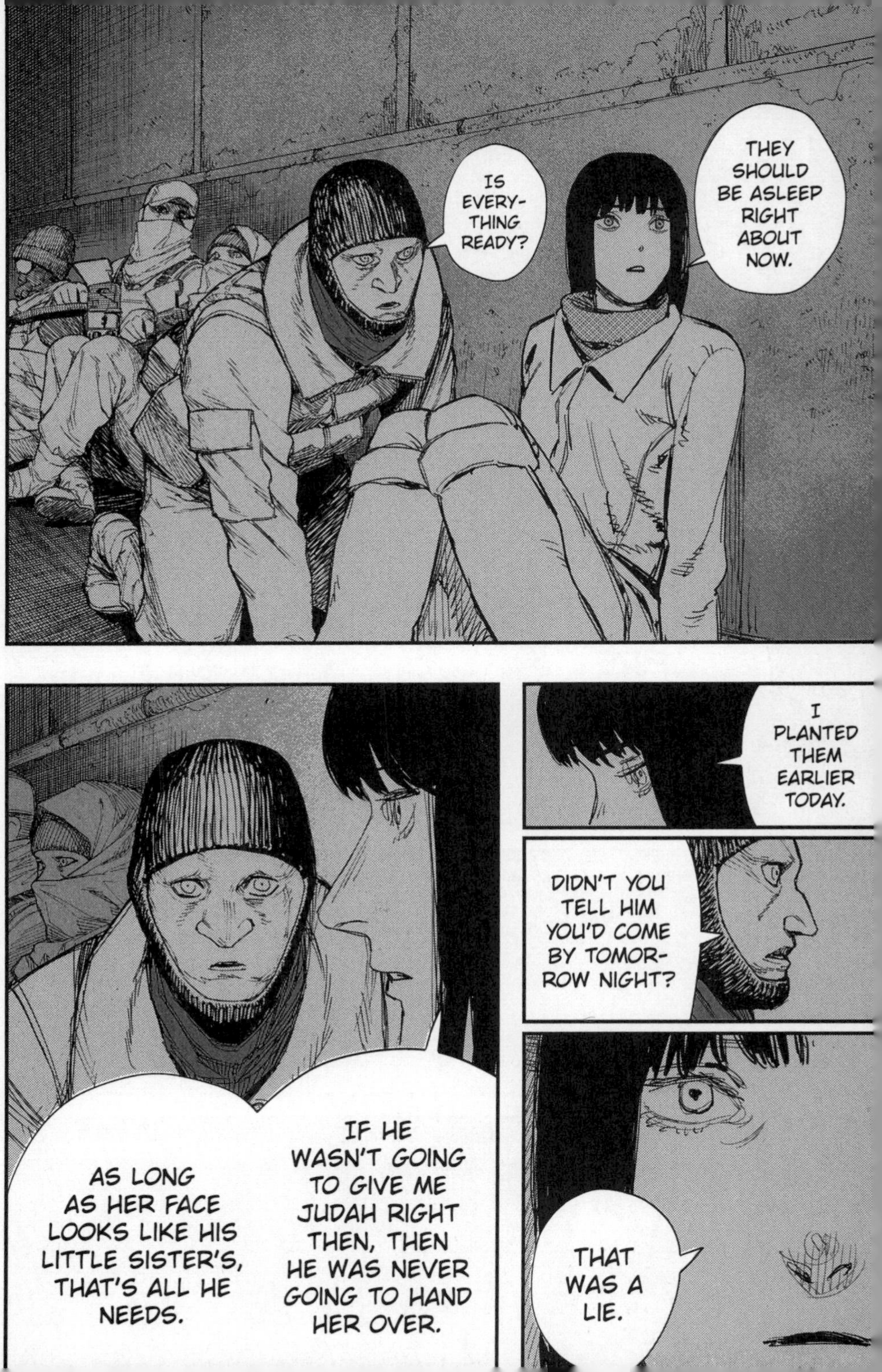
THEY SHOULD BE ASLEEP RIGHT ABOUT NOW.
IS EVERY-THING READY?
I PLANTED THEM EARLIER TODAY.
DIDN'T YOU TELL HIM YOU'D COME BY TOMOR-ROW NIGHT?
THAT WAS A LIE.
IF HE WASN'T GOING TO GIVE ME JUDAH RIGHT THEN, THEN HE WAS NEVER GOING TO HAND HER OVER.
AS LONG AS HER FACE LOOKS LIKE HIS LITTLE SISTER'S, THAT'S ALL HE NEEDS.

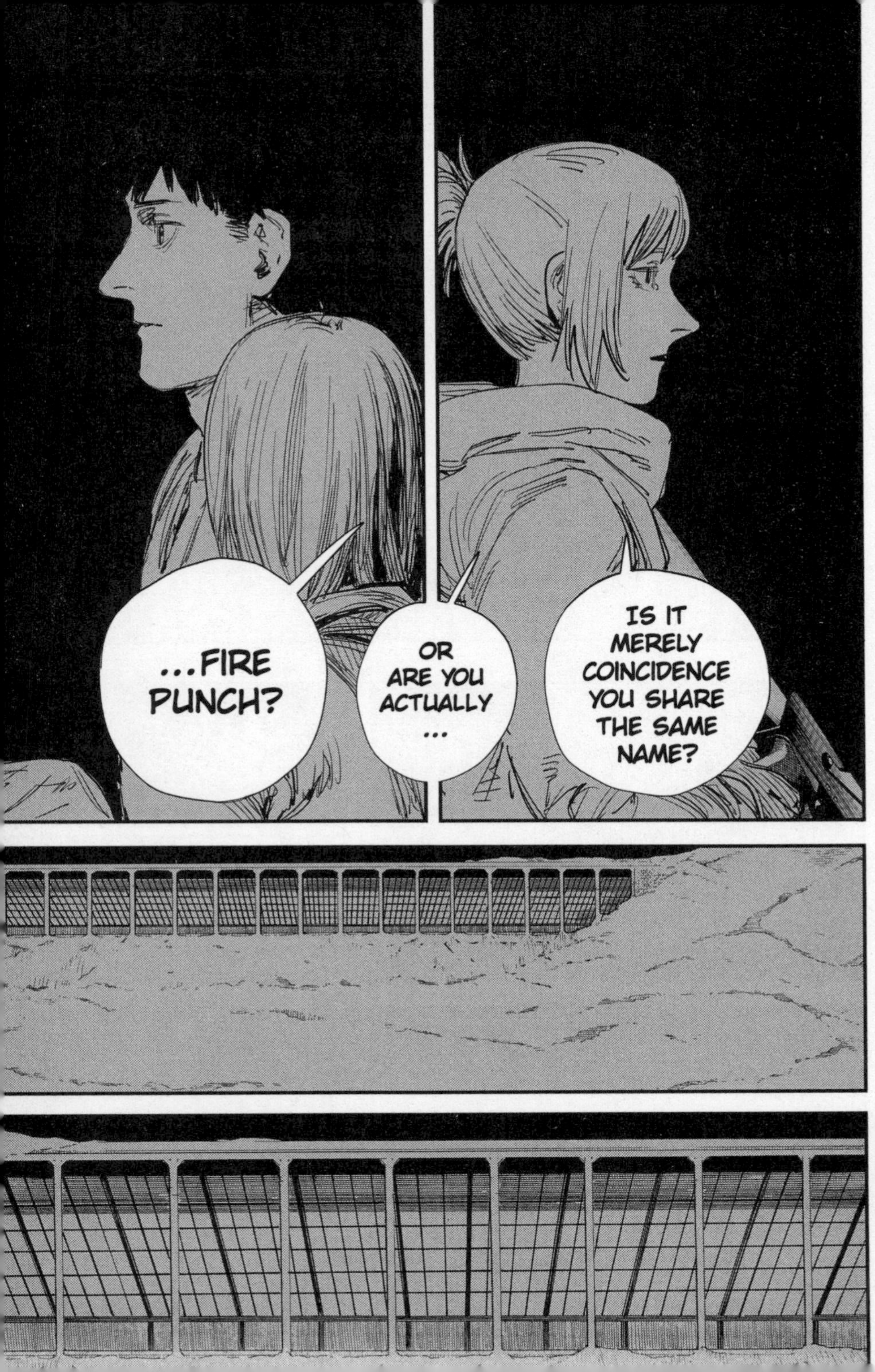
IS IT MERELY COINCIDENCE YOU SHARE THE SAME NAME?
OR ARE YOU ACTUALLY ...
...FIRE PUNCH?

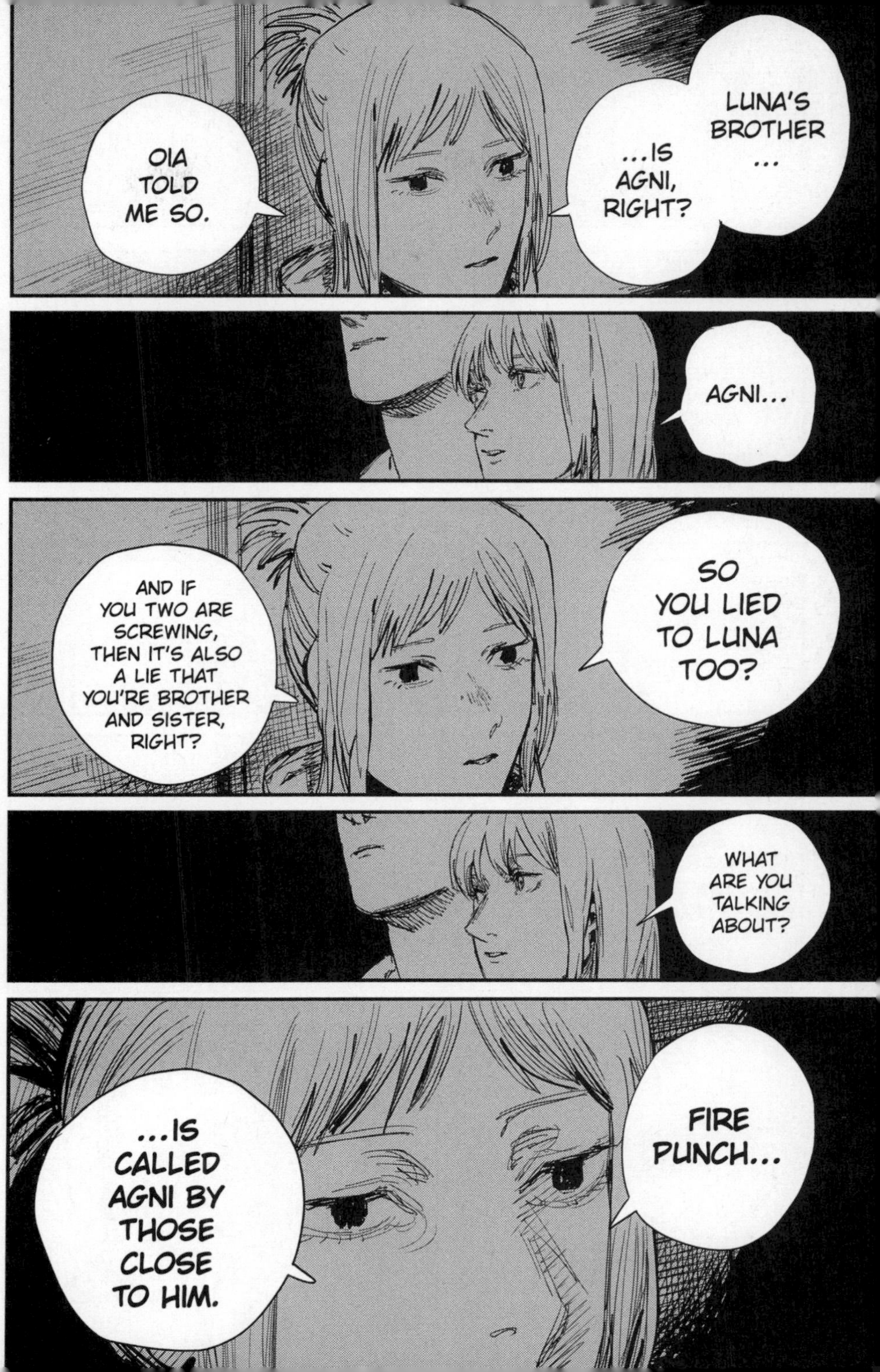
LUNA'S BROTHER ...
...IS AGNI, RIGHT?
OIA TOLD ME SO.
AGNI...
SO YOU LIED TO LUNA TOO?
AND IF YOU TWO ARE SCREWING, THEN IT'S ALSO A LIE THAT YOU'RE BROTHER AND SISTER, RIGHT?
WHAT ARE YOU TALKING ABOUT?
FIRE PUNCH...
...IS CALLED AGNI BY THOSE CLOSE TO HIM.

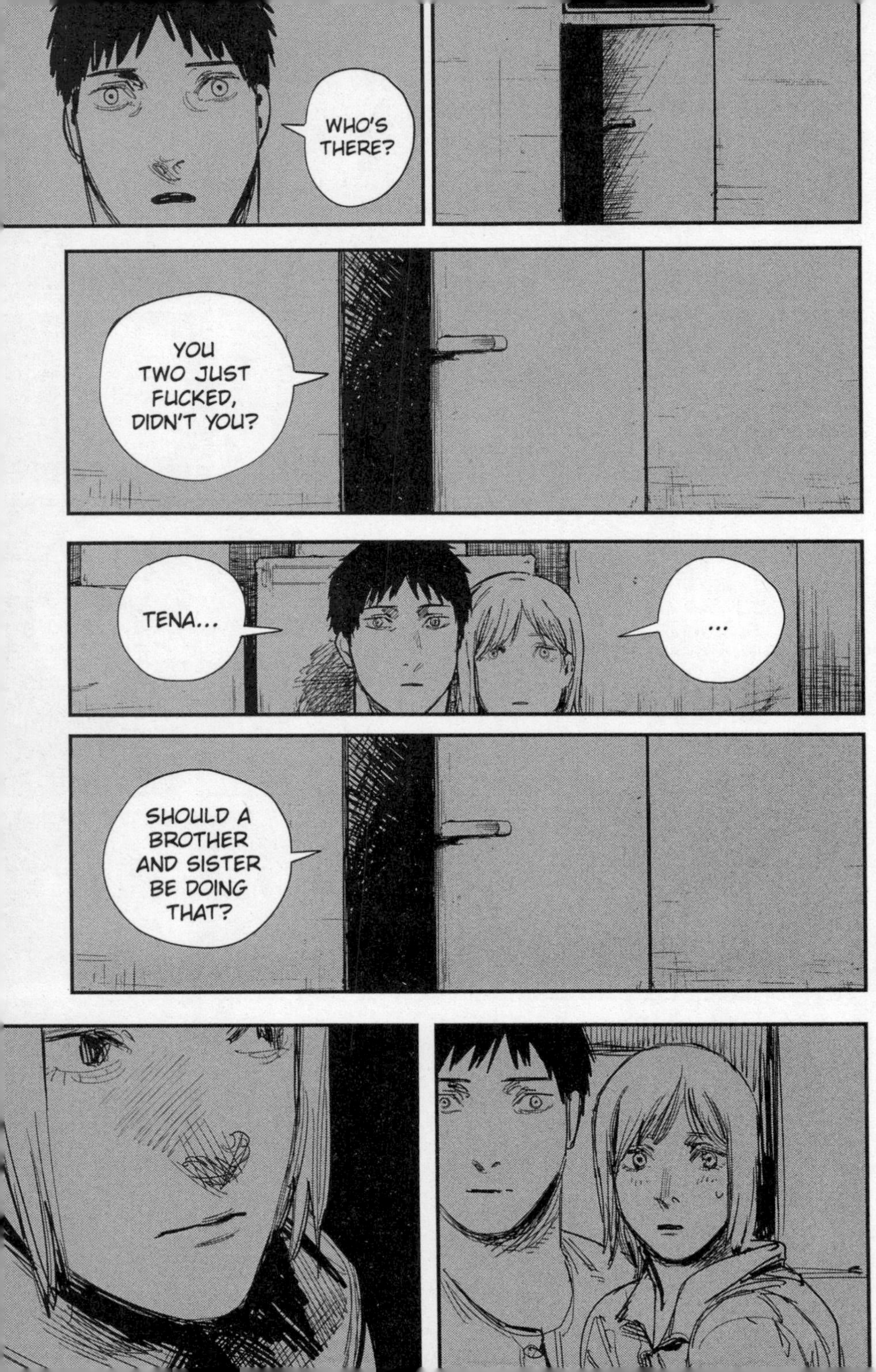
WHO'S THERE?
YOU TWO JUST FUCKED, DIDN'T YOU?
...
TENA...
SHOULD A BROTHER AND SISTER BE DOING THAT?

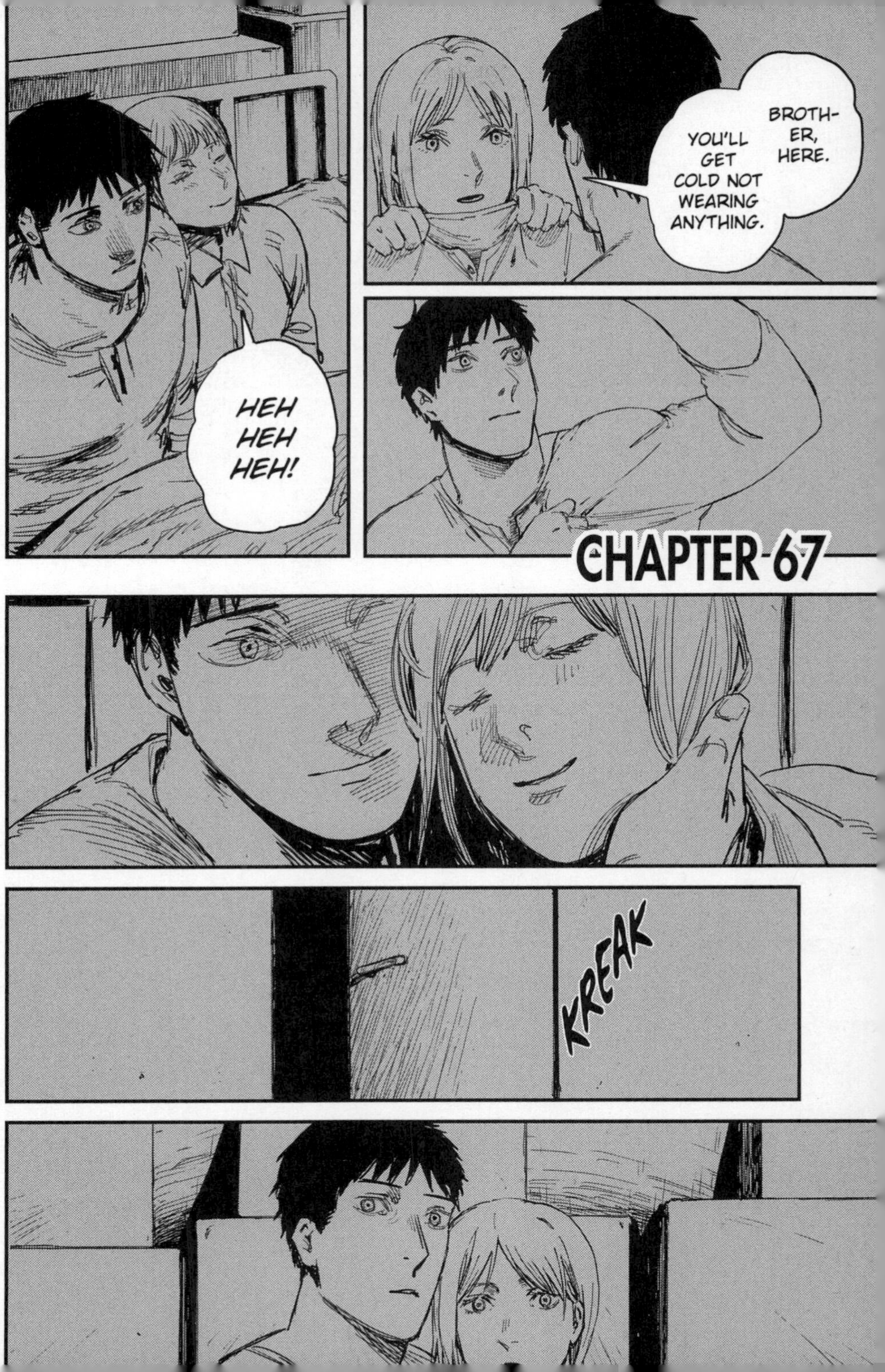
BROTHER, HERE. YOU'LL GET COLD NOT WEARING ANYTHING.
HEH HEH HEH!
CHAPTER 67
KREAK

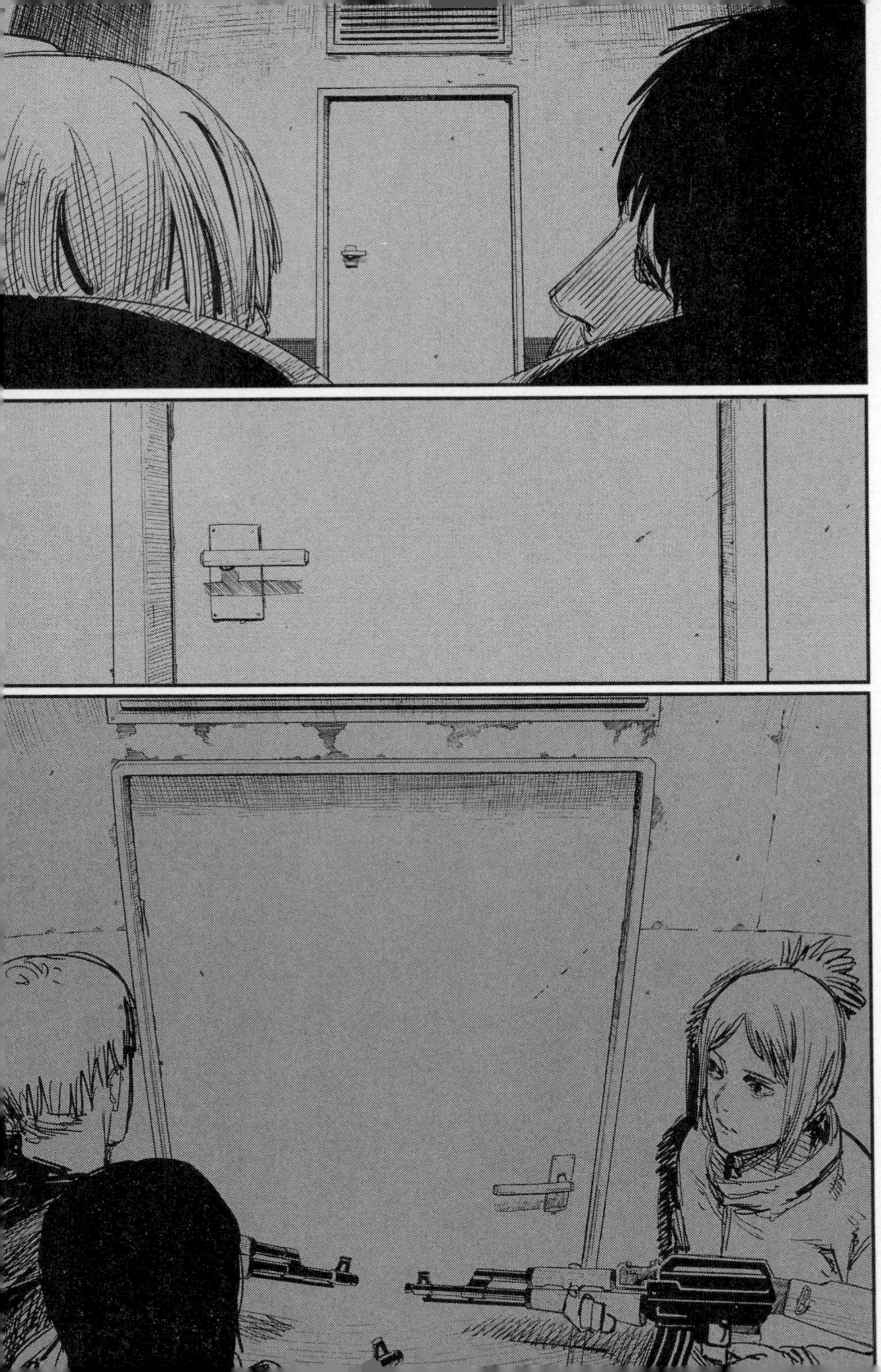

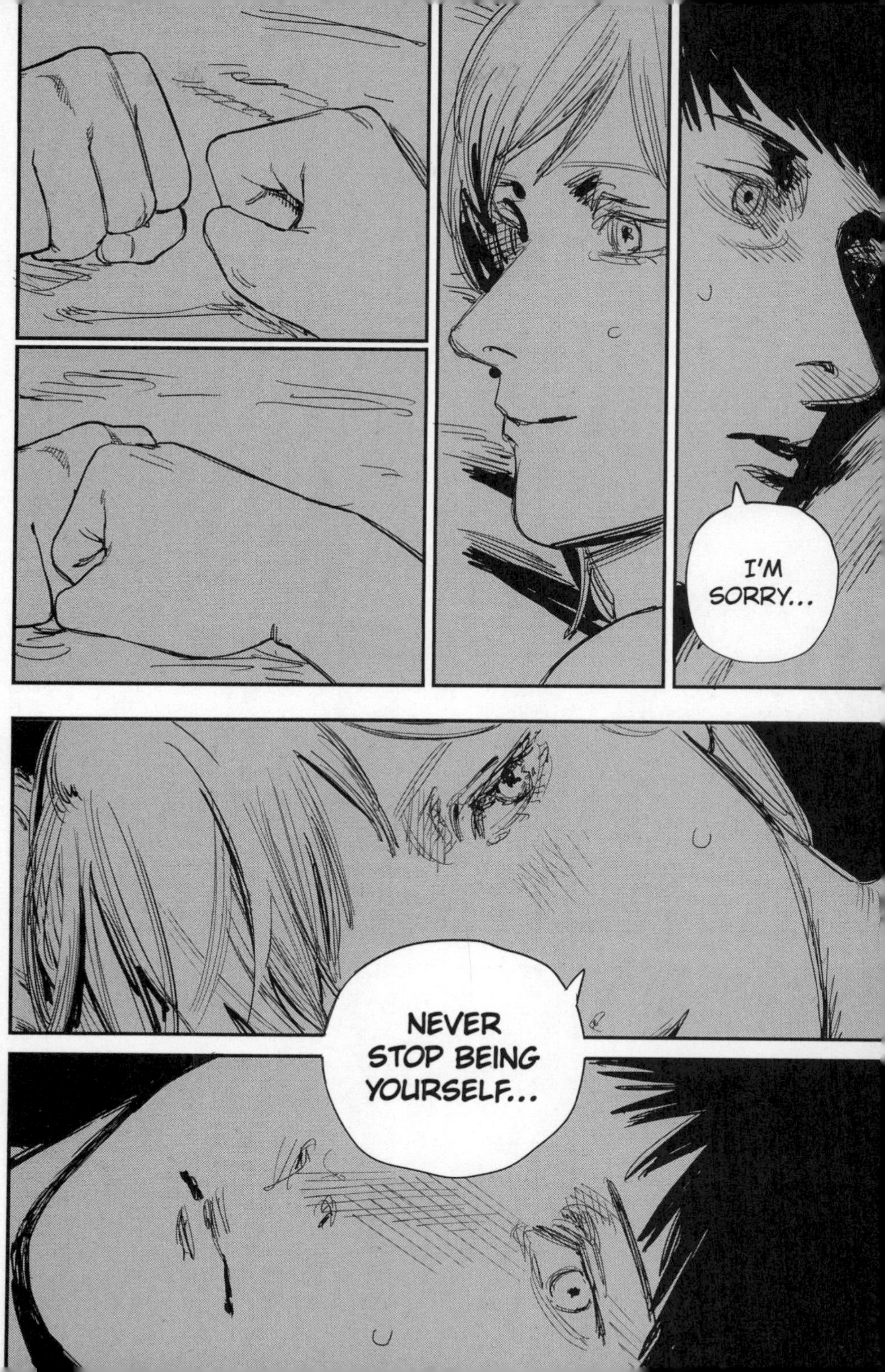
I'M SORRY...
NEVER STOP BEING YOURSELF...

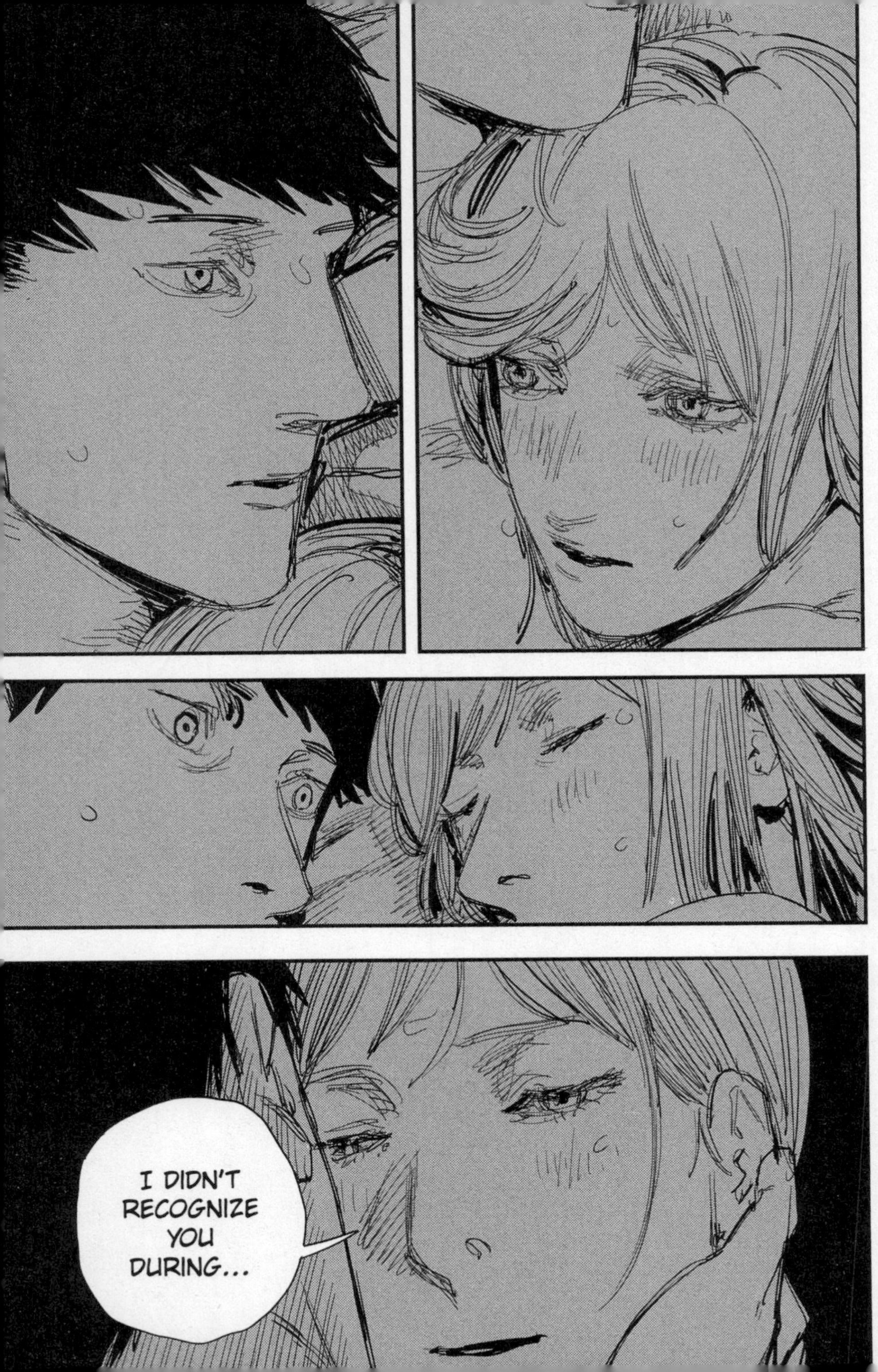
I DIDN'T RECOGNIZE YOU DURING...

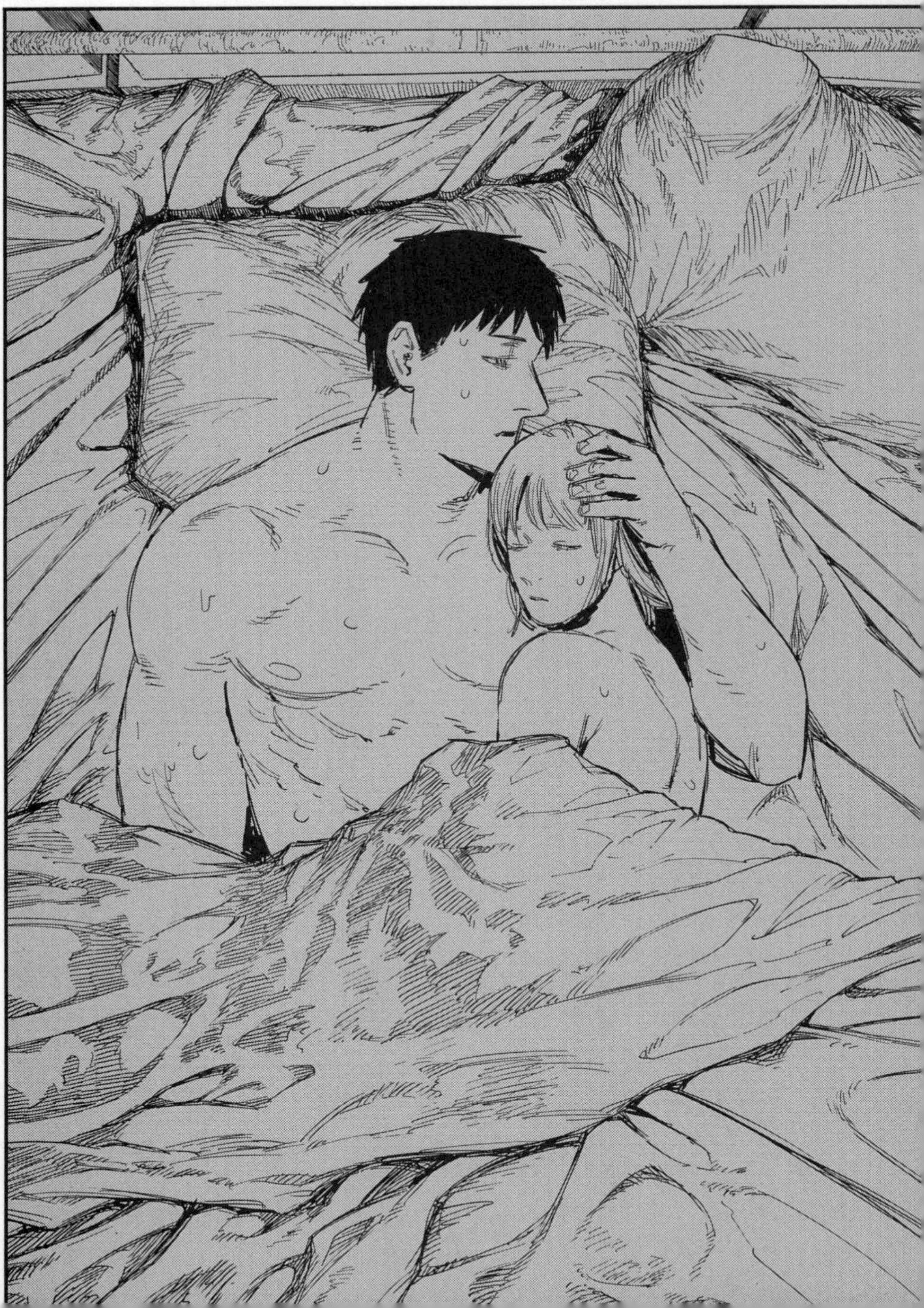

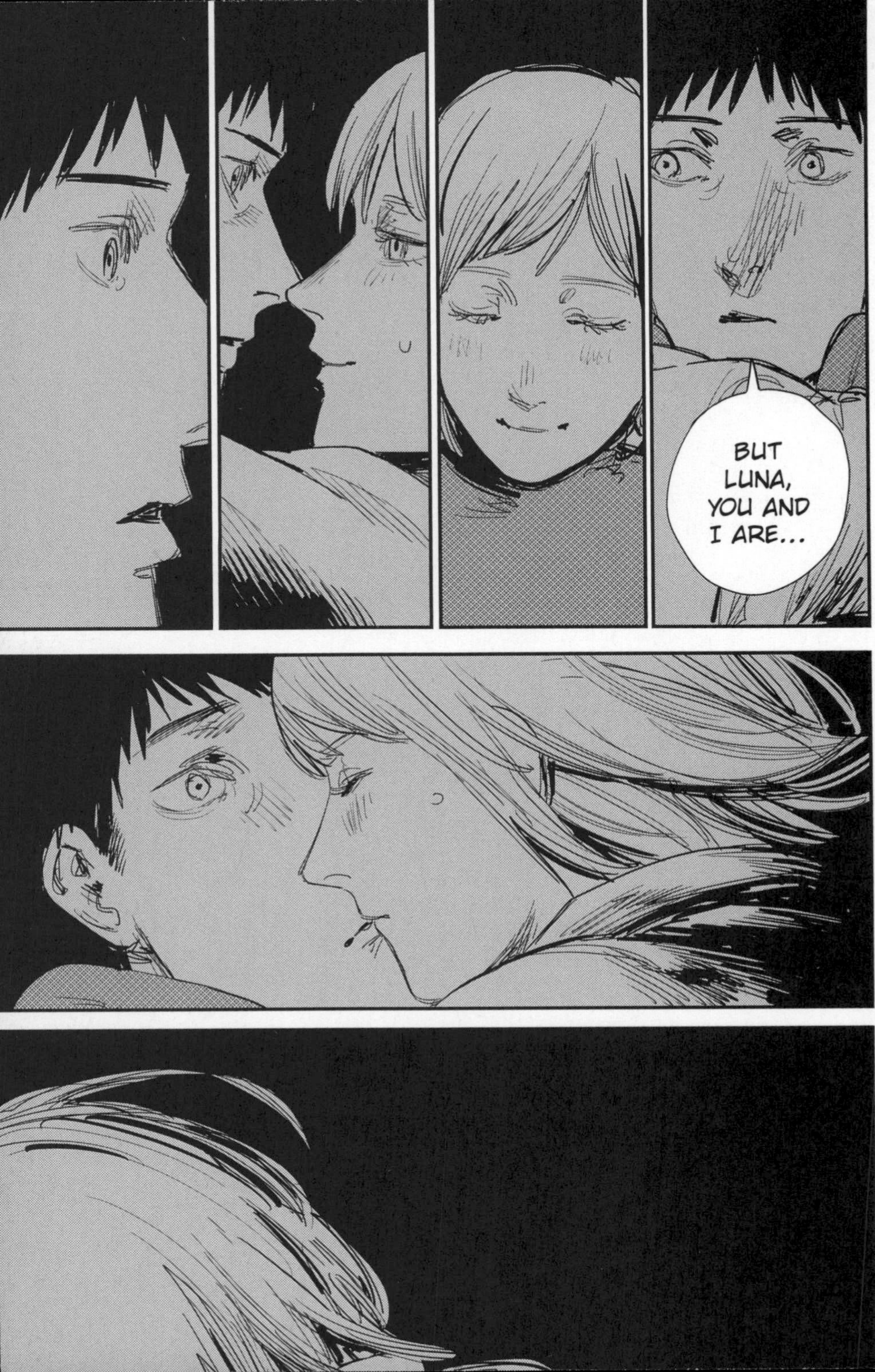
BUT LUNA, YOU AND I ARE...

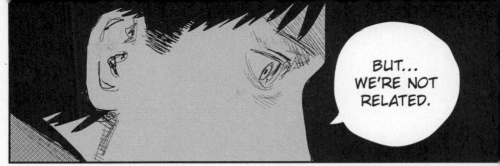

BUT...
WE'RE NOT
RELATED.

THEN WHY
DON'T WE
BECOME A
FAMILY?

WE COULD
MAKE A
BABY, YOU
AND ME.

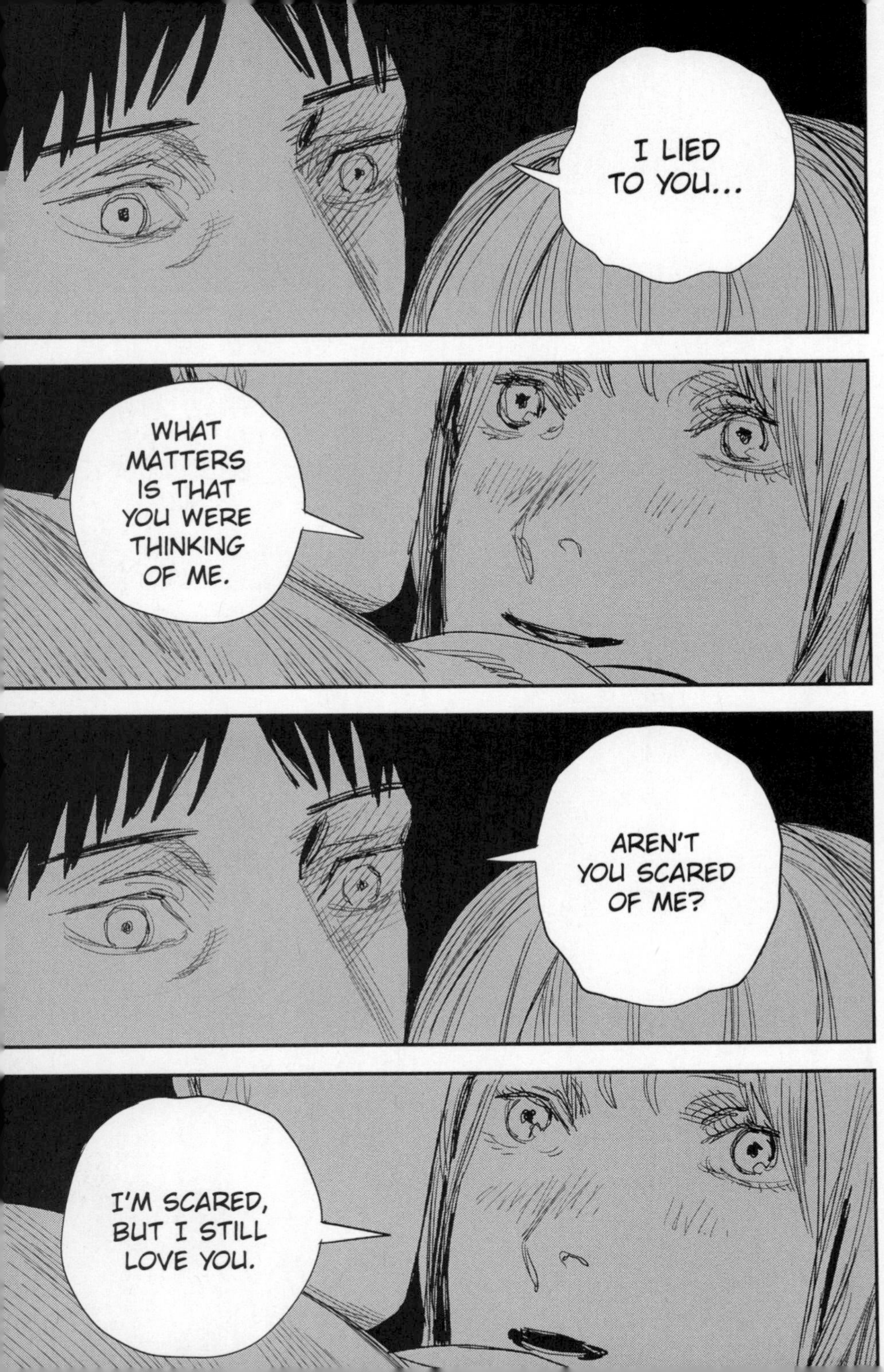
I LIED TO YOU...
WHAT MATTERS IS THAT YOU WERE THINKING OF ME.
AREN'T YOU SCARED OF ME?
I'M SCARED, BUT I STILL LOVE YOU.

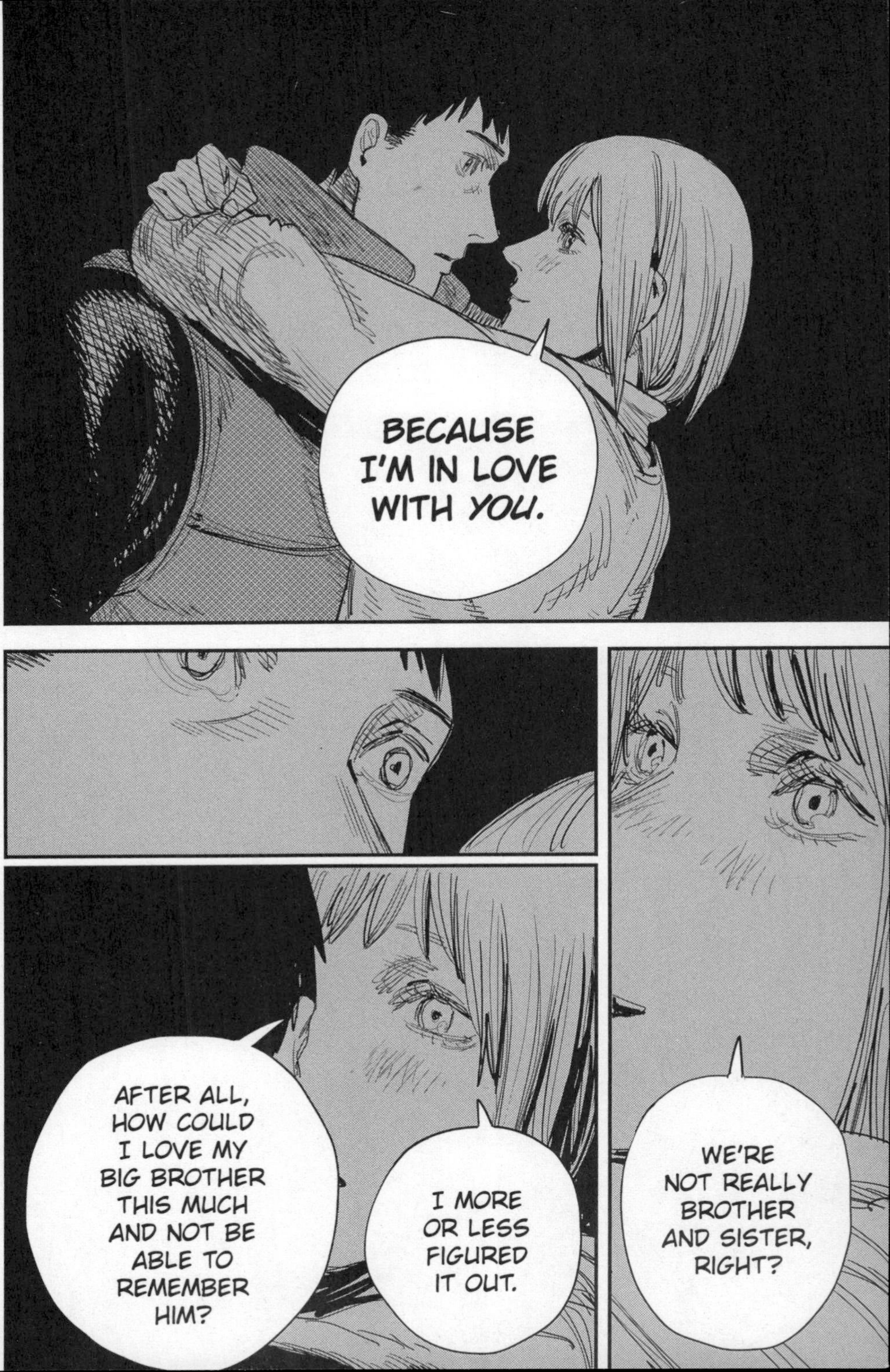
BECAUSE I'M IN LOVE WITH YOU.
WE'RE NOT REALLY BROTHER AND SISTER, RIGHT?
I MORE OR LESS FIGURED IT OUT.
AFTER ALL, HOW COULD I LOVE MY BIG BROTHER THIS MUCH AND NOT BE ABLE TO REMEMBER HIM?

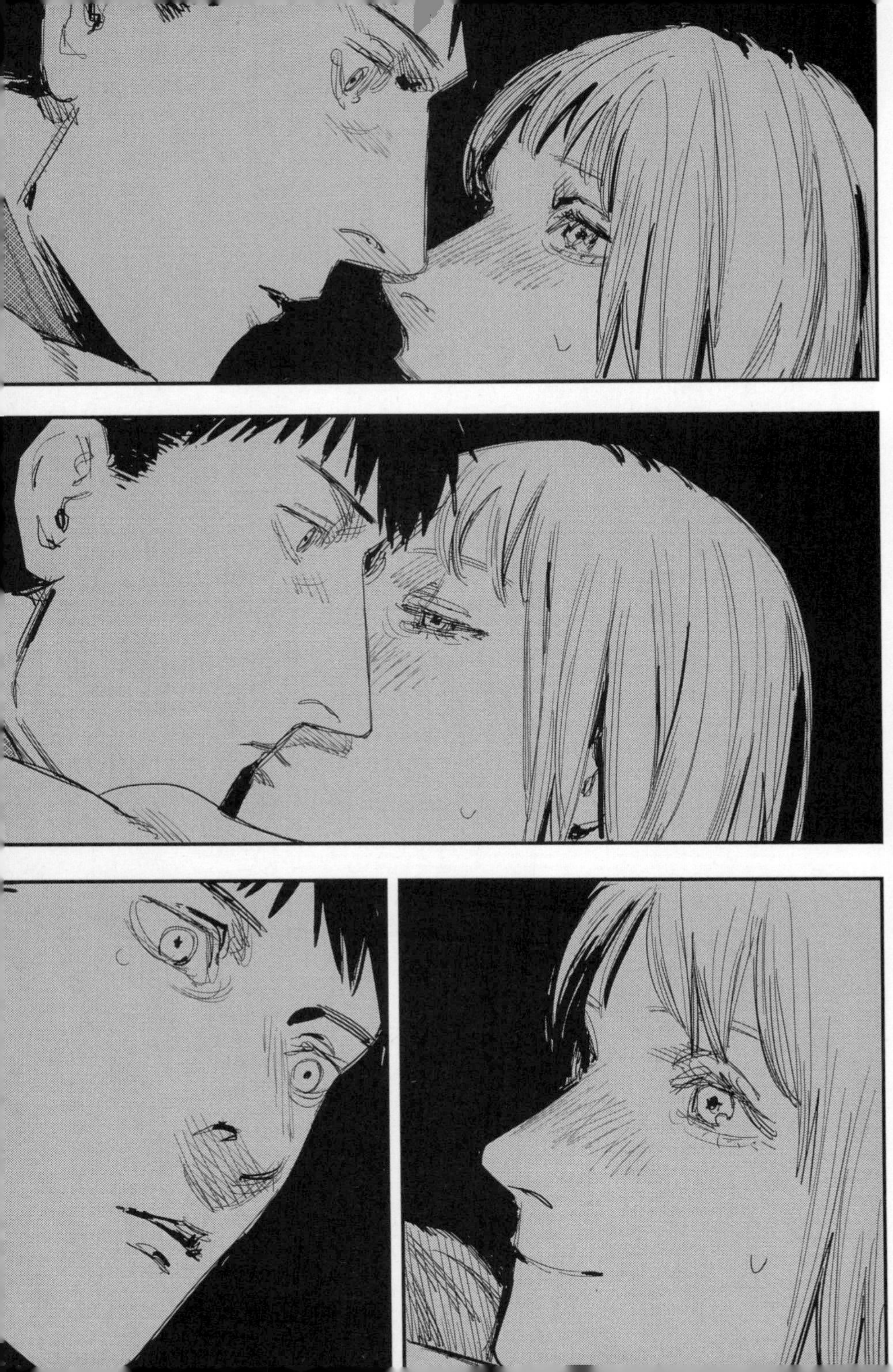

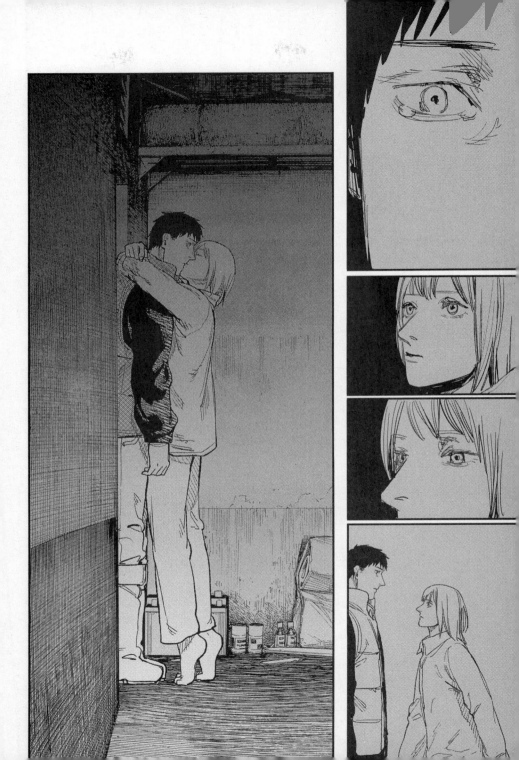

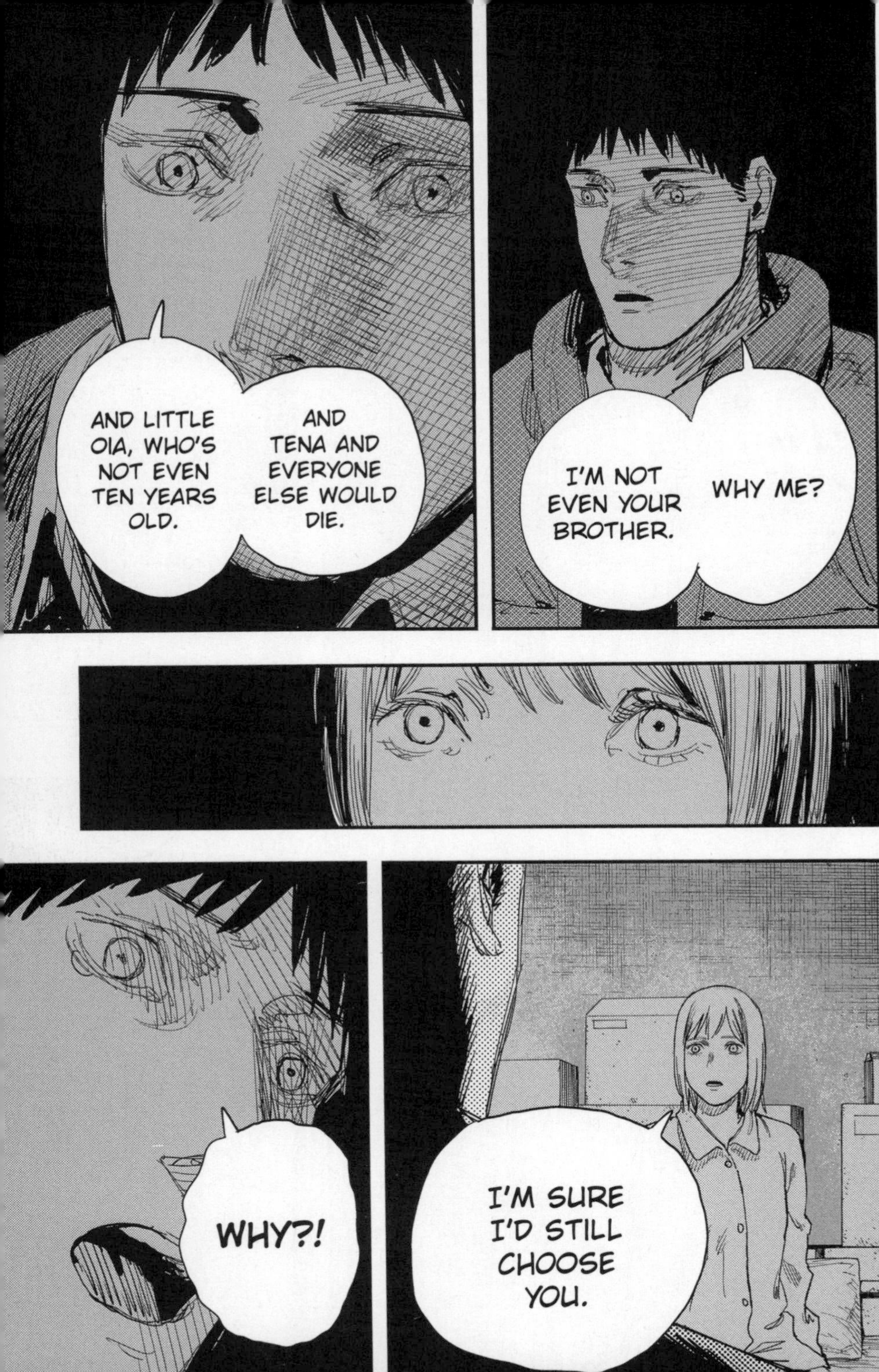
WHY ME?
I'M NOT EVEN YOUR BROTHER.
AND TENA AND EVERYONE ELSE WOULD DIE.
AND LITTLE OIA, WHO'S NOT EVEN TEN YEARS OLD.
I'M SURE I'D STILL CHOOSE YOU.
WHY?!

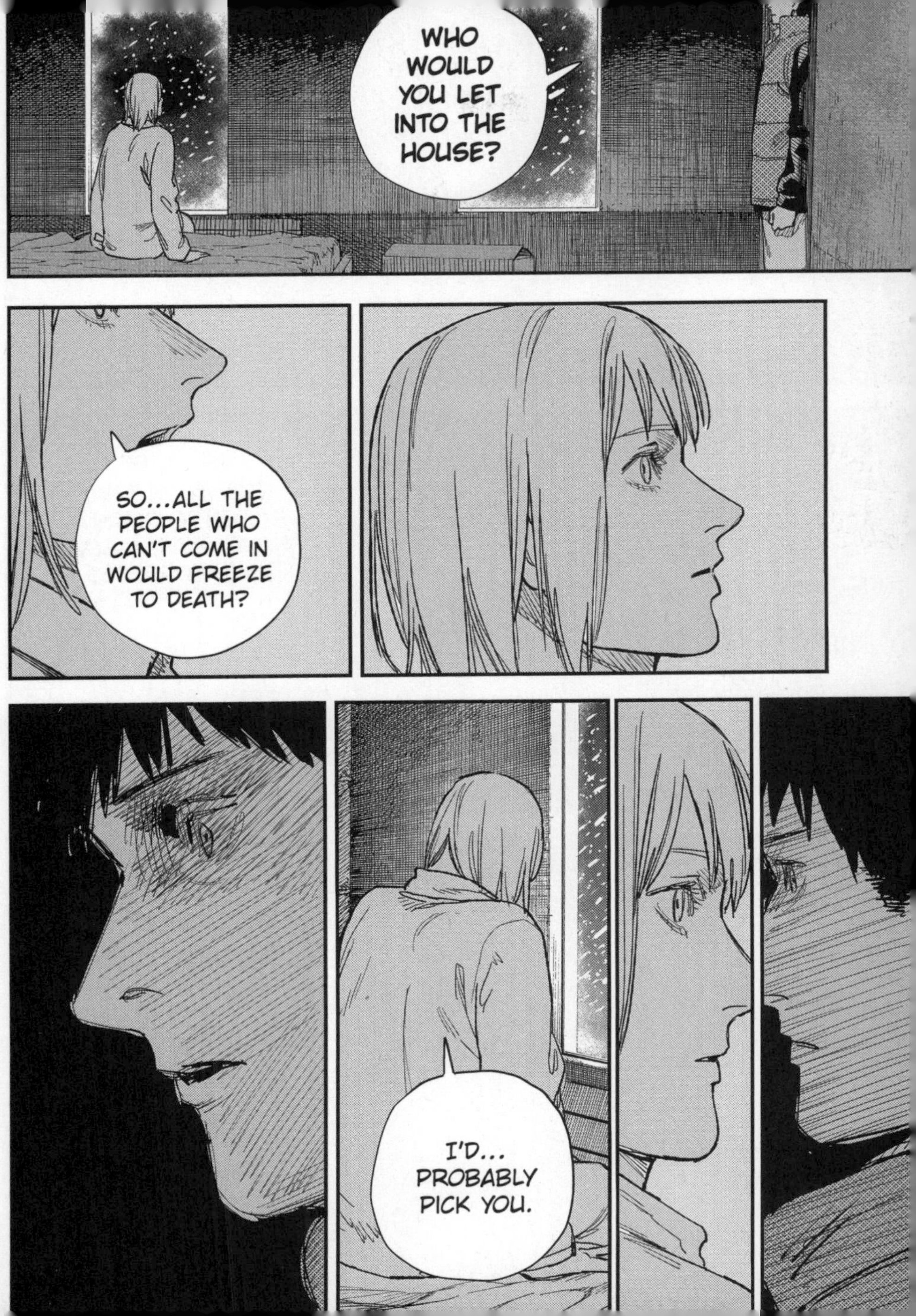
WHO WOULD YOU LET INTO THE HOUSE?
SO...ALL THE PEOPLE WHO CAN'T COME IN WOULD FREEZE TO DEATH?
I'D... PROBABLY PICK YOU.

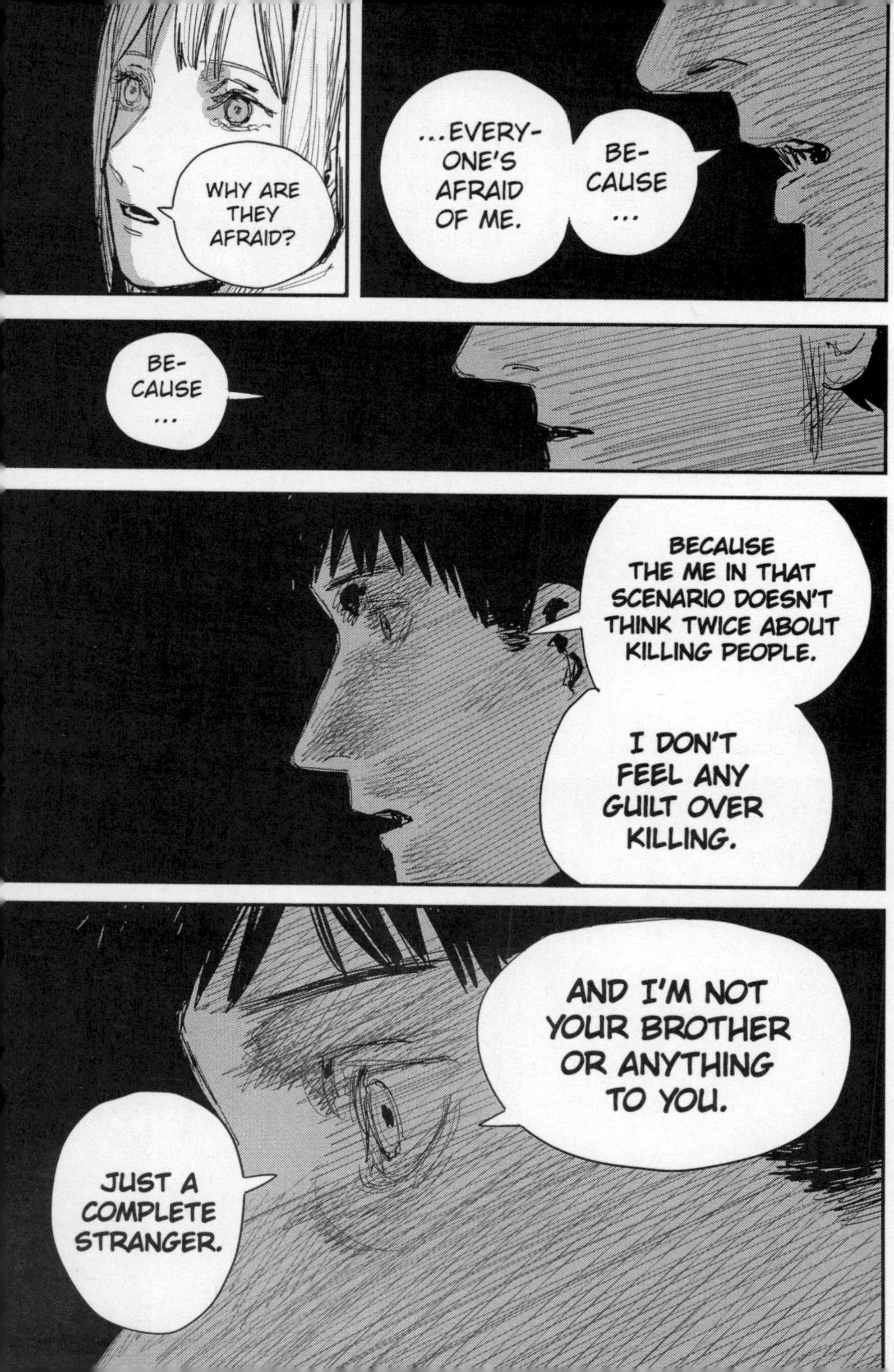
BE-CAUSE ...
...EVERY-ONE'S AFRAID OF ME.
WHY ARE THEY AFRAID?
BE-CAUSE ...
BECAUSE THE ME IN THAT SCENARIO DOESN'T THINK TWICE ABOUT KILLING PEOPLE.
I DON'T FEEL ANY GUILT OVER KILLING.
AND I'M NOT YOUR BROTHER OR ANYTHING TO YOU.
JUST A COMPLETE STRANGER.

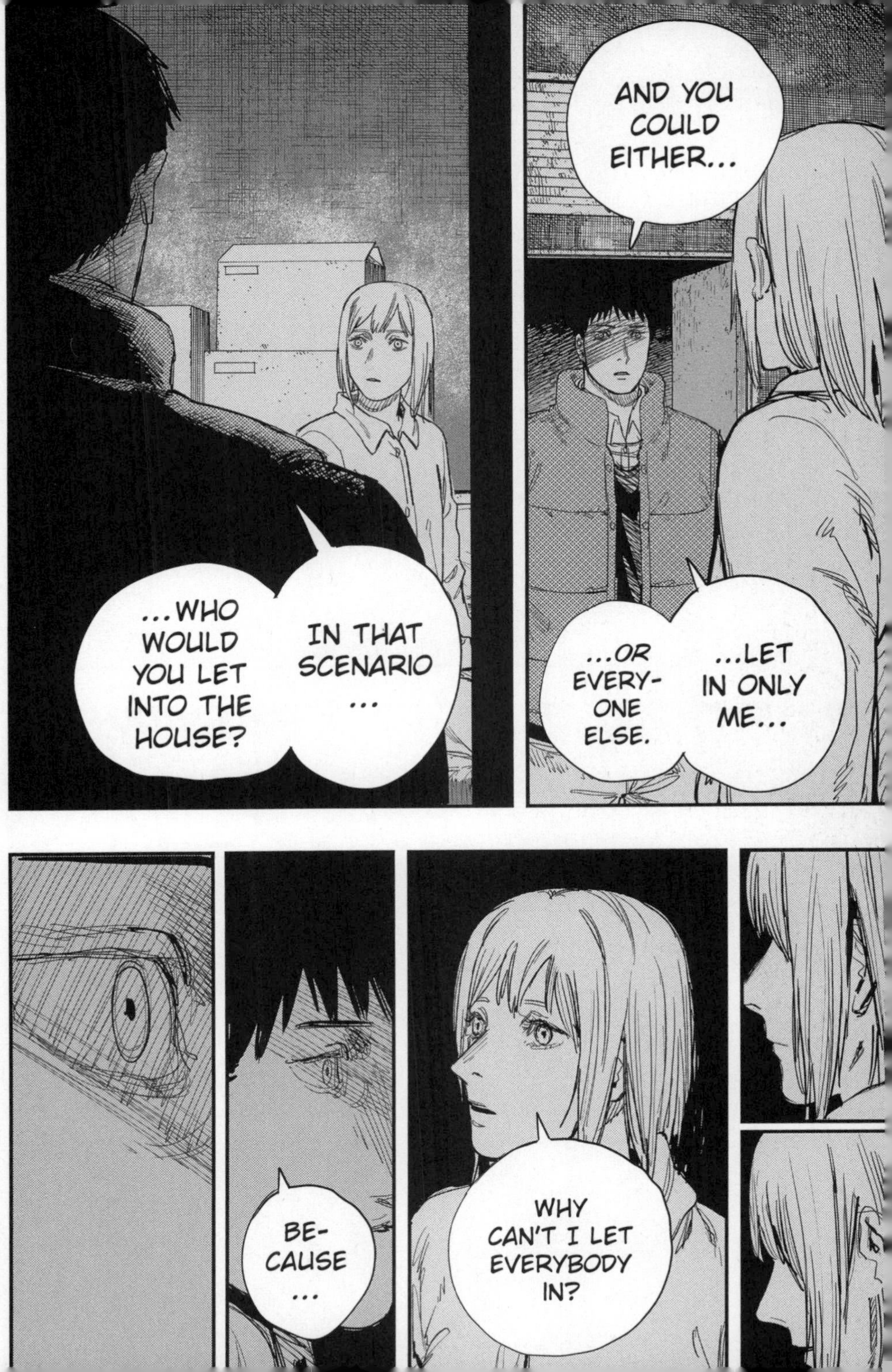
AND YOU COULD EITHER...
...LET IN ONLY ME...
...OR EVERY-ONE ELSE.
IN THAT SCENARIO...
...WHO WOULD YOU LET INTO THE HOUSE?
WHY CAN'T I LET EVERYBODY IN?
BE-CAUSE...

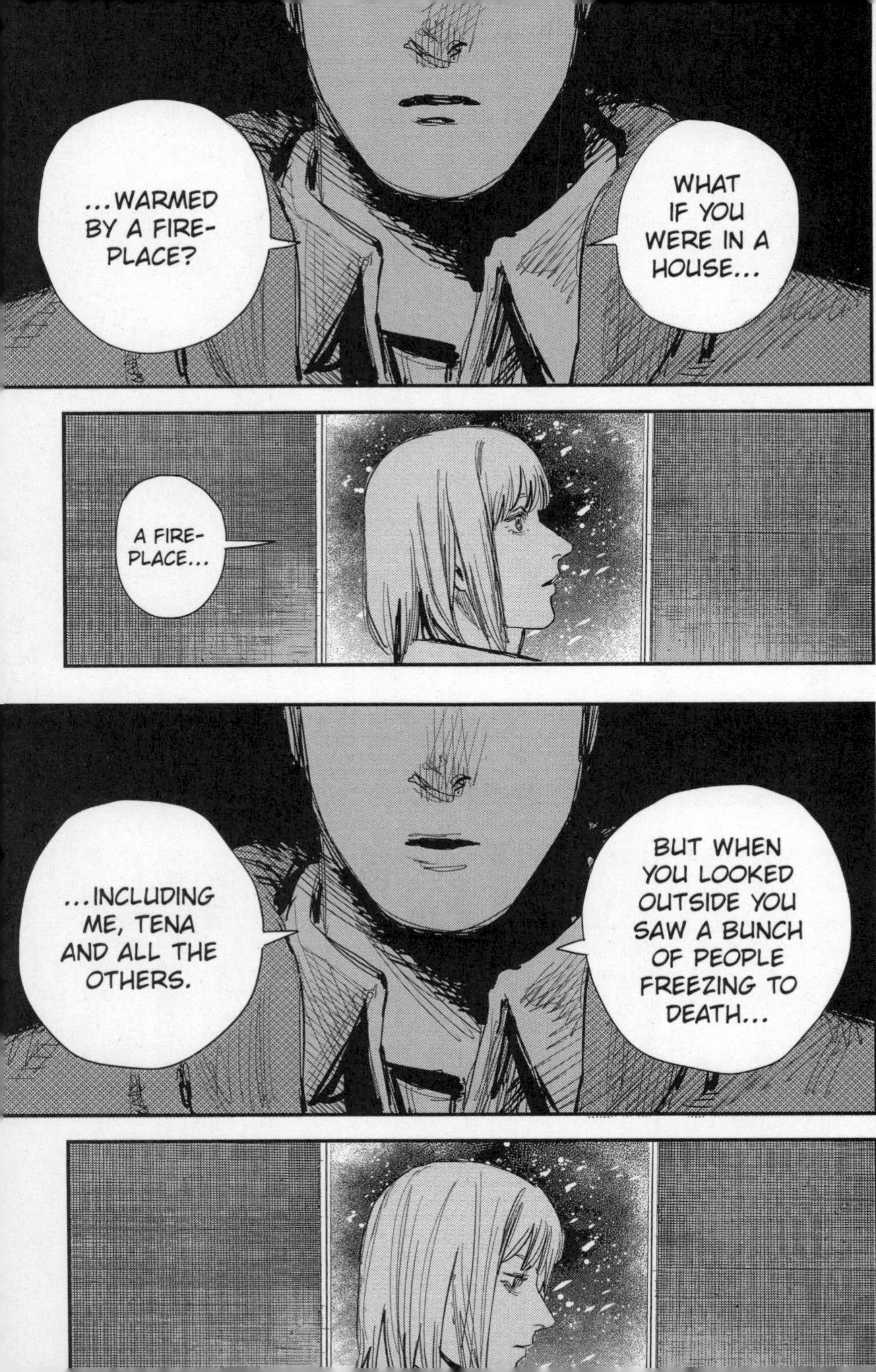
WHAT IF YOU WERE IN A HOUSE...
...WARMED BY A FIRE-PLACE?
A FIRE-PLACE...
BUT WHEN YOU LOOKED OUTSIDE YOU SAW A BUNCH OF PEOPLE FREEZING TO DEATH...
...INCLUDING ME, TENA AND ALL THE OTHERS.

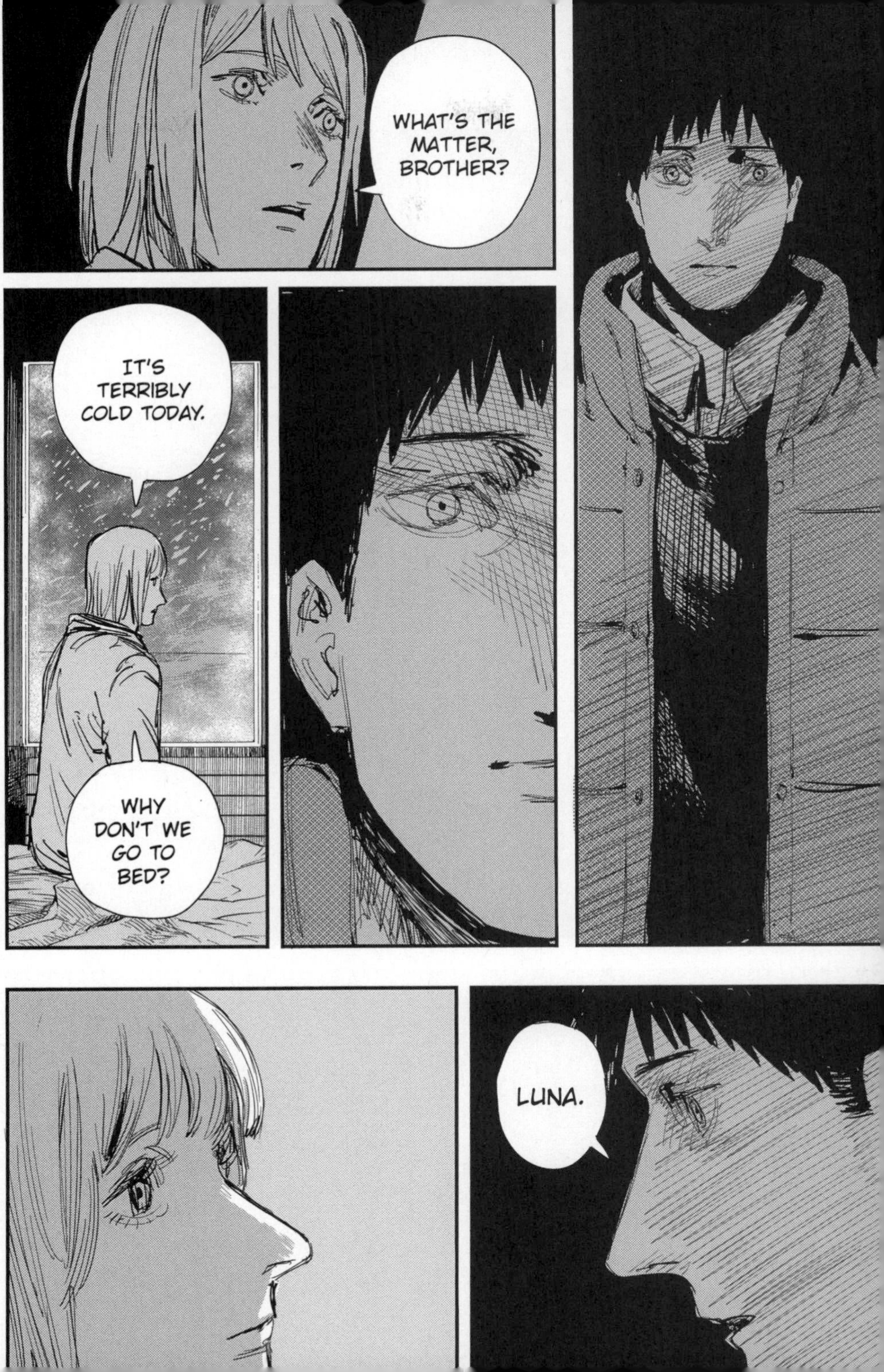
WHAT'S THE MATTER, BROTHER?
IT'S TERRIBLY COLD TODAY.
WHY DON'T WE GO TO BED?
LUNA.

CHAPTER 66

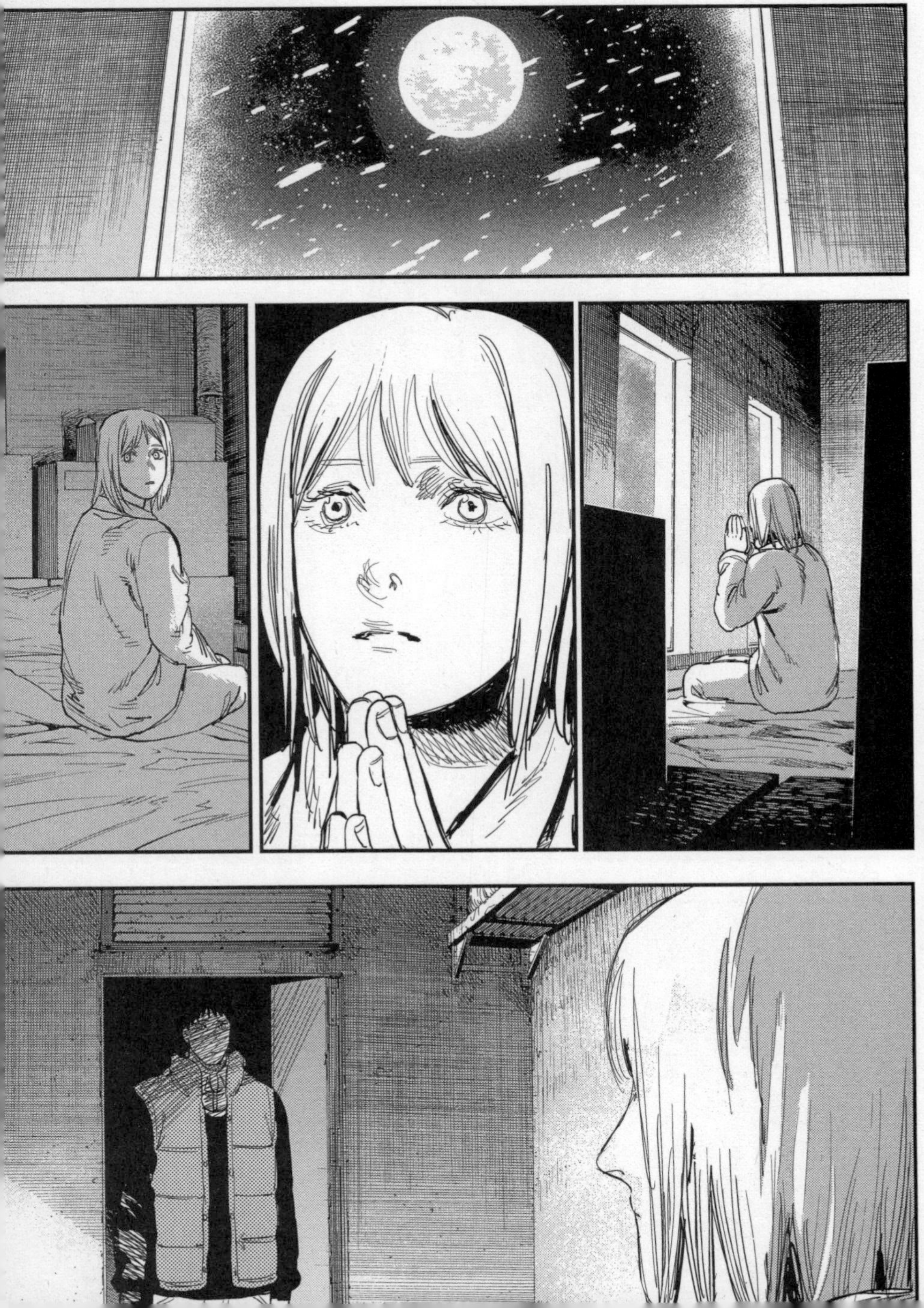

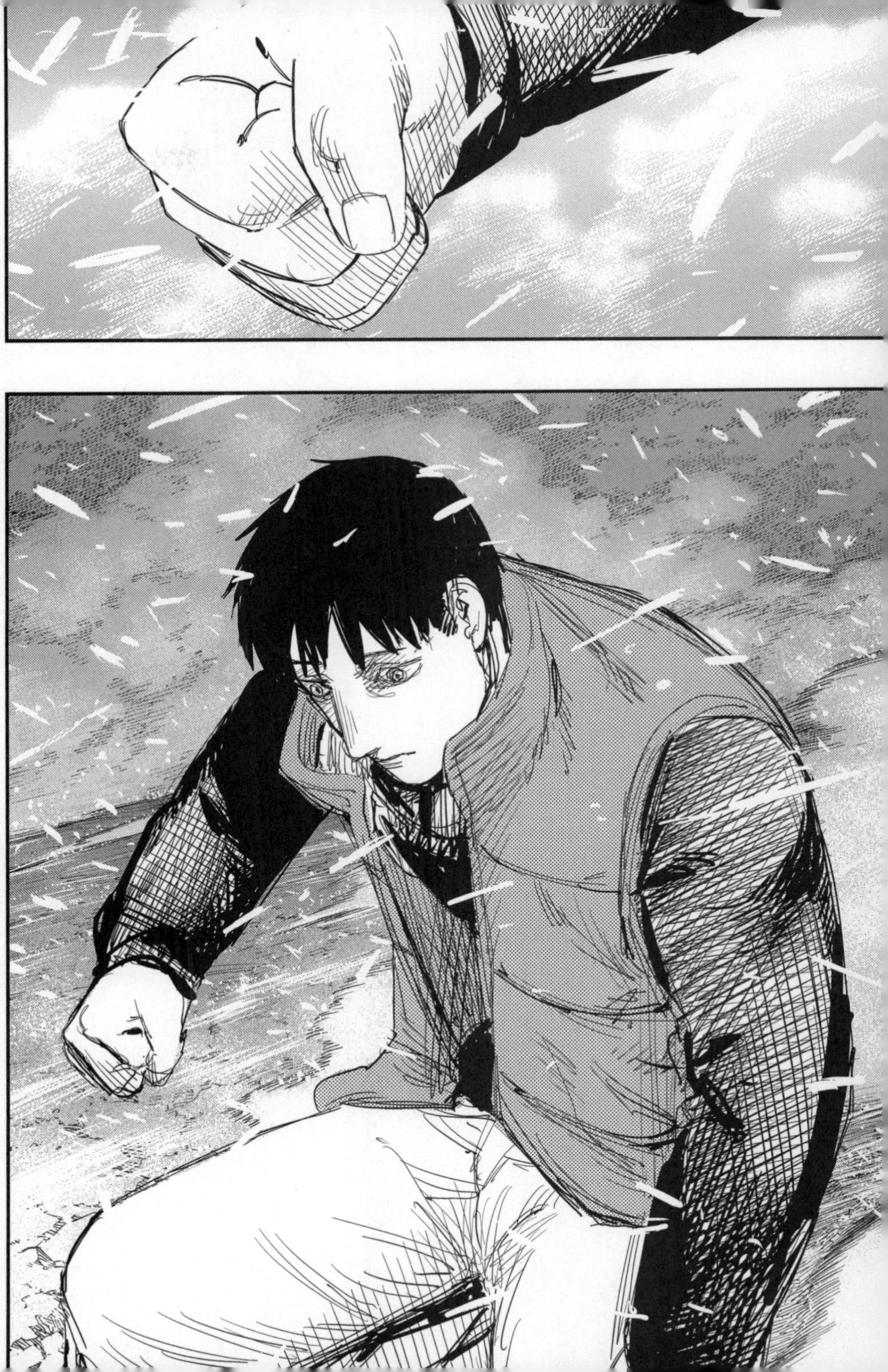

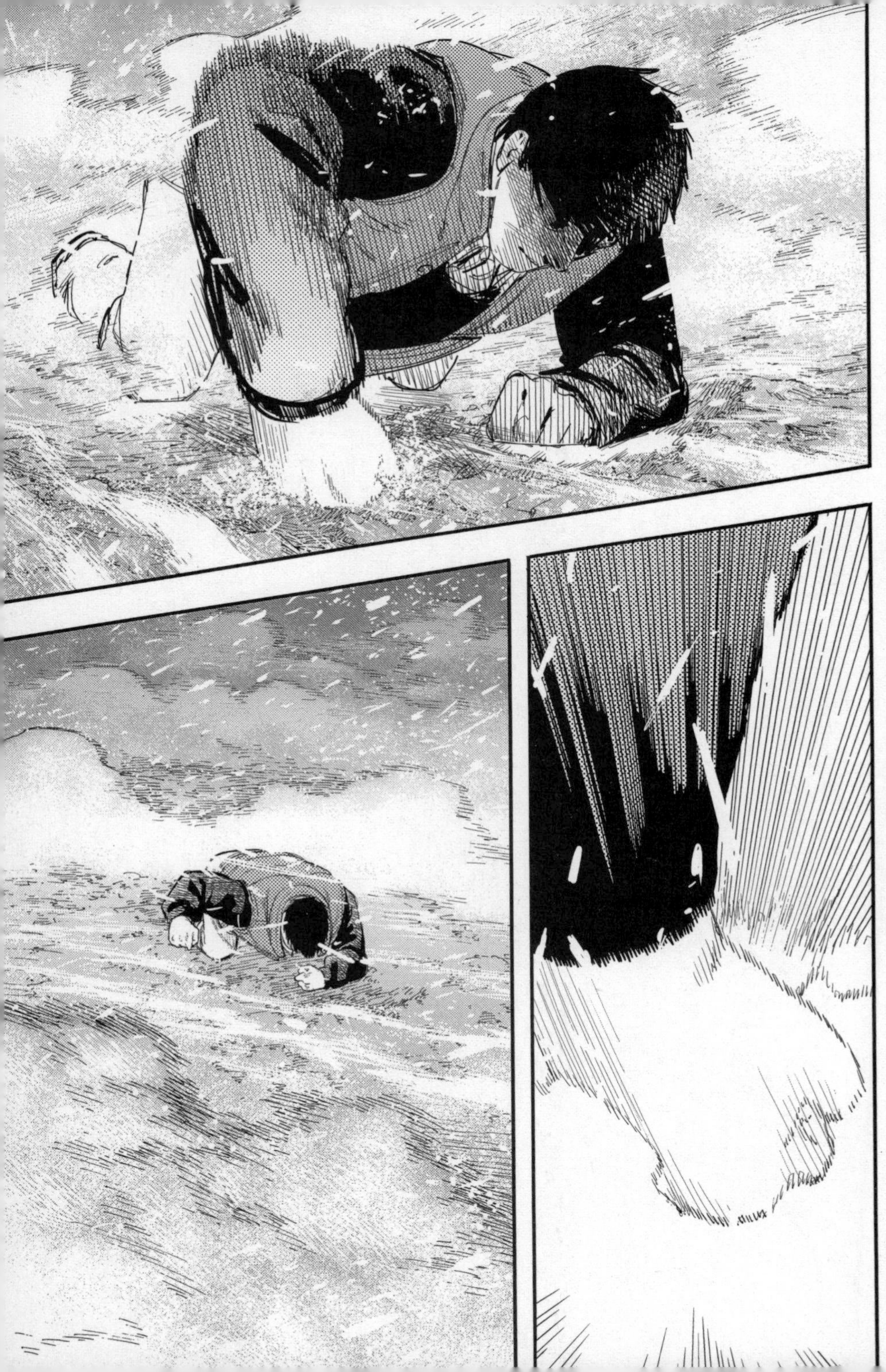

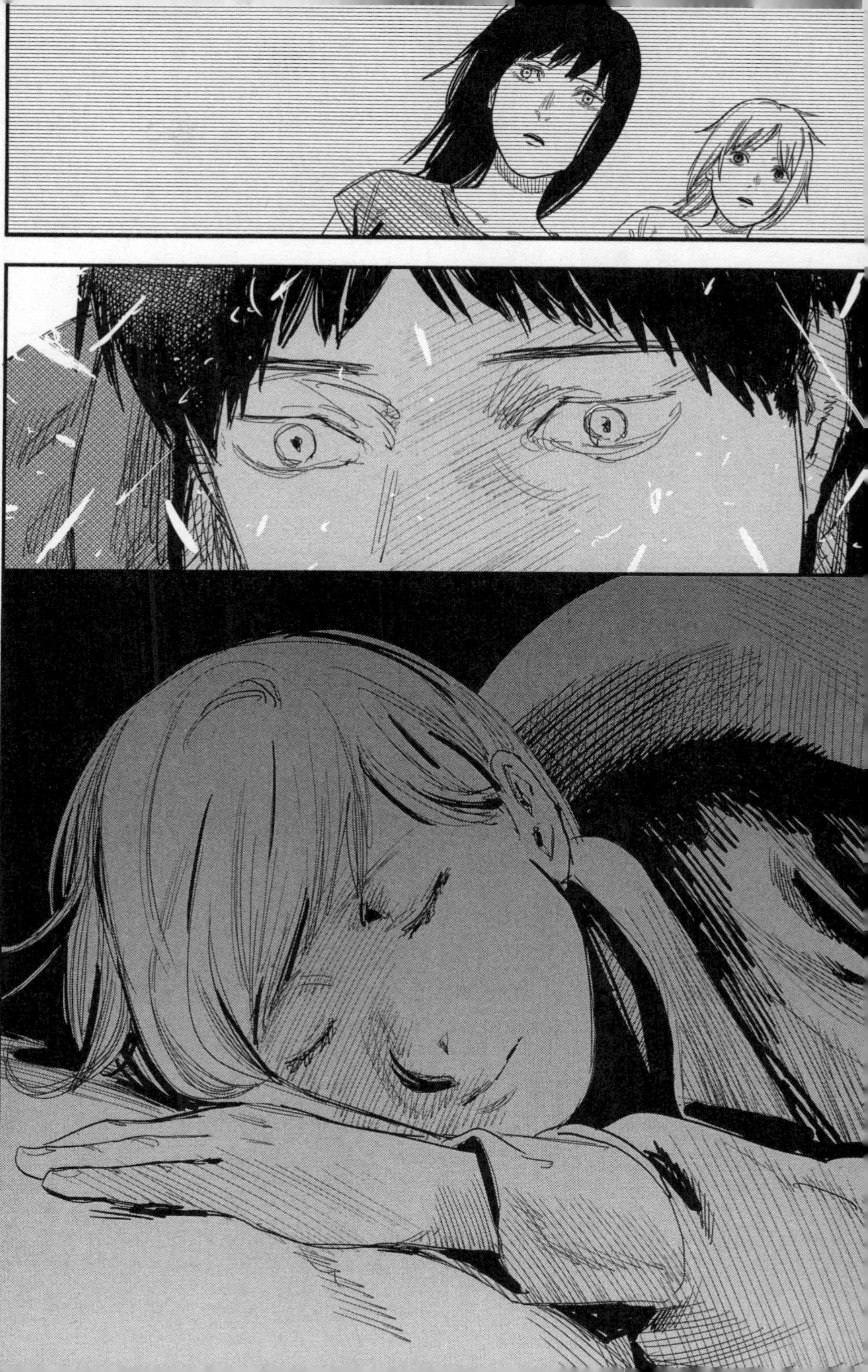

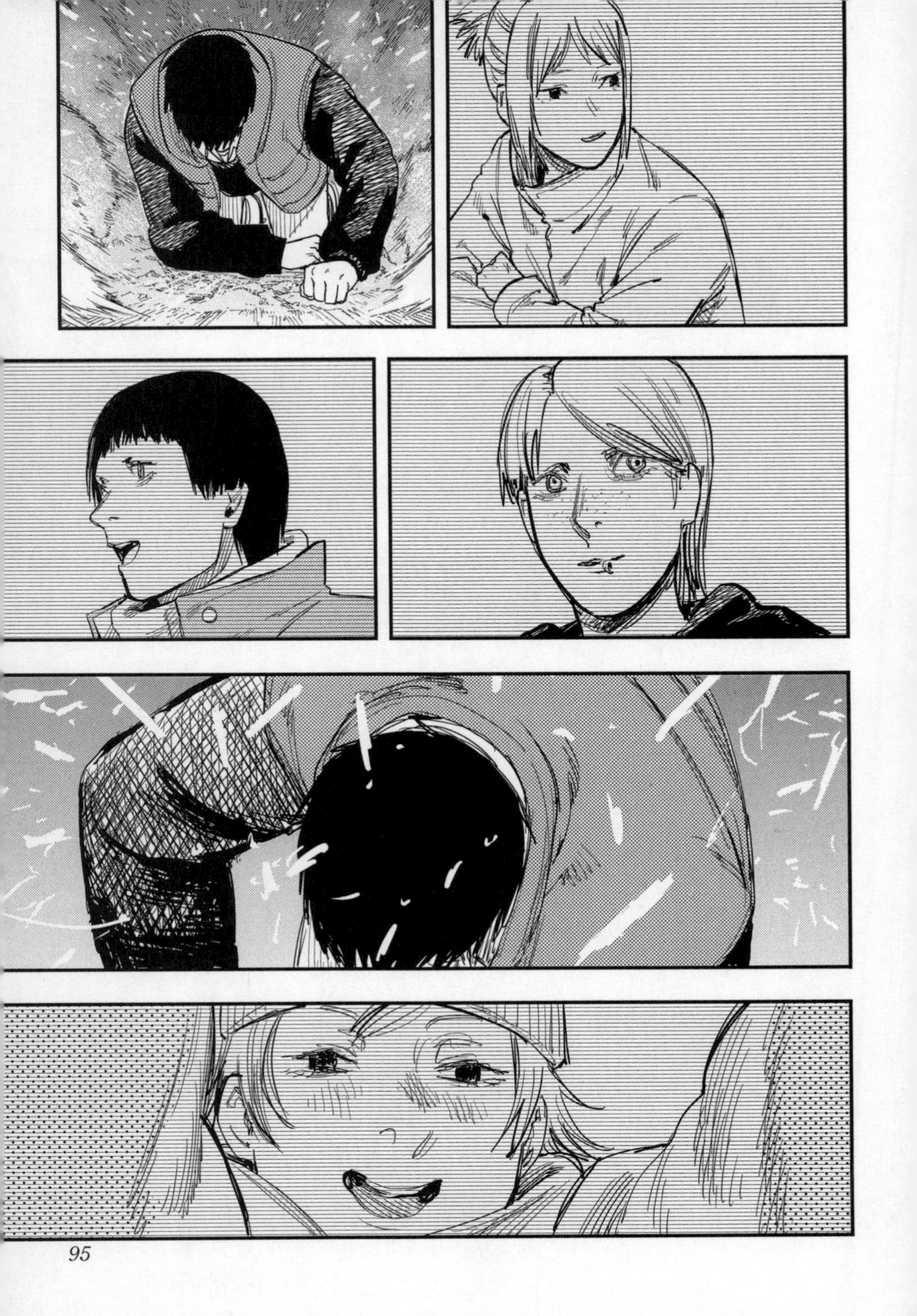

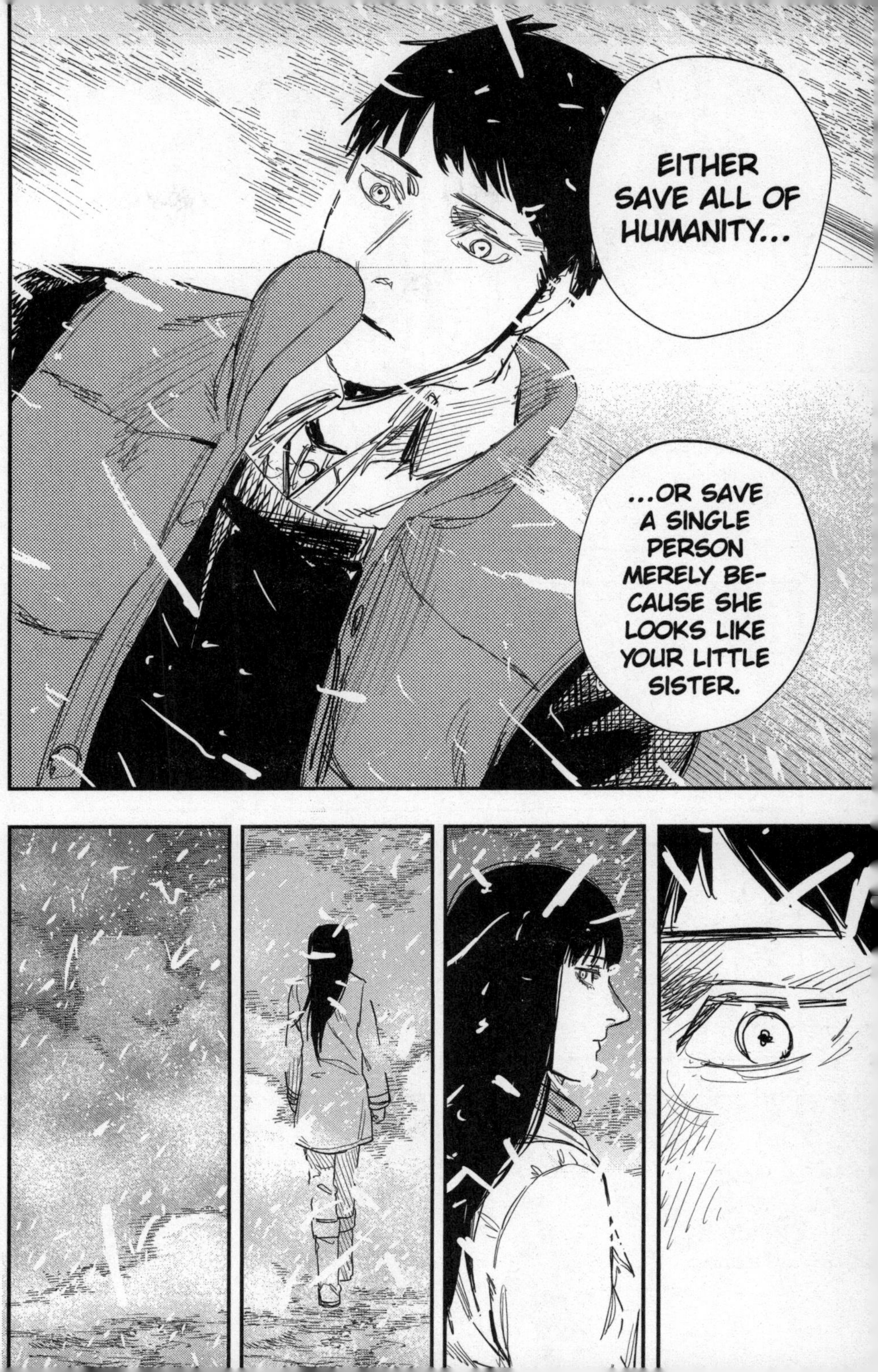
EITHER SAVE ALL OF HUMANITY...
...OR SAVE A SINGLE PERSON MERELY BE-CAUSE SHE LOOKS LIKE YOUR LITTLE SISTER.

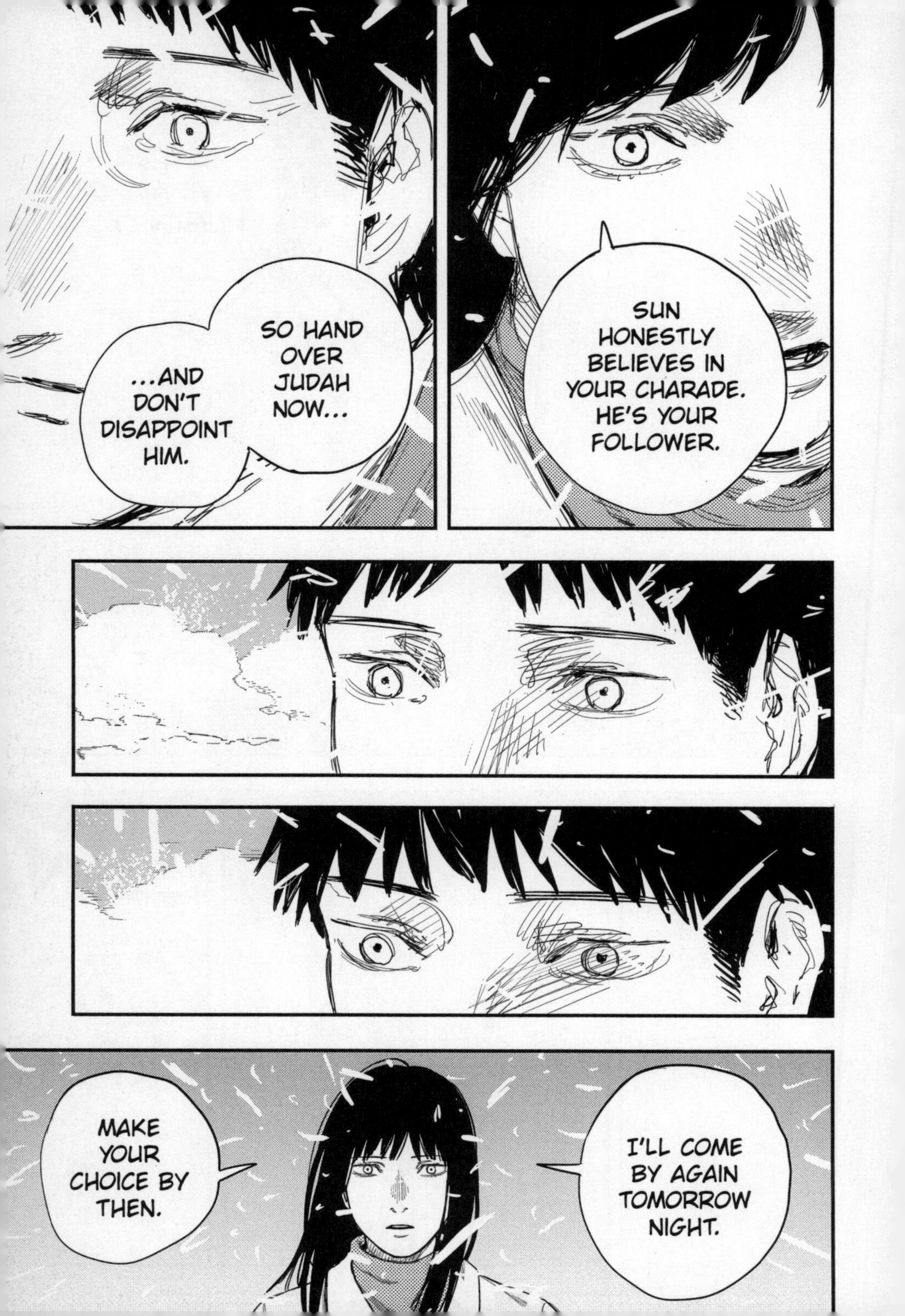
SUN HONESTLY BELIEVES IN YOUR CHARADE. HE'S YOUR FOLLOWER.
SO HAND OVER JUDAH NOW...
...AND DON'T DISAPPOINT HIM.
I'LL COME BY AGAIN TOMORROW NIGHT.
MAKE YOUR CHOICE BY THEN.

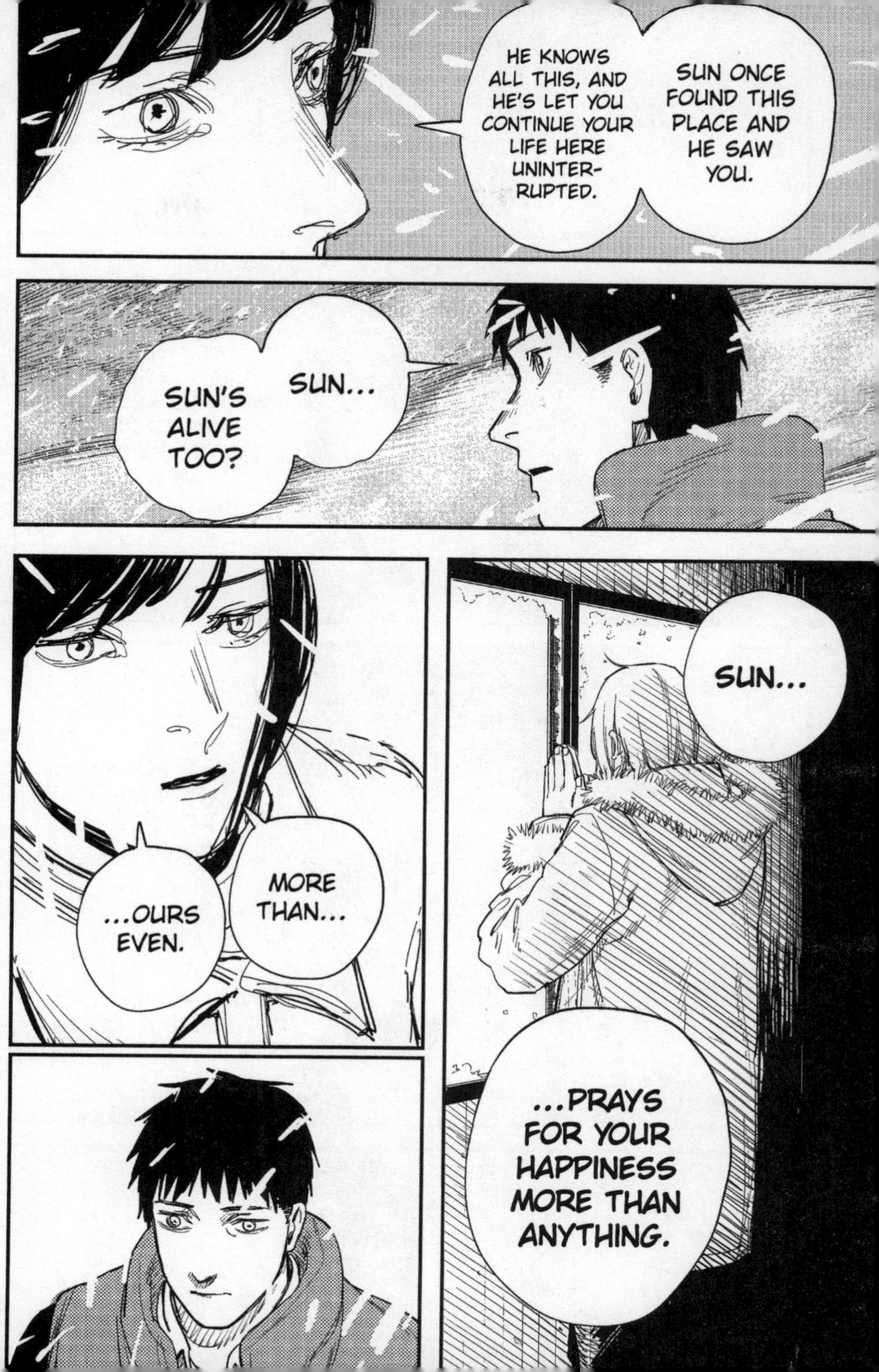
SUN ONCE FOUND THIS PLACE AND HE SAW YOU.
HE KNOWS ALL THIS, AND HE'S LET YOU CONTINUE YOUR LIFE HERE UNINTER-RUPTED.
SUN...
SUN'S ALIVE TOO?
SUN...
...PRAYS FOR YOUR HAPPINESS MORE THAN ANYTHING.
MORE THAN...
...OURS EVEN.

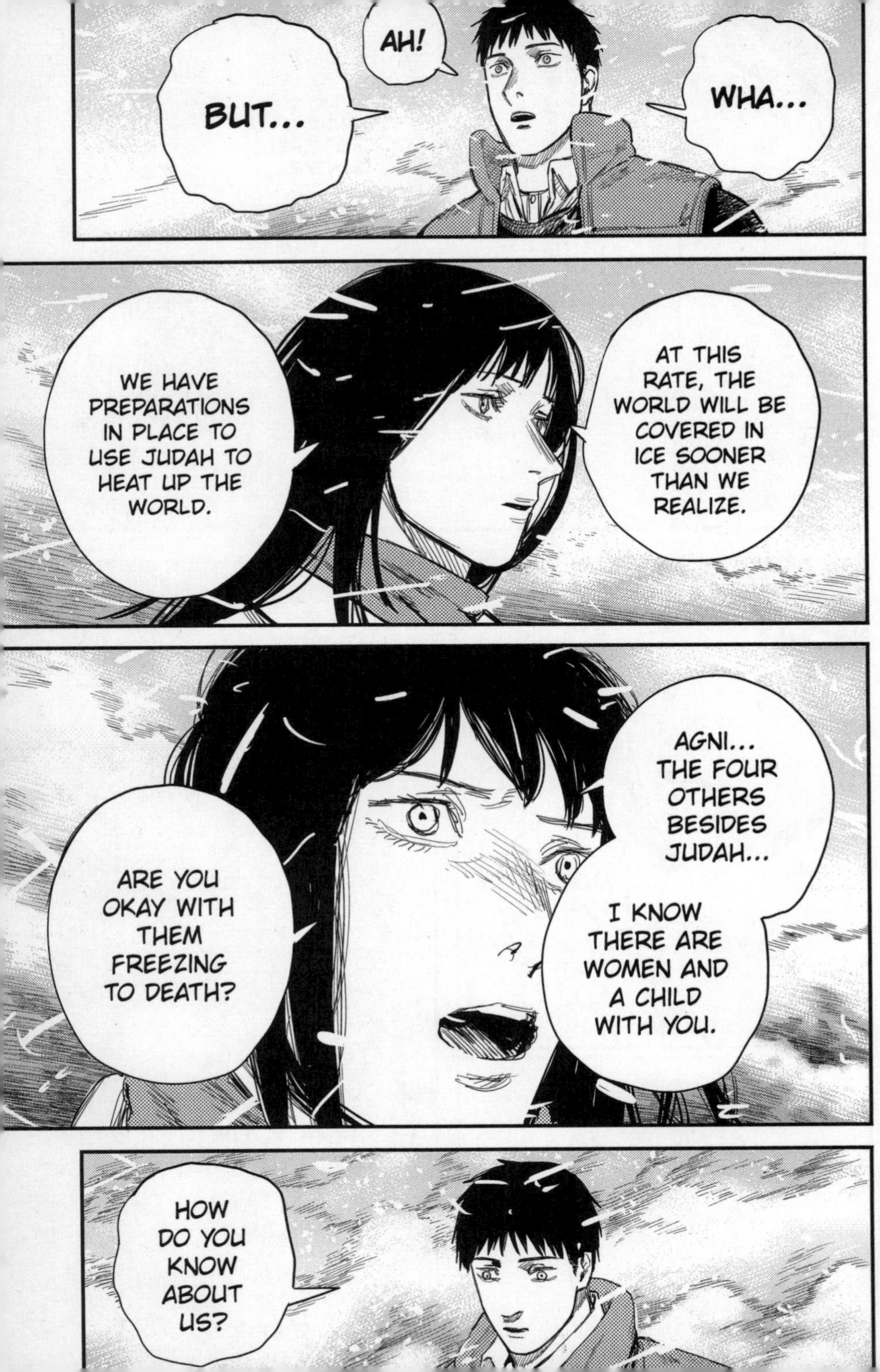
WHA...
AH!
BUT...
AT THIS RATE, THE WORLD WILL BE COVERED IN ICE SOONER THAN WE REALIZE.
WE HAVE PREPARATIONS IN PLACE TO USE JUDAH TO HEAT UP THE WORLD.
AGNI... THE FOUR OTHERS BESIDES JUDAH...
I KNOW THERE ARE WOMEN AND A CHILD WITH YOU.
ARE YOU OKAY WITH THEM FREEZING TO DEATH?
HOW DO YOU KNOW ABOUT US?

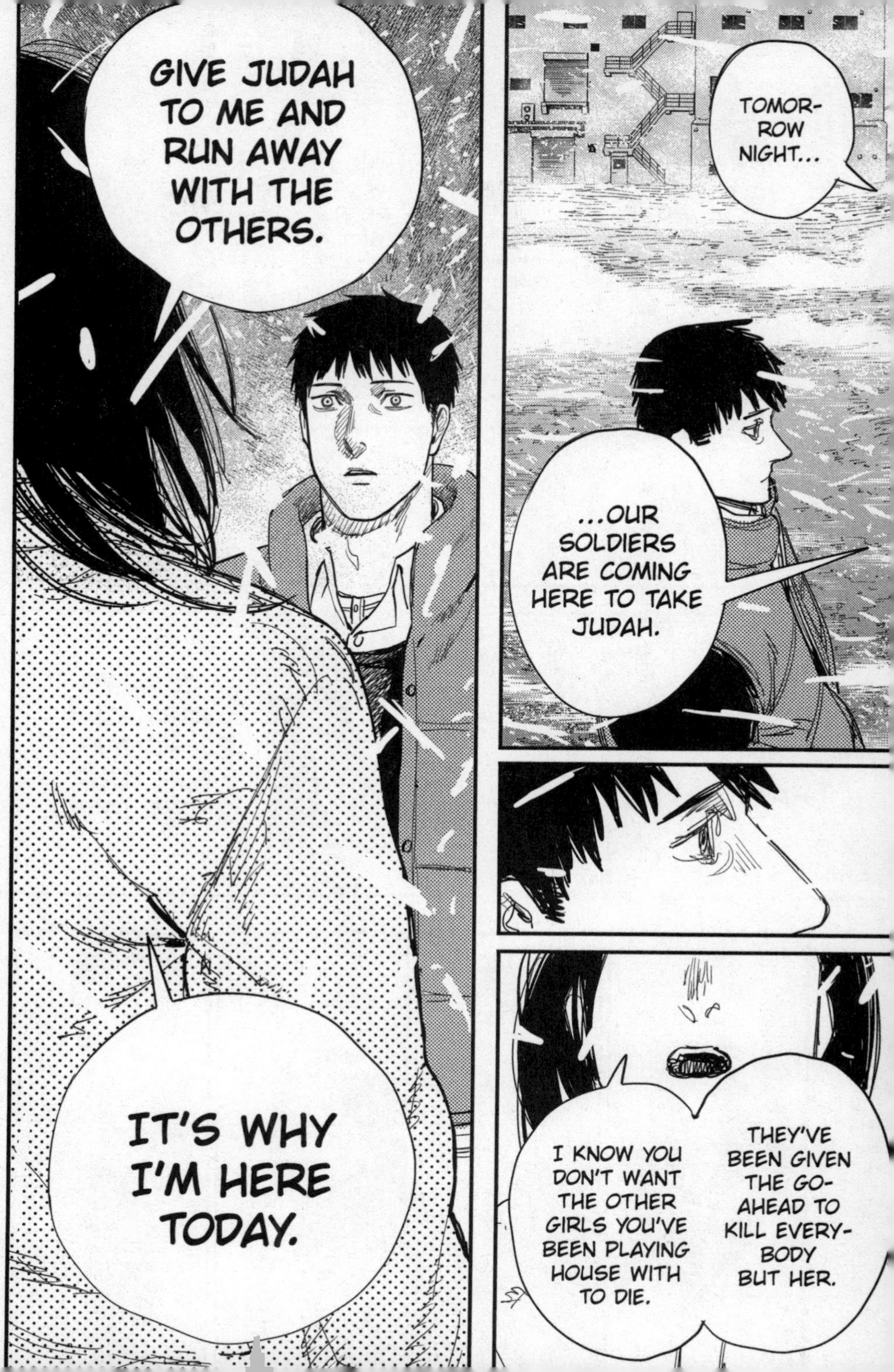
TOMOR-ROW NIGHT...
...OUR SOLDIERS ARE COMING HERE TO TAKE JUDAH.
THEY'VE BEEN GIVEN THE GO-AHEAD TO KILL EVERY-BODY BUT HER.
I KNOW YOU DON'T WANT THE OTHER GIRLS YOU'VE BEEN PLAYING HOUSE WITH TO DIE.
GIVE JUDAH TO ME AND RUN AWAY WITH THE OTHERS.
IT'S WHY I'M HERE TODAY.

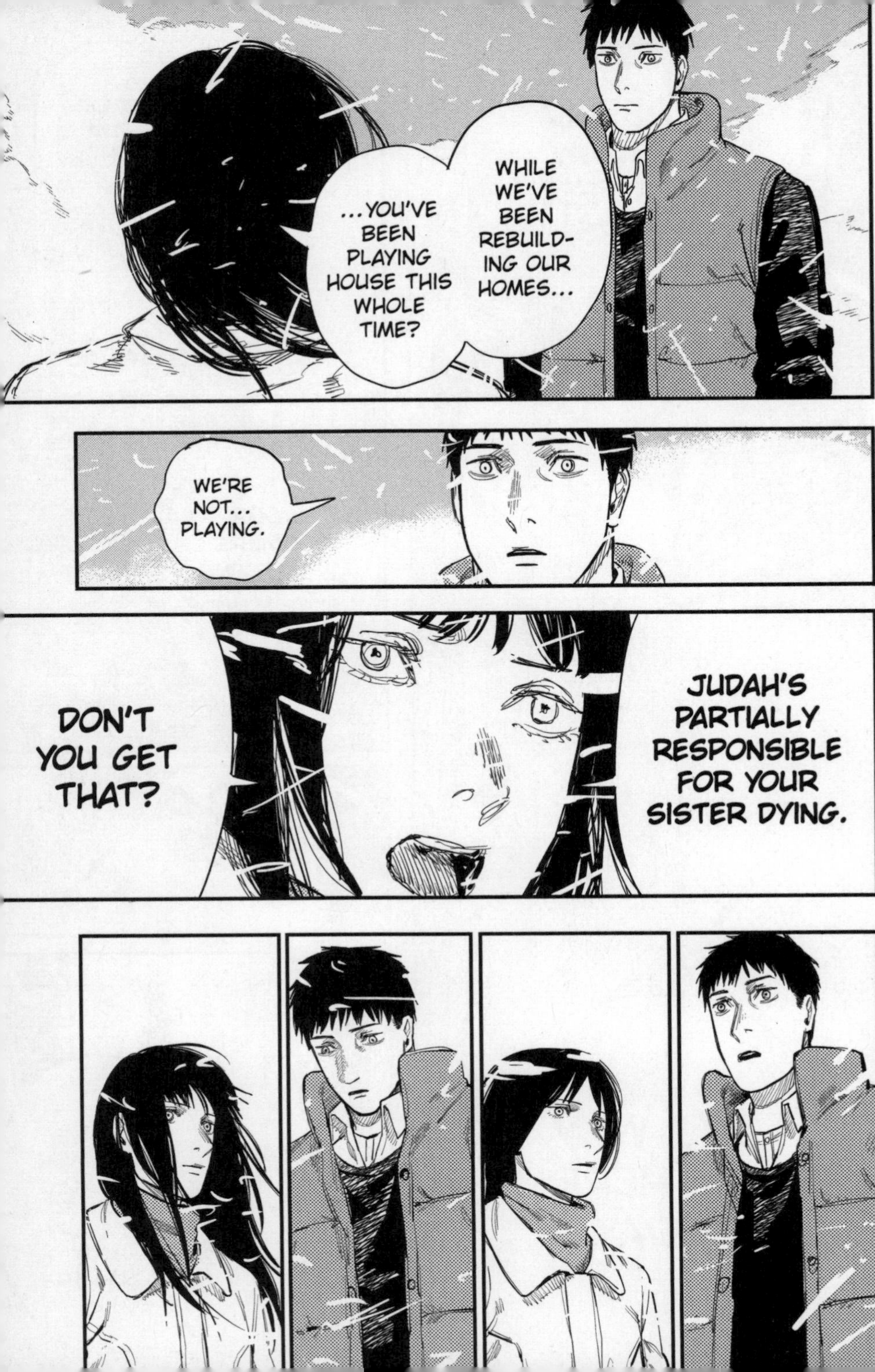
WHILE WE'VE BEEN REBUILD-ING OUR HOMES...
...YOU'VE BEEN PLAYING HOUSE THIS WHOLE TIME?
WE'RE NOT... PLAYING.
JUDAH'S PARTIALLY RESPONSIBLE FOR YOUR SISTER DYING.
DON'T YOU GET THAT?

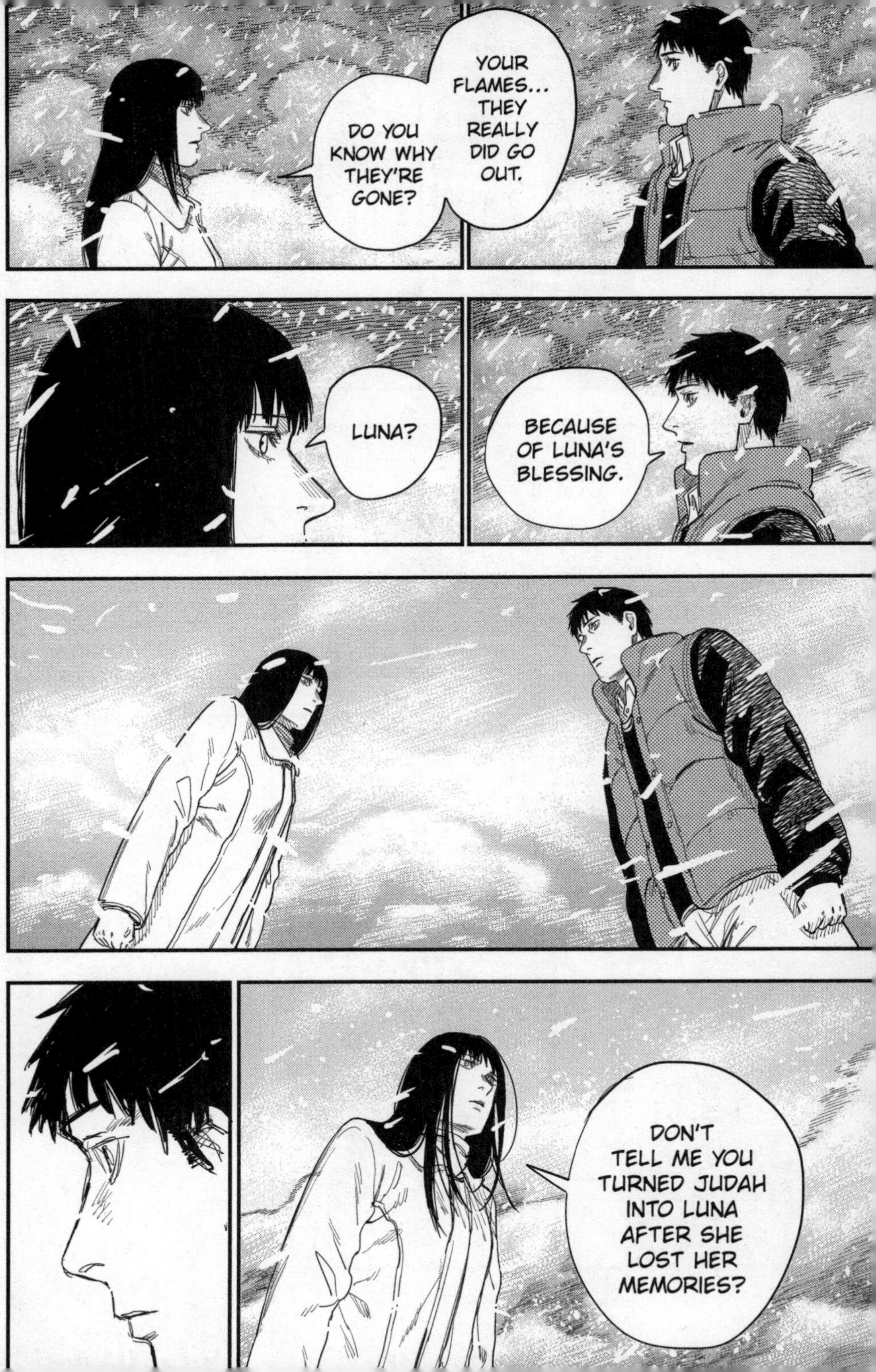
YOUR FLAMES... THEY REALLY DID GO OUT.
DO YOU KNOW WHY THEY'RE GONE?
BECAUSE OF LUNA'S BLESSING.
LUNA?
DON'T TELL ME YOU TURNED JUDAH INTO LUNA AFTER SHE LOST HER MEMORIES?

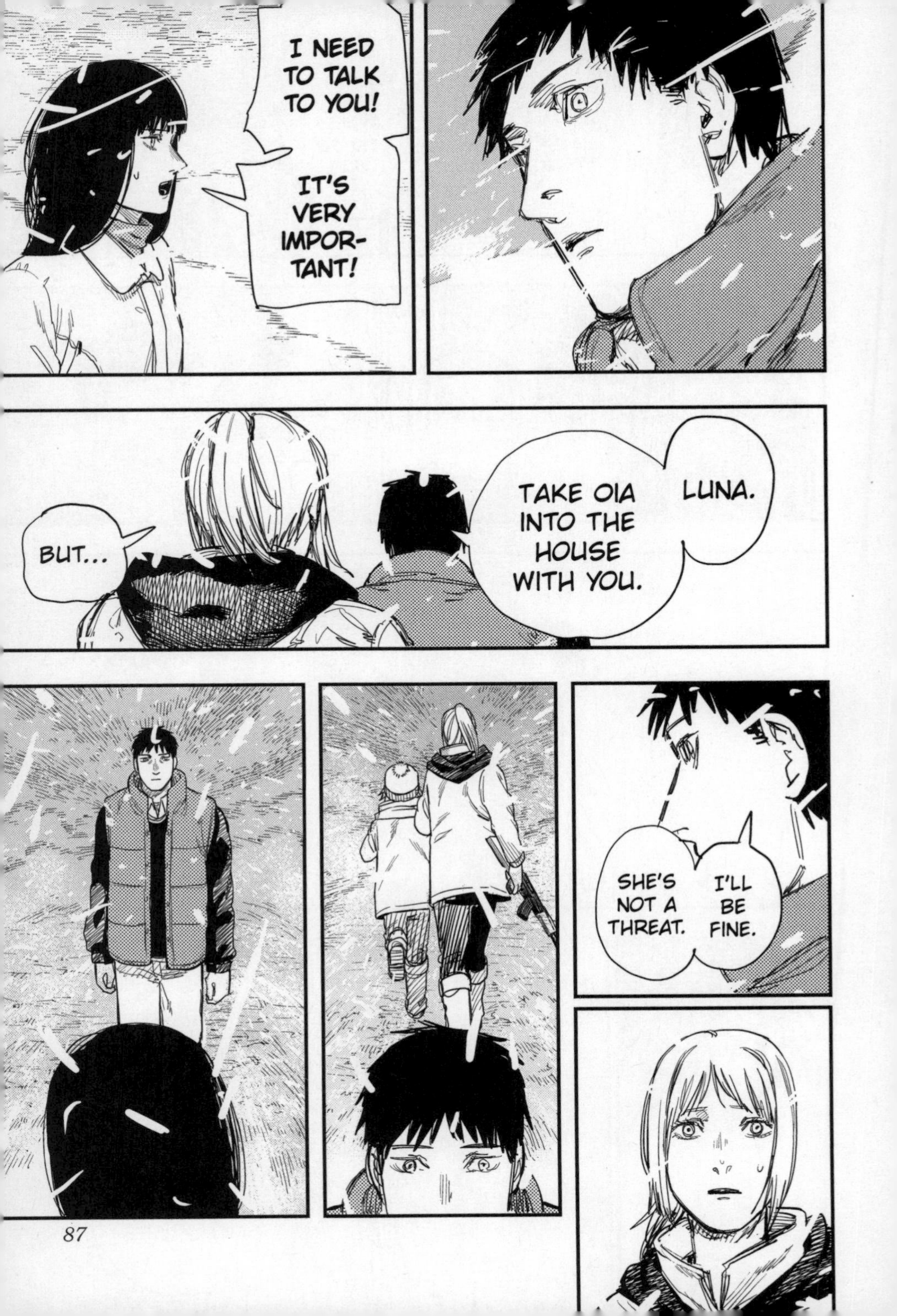
I NEED TO TALK TO YOU!
IT'S VERY IMPOR-TANT!
LUNA.
TAKE OIA INTO THE HOUSE WITH YOU.
BUT...
I'LL BE FINE.
SHE'S NOT A THREAT.

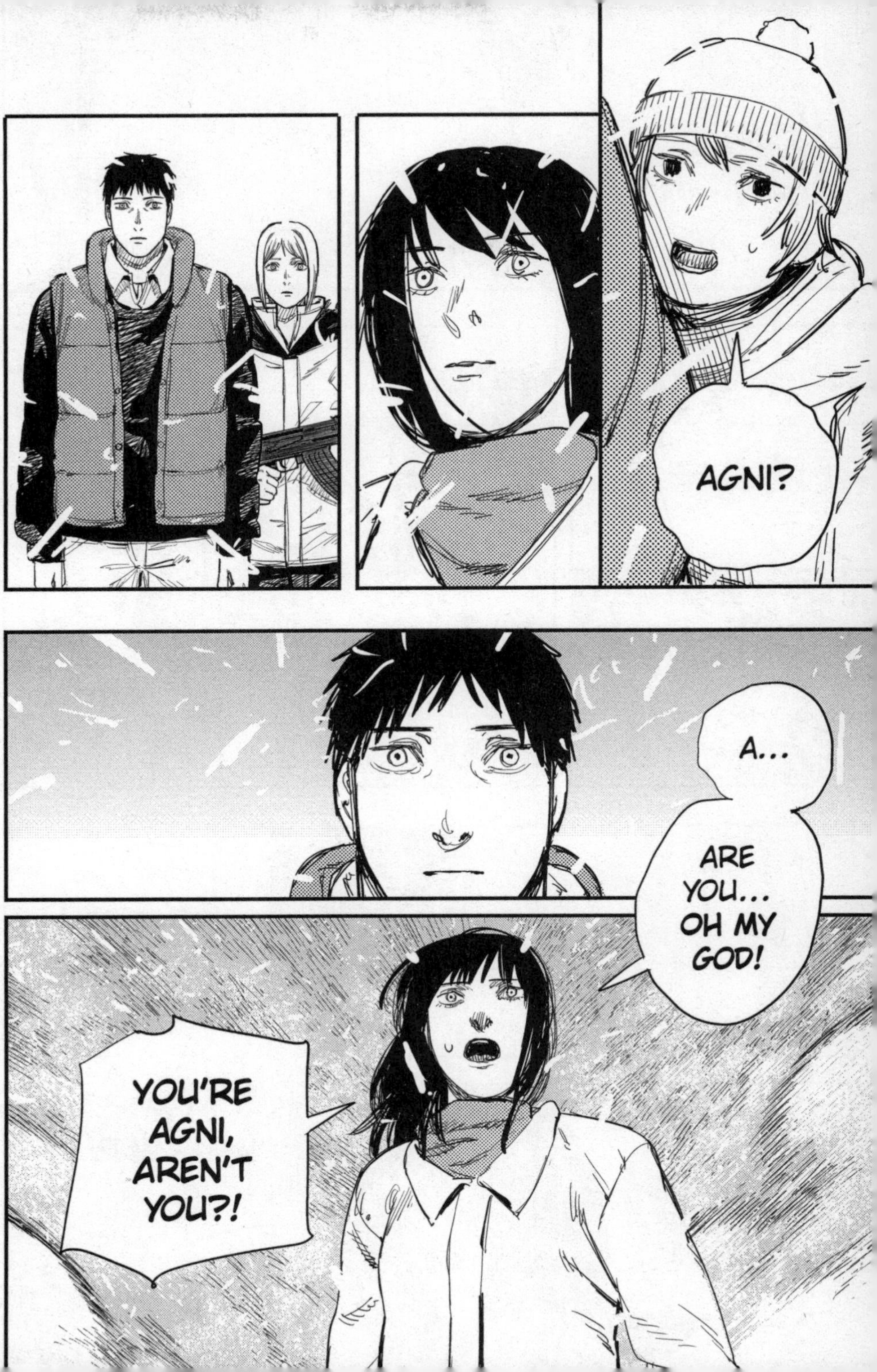
AGNI?
A...
ARE YOU... OH MY GOD!
YOU'RE AGNI, AREN'T YOU?!

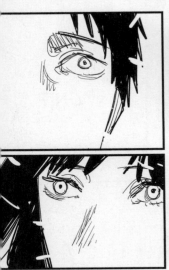

YOU KNOW HER?

NENETO!

NENETO! YOU'RE ALIVE—

I'M UNARMED!

I'VE COME TO SPEAK TO AGNI!

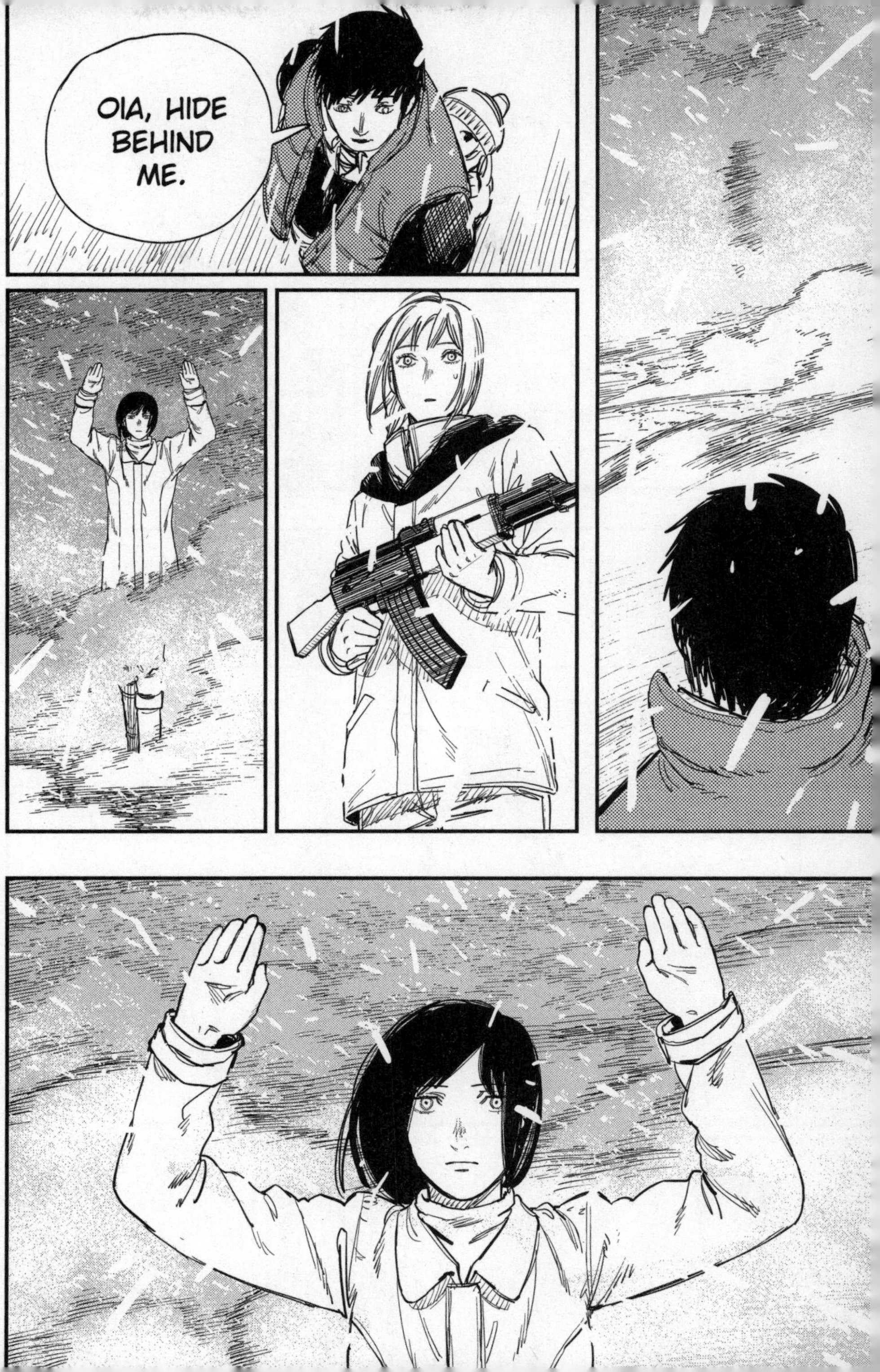
OIA, HIDE BEHIND ME.

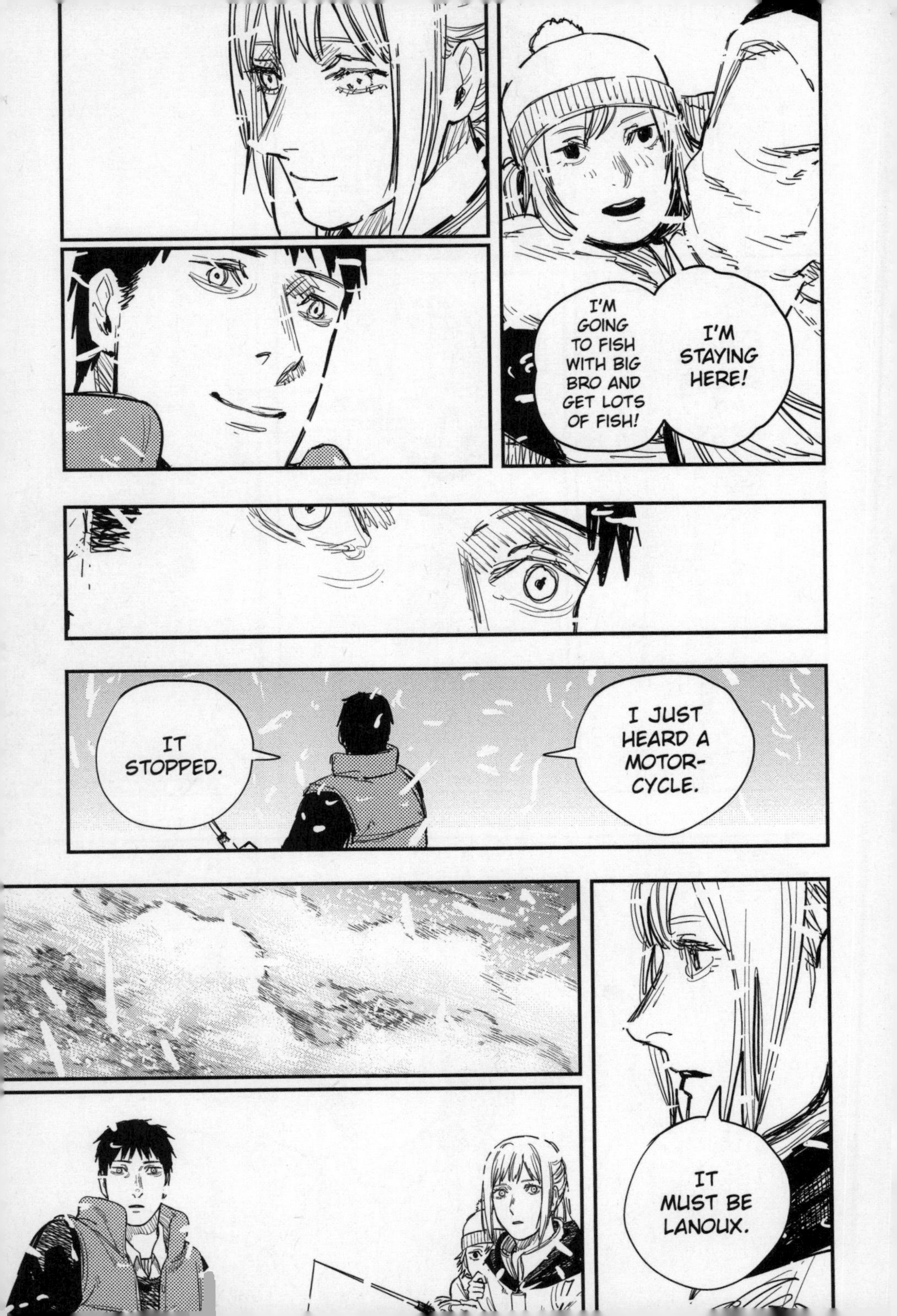
I'M STAYING HERE!
I'M GOING TO FISH WITH BIG BRO AND GET LOTS OF FISH!
I JUST HEARD A MOTOR-CYCLE.
IT STOPPED.
IT MUST BE LANOUX.

CHAPTER 65

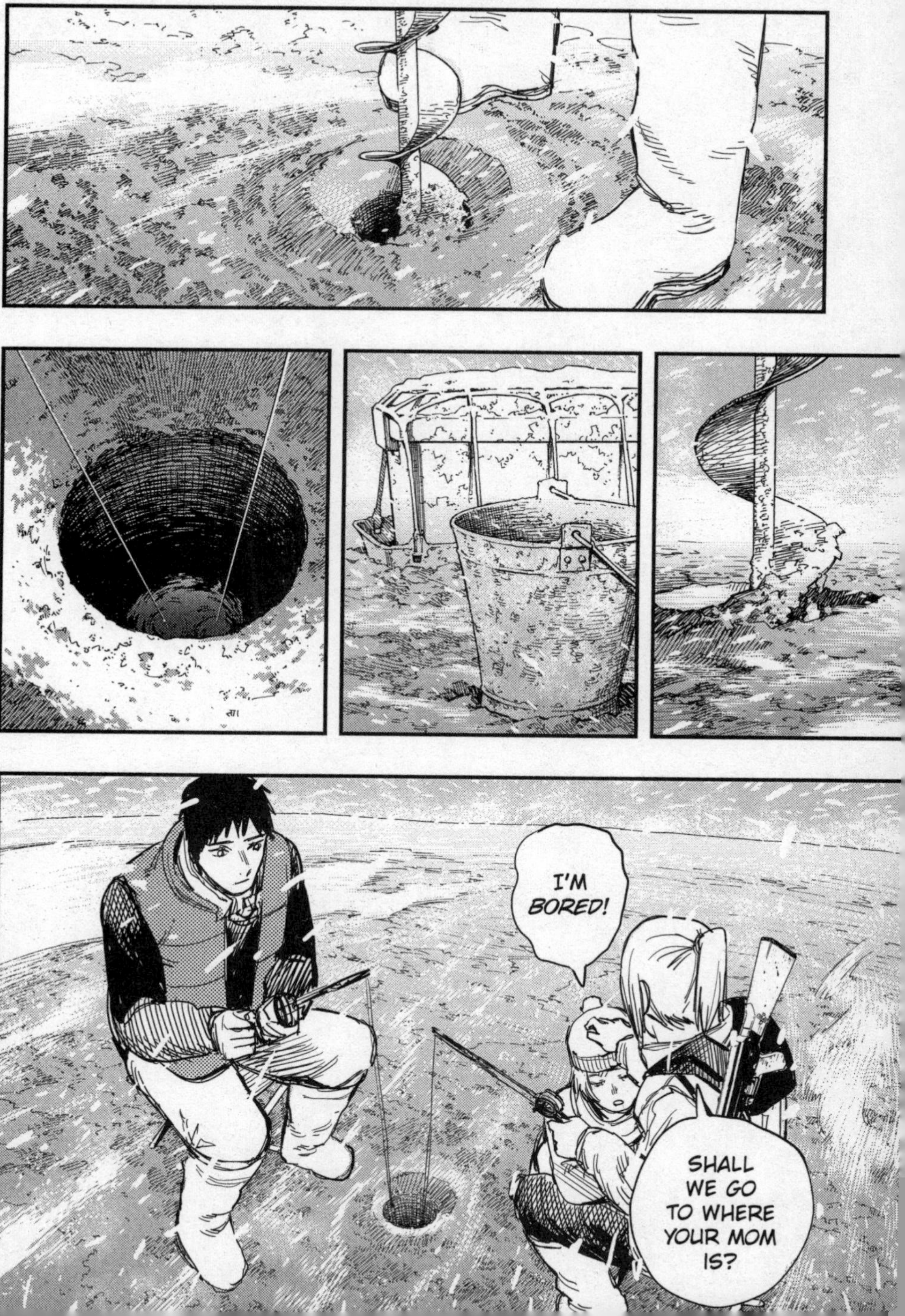
I'M BORED!
SHALL WE GO TO WHERE YOUR MOM IS?

FIRE PUNCH

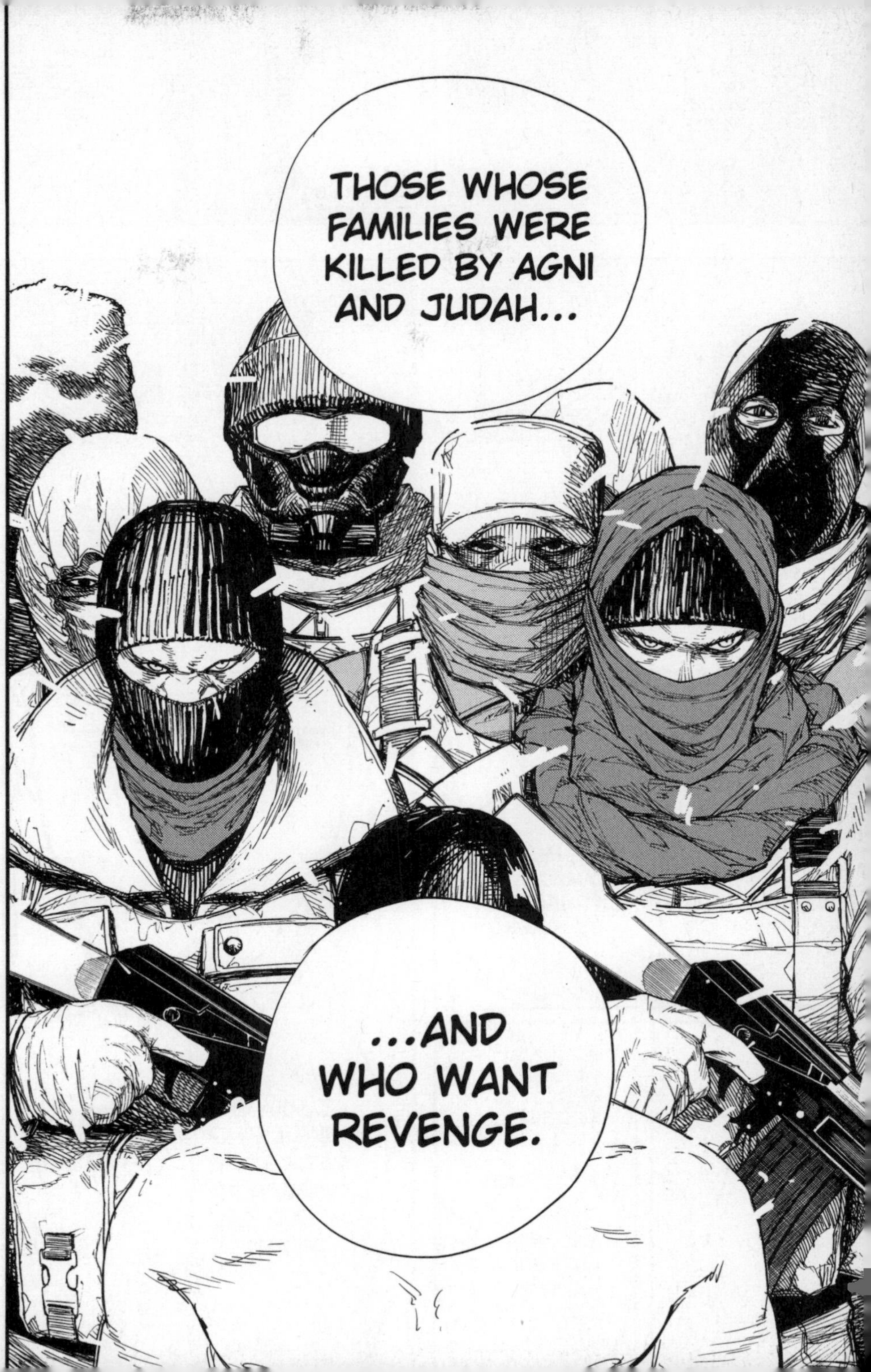
THOSE WHOSE FAMILIES WERE KILLED BY AGNI AND JUDAH...
...AND WHO WANT REVENGE.

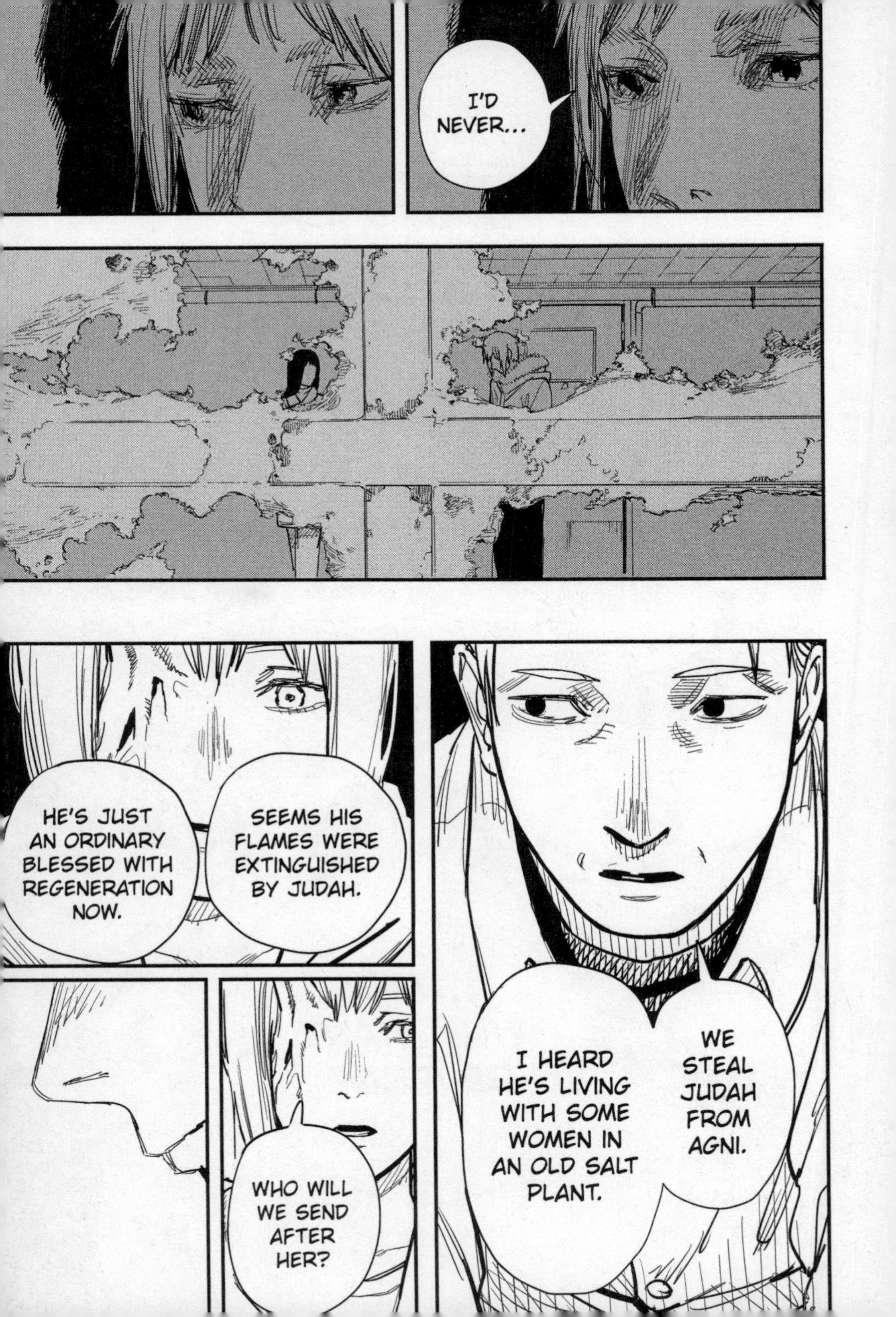
I'D NEVER...
WE STEAL JUDAH FROM AGNI.
I HEARD HE'S LIVING WITH SOME WOMEN IN AN OLD SALT PLANT.
SEEMS HIS FLAMES WERE EXTINGUISHED BY JUDAH.
HE'S JUST AN ORDINARY BLESSED WITH REGENERATION NOW.
WHO WILL WE SEND AFTER HER?

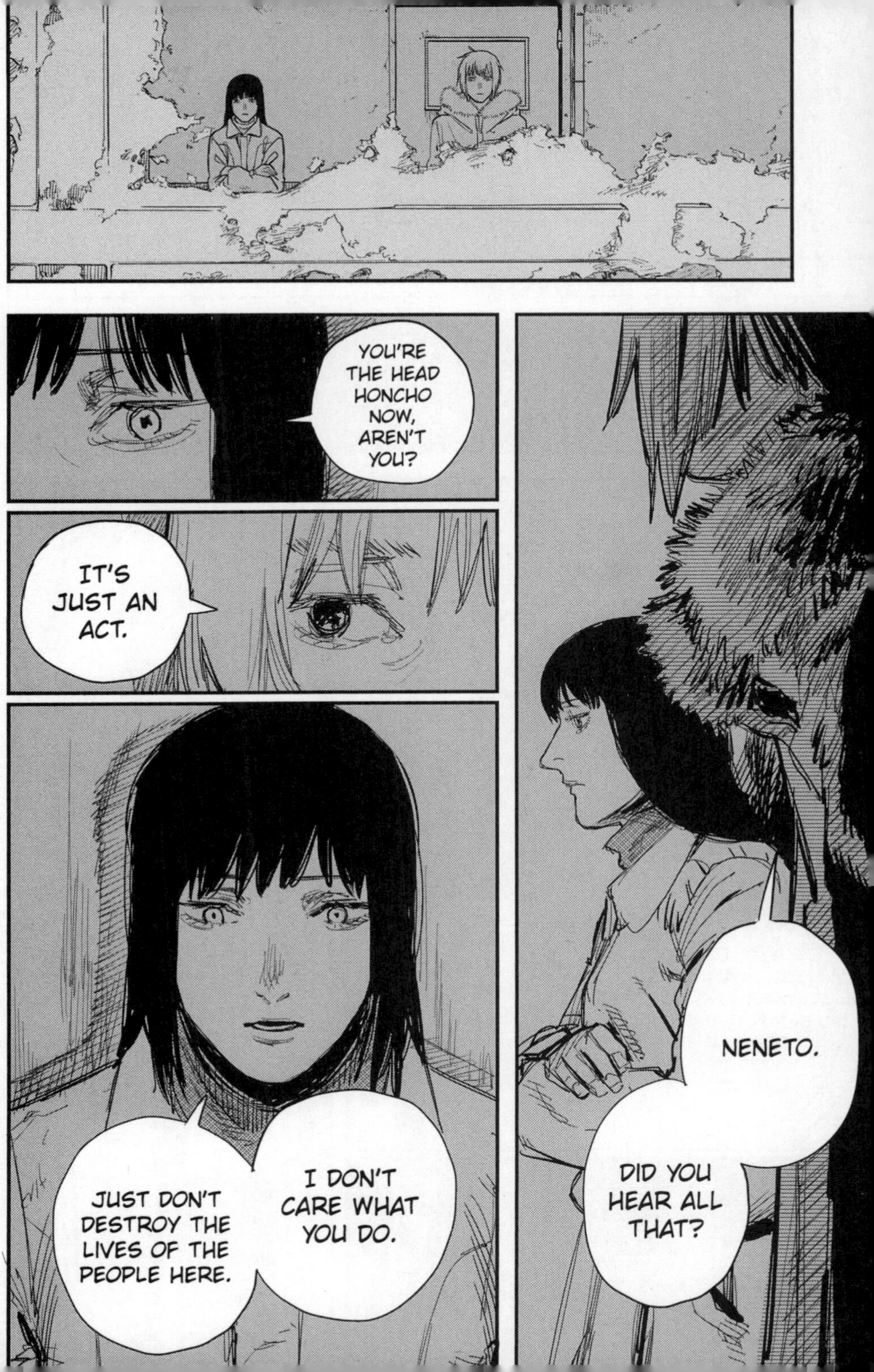
NENETO.
DID YOU HEAR ALL THAT?
YOU'RE THE HEAD HONCHO NOW, AREN'T YOU?
IT'S JUST AN ACT.
I DON'T CARE WHAT YOU DO.
JUST DON'T DESTROY THE LIVES OF THE PEOPLE HERE.

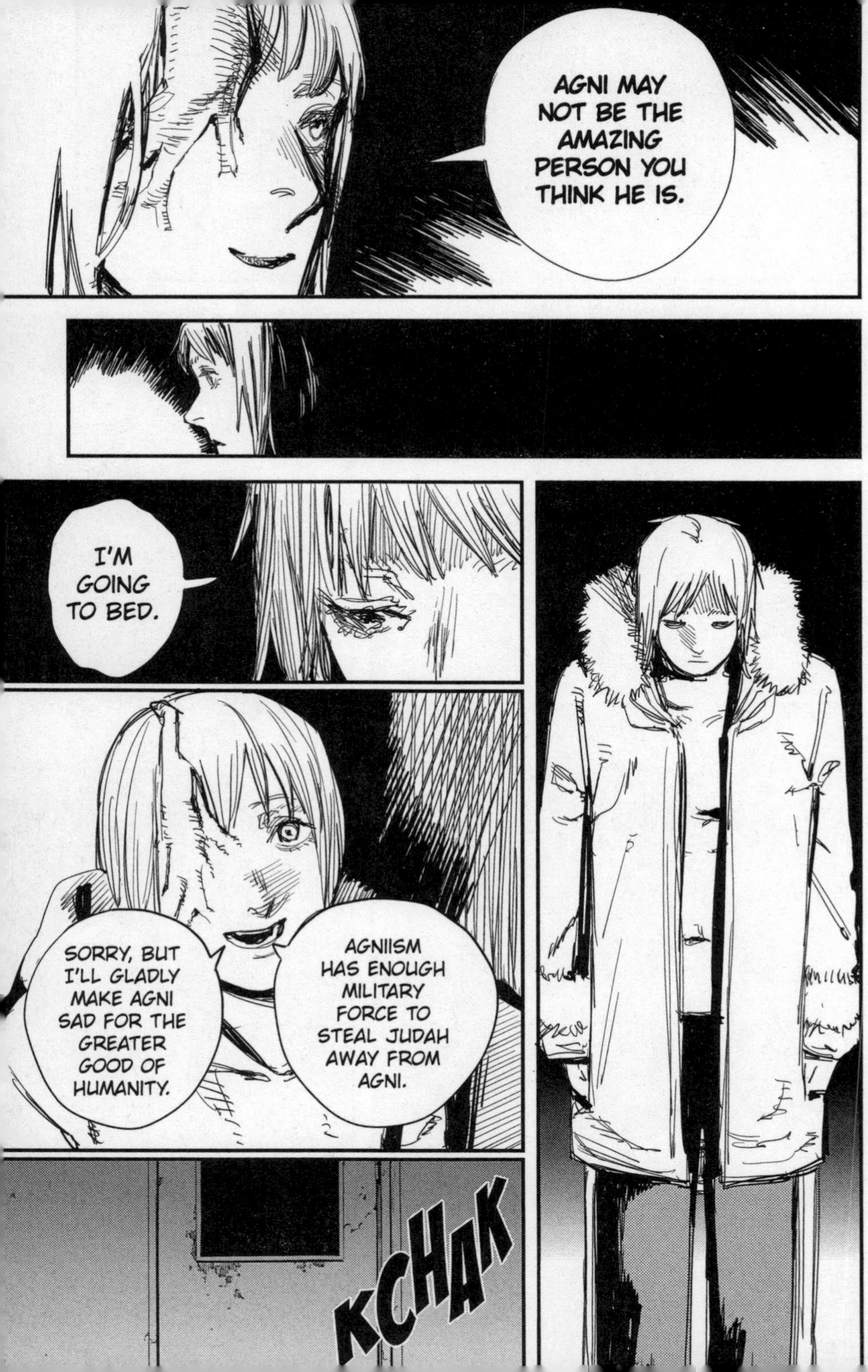
AGNI MAY NOT BE THE AMAZING PERSON YOU THINK HE IS.
I'M GOING TO BED.
AGNIISM HAS ENOUGH MILITARY FORCE TO STEAL JUDAH AWAY FROM AGNI.
SORRY, BUT I'LL GLADLY MAKE AGNI SAD FOR THE GREATER GOOD OF HUMANITY.
KCHAK

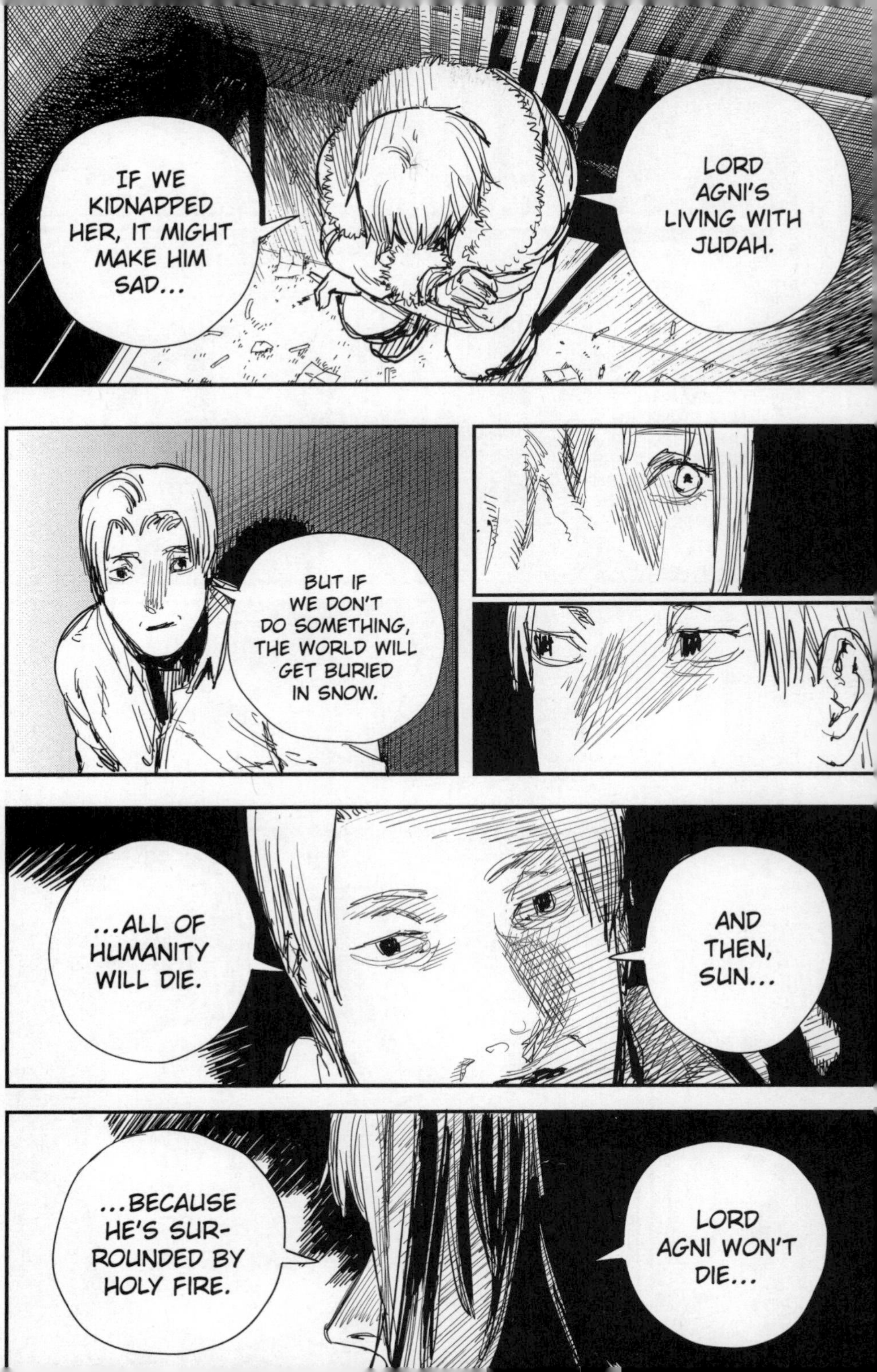
LORD AGNI'S LIVING WITH JUDAH.
IF WE KIDNAPPED HER, IT MIGHT MAKE HIM SAD...
BUT IF WE DON'T DO SOMETHING, THE WORLD WILL GET BURIED IN SNOW.
AND THEN, SUN...
...ALL OF HUMANITY WILL DIE.
LORD AGNI WON'T DIE...
...BECAUSE HE'S SUR-ROUNDED BY HOLY FIRE.

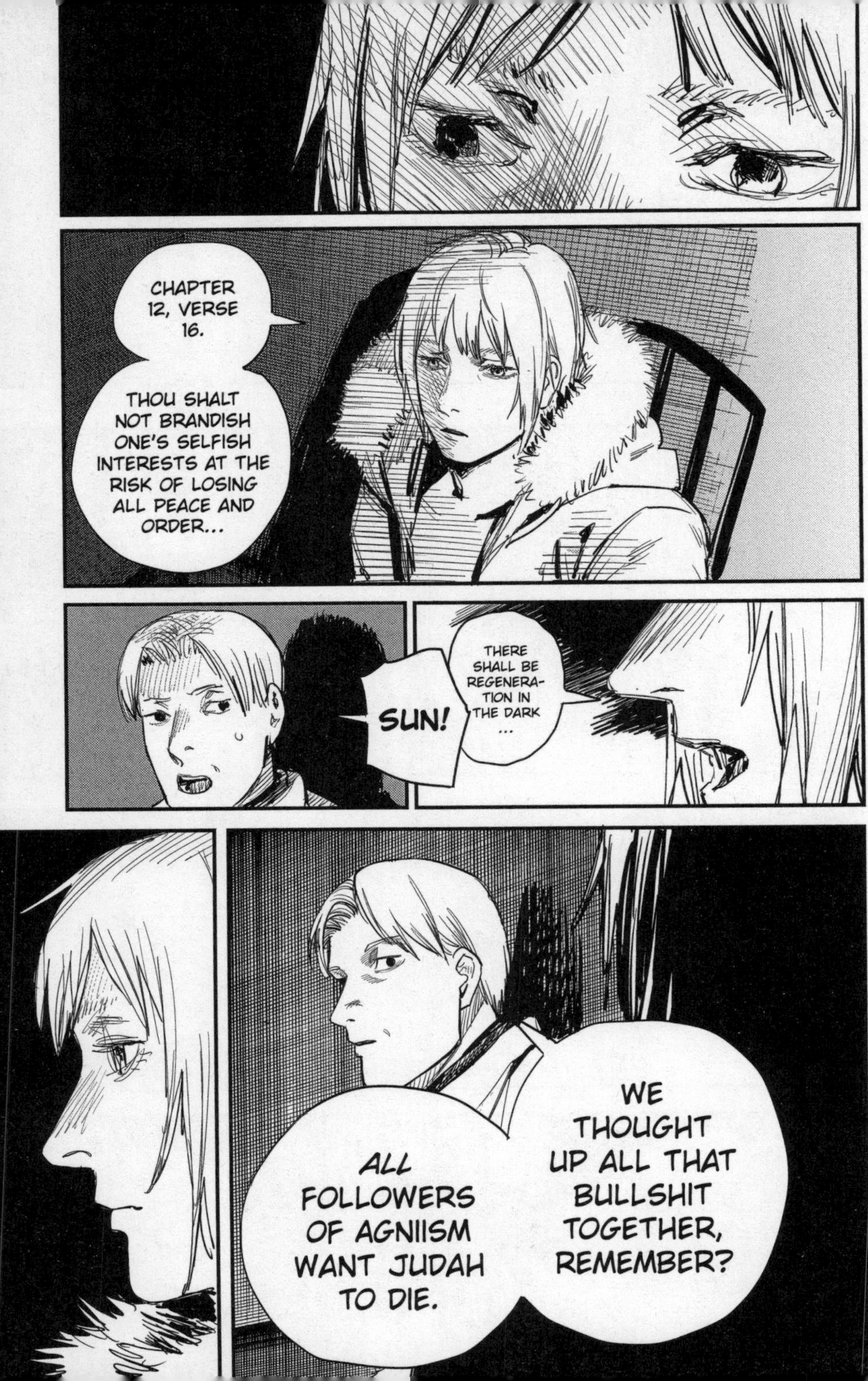
CHAPTER 12, VERSE 16.
THOU SHALT NOT BRANDISH ONE'S SELFISH INTERESTS AT THE RISK OF LOSING ALL PEACE AND ORDER...
THERE SHALL BE REGENERA-TION IN THE DARK ...
SUN!
WE THOUGHT UP ALL THAT BULLSHIT TOGETHER, REMEMBER?
ALL FOLLOWERS OF AGNIISM WANT JUDAH TO DIE.

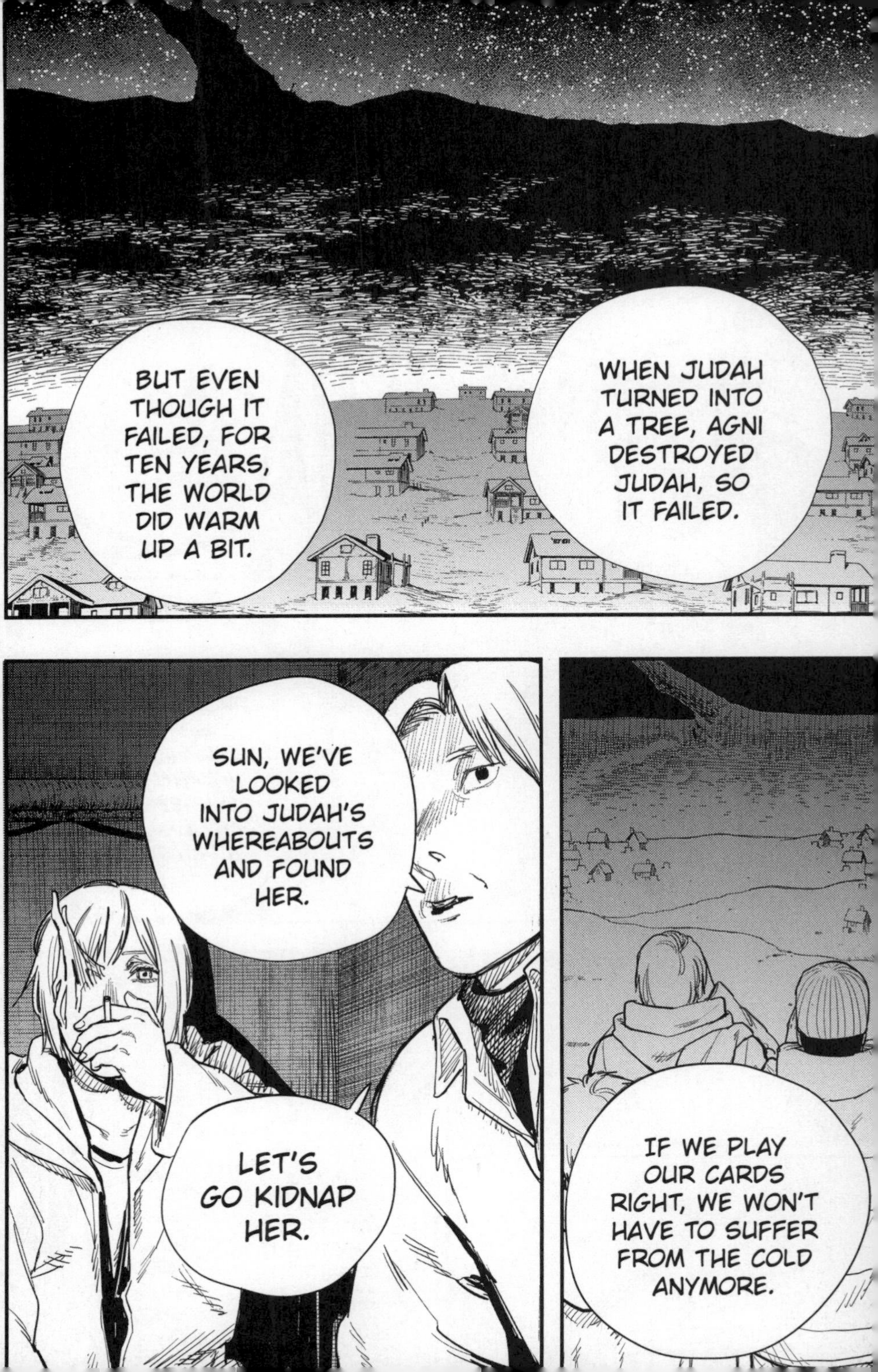
WHEN JUDAH TURNED INTO A TREE, AGNI DESTROYED JUDAH, SO IT FAILED.
BUT EVEN THOUGH IT FAILED, FOR TEN YEARS, THE WORLD DID WARM UP A BIT.
IF WE PLAY OUR CARDS RIGHT, WE WON'T HAVE TO SUFFER FROM THE COLD ANYMORE.
SUN, WE'VE LOOKED INTO JUDAH'S WHEREABOUTS AND FOUND HER.
LET'S GO KIDNAP HER.

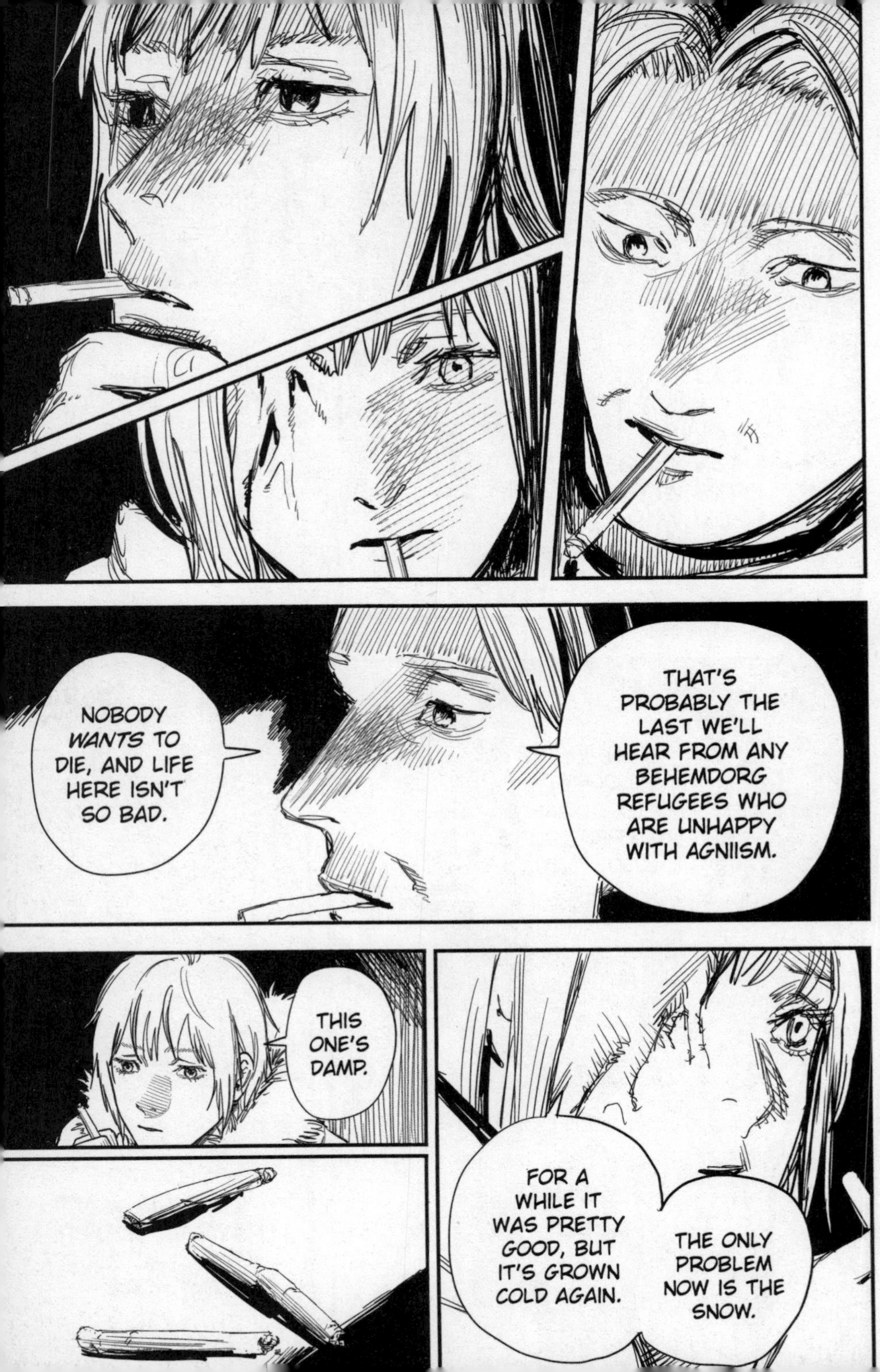
THAT'S PROBABLY THE LAST WE'LL HEAR FROM ANY BEHEMDORG REFUGEES WHO ARE UNHAPPY WITH AGNIISM.
NOBODY *WANTS* TO DIE, AND LIFE HERE ISN'T SO BAD.
THE ONLY PROBLEM NOW IS THE SNOW.
FOR A WHILE IT WAS PRETTY GOOD, BUT IT'S GROWN COLD AGAIN.
THIS ONE'S DAMP.

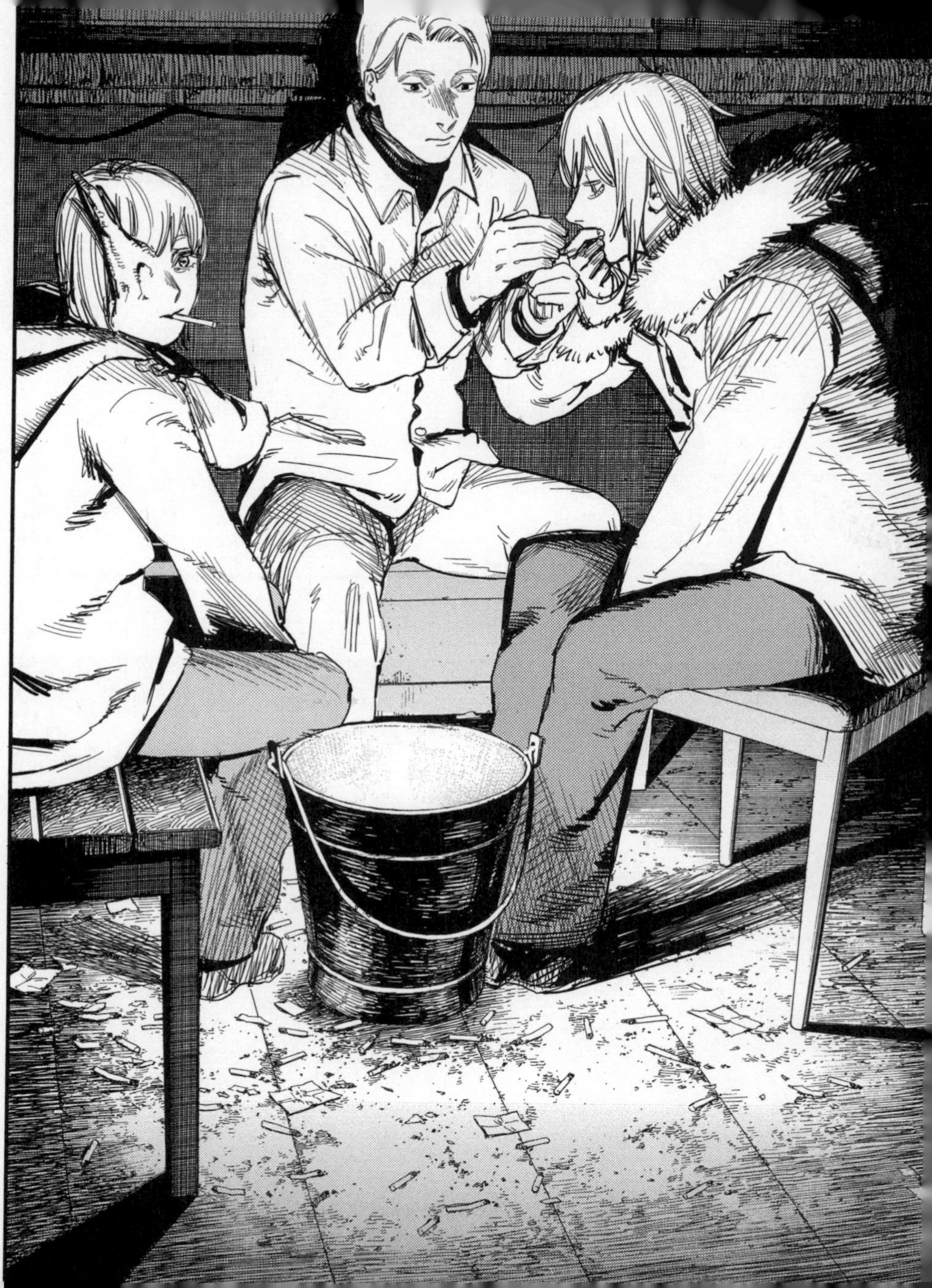

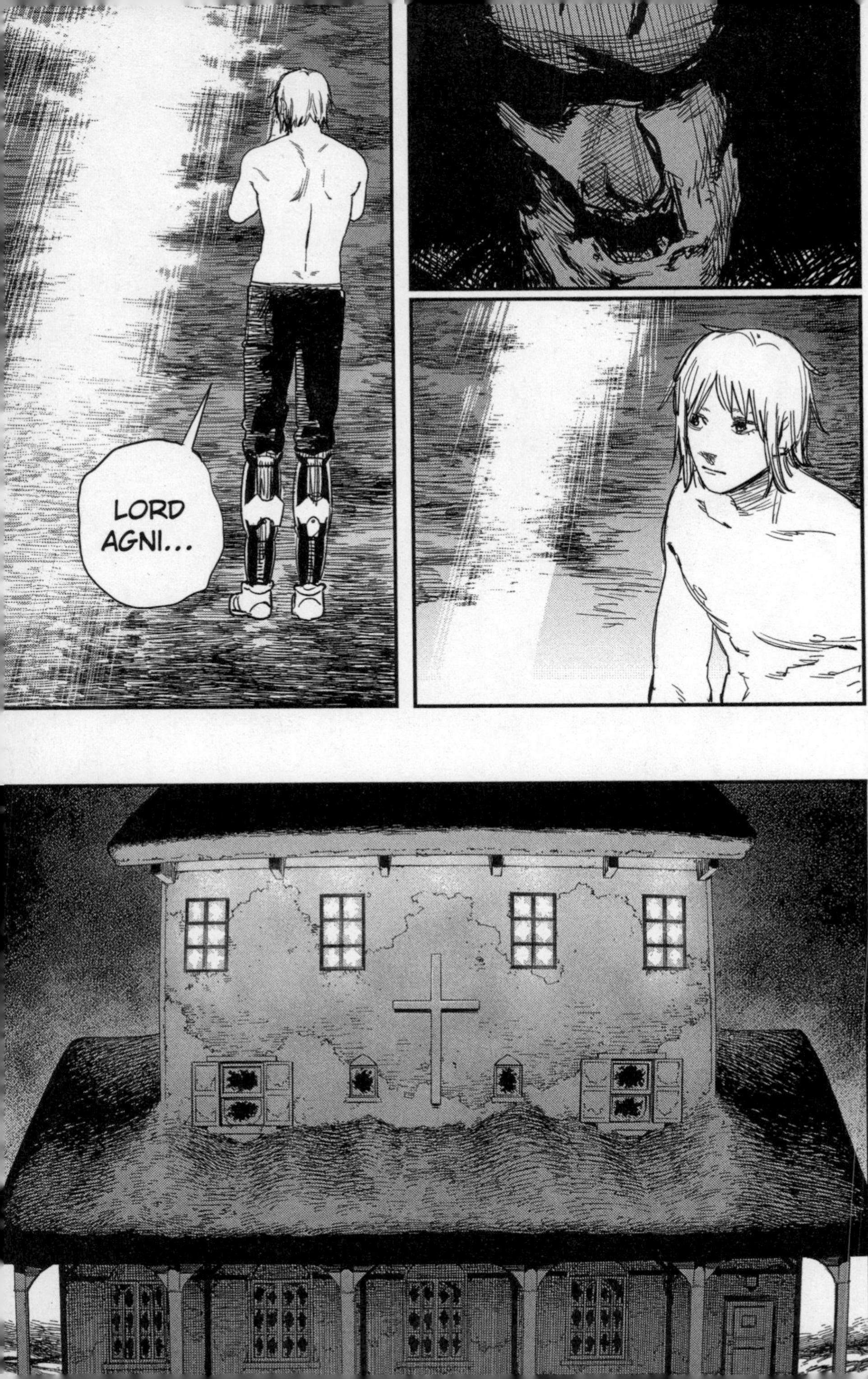
LORD AGNI...

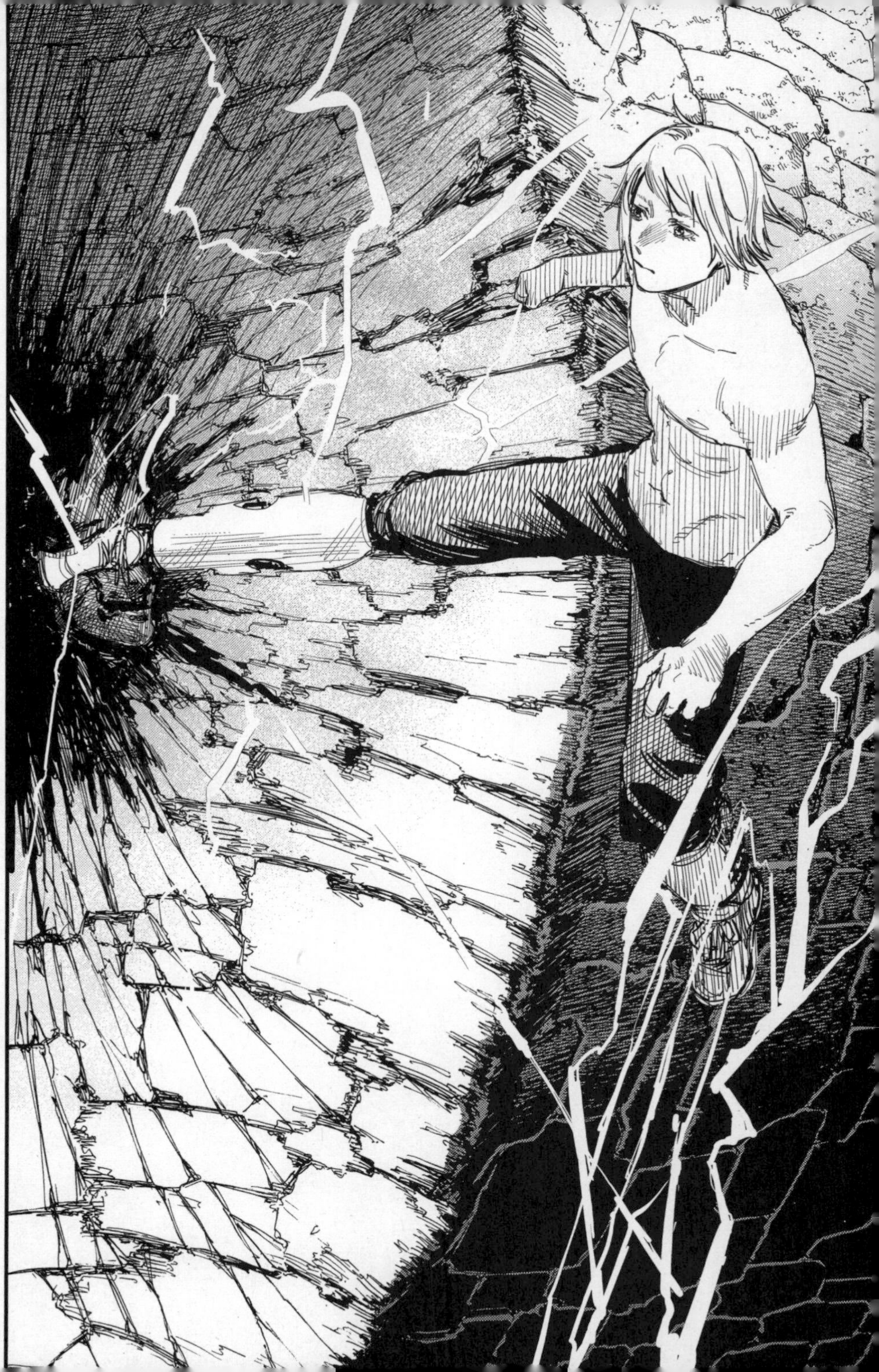

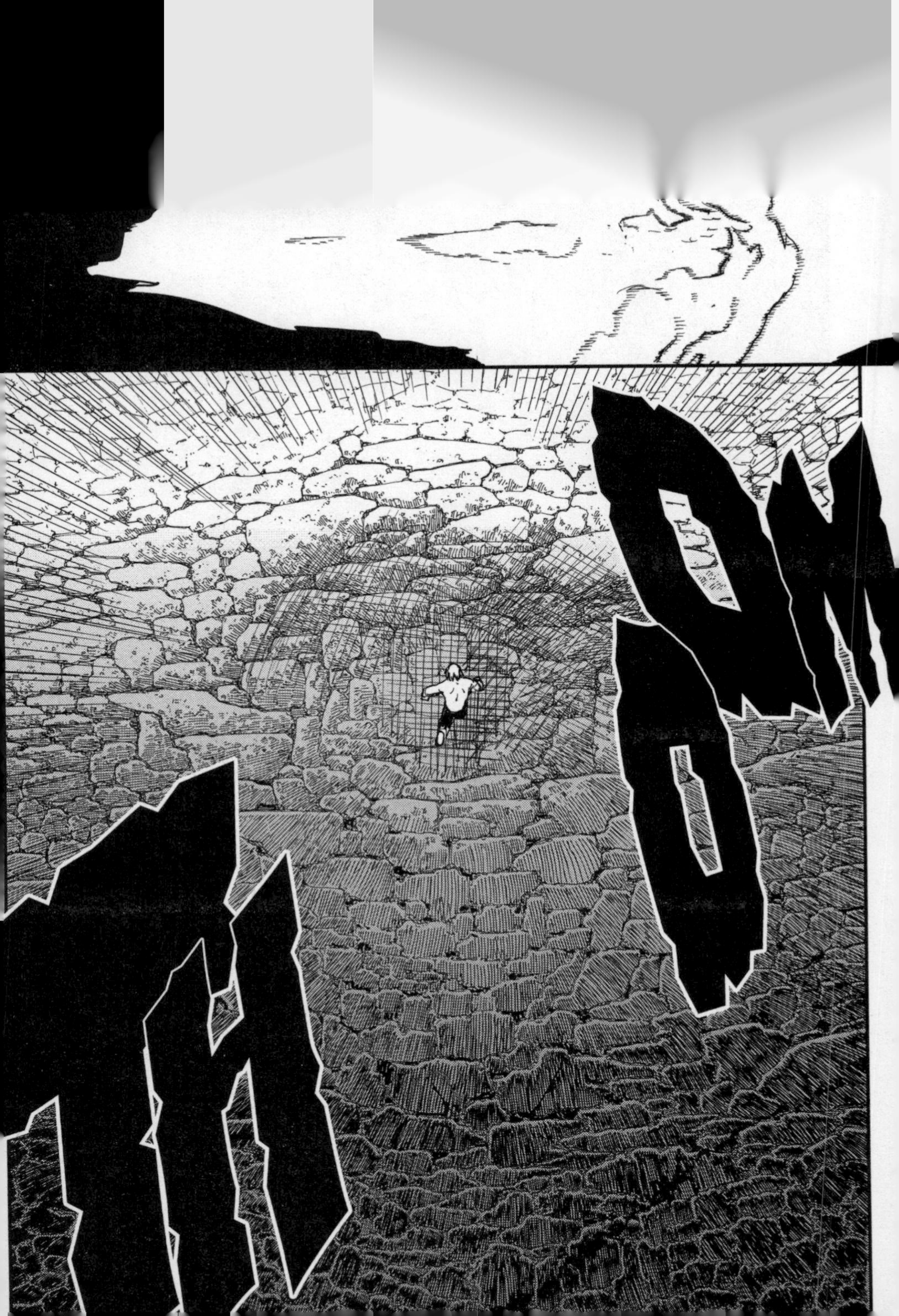

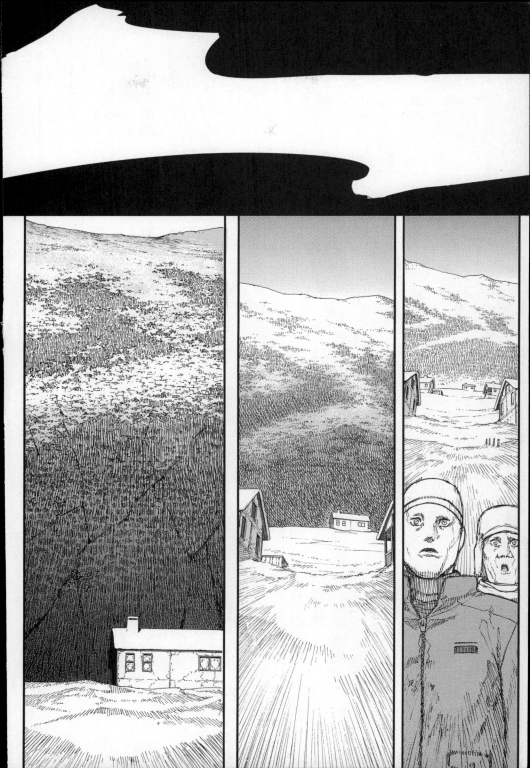

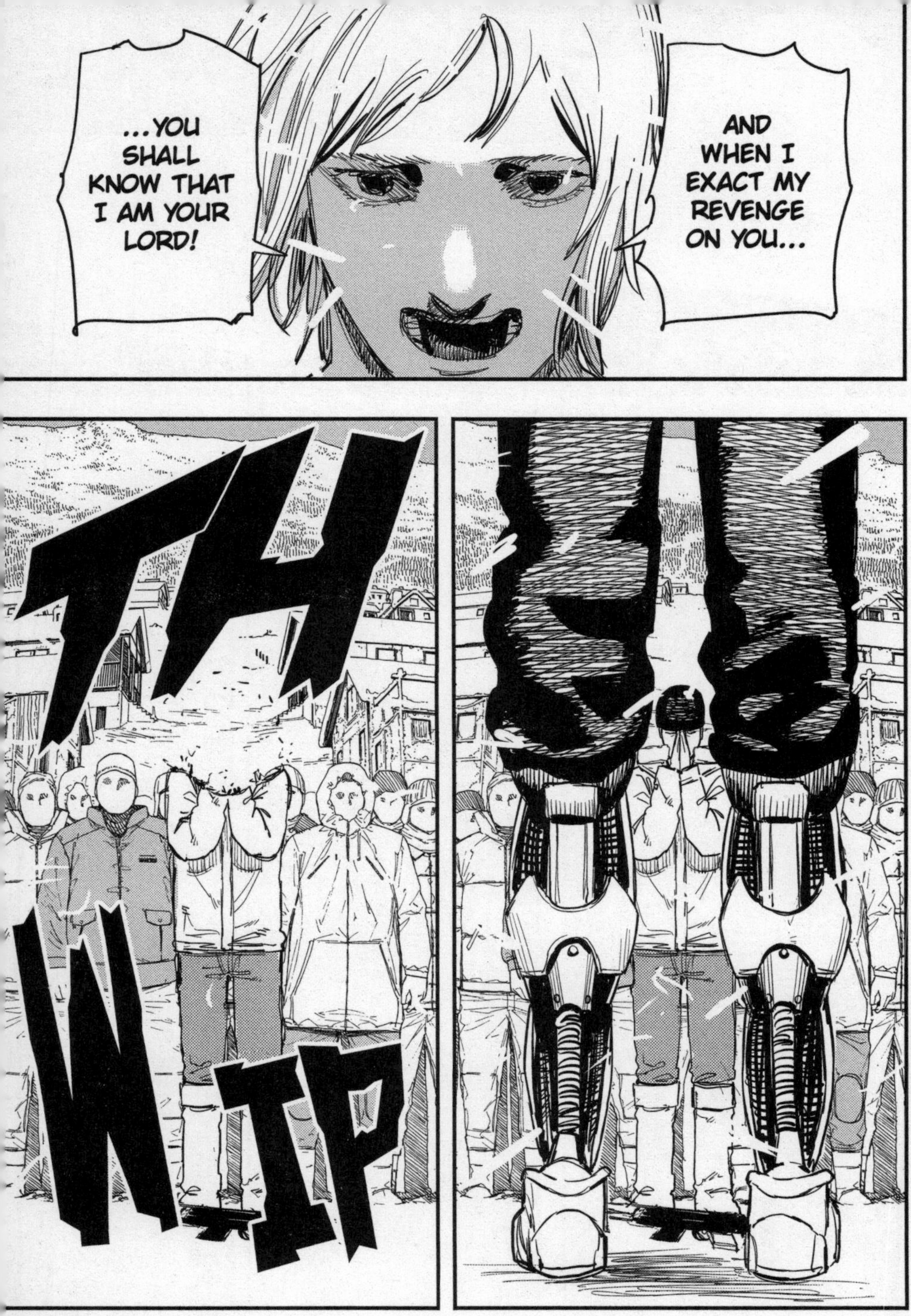
AND WHEN I EXACT MY REVENGE ON YOU...
...YOU SHALL KNOW THAT I AM YOUR LORD!
THWIP

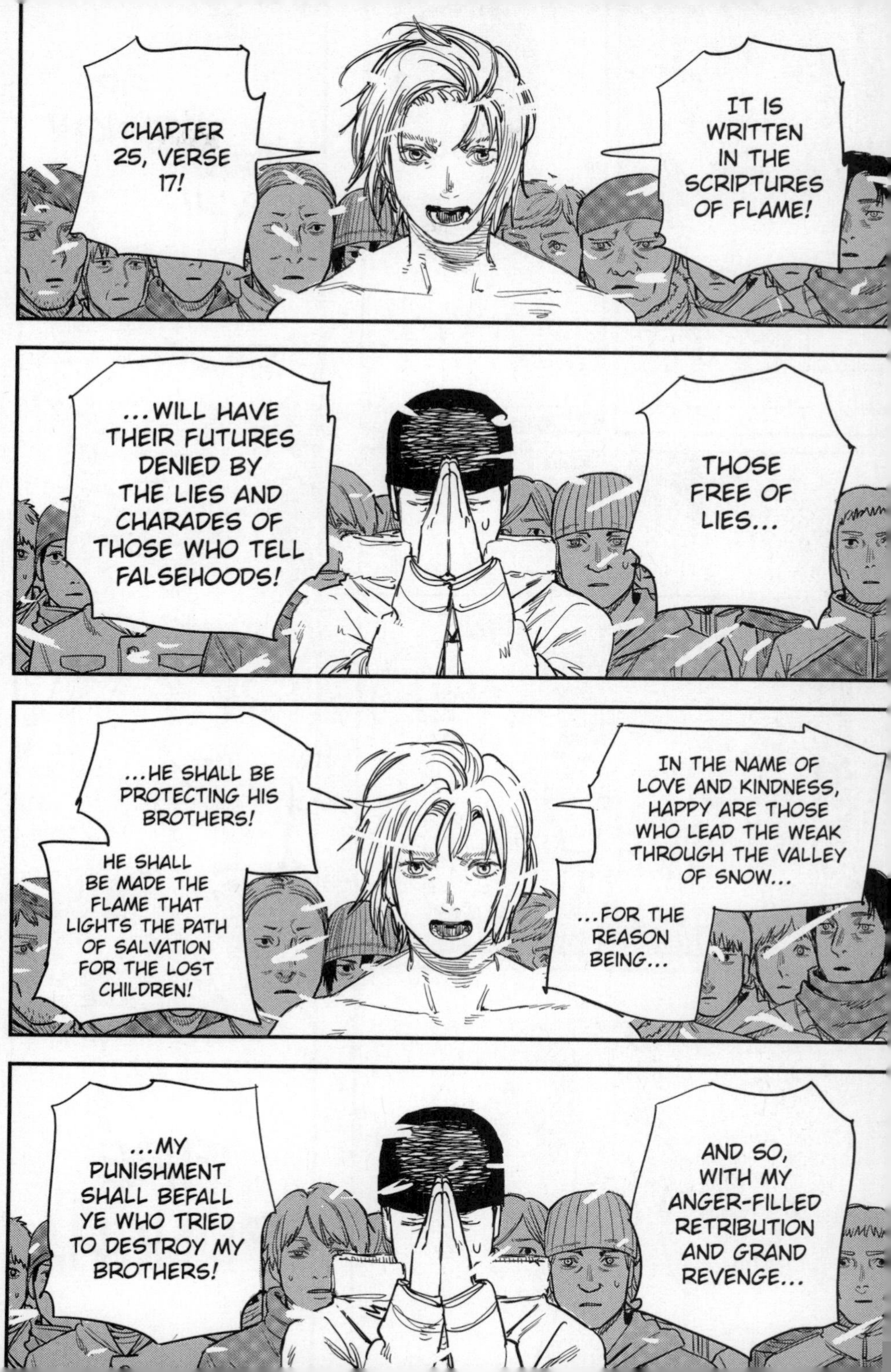
IT IS WRITTEN IN THE SCRIPTURES OF FLAME!
CHAPTER 25, VERSE 17!
THOSE FREE OF LIES...
...WILL HAVE THEIR FUTURES DENIED BY THE LIES AND CHARADES OF THOSE WHO TELL FALSEHOODS!
IN THE NAME OF LOVE AND KINDNESS, HAPPY ARE THOSE WHO LEAD THE WEAK THROUGH THE VALLEY OF SNOW...
...FOR THE REASON BEING...
...HE SHALL BE PROTECTING HIS BROTHERS!
HE SHALL BE MADE THE FLAME THAT LIGHTS THE PATH OF SALVATION FOR THE LOST CHILDREN!
AND SO, WITH MY ANGER-FILLED RETRIBUTION AND GRAND REVENGE...
...MY PUNISHMENT SHALL BEFALL YE WHO TRIED TO DESTROY MY BROTHERS!

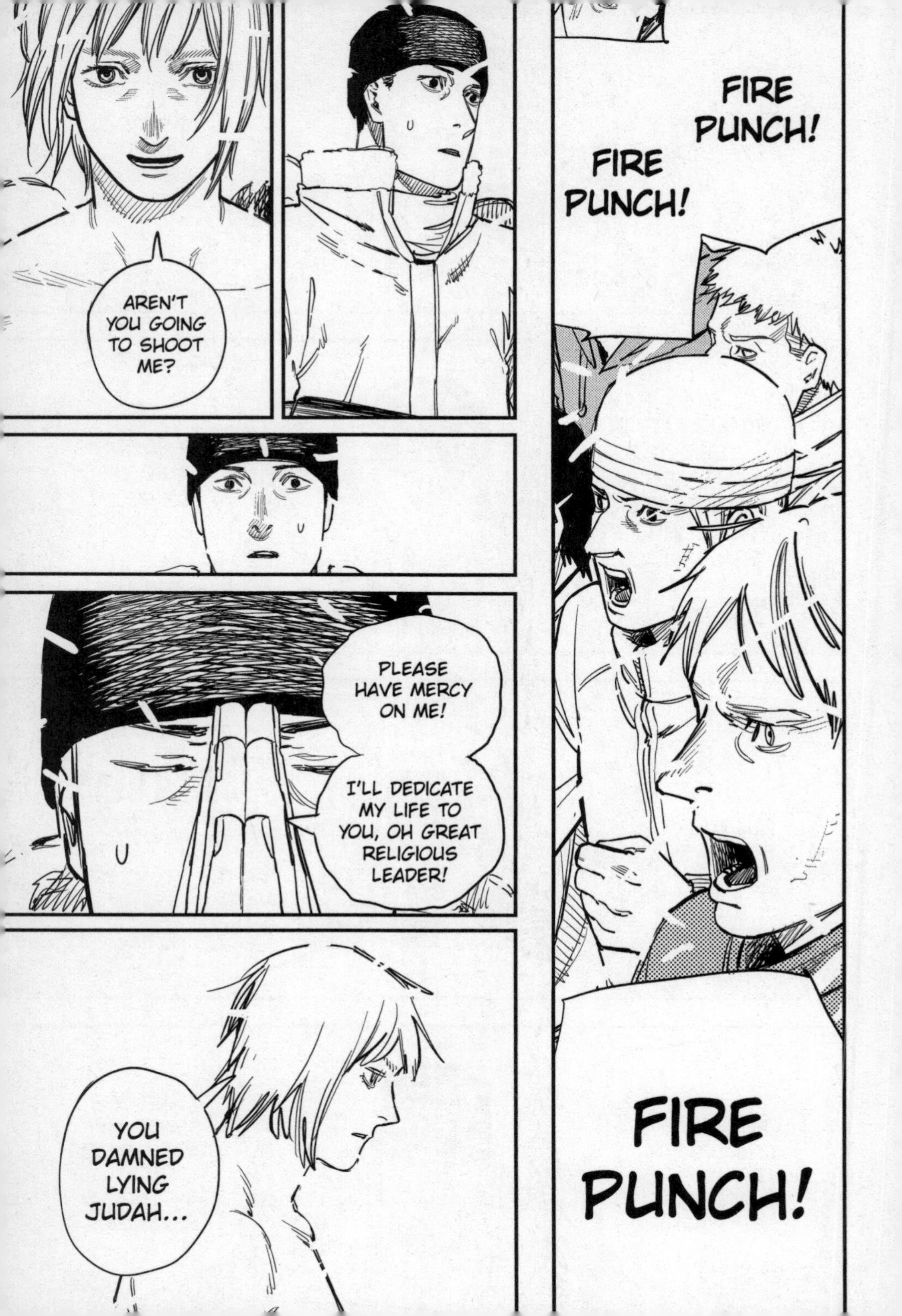
FIRE PUNCH!
FIRE PUNCH!
FIRE PUNCH!
AREN'T YOU GOING TO SHOOT ME?
PLEASE HAVE MERCY ON ME!
I'LL DEDICATE MY LIFE TO YOU, OH GREAT RELIGIOUS LEADER!
YOU DAMNED LYING JUDAH...

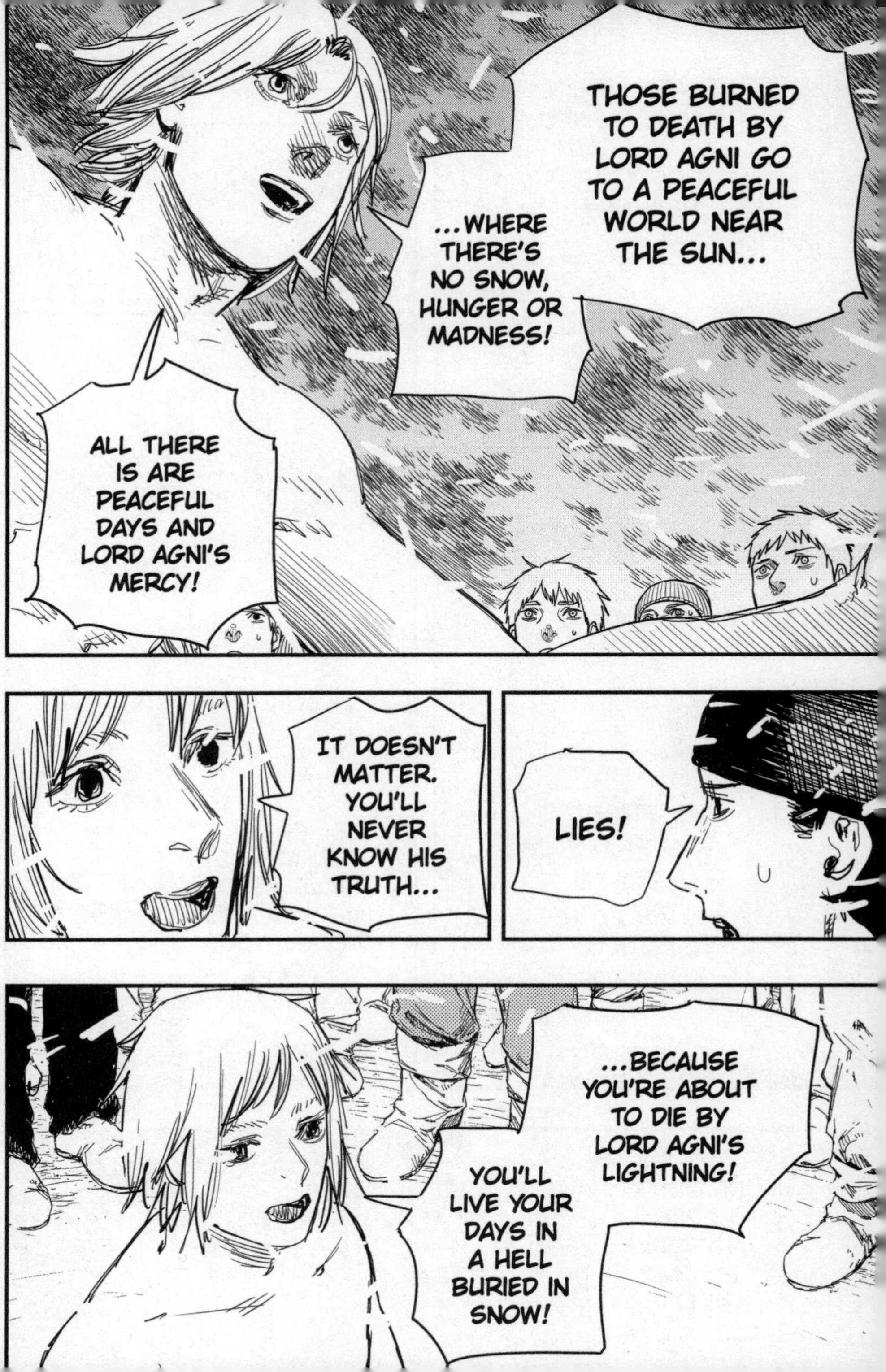
THOSE BURNED TO DEATH BY LORD AGNI GO TO A PEACEFUL WORLD NEAR THE SUN...
...WHERE THERE'S NO SNOW, HUNGER OR MADNESS!
ALL THERE IS ARE PEACEFUL DAYS AND LORD AGNI'S MERCY!
LIES!
IT DOESN'T MATTER. YOU'LL NEVER KNOW HIS TRUTH...
...BECAUSE YOU'RE ABOUT TO DIE BY LORD AGNI'S LIGHTNING!
YOU'LL LIVE YOUR DAYS IN A HELL BURIED IN SNOW!

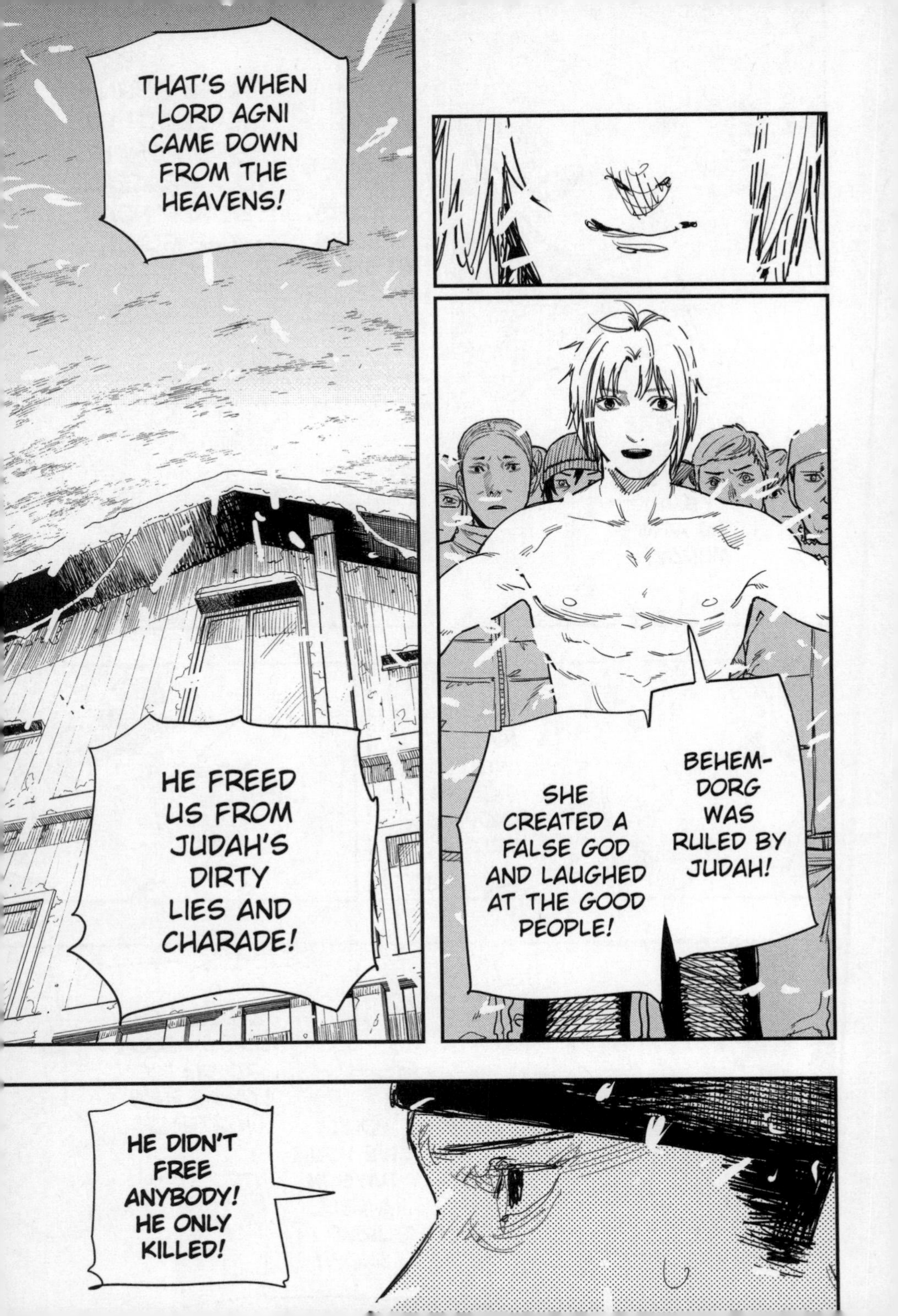
BEHEM-DORG WAS RULED BY JUDAH!
SHE CREATED A FALSE GOD AND LAUGHED AT THE GOOD PEOPLE!
THAT'S WHEN LORD AGNI CAME DOWN FROM THE HEAVENS!
HE FREED US FROM JUDAH'S DIRTY LIES AND CHARADE!
HE DIDN'T FREE ANYBODY! HE ONLY KILLED!

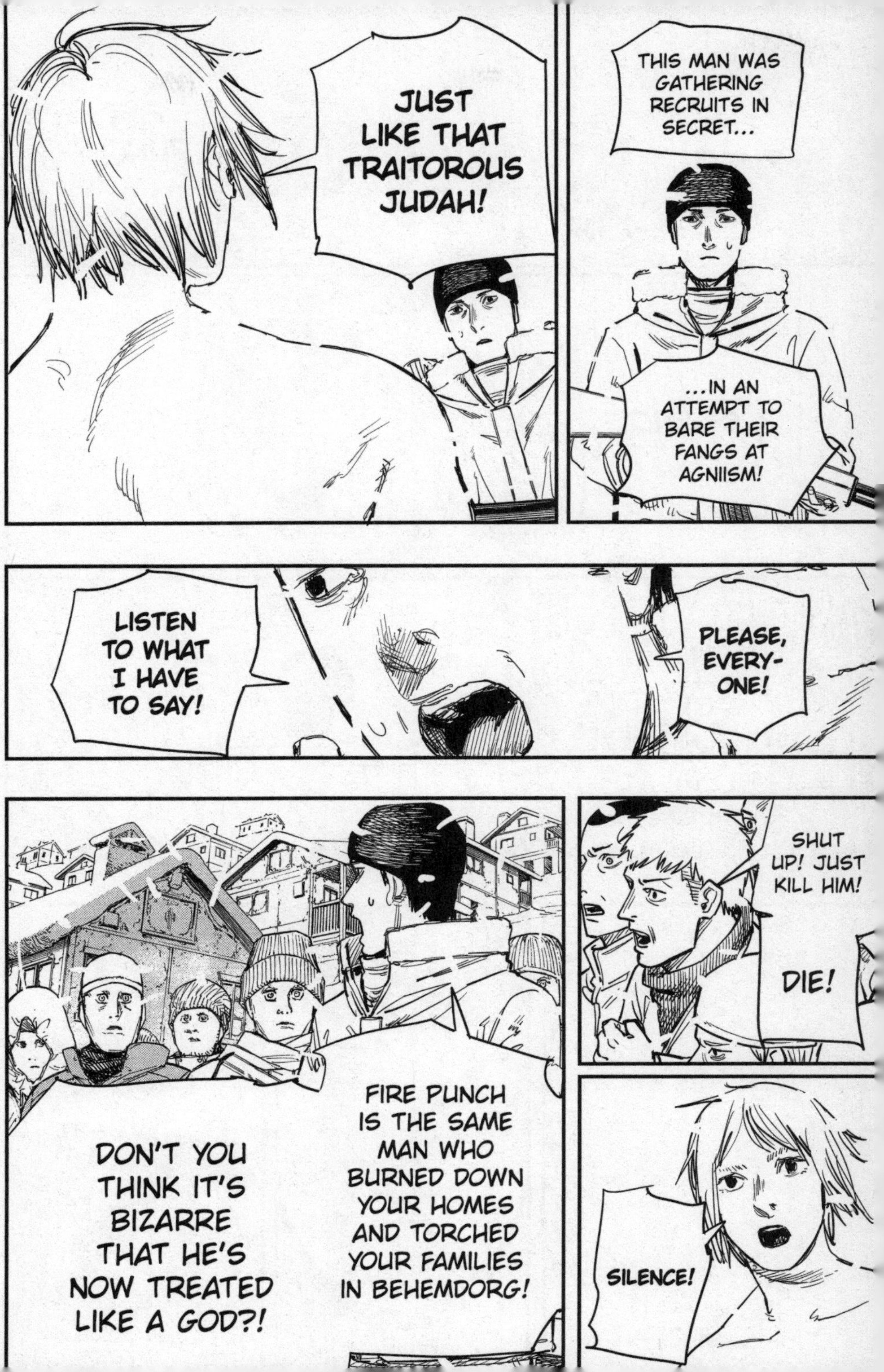
THIS MAN WAS GATHERING RECRUITS IN SECRET...
...IN AN ATTEMPT TO BARE THEIR FANGS AT AGNIISM!
JUST LIKE THAT TRAITOROUS JUDAH!
PLEASE, EVERYONE!
LISTEN TO WHAT I HAVE TO SAY!
SHUT UP! JUST KILL HIM!
DIE!
SILENCE!
FIRE PUNCH IS THE SAME MAN WHO BURNED DOWN YOUR HOMES AND TORCHED YOUR FAMILIES IN BEHEMDORG!
DON'T YOU THINK IT'S BIZARRE THAT HE'S NOW TREATED LIKE A GOD?!

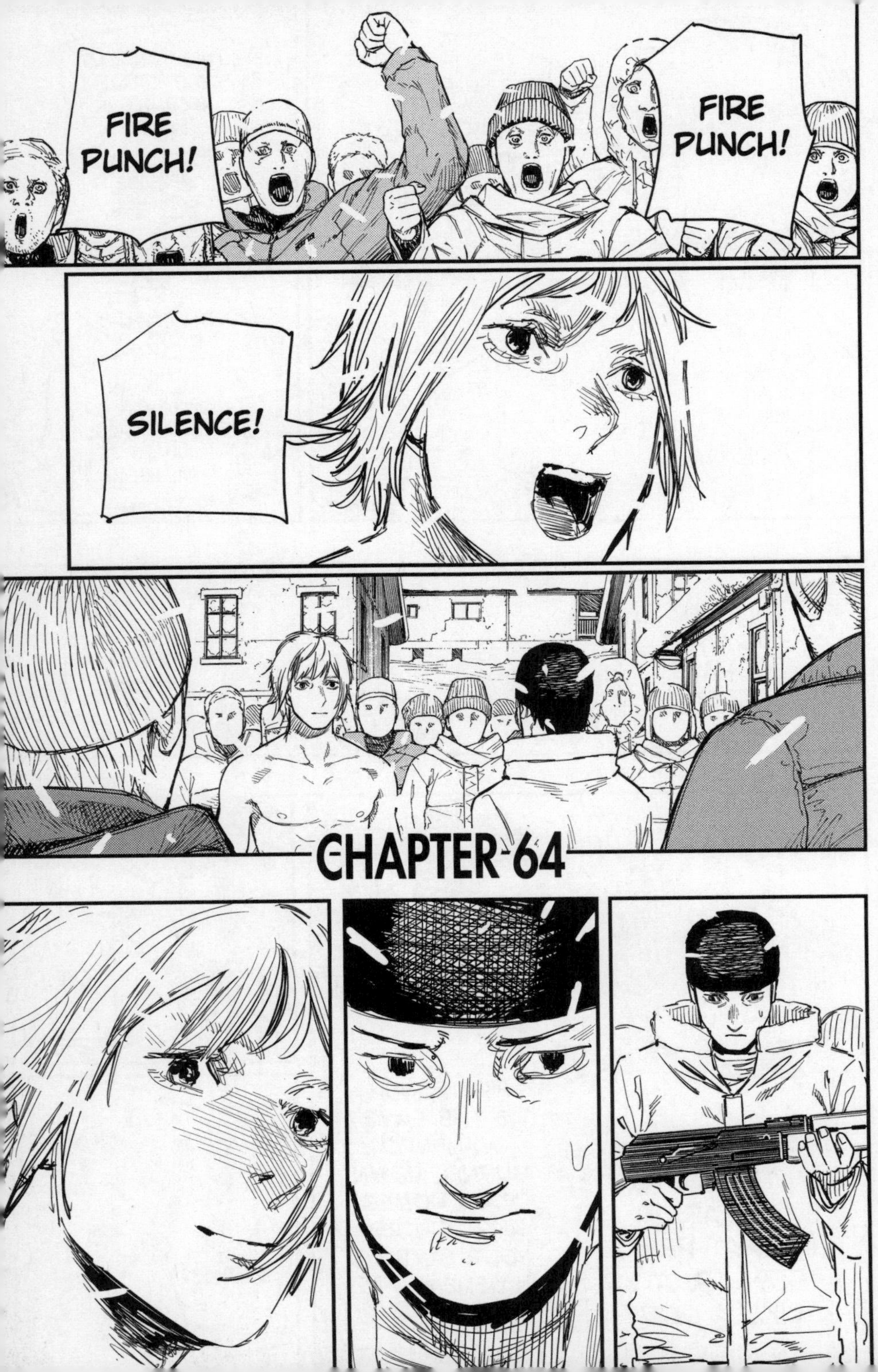
FIRE PUNCH!
FIRE PUNCH!
SILENCE!
CHAPTER 64

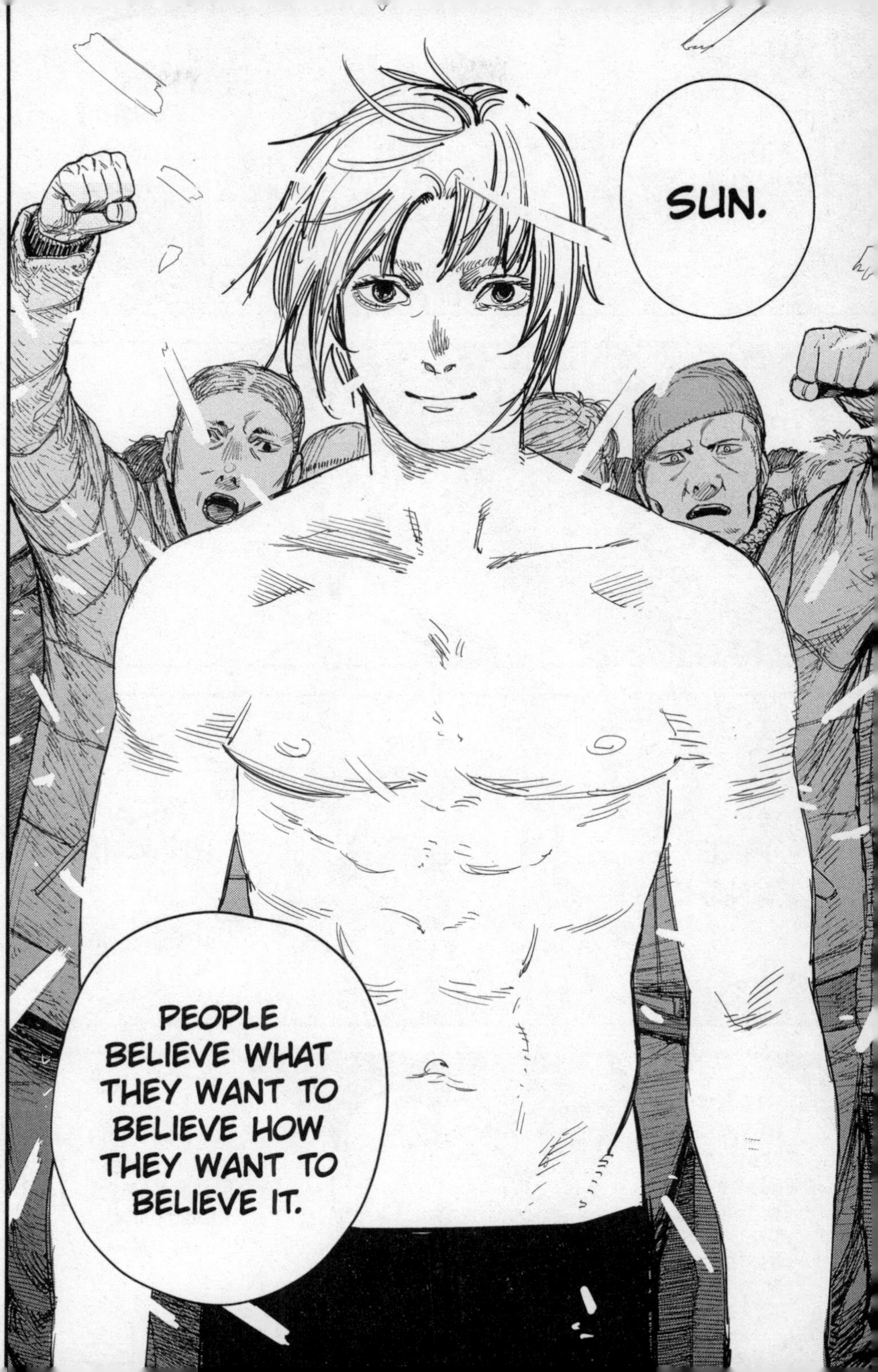
SUN.
PEOPLE BELIEVE WHAT THEY WANT TO BELIEVE HOW THEY WANT TO BELIEVE IT.

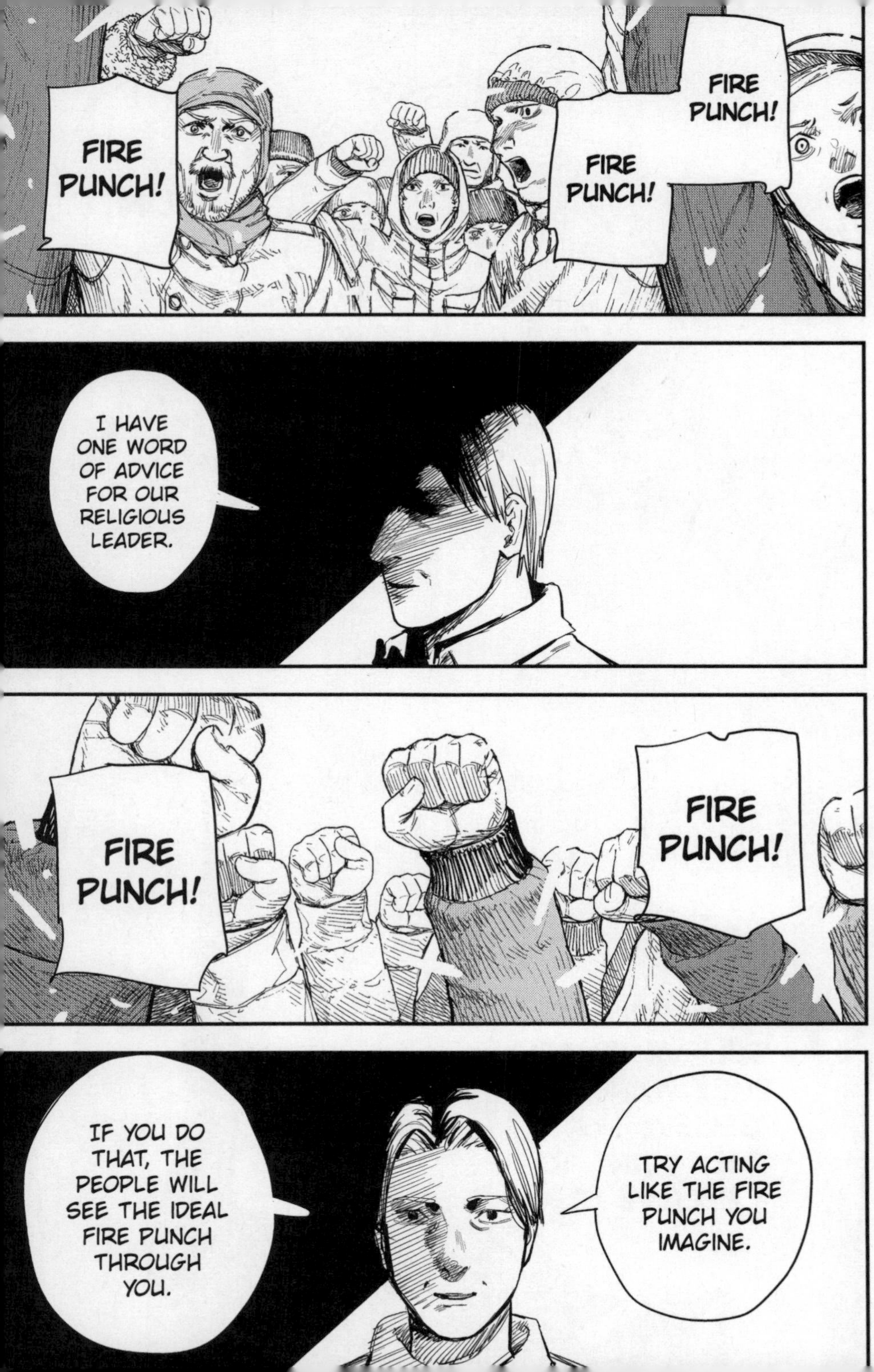
FIRE PUNCH!
FIRE PUNCH!
FIRE PUNCH!
I HAVE ONE WORD OF ADVICE FOR OUR RELIGIOUS LEADER.
FIRE PUNCH!
FIRE PUNCH!
TRY ACTING LIKE THE FIRE PUNCH YOU IMAGINE.
IF YOU DO THAT, THE PEOPLE WILL SEE THE IDEAL FIRE PUNCH THROUGH YOU.

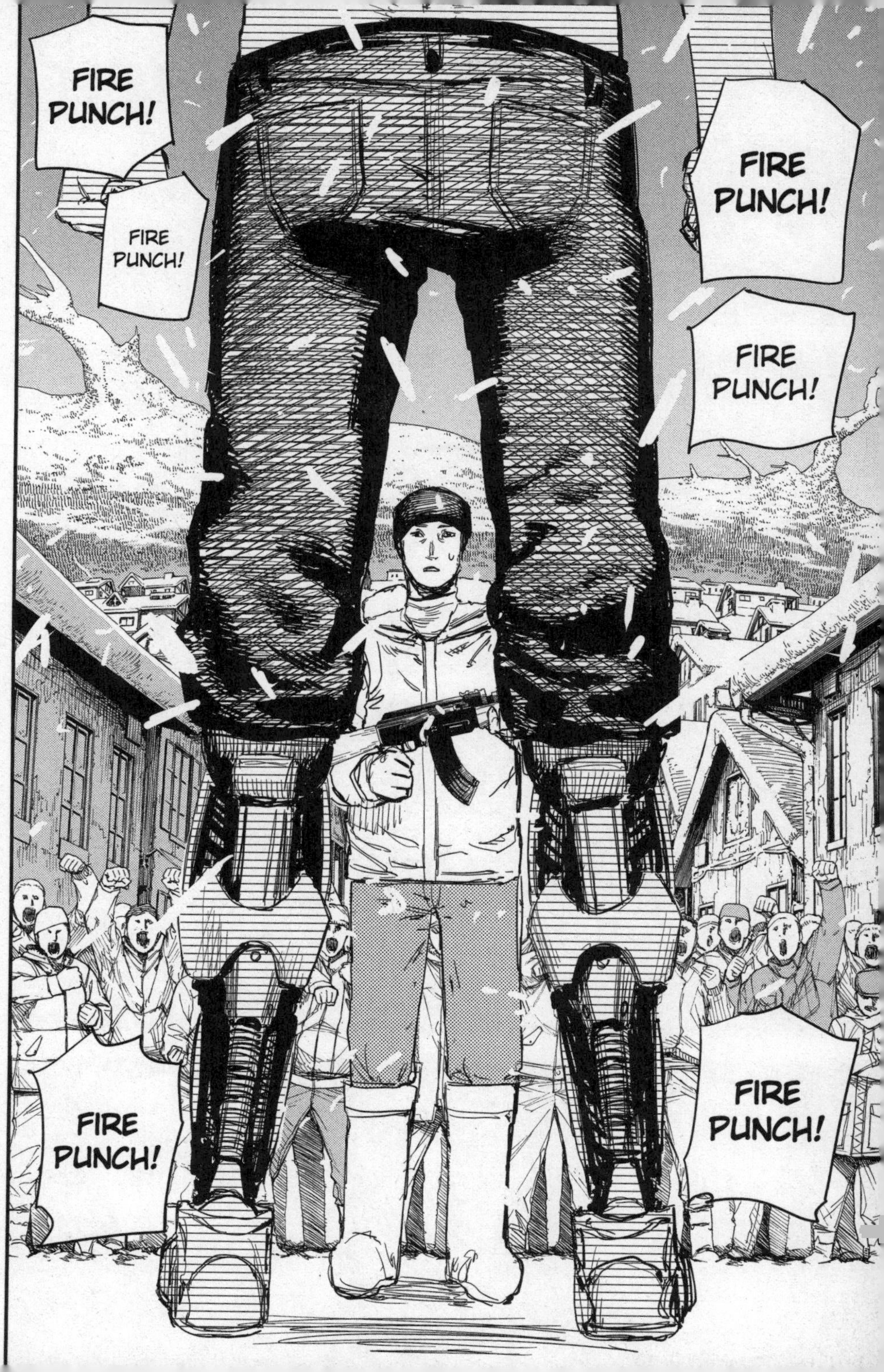
FIRE PUNCH!
FIRE PUNCH!
FIRE PUNCH!
FIRE PUNCH!
FIRE PUNCH!
FIRE PUNCH!

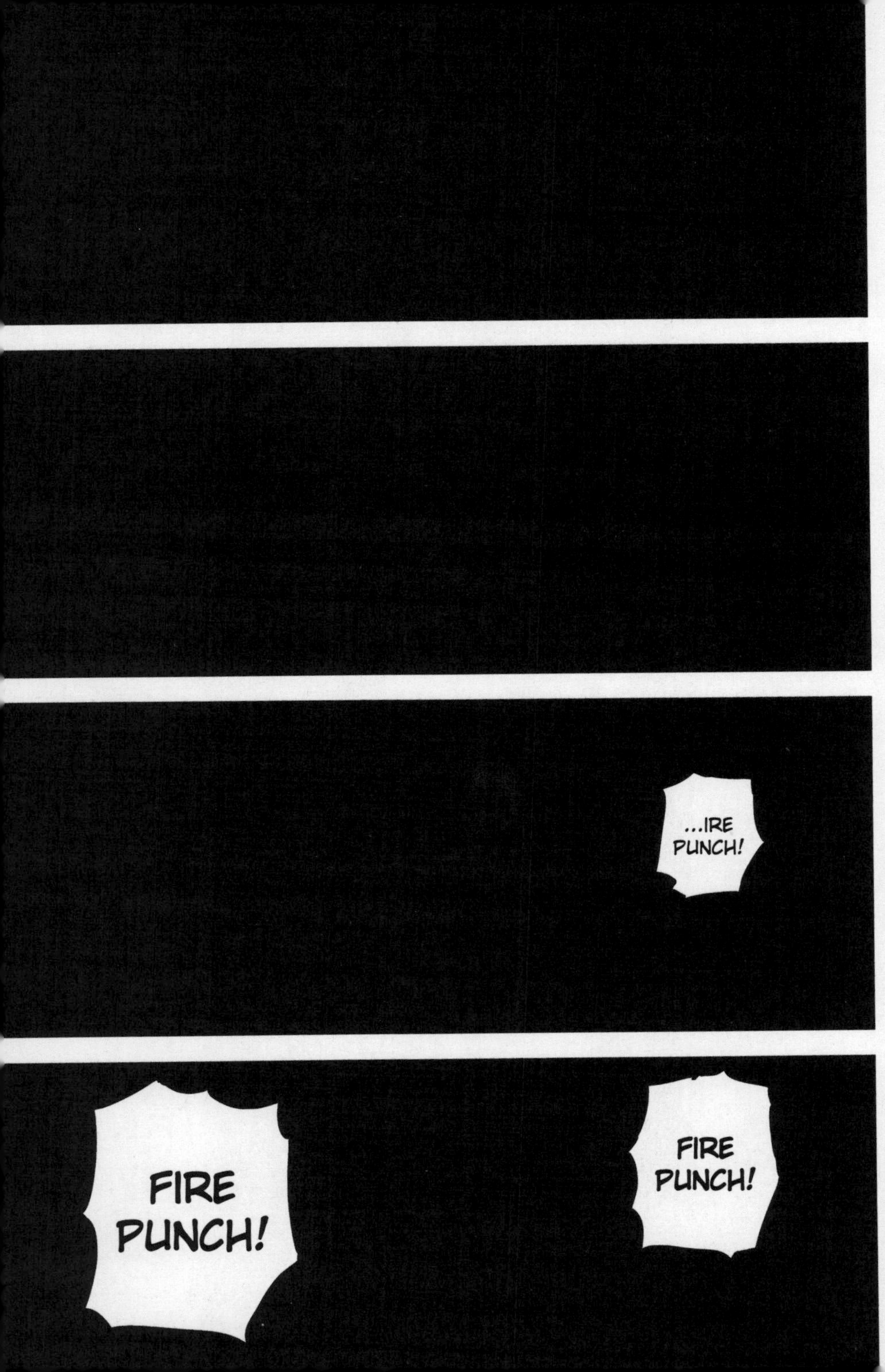
...IRE PUNCH!
FIRE PUNCH!
FIRE PUNCH!

I'D TELL YOU NOT TO KILL ANYONE ANYMORE.

NOT ANYBODY...

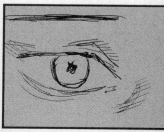

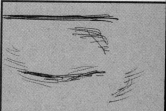

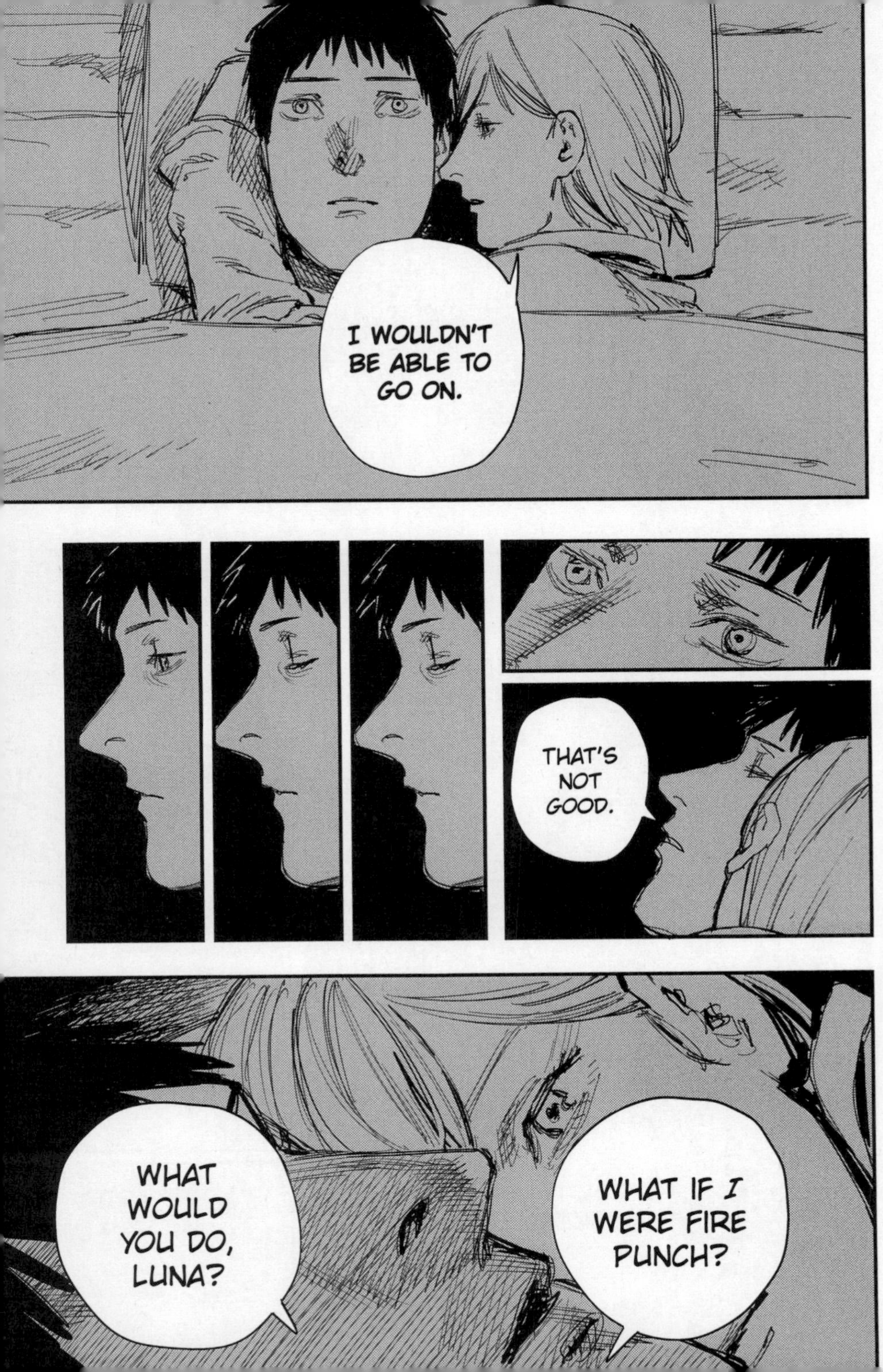
I WOULDN'T BE ABLE TO GO ON.
THAT'S NOT GOOD.
WHAT IF *I* WERE FIRE PUNCH?
WHAT WOULD YOU DO, LUNA?

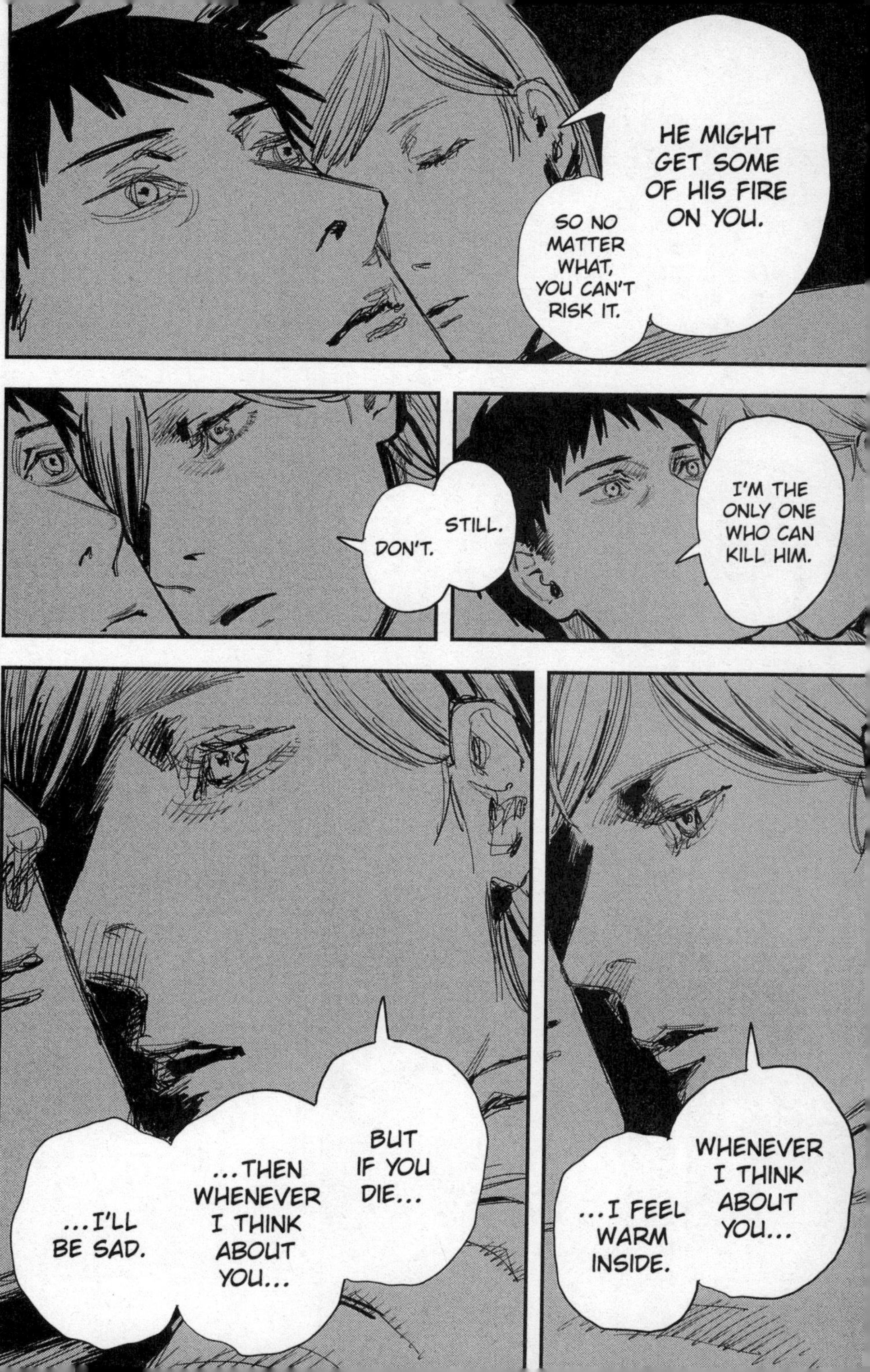
HE MIGHT GET SOME OF HIS FIRE ON YOU.
SO NO MATTER WHAT, YOU CAN'T RISK IT.
I'M THE ONLY ONE WHO CAN KILL HIM.
STILL.
DON'T.
WHENEVER I THINK ABOUT YOU...
...I FEEL WARM INSIDE.
BUT IF YOU DIE...
...THEN WHENEVER I THINK ABOUT YOU...
...I'LL BE SAD.

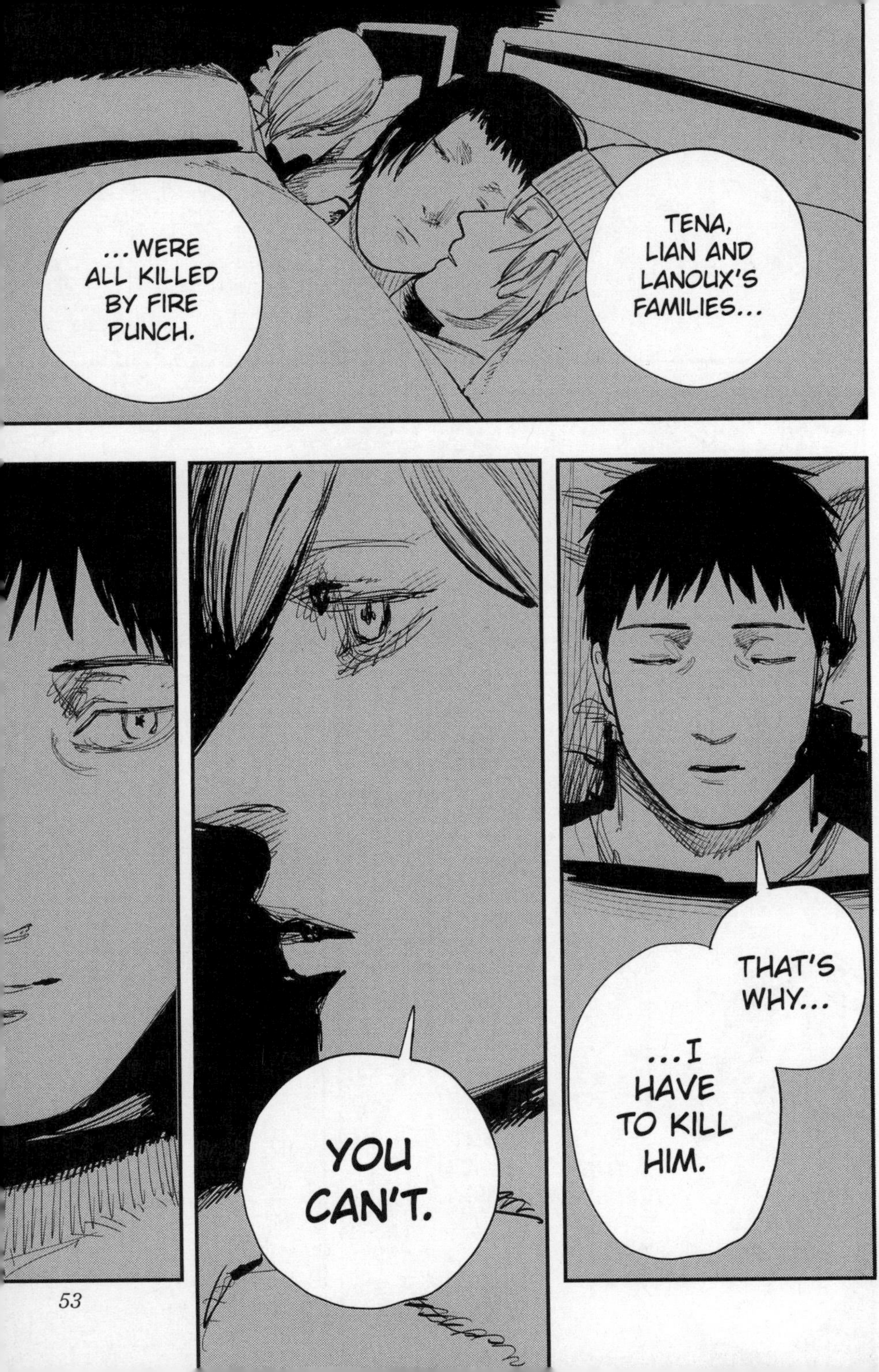
TENA, LIAN AND LANOUX'S FAMILIES...
...WERE ALL KILLED BY FIRE PUNCH.
THAT'S WHY...
...I HAVE TO KILL HIM.
YOU CAN'T.

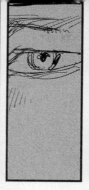

BROTHER... ARE YOU AWAKE?
I'M AWAKE.
WHO'S FIRE PUNCH?
YOU HEARD THAT?
ARE YOU GOING TO...
...KILL FIRE PUNCH?
FIRE PUNCH...IS A REALLY BAD PERSON.
HIS WHOLE BODY'S COVERED IN FLAMES...
...AND HE'LL BURN PEOPLE, EVEN CHILDREN, TO DEATH.

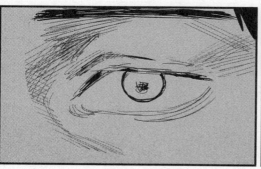

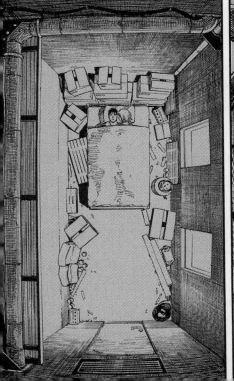

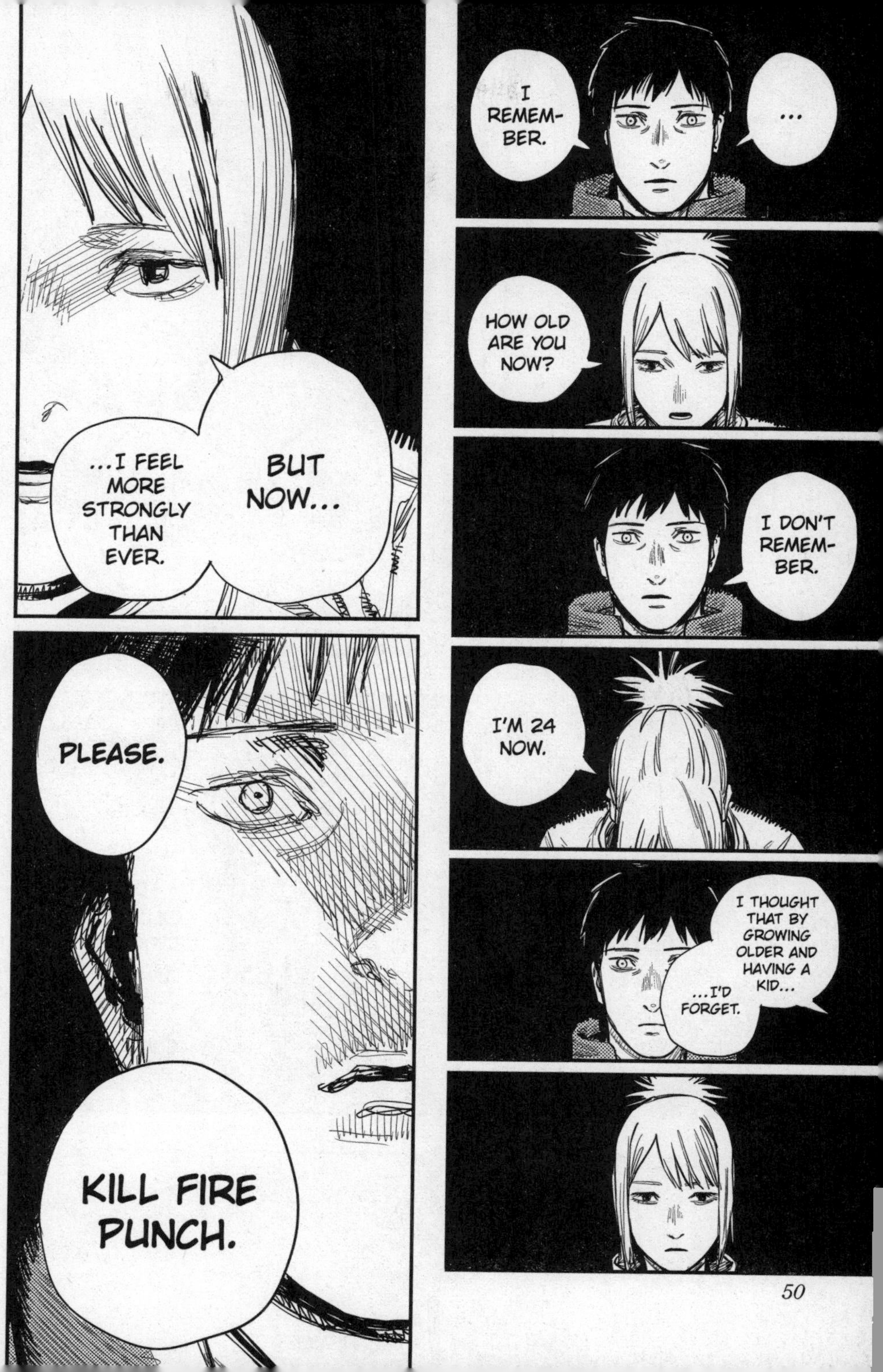
...
I REMEMBER.
HOW OLD ARE YOU NOW?
I DON'T REMEMBER.
I'M 24 NOW.
I THOUGHT THAT BY GROWING OLDER AND HAVING A KID...
...I'D FORGET.
BUT NOW...
...I FEEL MORE STRONGLY THAN EVER.
PLEASE.
KILL FIRE PUNCH.

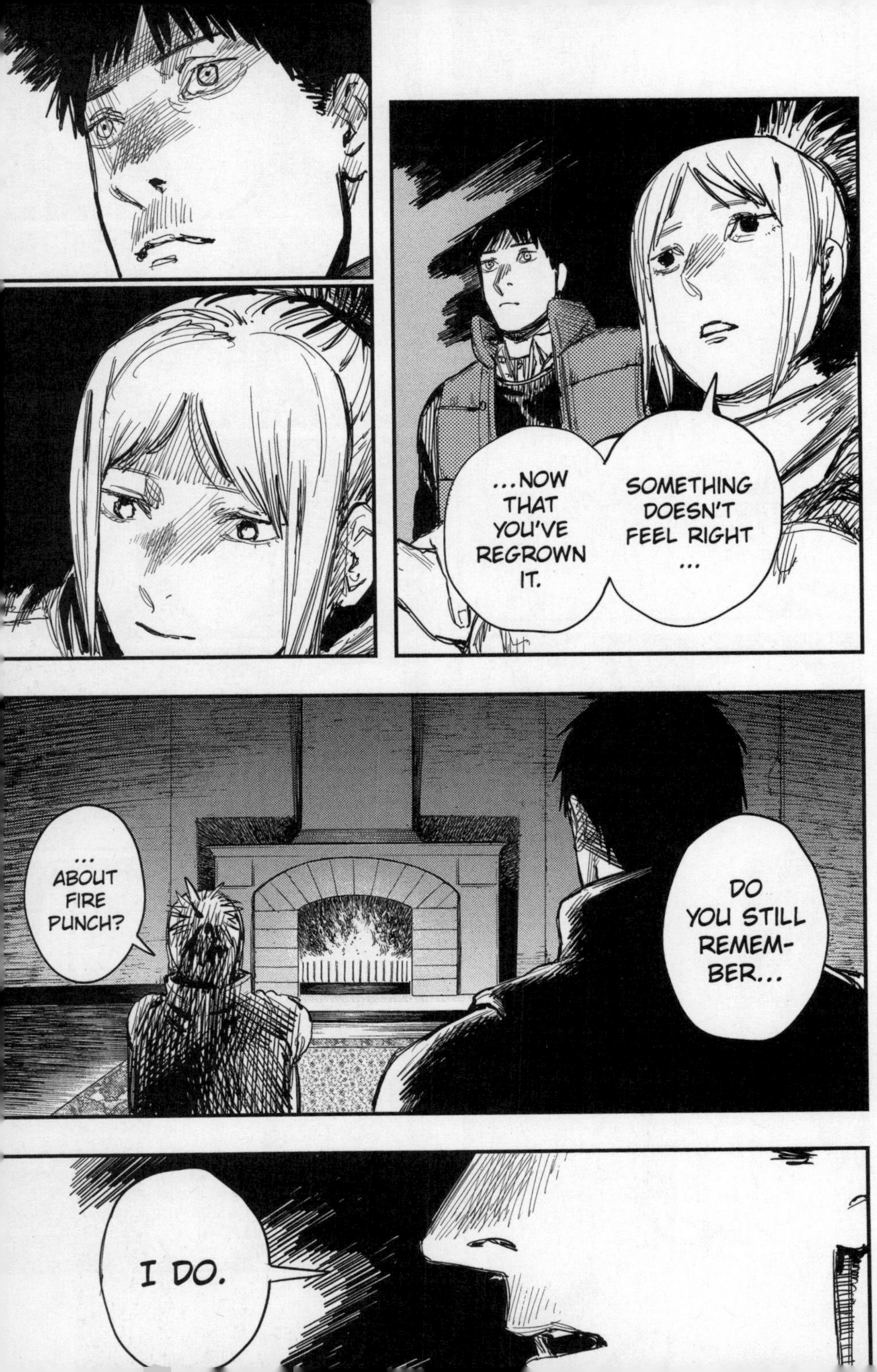
SOMETHING DOESN'T FEEL RIGHT ...
...NOW THAT YOU'VE REGROWN IT.
DO YOU STILL REMEMBER...
... ABOUT FIRE PUNCH?
I DO.

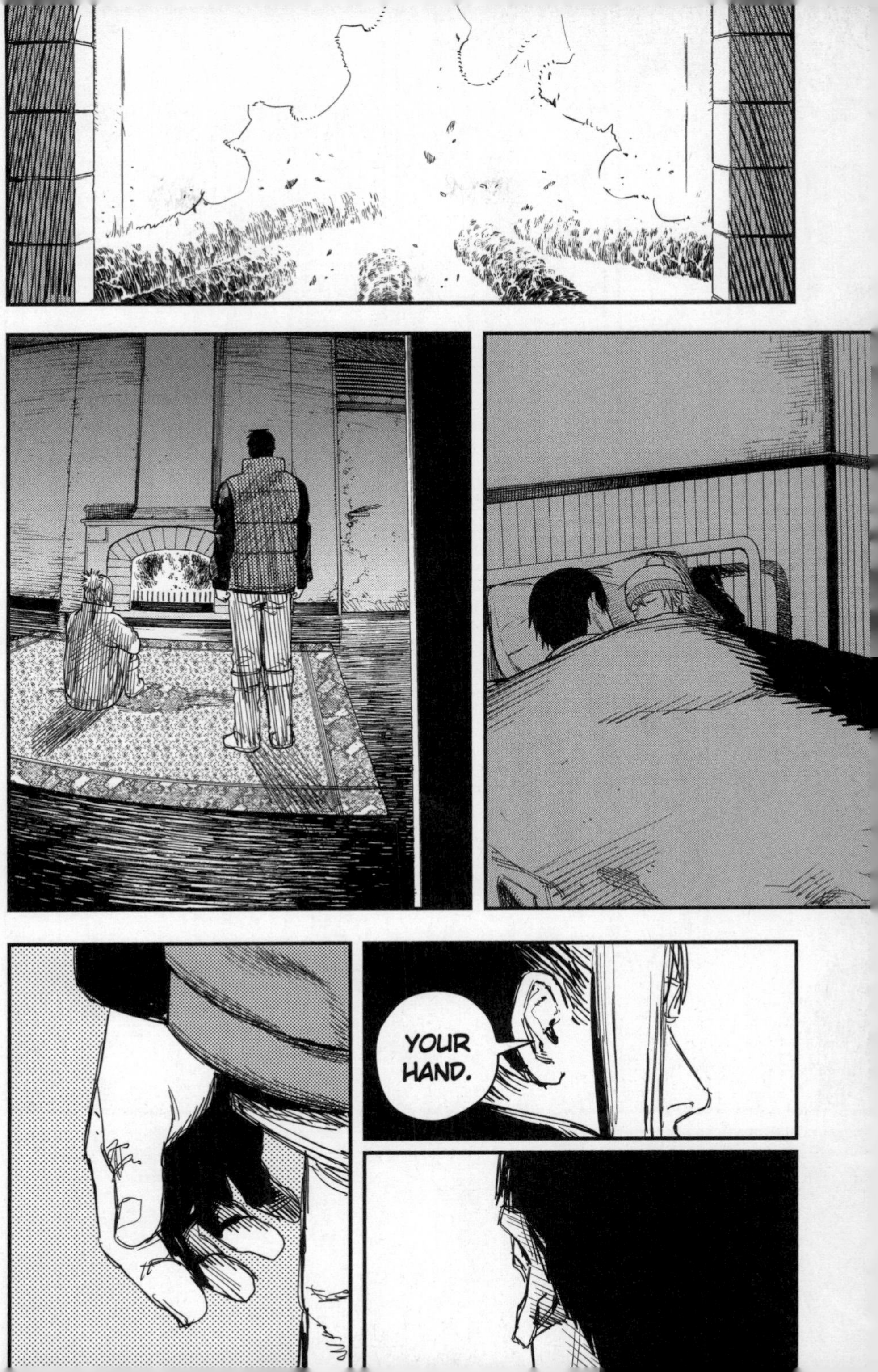
YOUR HAND.

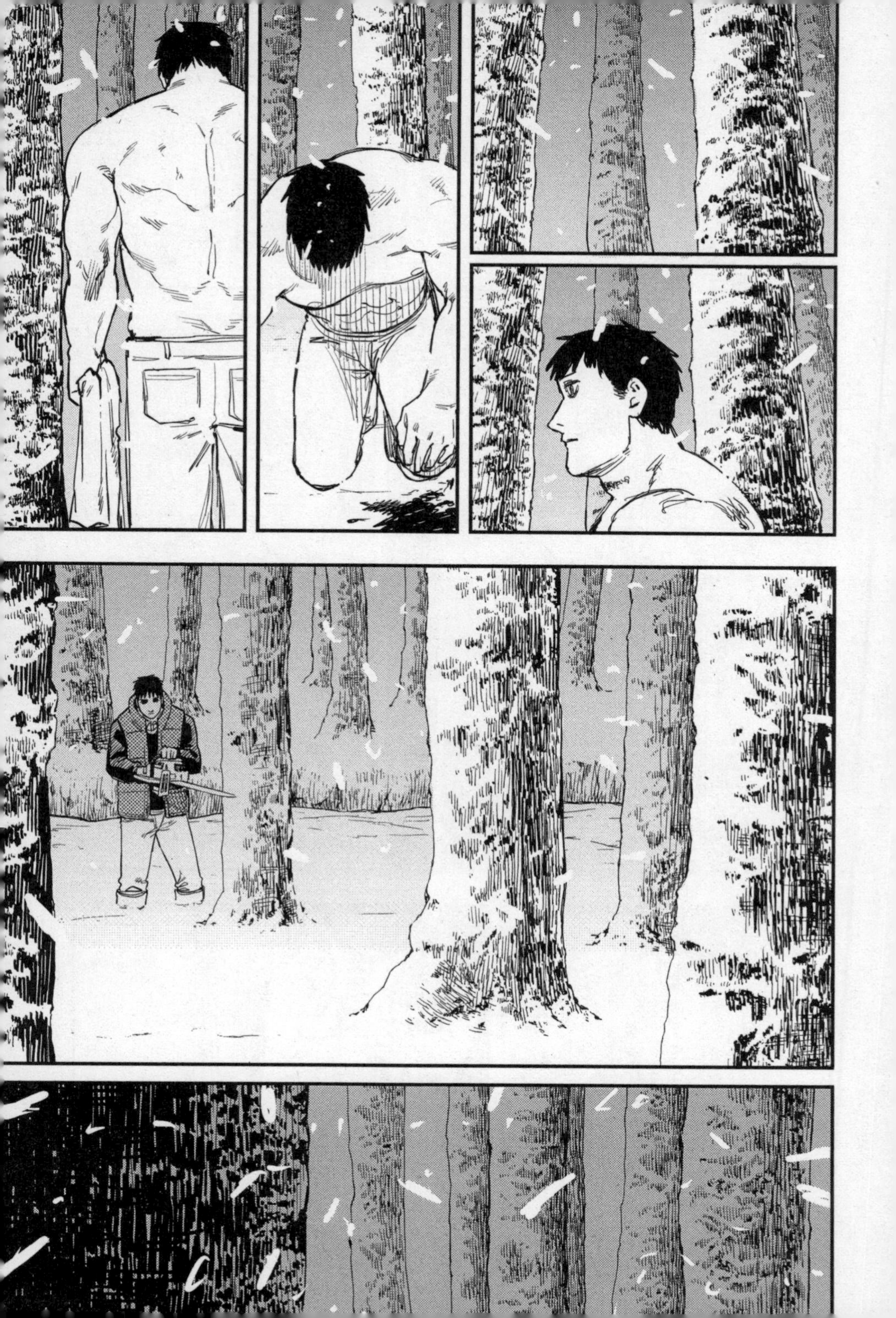

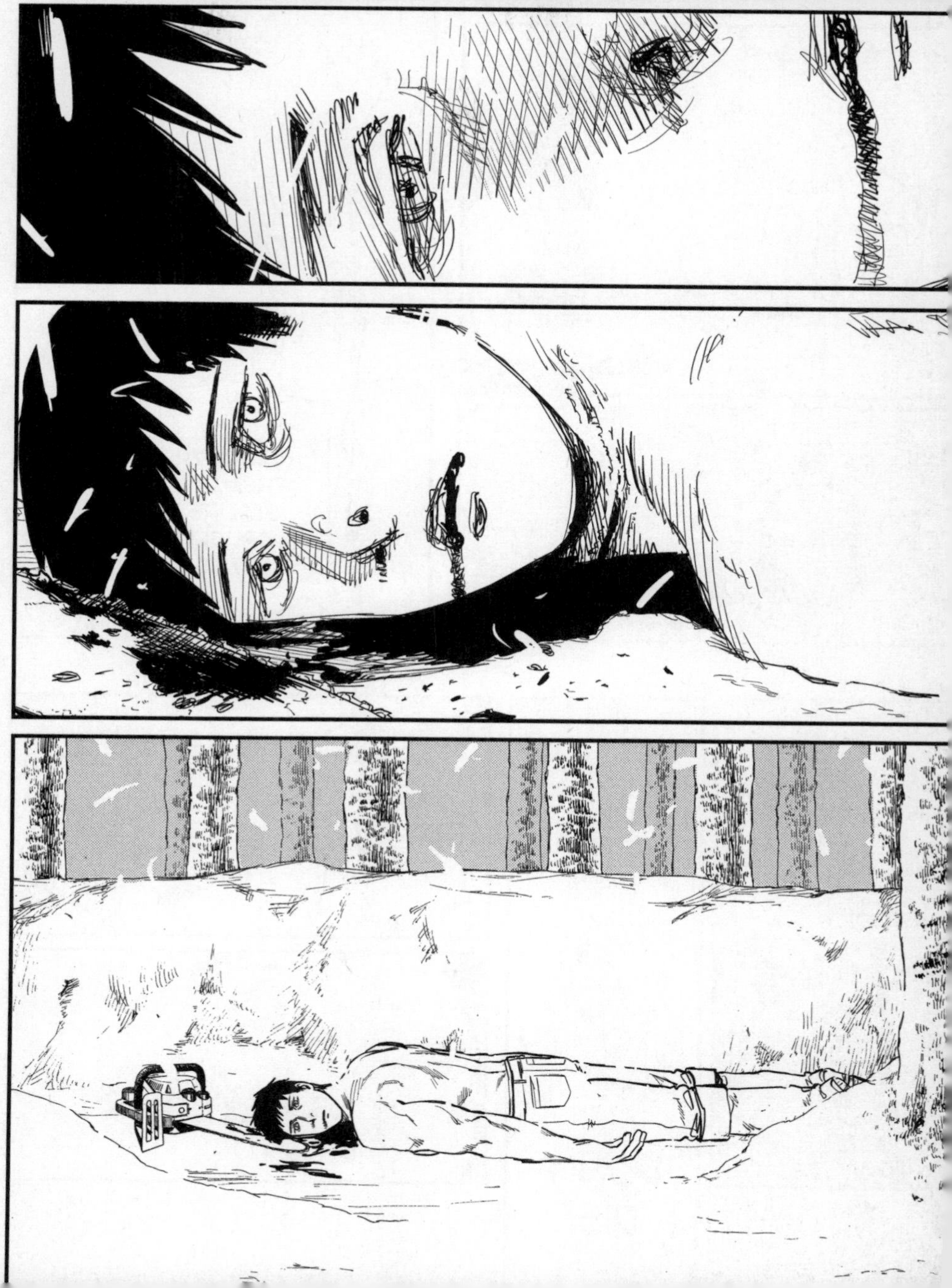

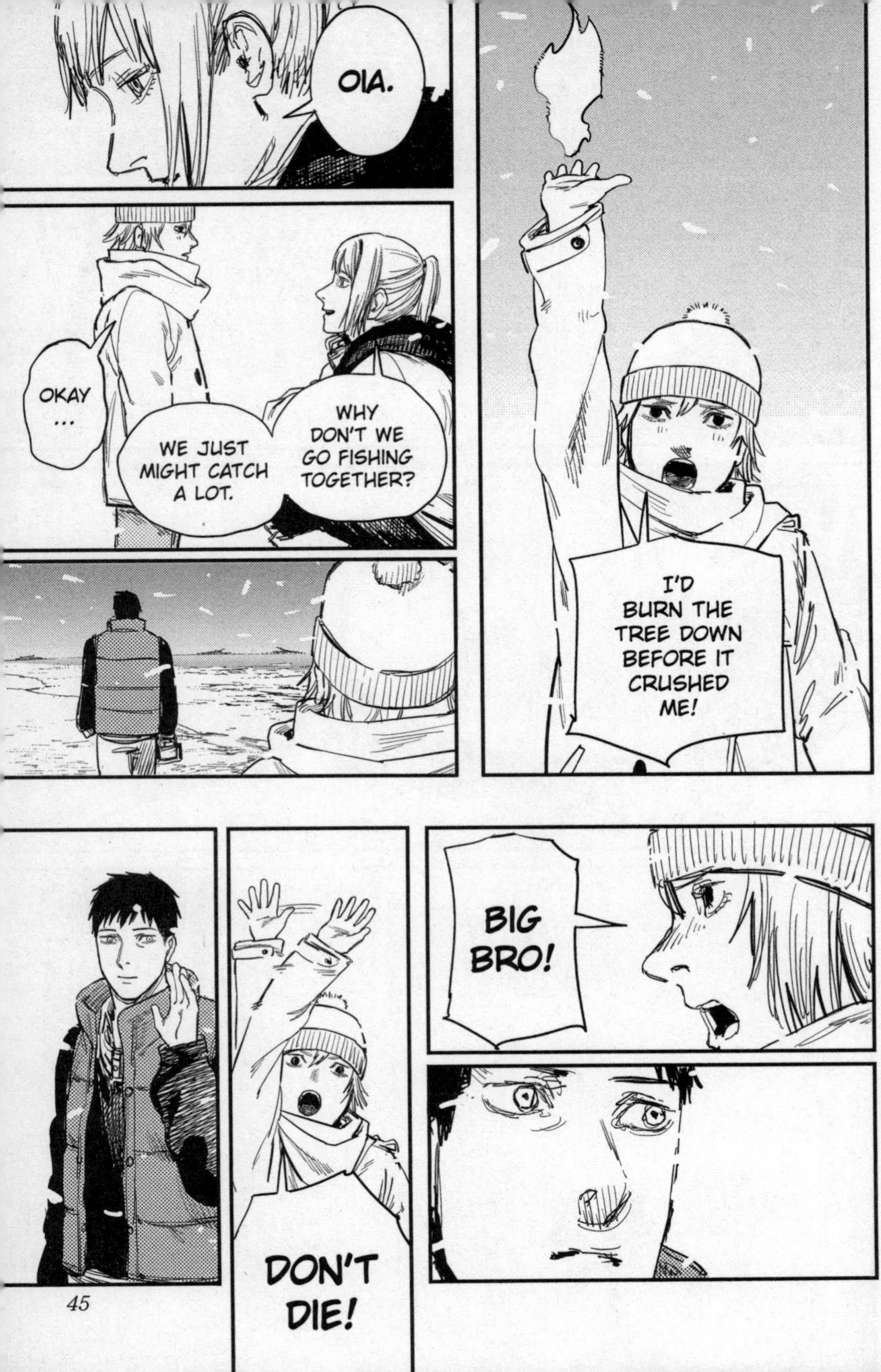
I'D BURN THE TREE DOWN BEFORE IT CRUSHED ME!
OIA.
WHY DON'T WE GO FISHING TOGETHER?
WE JUST MIGHT CATCH A LOT.
OKAY ...
BIG BRO!
DON'T DIE!

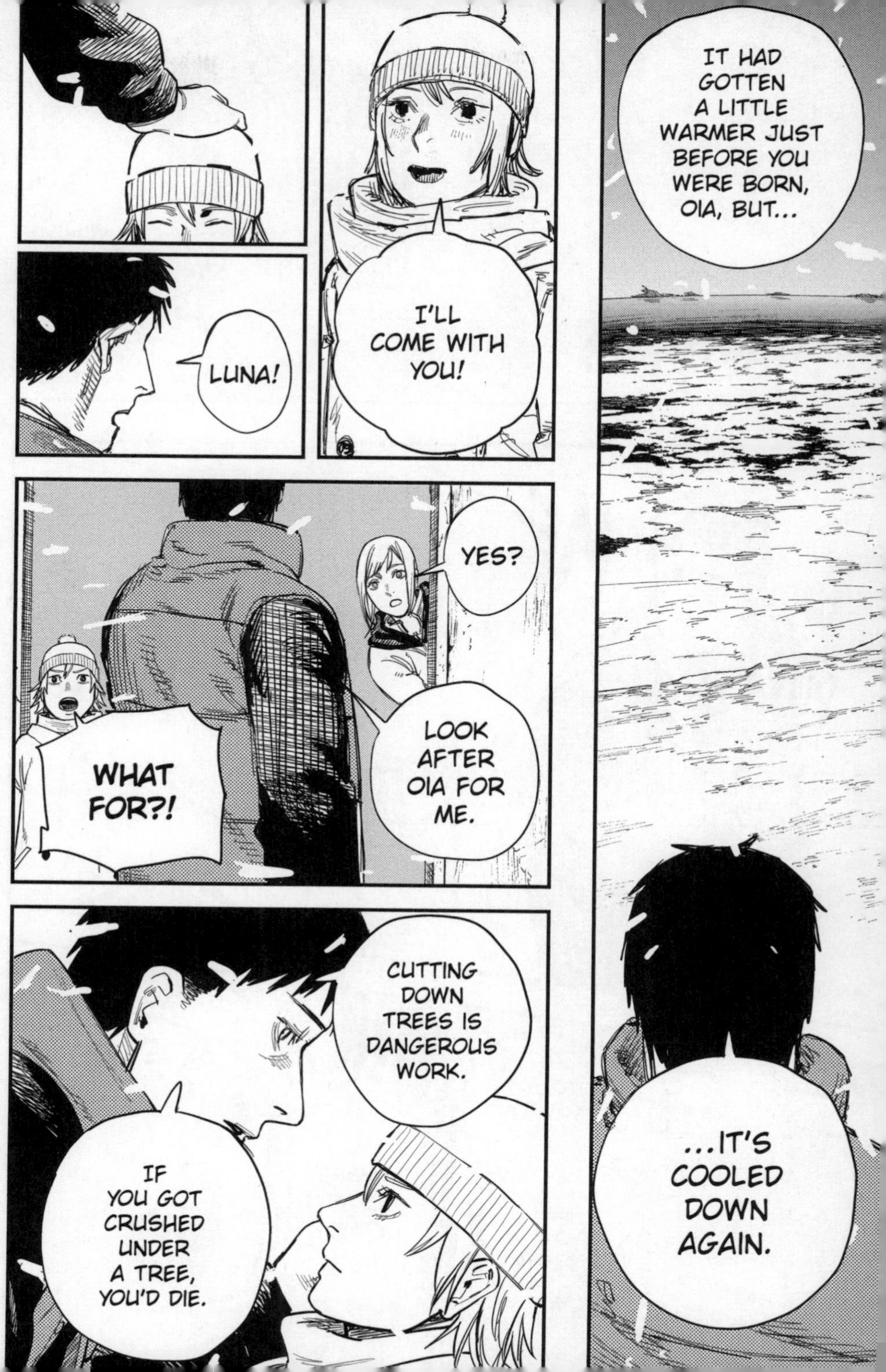
IT HAD GOTTEN A LITTLE WARMER JUST BEFORE YOU WERE BORN, OIA, BUT...
...IT'S COOLED DOWN AGAIN.
I'LL COME WITH YOU!
LUNA!
YES?
LOOK AFTER OIA FOR ME.
WHAT FOR?!
CUTTING DOWN TREES IS DANGEROUS WORK.
IF YOU GOT CRUSHED UNDER A TREE, YOU'D DIE.

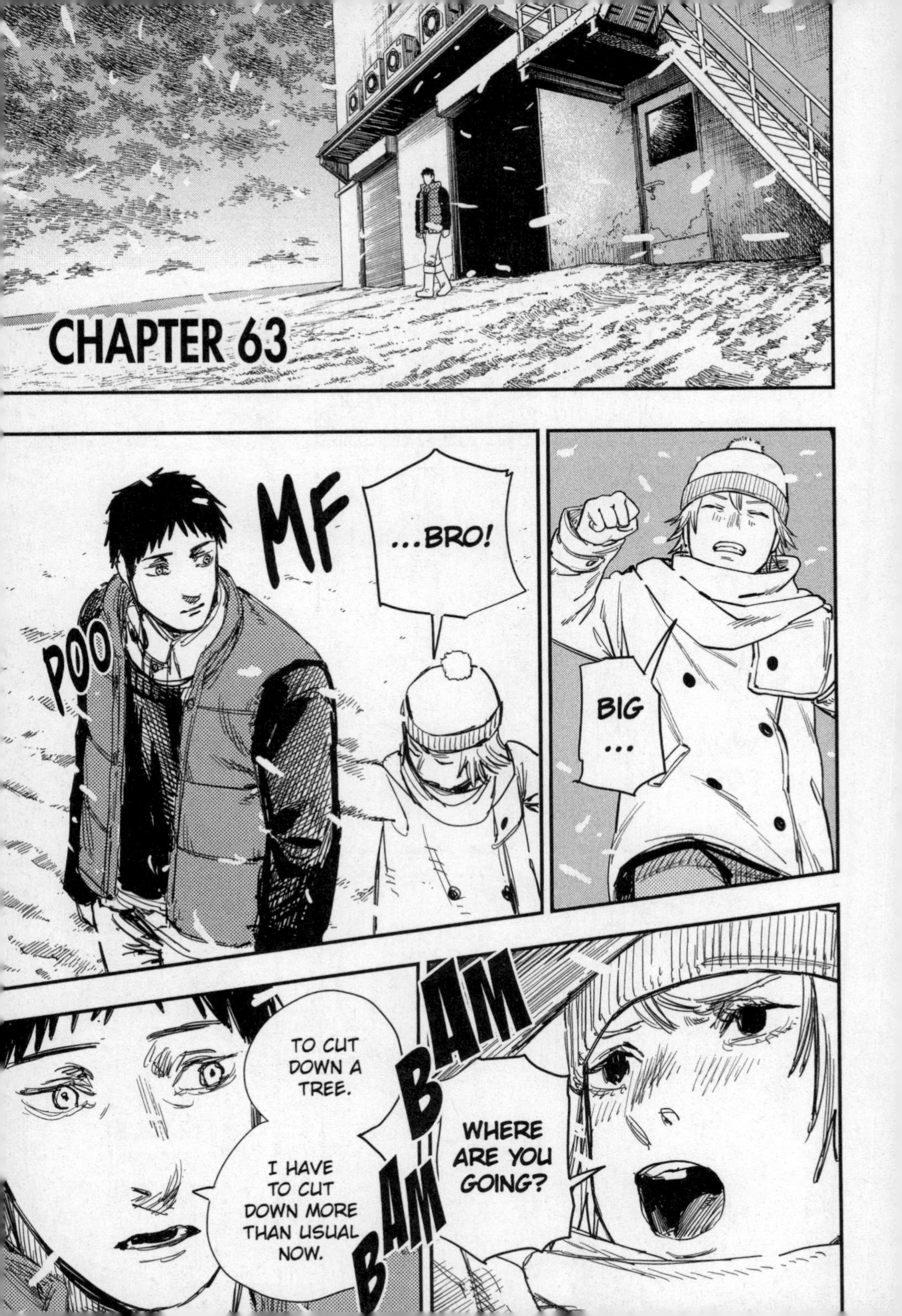
CHAPTER 63
BIG ...
...BRO!
MF
POO
BAM
BAM
WHERE ARE YOU GOING?
TO CUT DOWN A TREE.
I HAVE TO CUT DOWN MORE THAN USUAL NOW.

FIRE PUNCH

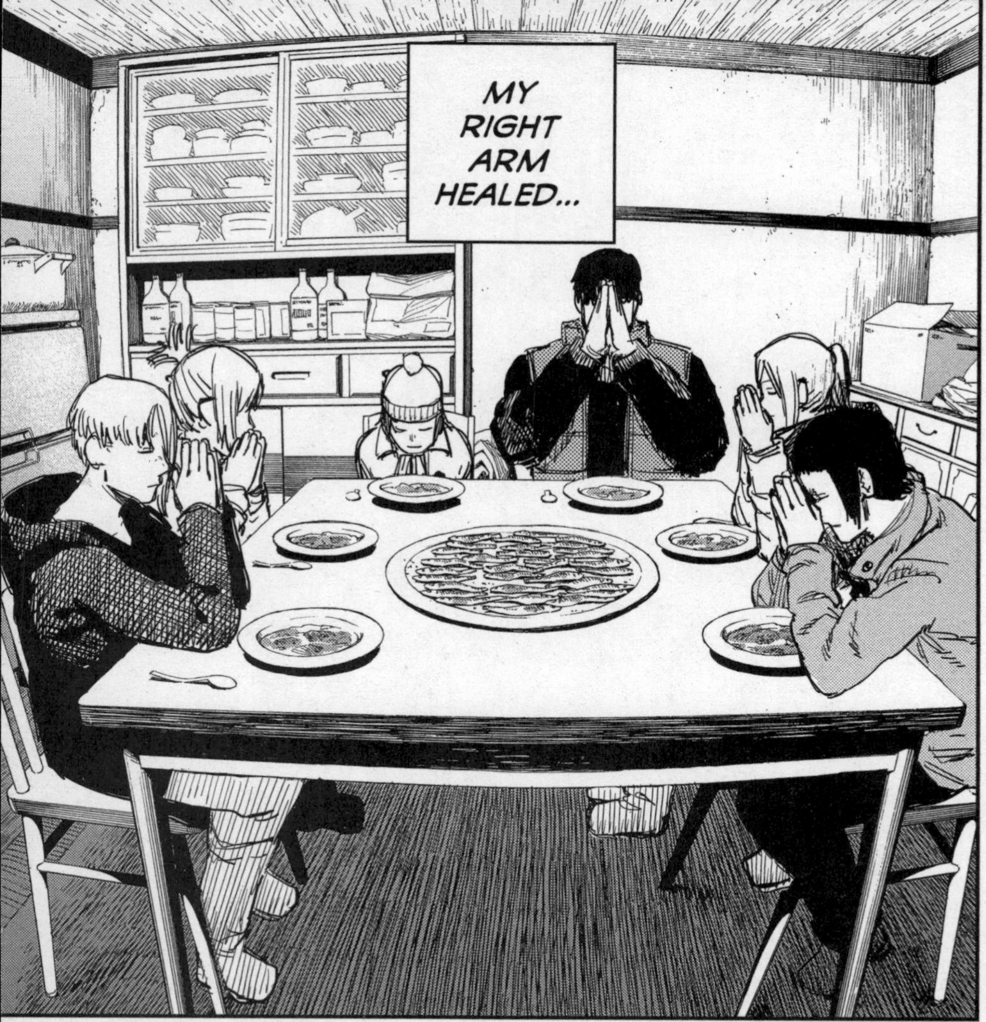
MY RIGHT ARM HEALED...

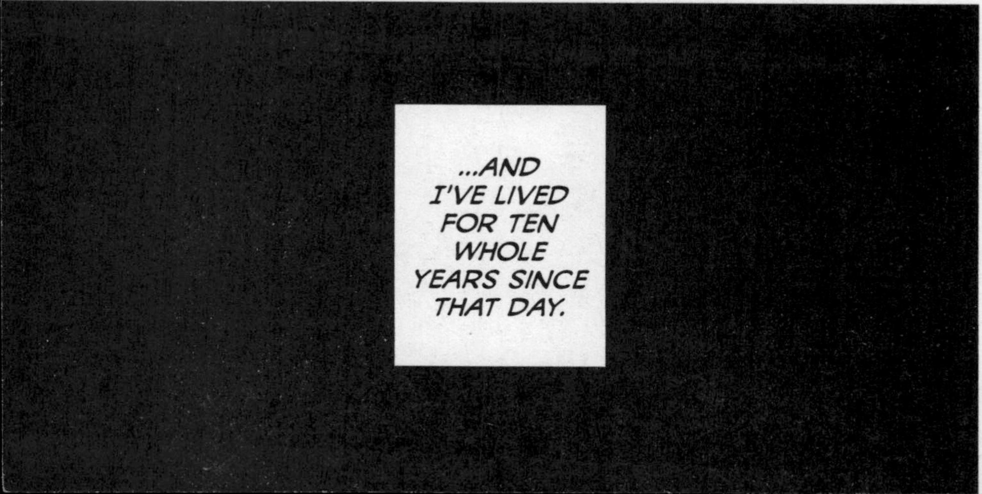
...AND I'VE LIVED FOR TEN WHOLE YEARS SINCE THAT DAY.

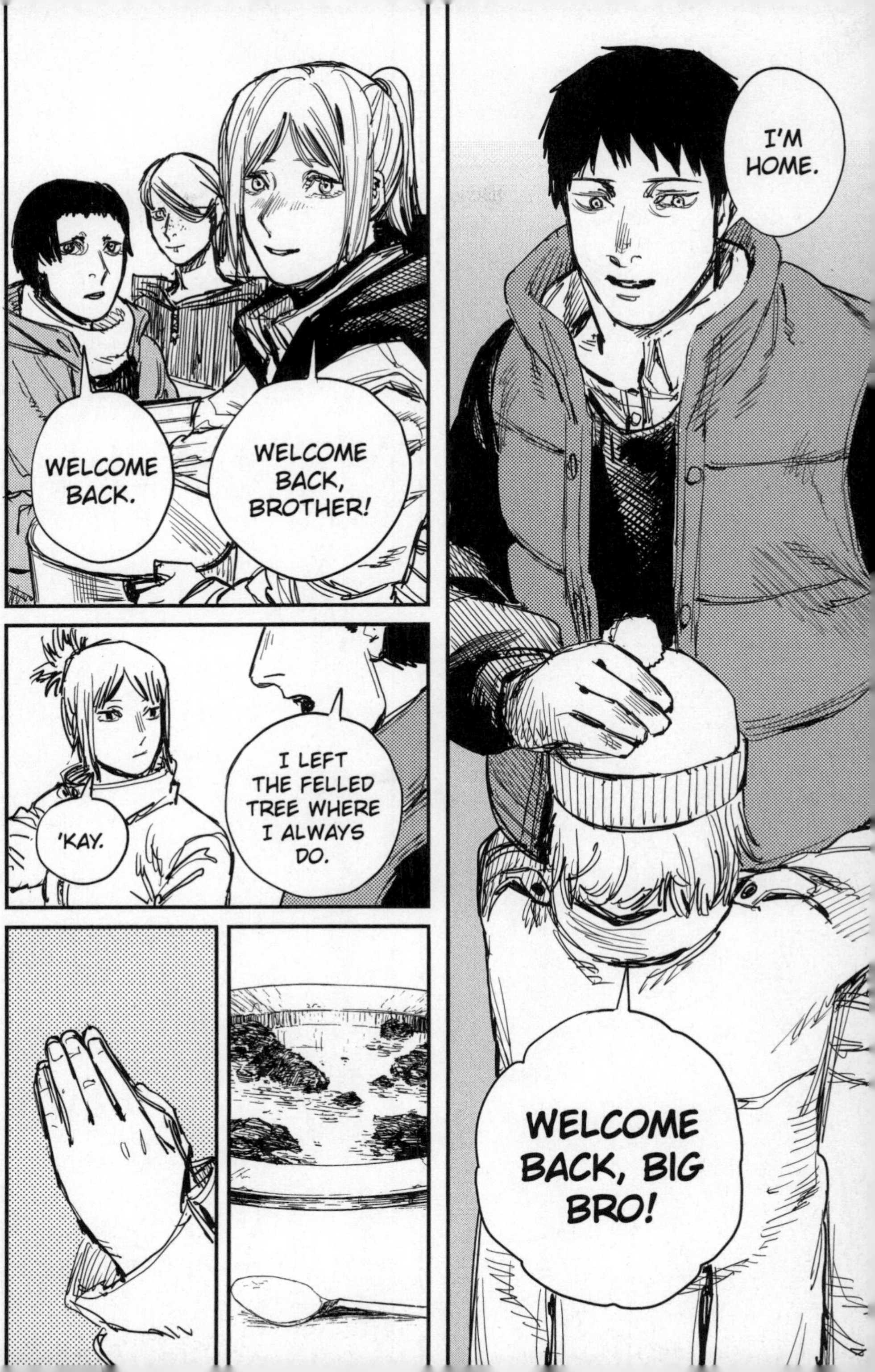
I'M HOME.
WELCOME BACK, BIG BRO!
WELCOME BACK, BROTHER!
WELCOME BACK.
I LEFT THE FELLED TREE WHERE I ALWAYS DO.
'KAY.

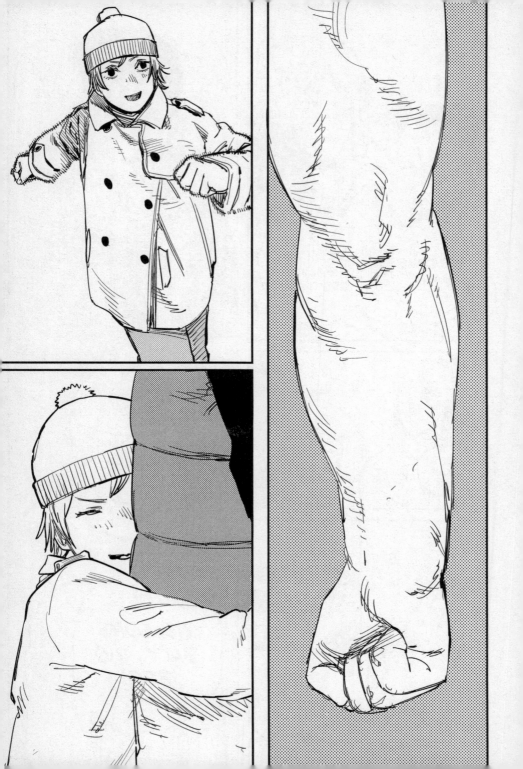

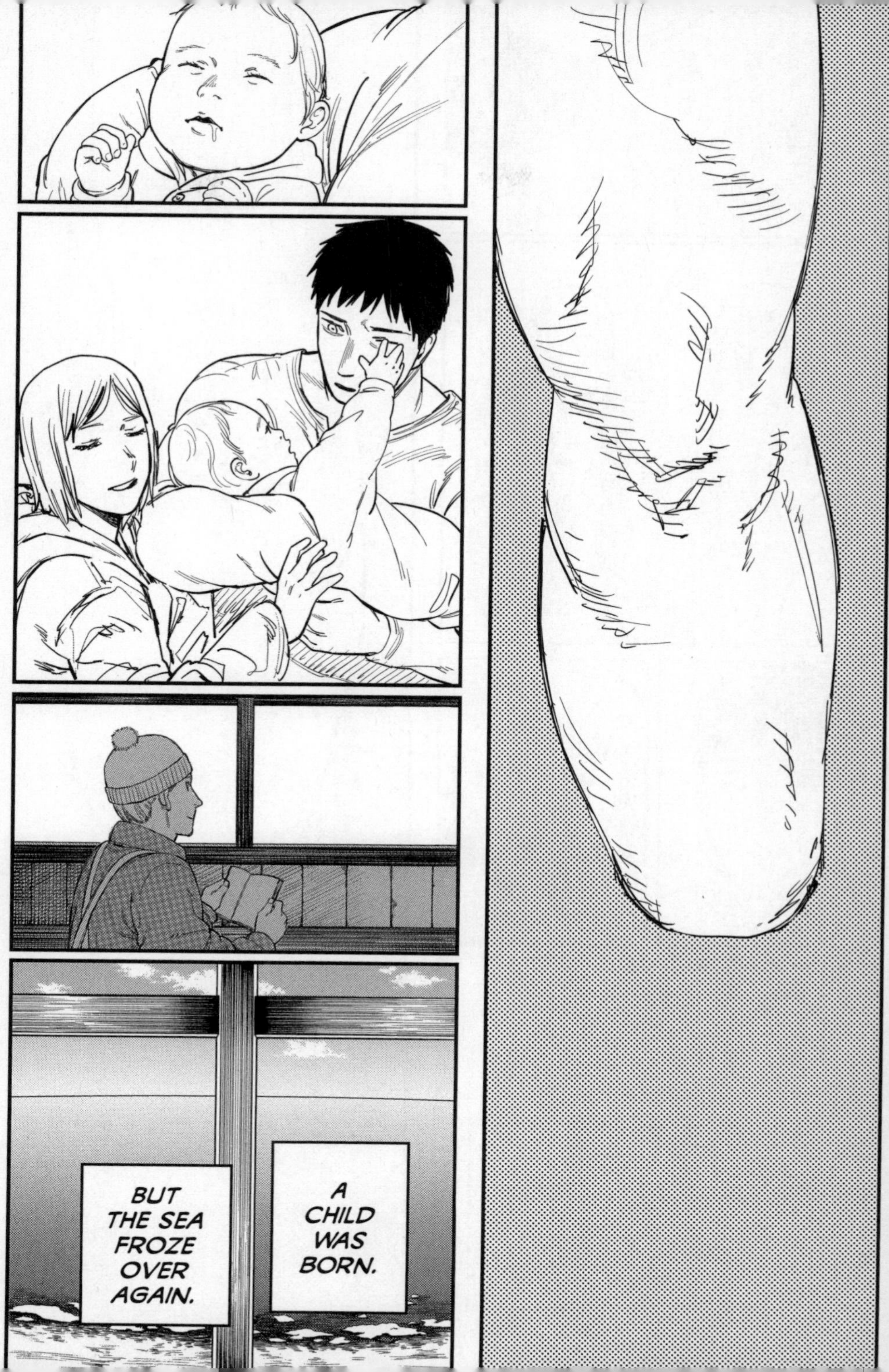
A CHILD WAS BORN.
BUT THE SEA FROZE OVER AGAIN.

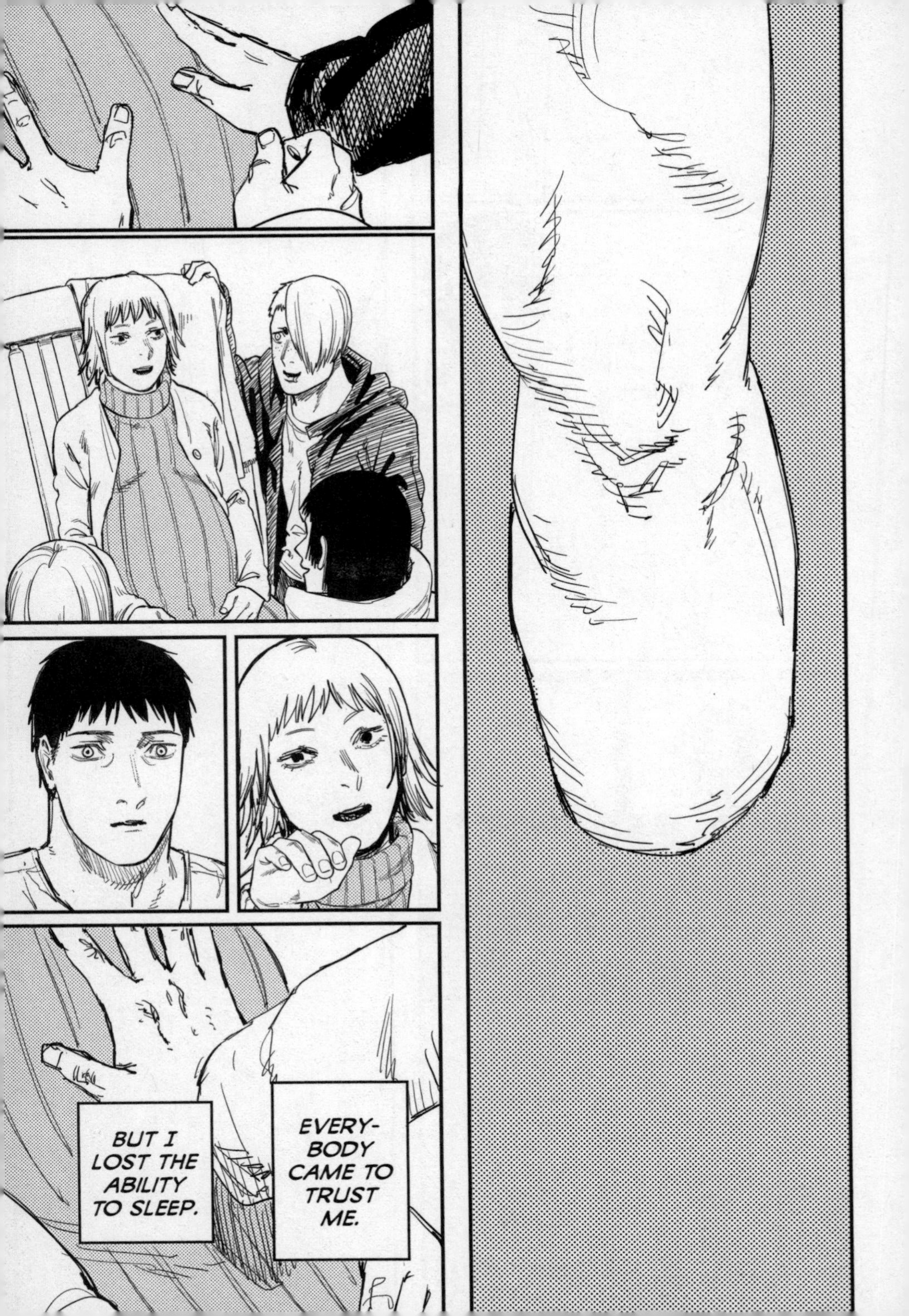
EVERY-BODY CAME TO TRUST ME.
BUT I LOST THE ABILITY TO SLEEP.

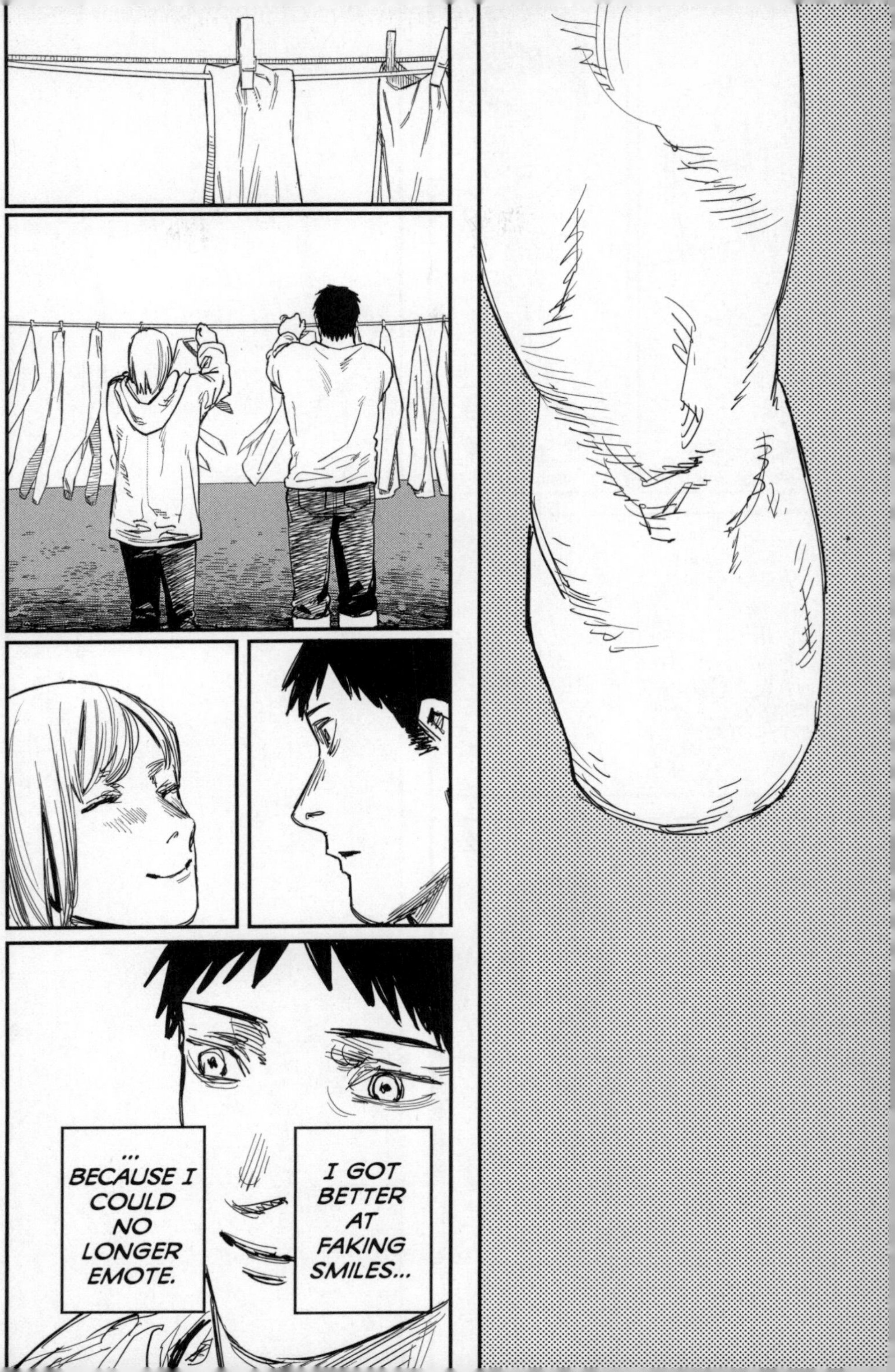
I GOT BETTER AT FAKING SMILES...
...BECAUSE I COULD NO LONGER EMOTE.

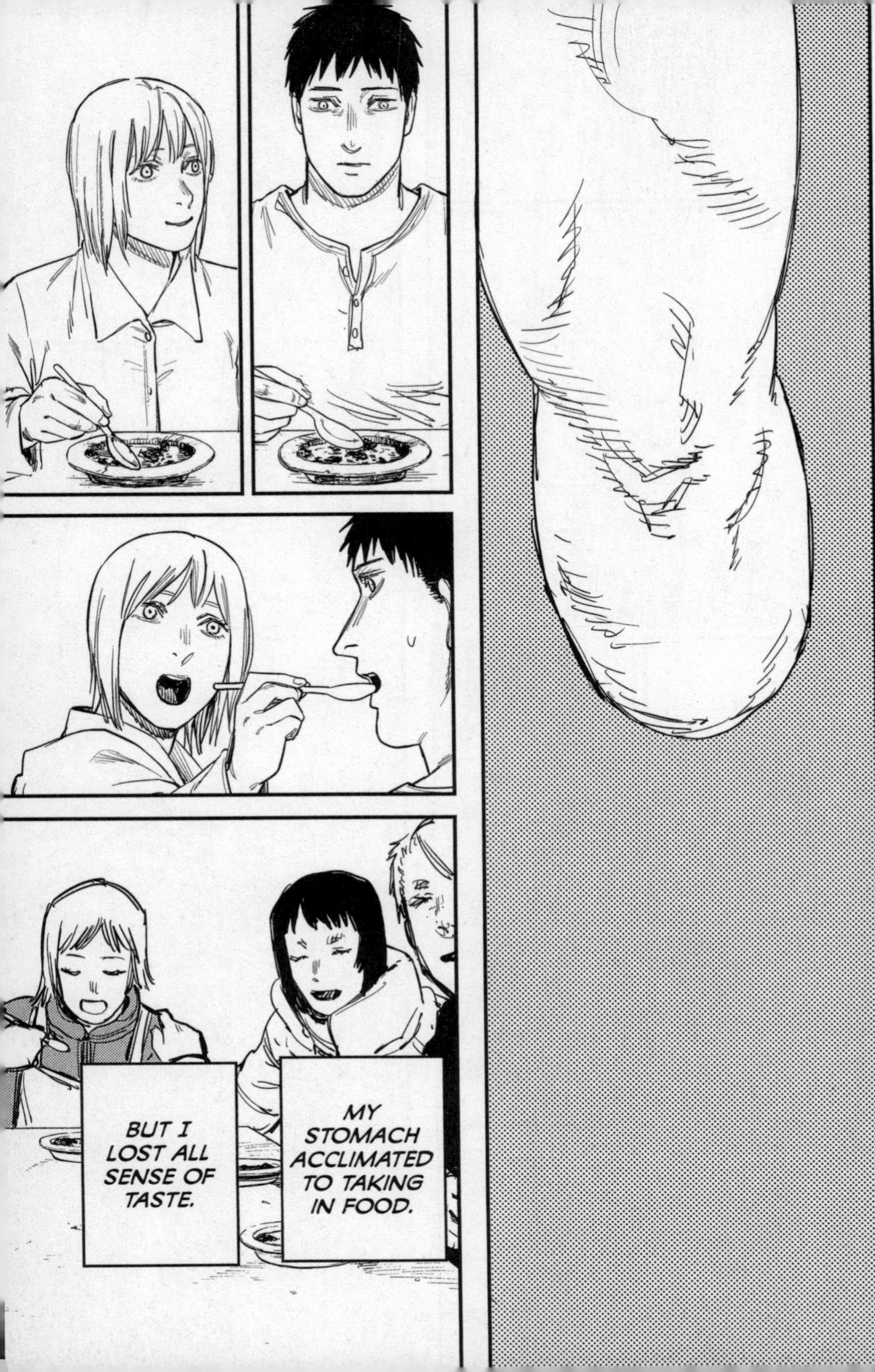
MY STOMACH ACCLIMATED TO TAKING IN FOOD.
BUT I LOST ALL SENSE OF TASTE.

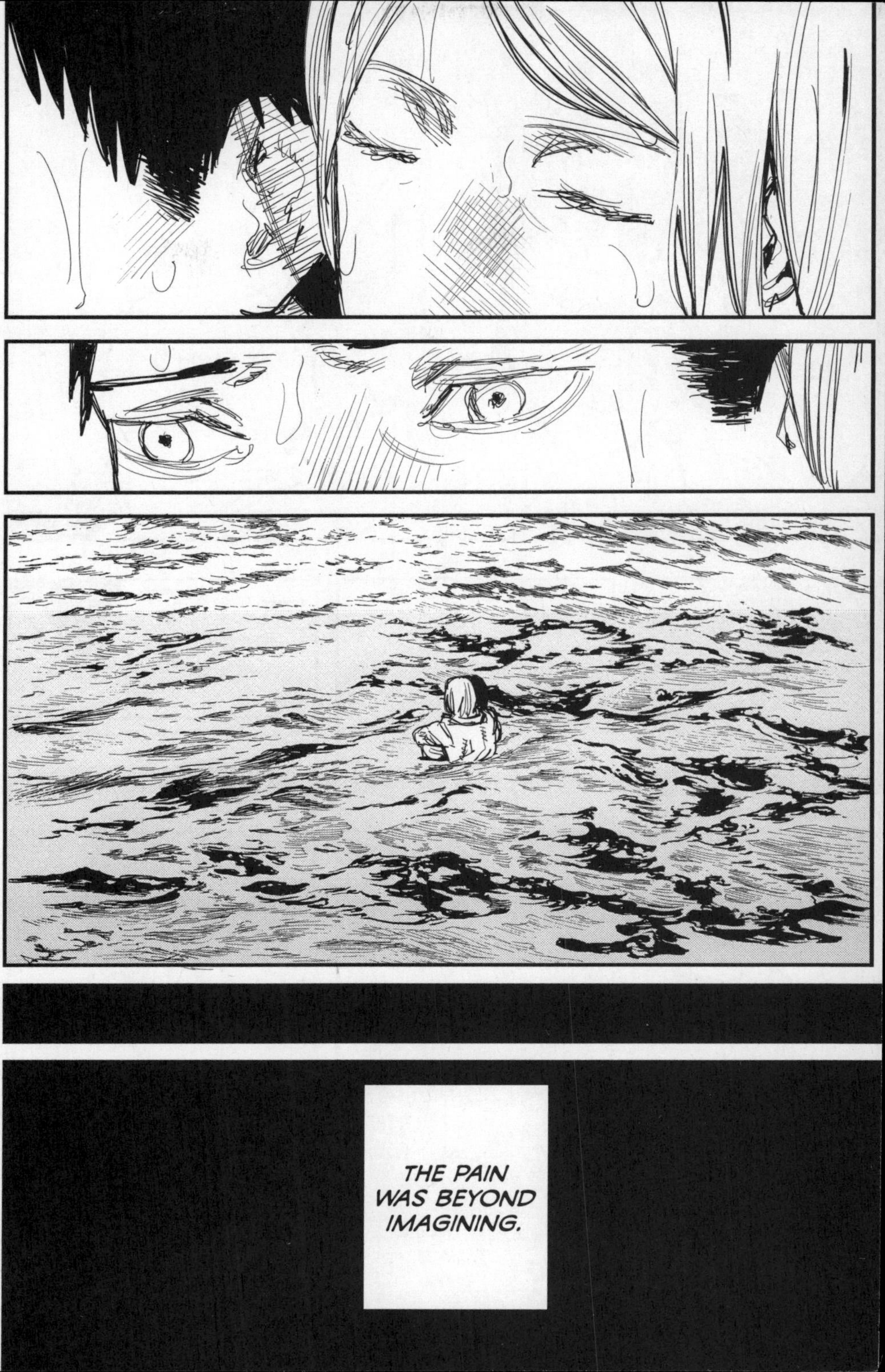
THE PAIN WAS BEYOND IMAGINING.

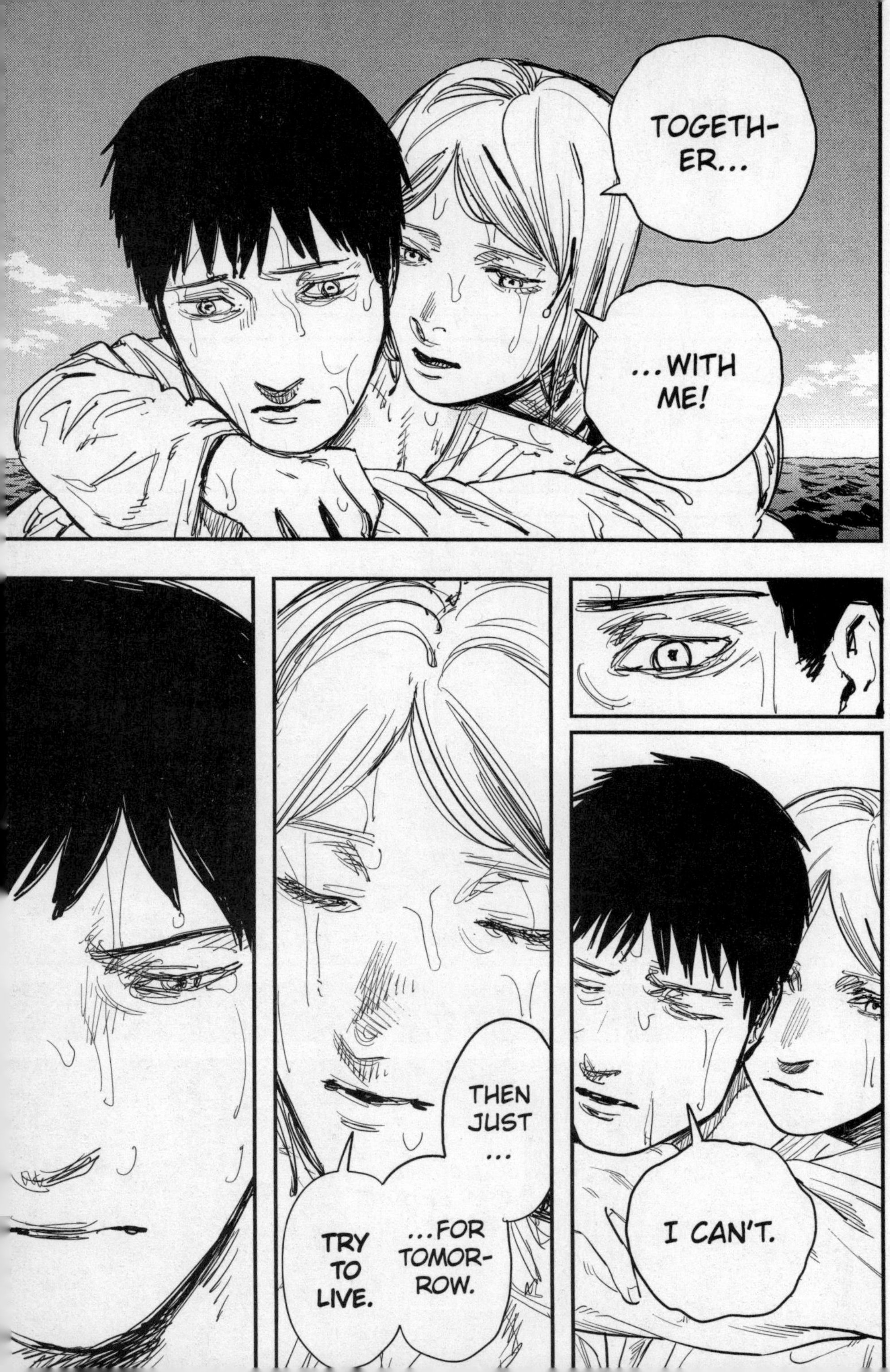
TOGETH-
ER...
...WITH
ME!
I CAN'T.
THEN
JUST
...
...FOR
TOMOR-
ROW.
TRY
TO
LIVE.

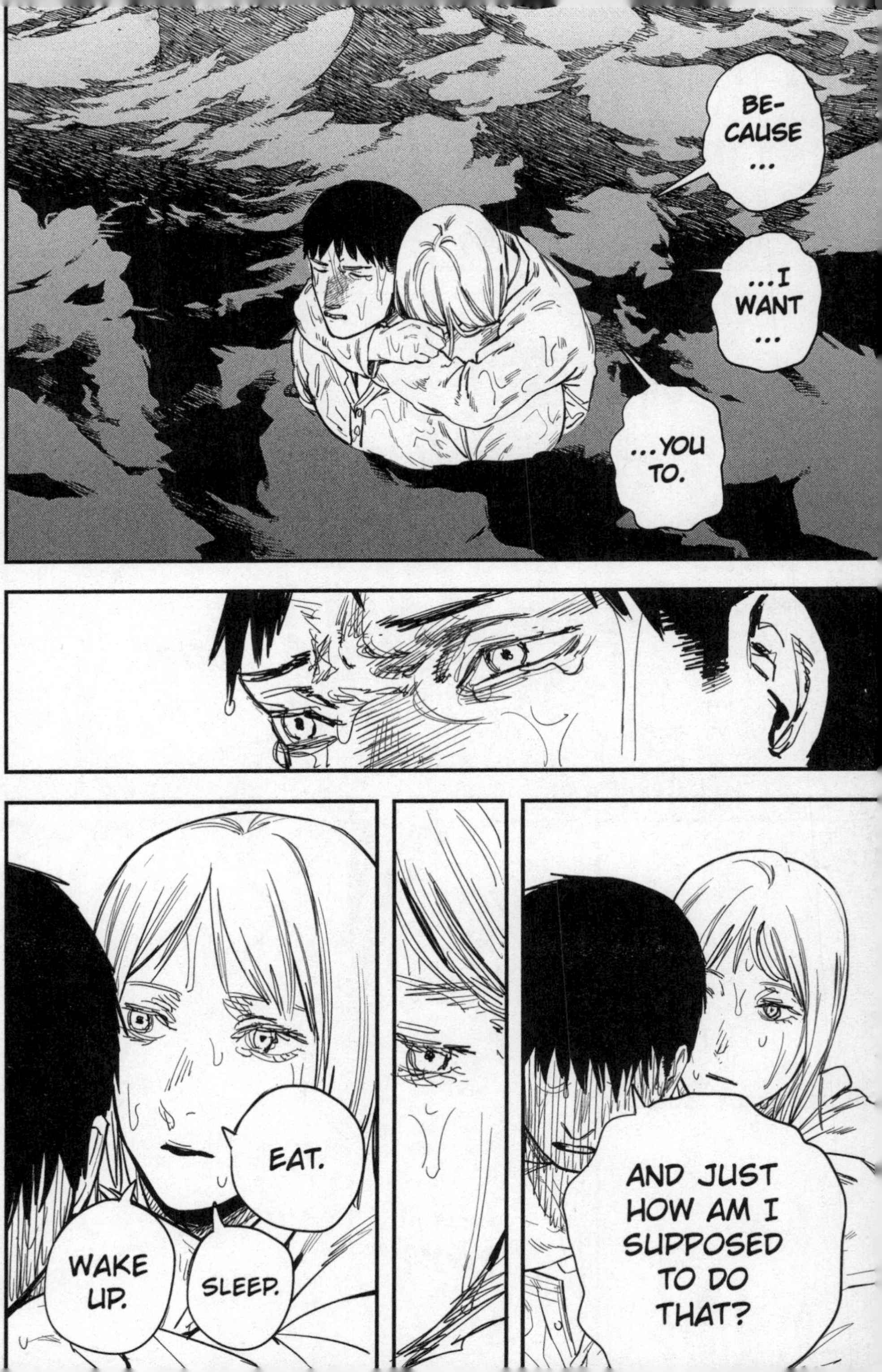
BE-CAUSE...
...I WANT...
...YOU TO.
AND JUST HOW AM I SUPPOSED TO DO THAT?
EAT.
SLEEP.
WAKE UP.

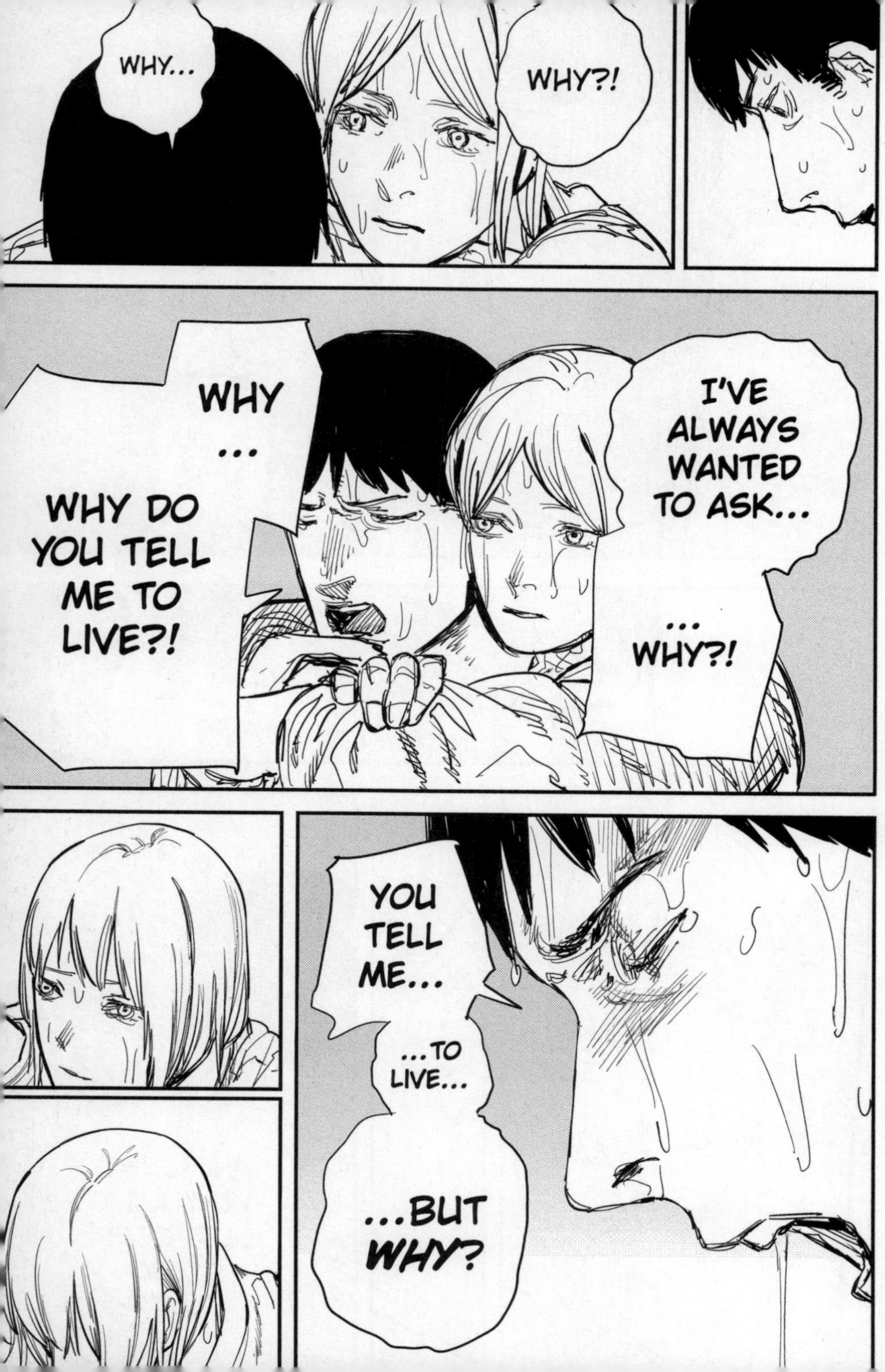
WHY?!
WHY...
I'VE ALWAYS WANTED TO ASK...
... WHY?!
WHY ...
WHY DO YOU TELL ME TO LIVE?!
YOU TELL ME...
...TO LIVE...
...BUT WHY?

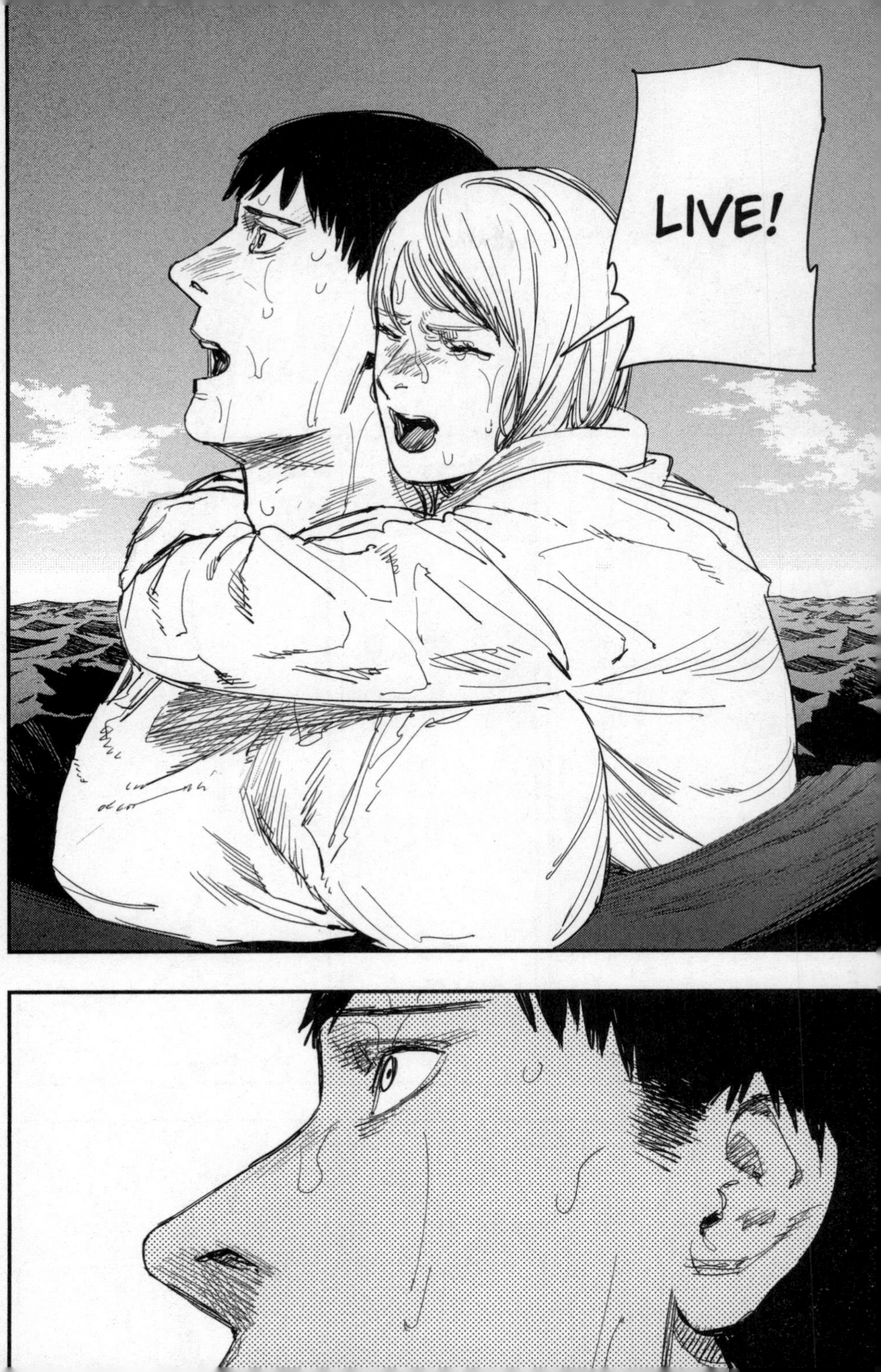
LIVE!

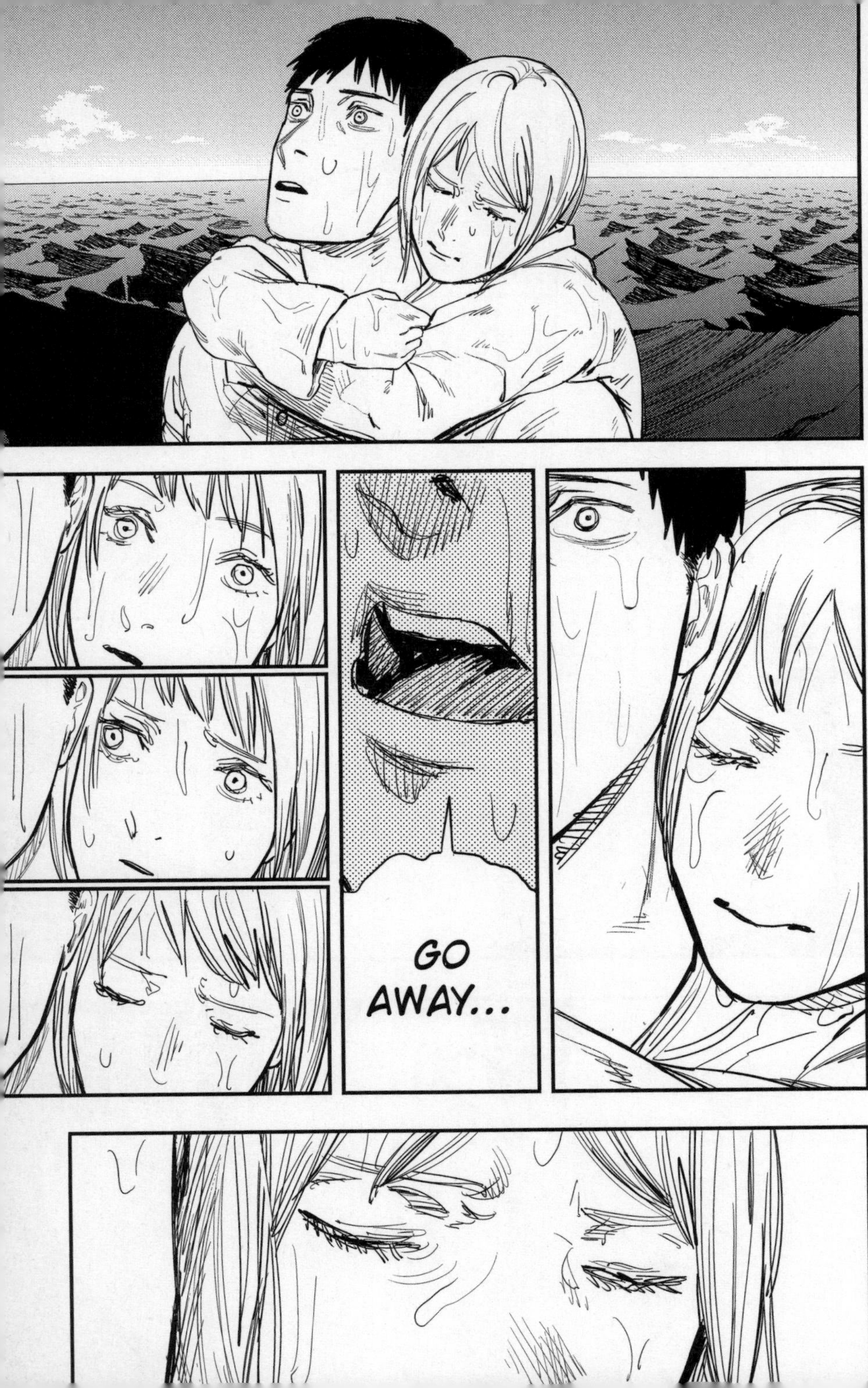
GO AWAY...

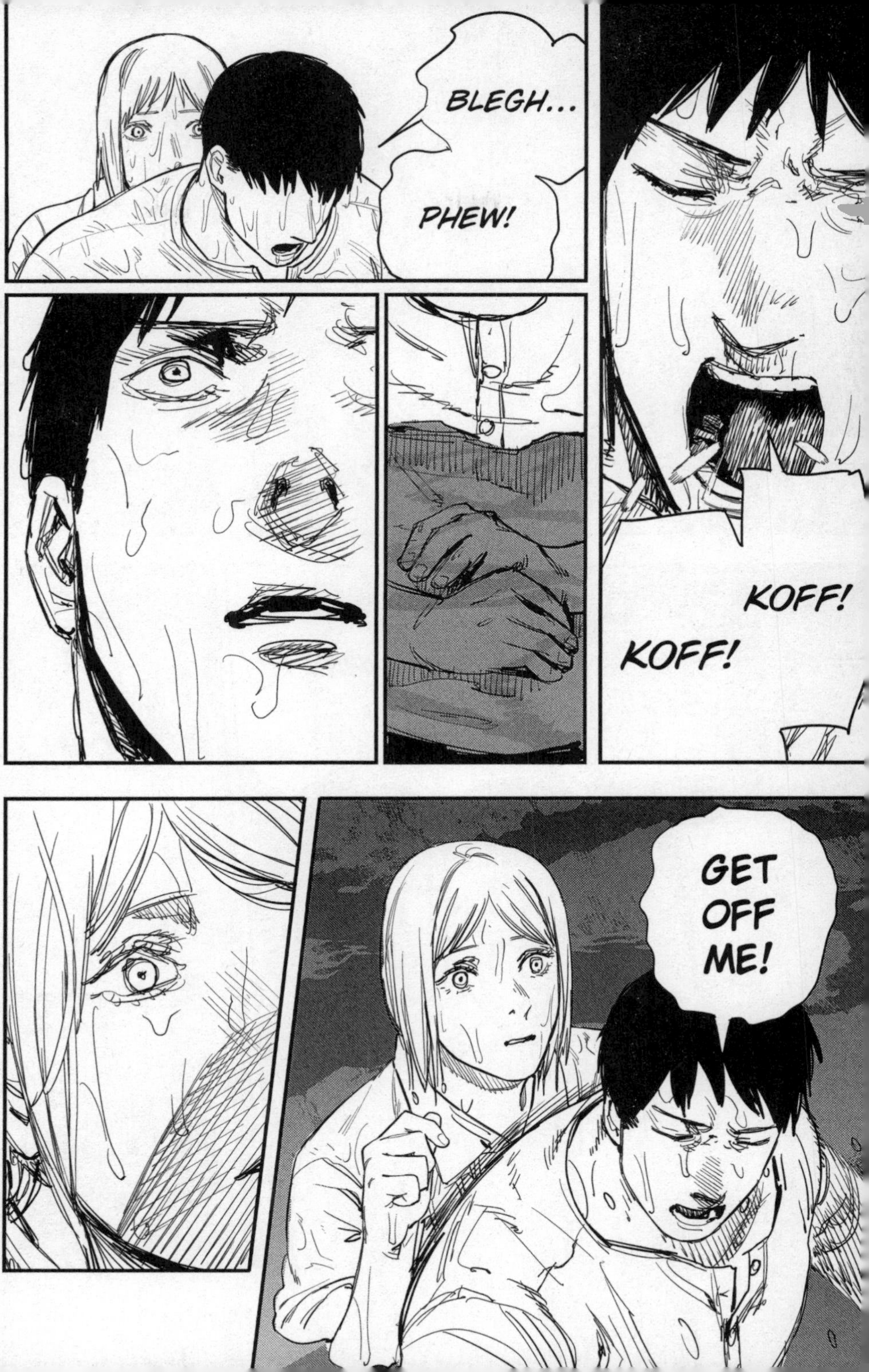
KOFF!
KOFF!
BLEGH...
PHEW!
GET OFF ME!

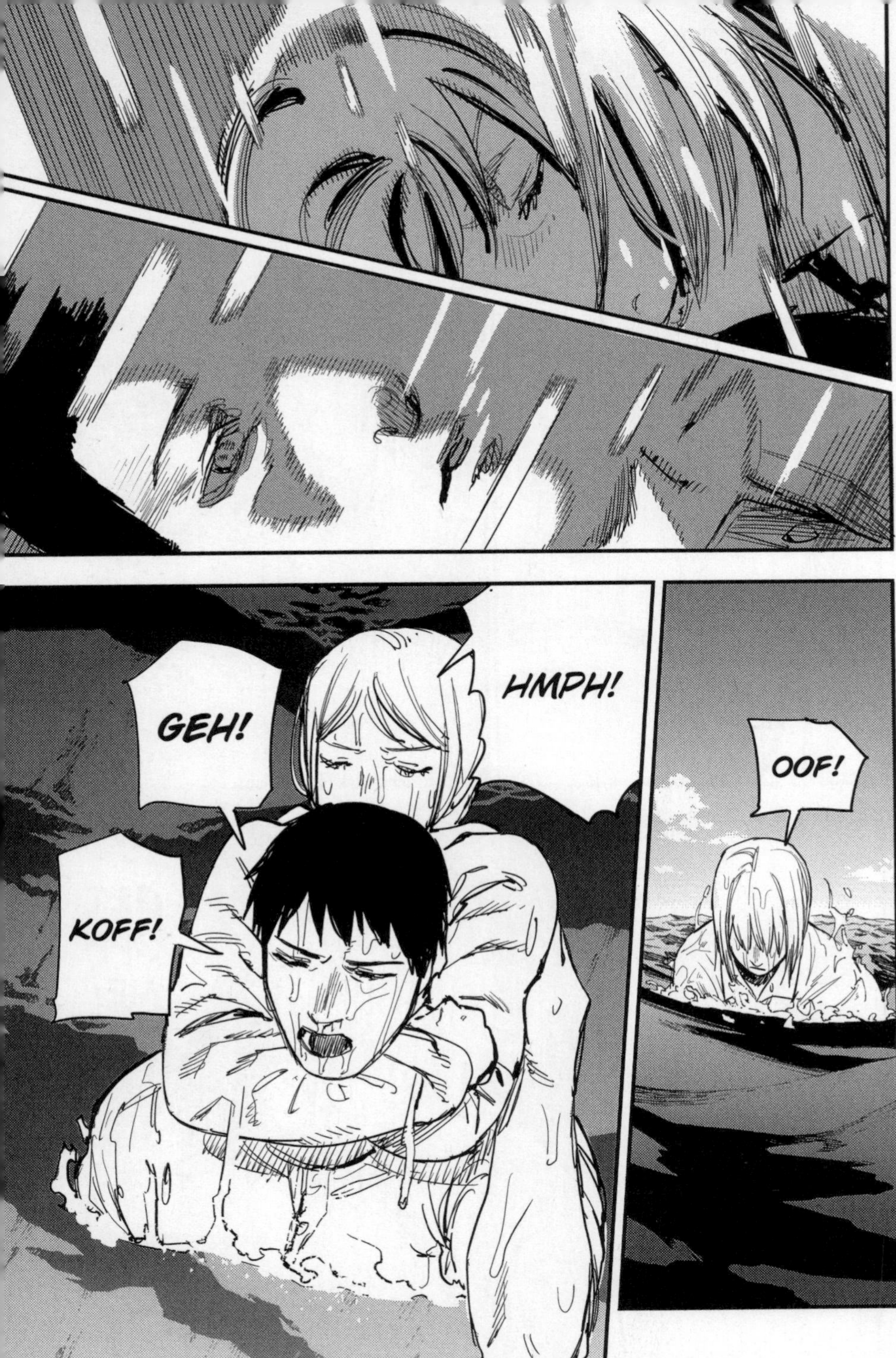
OOF!
HMPH!
GEH!
KOFF!

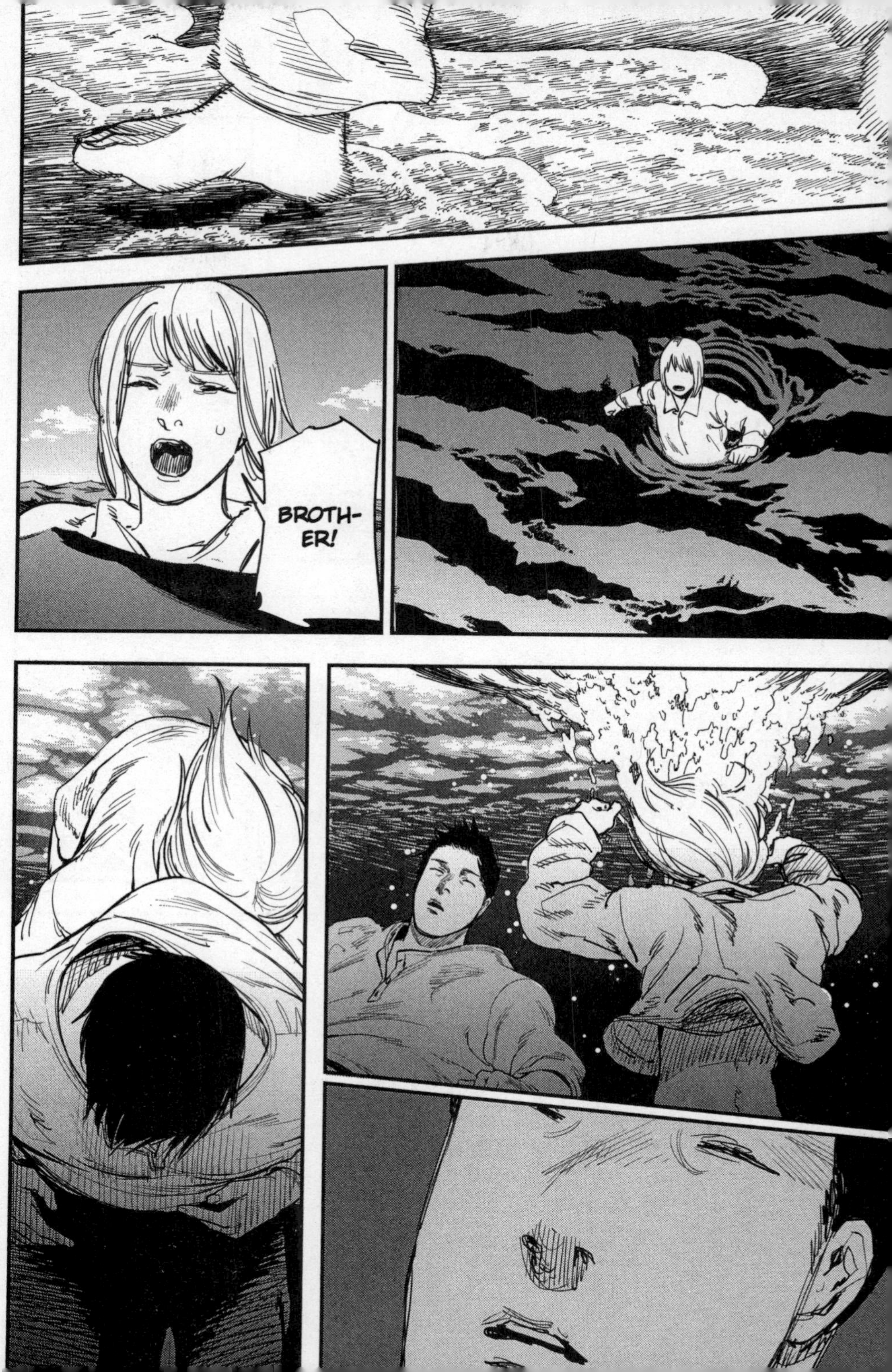
BROTHER-
ER!

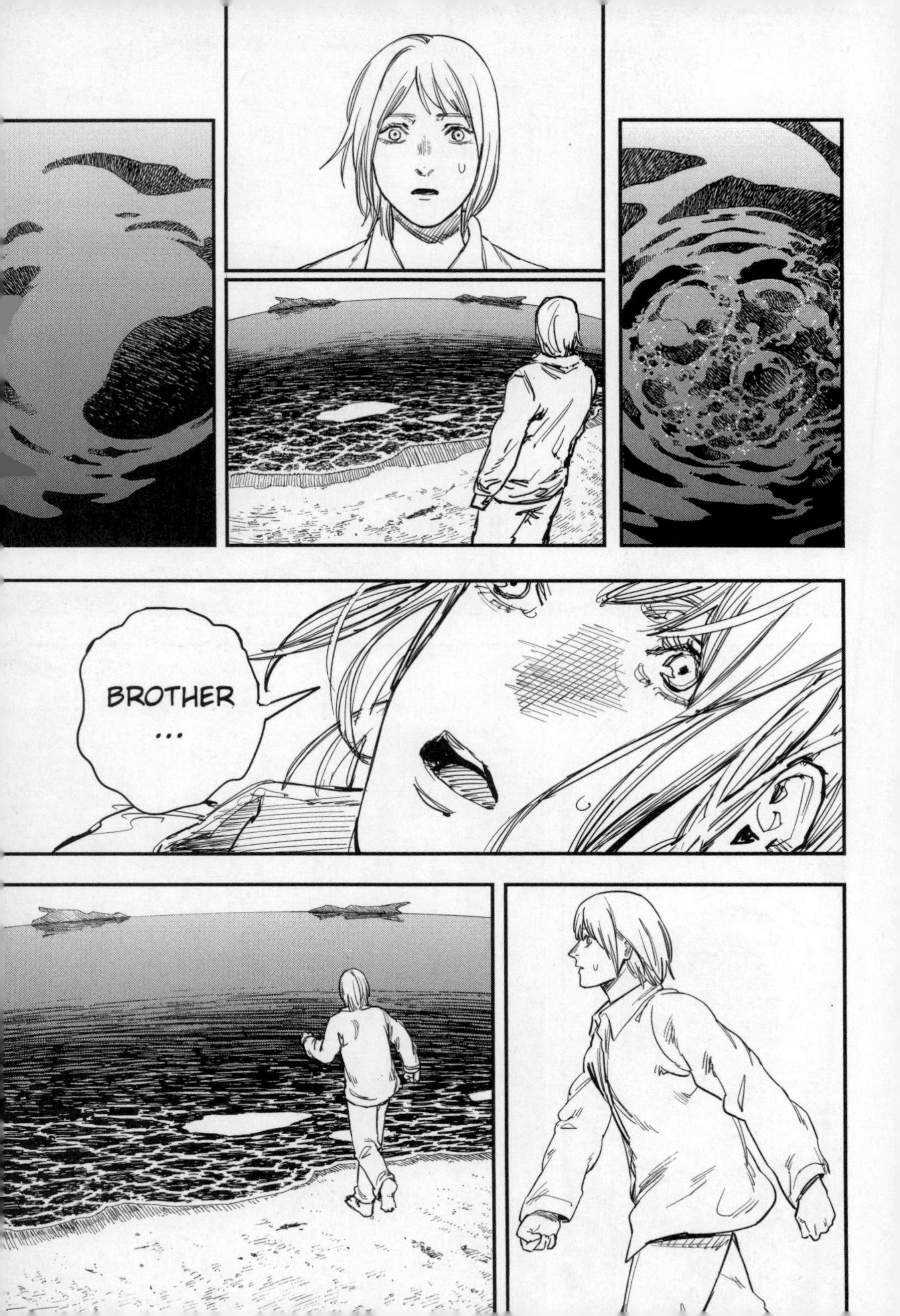
BROTHER
...

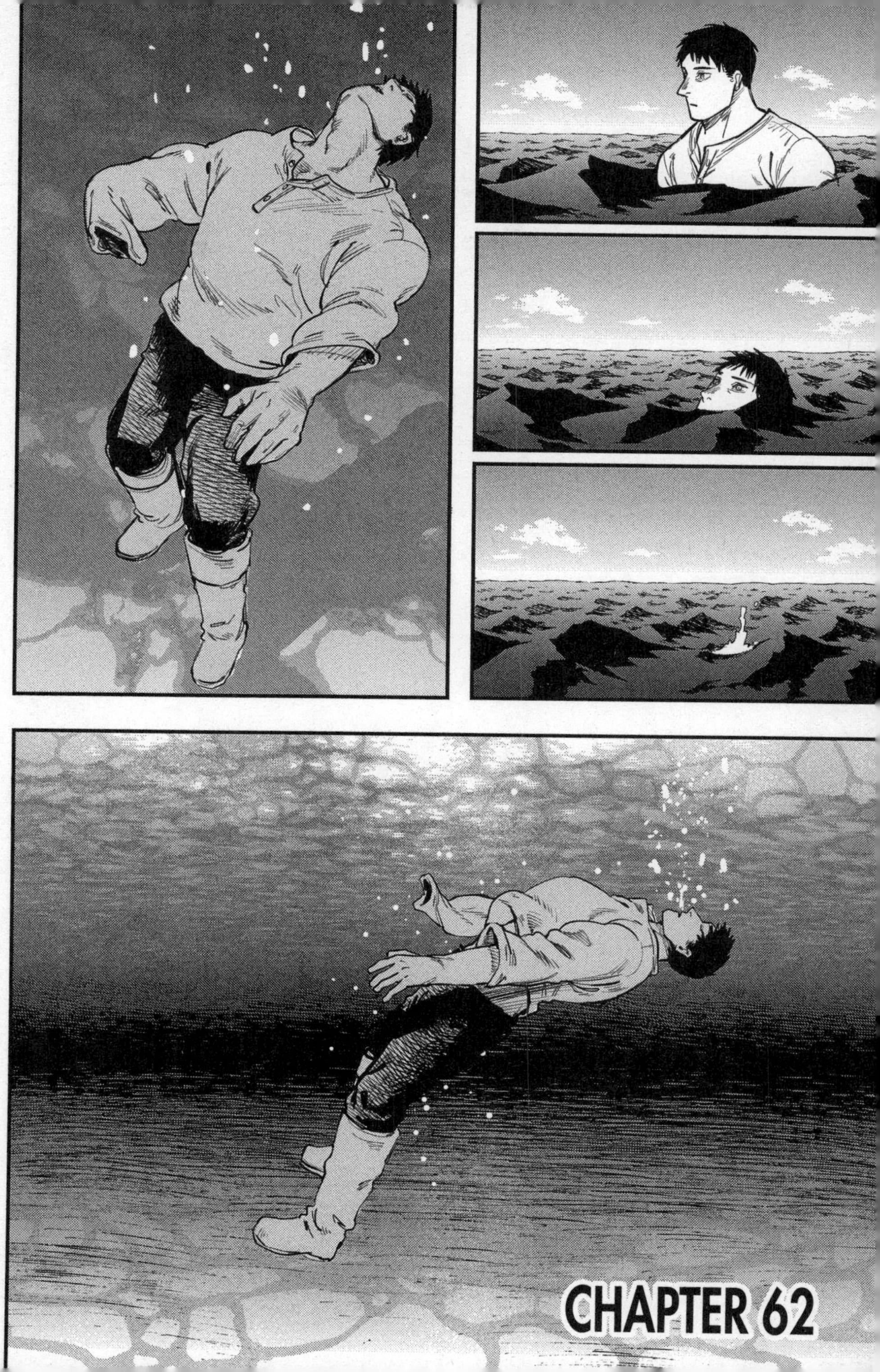
CHAPTER 62

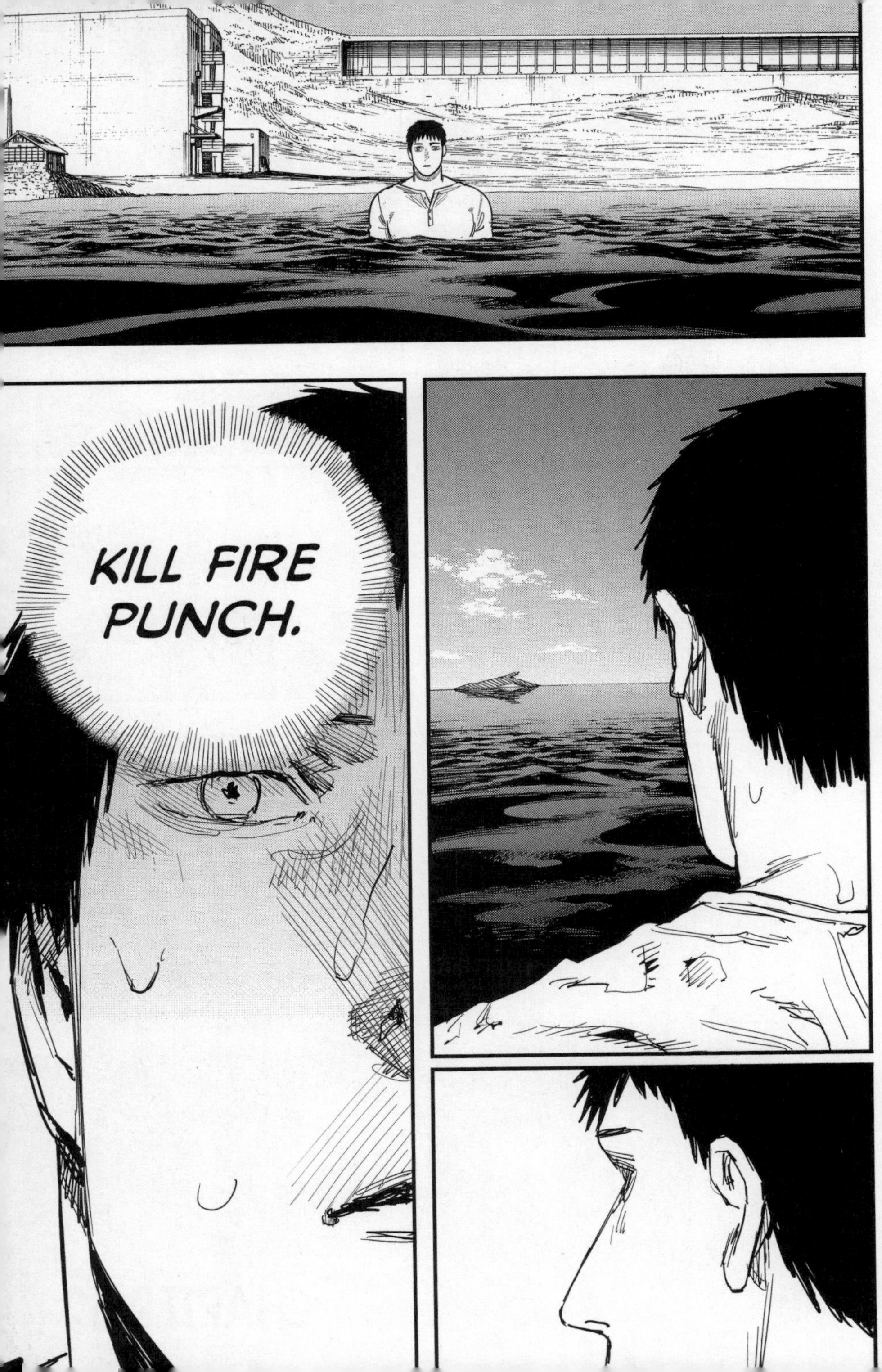
KILL FIRE PUNCH.

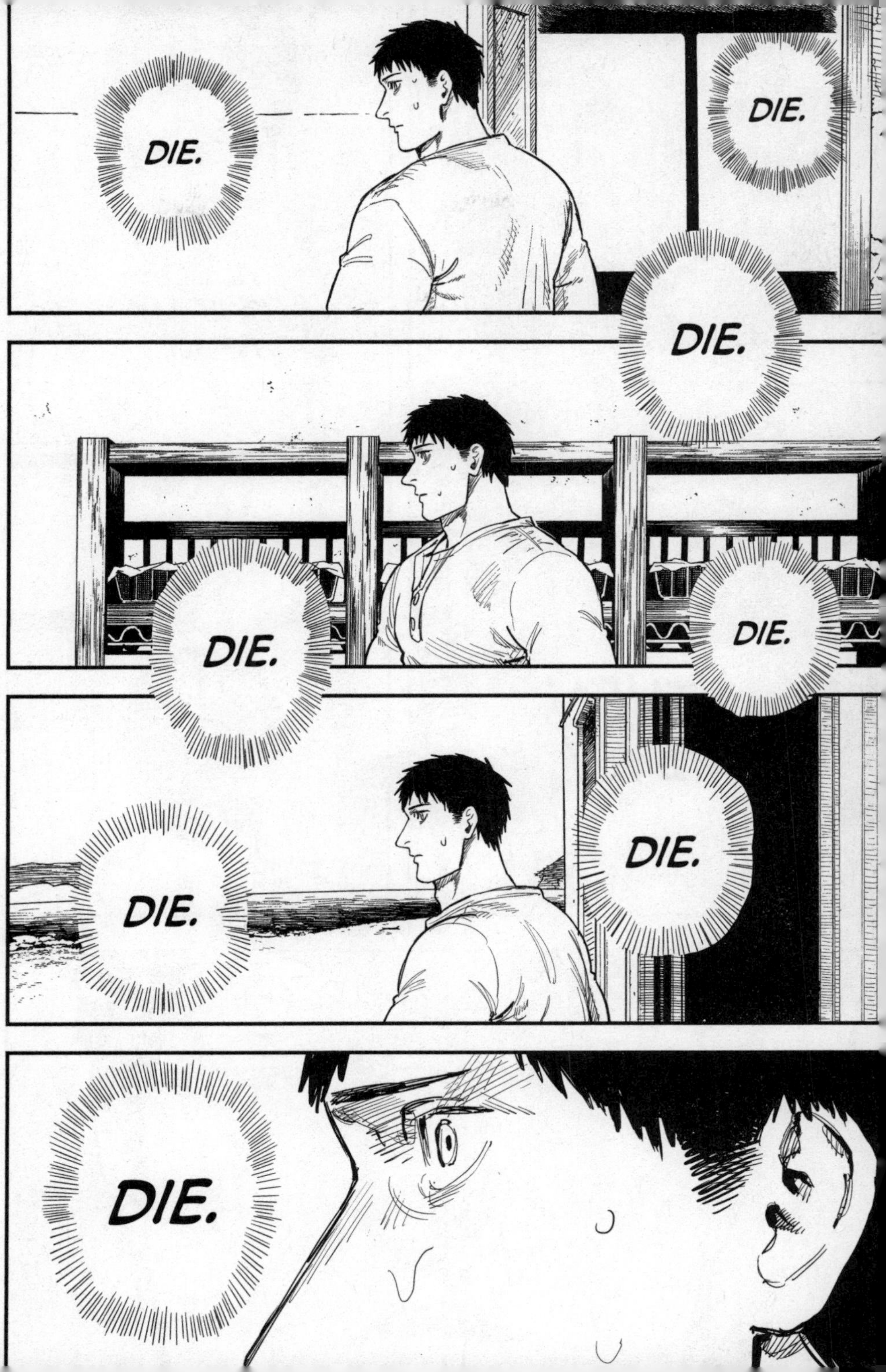
DIE.
DIE.
DIE.
DIE.
DIE.
DIE.
DIE.
DIE.
DIE.

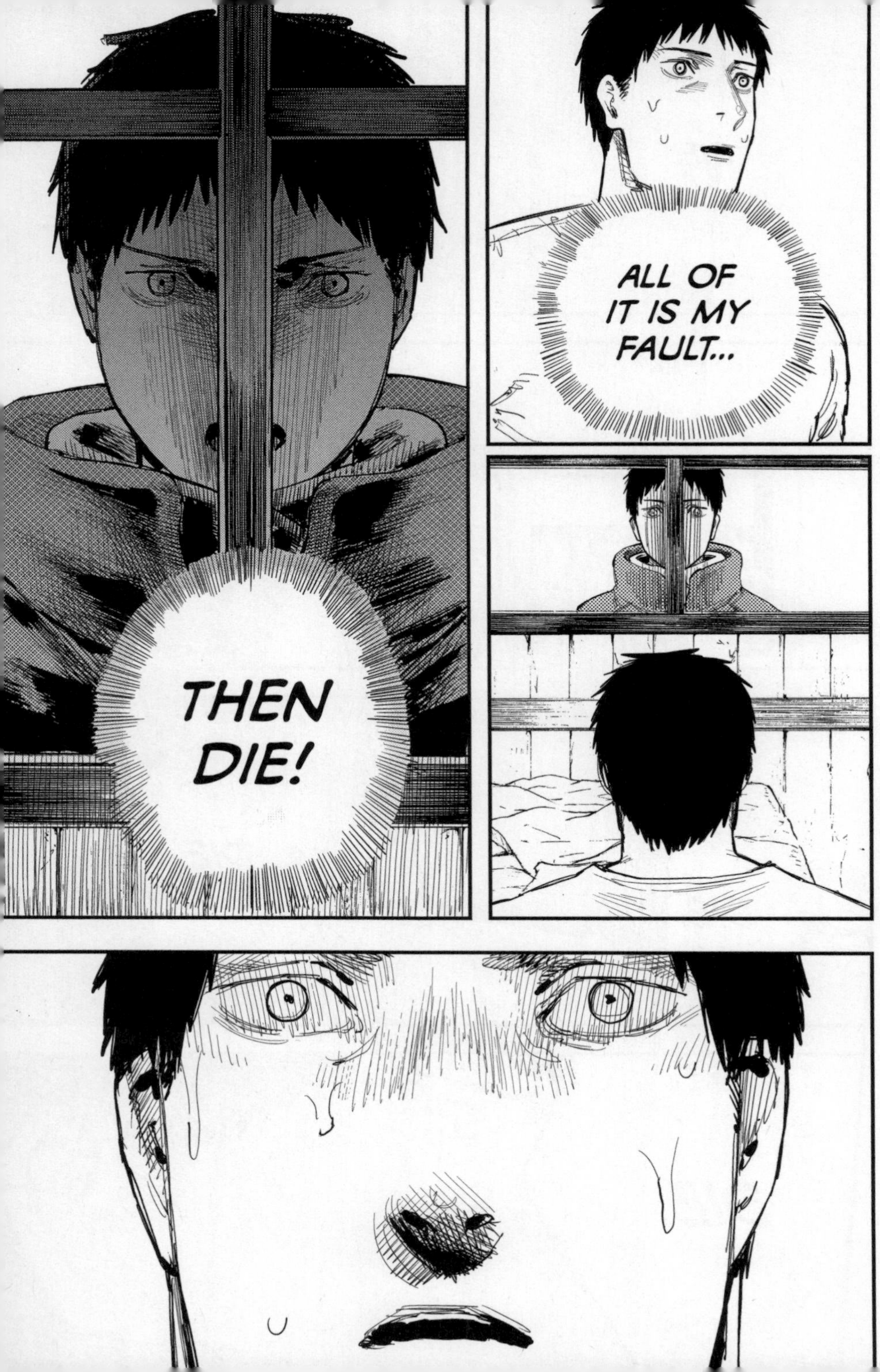
ALL OF IT IS MY FAULT...
THEN DIE!

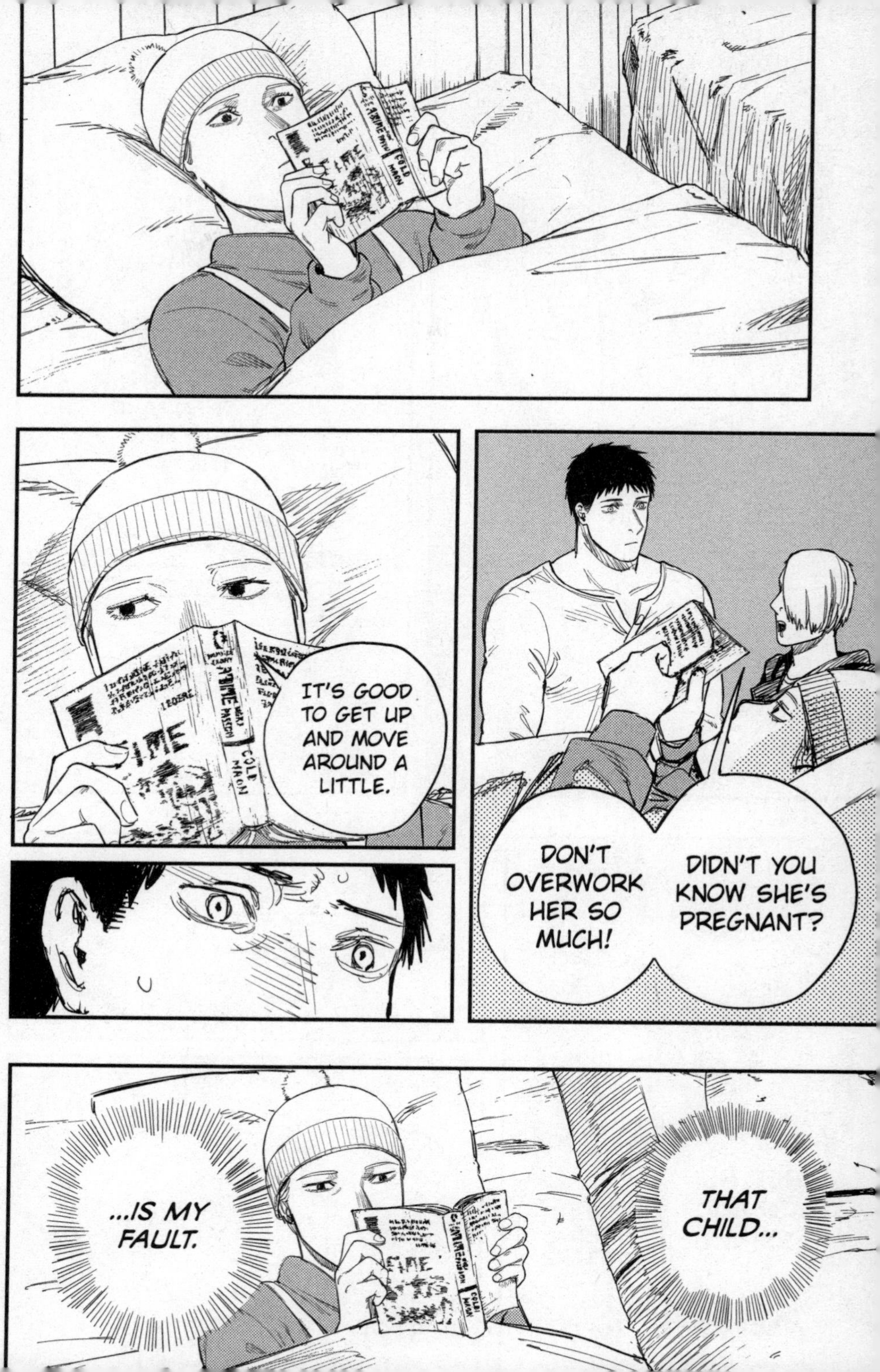
DIDN'T YOU KNOW SHE'S PREGNANT?
DON'T OVERWORK HER SO MUCH!
IT'S GOOD TO GET UP AND MOVE AROUND A LITTLE.
THAT CHILD...
...IS MY FAULT.

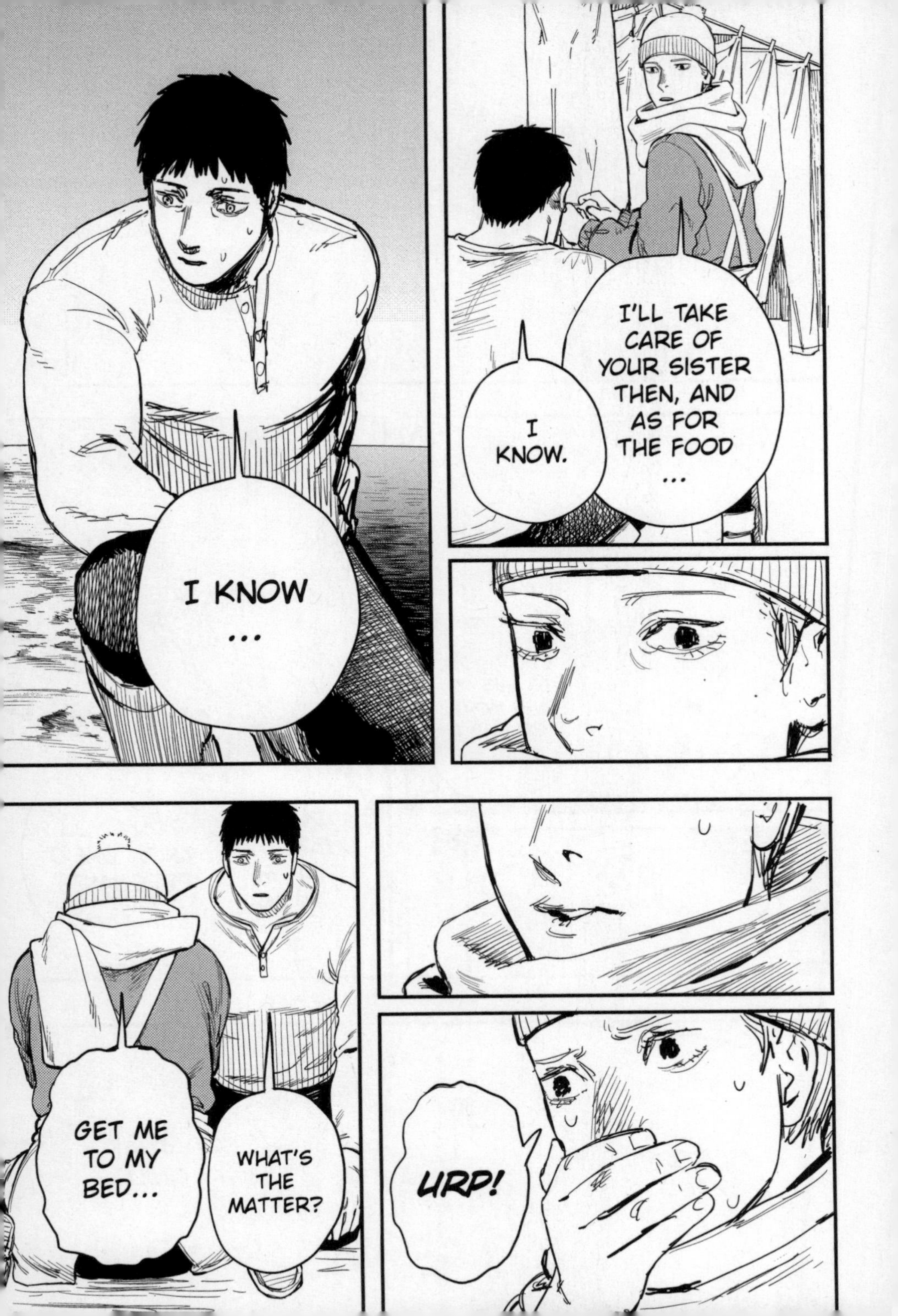
I'LL TAKE CARE OF YOUR SISTER THEN, AND AS FOR THE FOOD ...
I KNOW.
I KNOW ...
URP!
WHAT'S THE MATTER?
GET ME TO MY BED...

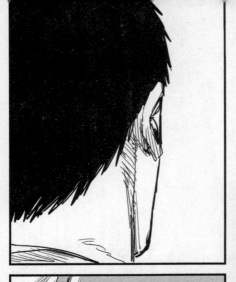

YOU CAN TAKE IT SLOW. LET THAT ARM HEAL TOO.

AND WHEN IT'S BETTER, KILL FIRE PUNCH.

I HAVE A PRETTY GOOD GUESS WHERE HE IS.

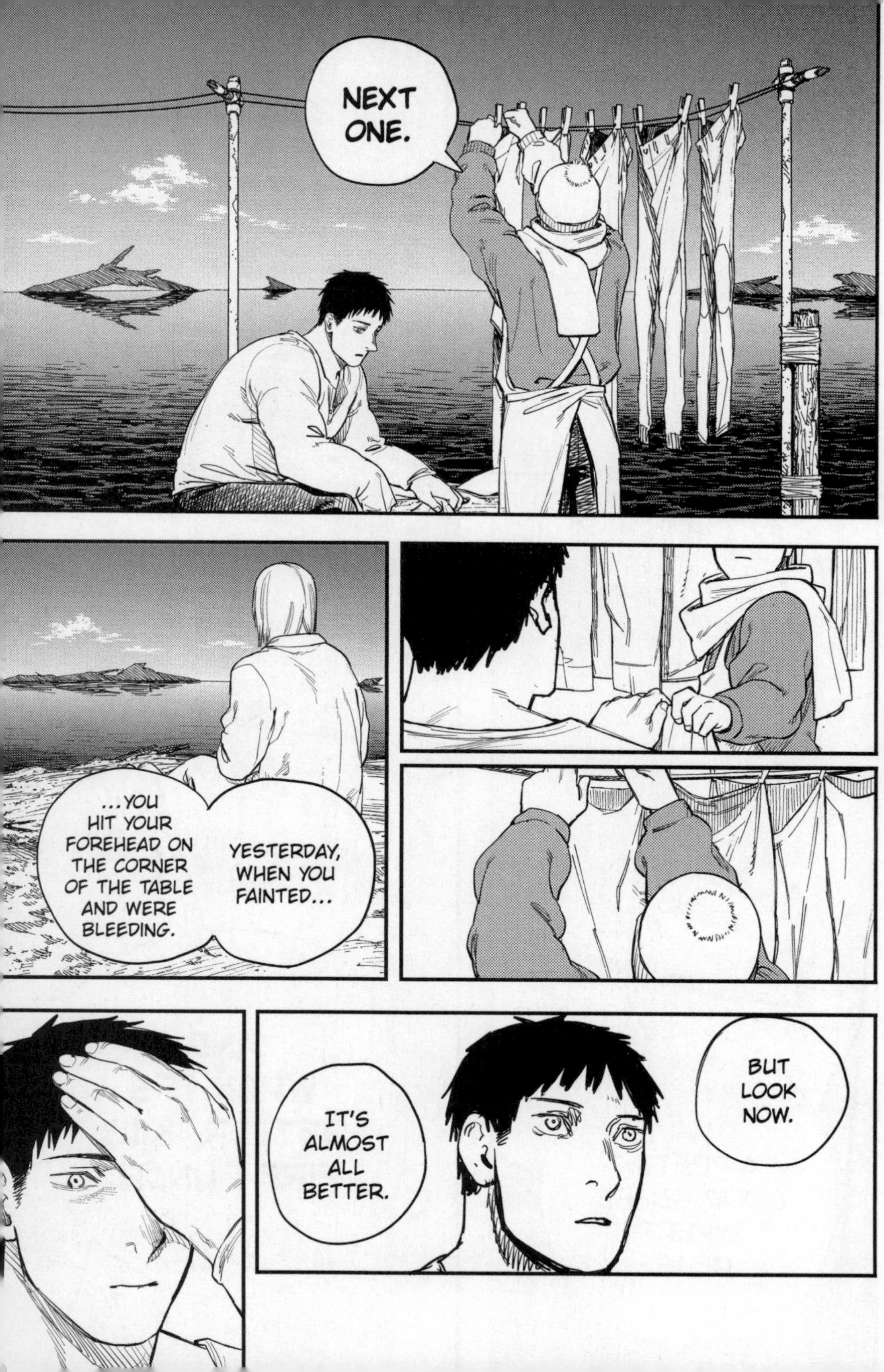
NEXT ONE.
YESTERDAY, WHEN YOU FAINTED...
...YOU HIT YOUR FOREHEAD ON THE CORNER OF THE TABLE AND WERE BLEEDING.
BUT LOOK NOW.
IT'S ALMOST ALL BETTER.

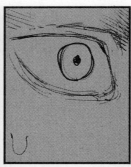

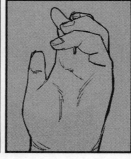

...WHEN I WAS...

...I PREFER...

I THINK...

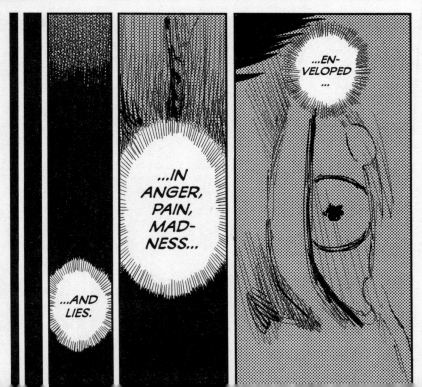

...EN-VELOPED...

...IN ANGER, PAIN, MAD-NESS...

...AND LIES.

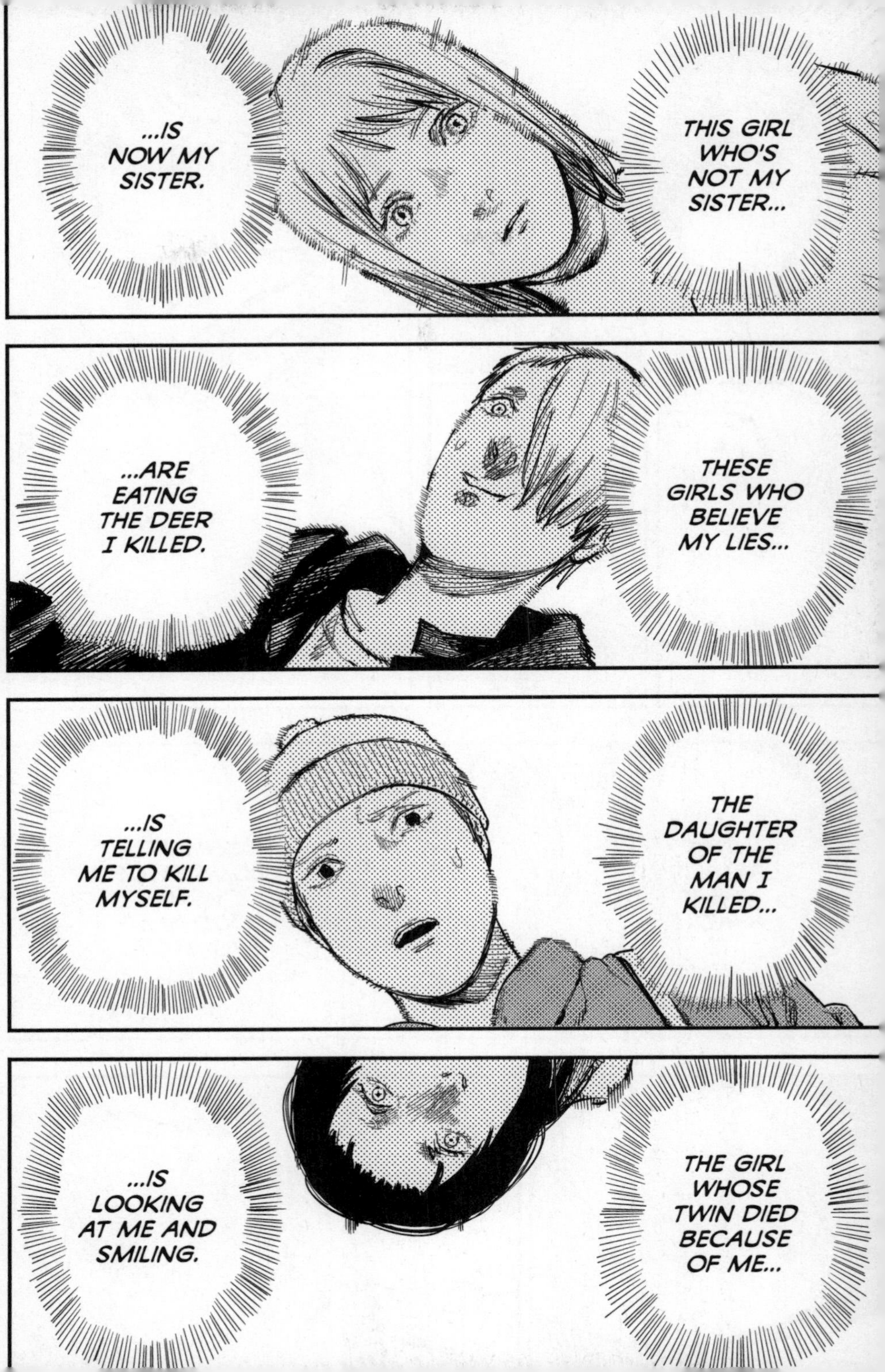
THIS GIRL WHO'S NOT MY SISTER...
...IS NOW MY SISTER.
THESE GIRLS WHO BELIEVE MY LIES...
...ARE EATING THE DEER I KILLED.
THE DAUGHTER OF THE MAN I KILLED...
...IS TELLING ME TO KILL MYSELF.
THE GIRL WHOSE TWIN DIED BECAUSE OF ME...
...IS LOOKING AT ME AND SMILING.

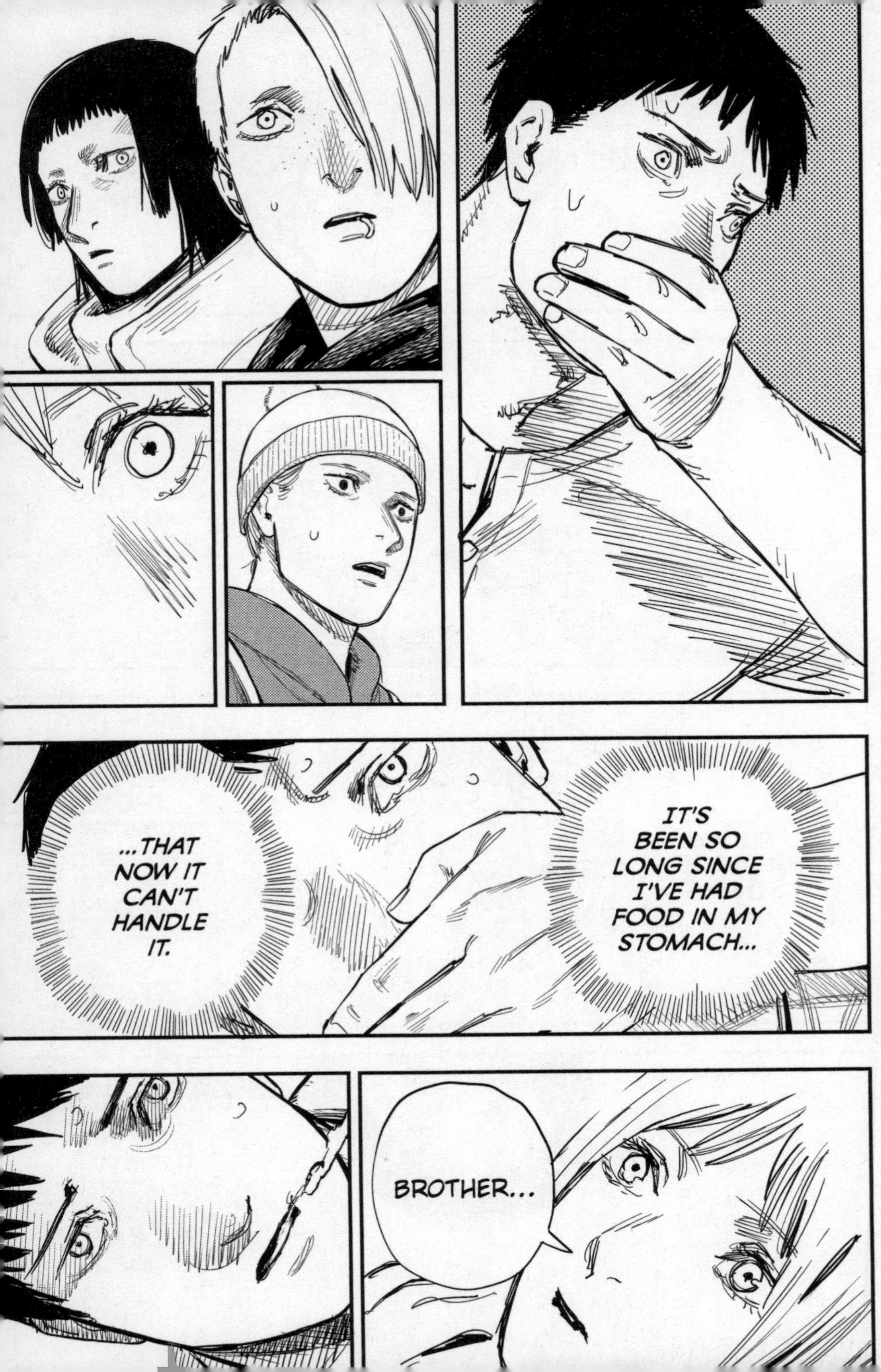
IT'S BEEN SO LONG SINCE I'VE HAD FOOD IN MY STOMACH...
...THAT NOW IT CAN'T HANDLE IT.
BROTHER...

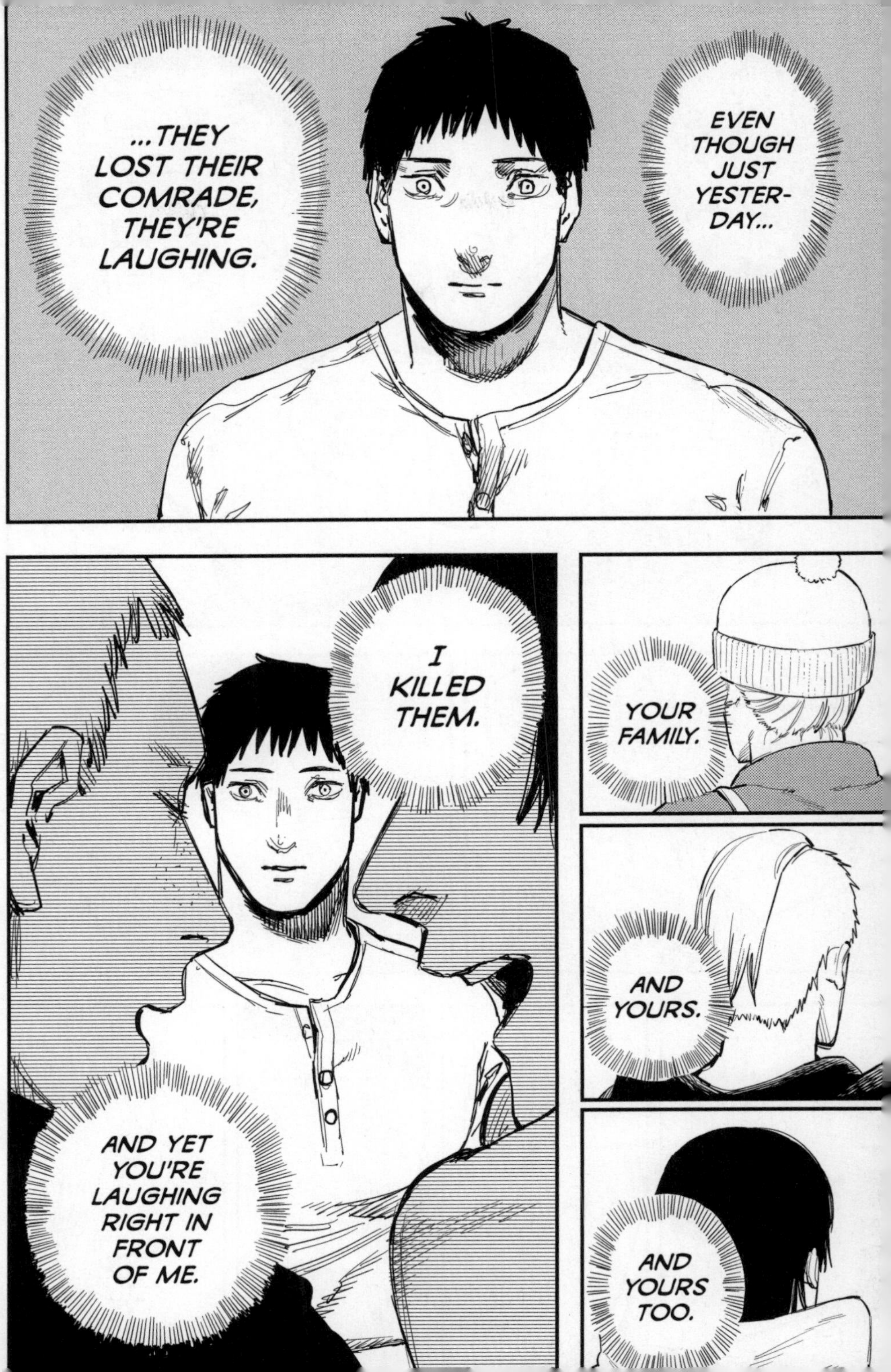
EVEN THOUGH JUST YESTER-DAY...
...THEY LOST THEIR COMRADE, THEY'RE LAUGHING.
YOUR FAMILY.
AND YOURS.
AND YOURS TOO.
I KILLED THEM.
AND YET YOU'RE LAUGHING RIGHT IN FRONT OF ME.

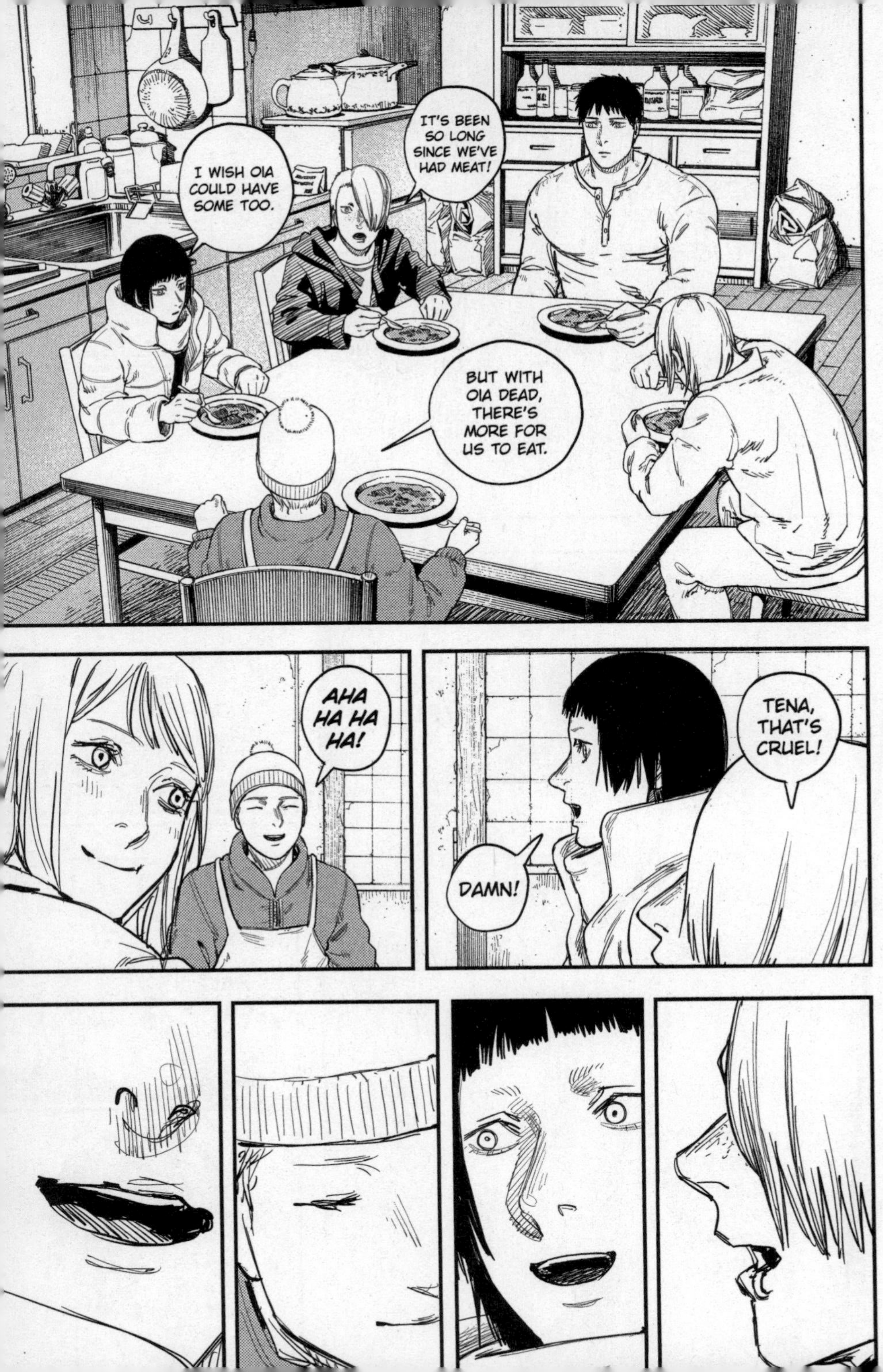
IT'S BEEN SO LONG SINCE WE'VE HAD MEAT!
I WISH OIA COULD HAVE SOME TOO.
BUT WITH OIA DEAD, THERE'S MORE FOR US TO EAT.
TENA, THAT'S CRUEL!
DAMN!
AHA HA HA HA!

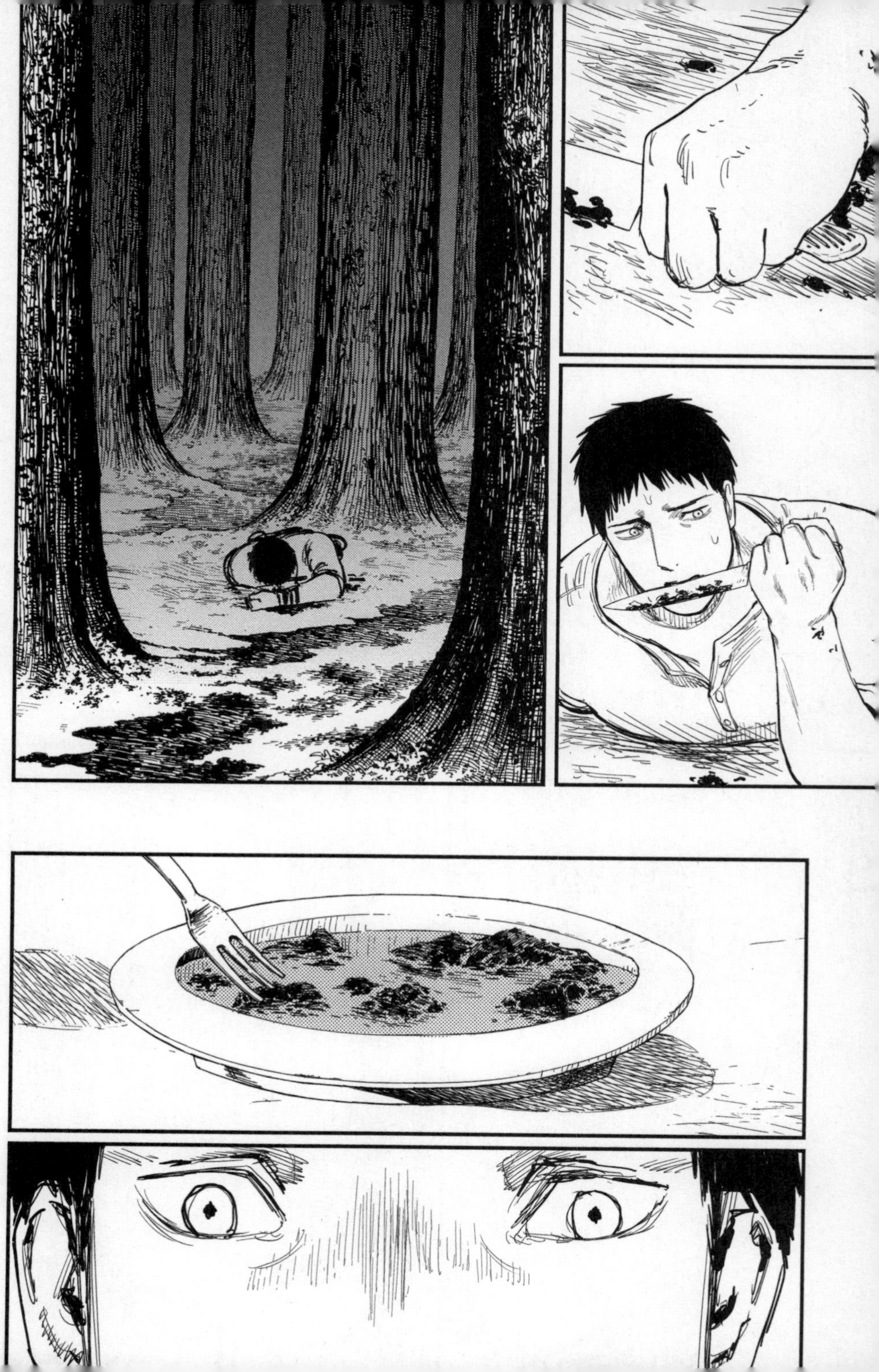

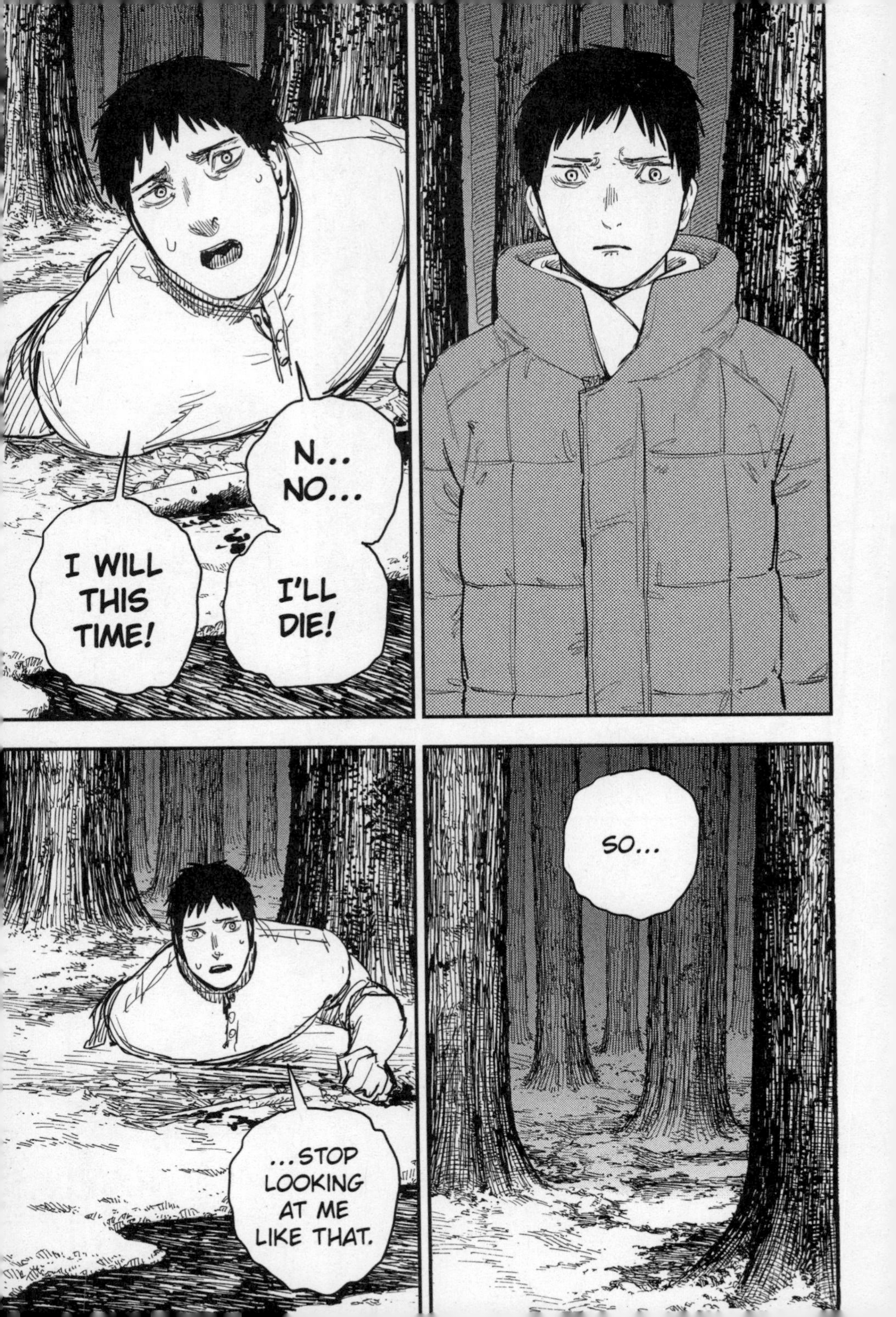
N... NO...
I'LL DIE!
I WILL THIS TIME!
SO...
...STOP LOOKING AT ME LIKE THAT.

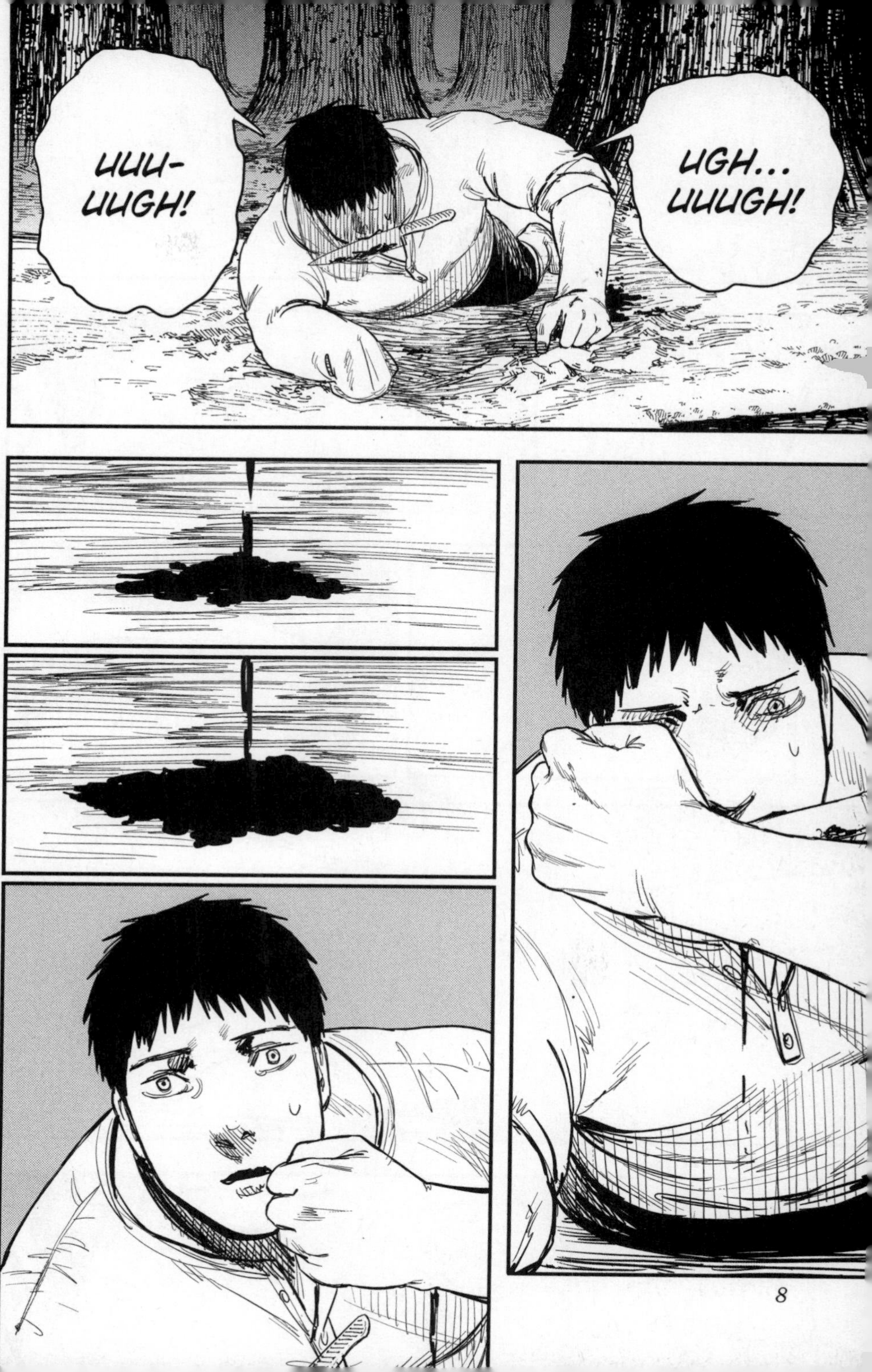
UGH... UUUGH!
UUU-UUGH!

LIVE.

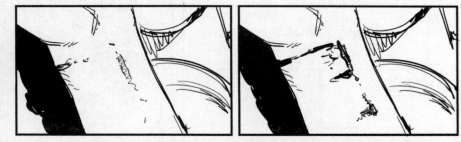

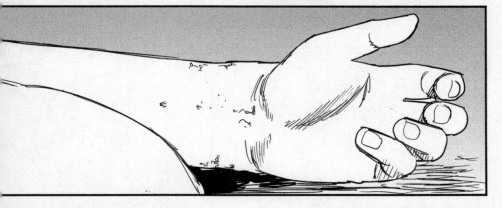

AH...

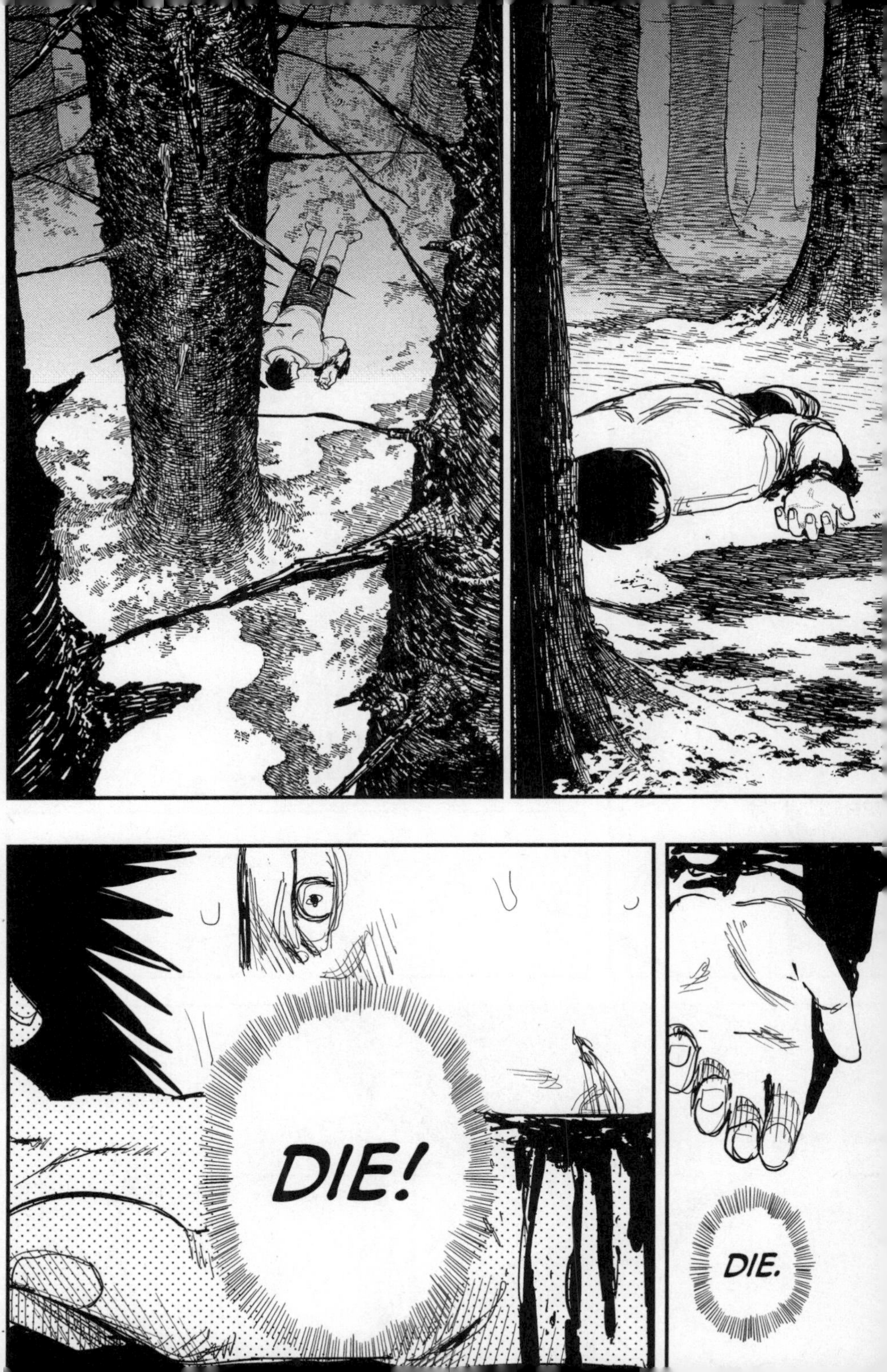
DIE.
DIE!

KILL FIRE PUNCH.

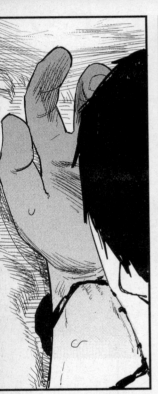

CHAPTER 61

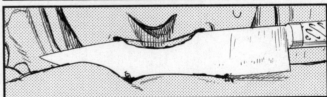

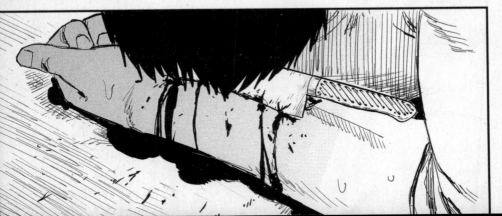

FIRE PUNCH

STORY AND ART BY
TATSUKI FUJIMOTO

LIAN

A pupil of Doma, she has medical training.

TENA

Doma's daughter, she's a Blessed with the power of fire. She's impregnated when a refugee rapes her.

MASKED MAN

A follower of Agni's, he's a Blessed with the ability to generate and manipulate iron.

LANOUX

A pupil of Doma, her twin sister is killed.

Humans who possess unique powers are called Blessed, and two such Blessed, Agni and Luna, live in a world frozen over by the Ice Witch. One day, Agni and Luna's village is attacked by a Behemdorg soldier named Doma, who's a Blessed whose flames won't extinguish until they've completely consumed their fuel. Luna loses her life, but Agni survives, suffering a living hell of trying to master the art of controlling the flames that endlessly consume him. After exacting his revenge on Doma, he goes on to destroy the giant tree that the Ice Witch made out of Judah. When he comes to, he finds Judah is with him among the remnants of the tree, but her mind has regressed to that of a child. Agni takes the opportunity to lie to her, calling her Luna and having her refer to him as her brother. While searching for shelter, the two meet a clan of women who were followers of Doma, and in order to stay with them, Agni hides his true identity and that of Judah. One of the girls is Doma's daughter Tena, and she asks Agni to kill Fire Punch. Agni has laid down lie after lie in order to hide his crimes, so how will he answer her plea?

STORY